THE COLLEGE BOARD
ACHIEVEMENT
TESTS

14 TESTS IN 13 SUBJECTS

COLLEGE ENTRANCE EXAMINATION BOARD
NEW YORK

The Admissions Testing Program is sponsored by the College Board, a nonprofit membership organization that provides tests and other educational services for students, schools, and colleges. The membership is composed of more than 2,500 colleges, schools, school systems, and education associations. Representatives of the members serve on the Board of Trustees and advisory councils and committees that consider the programs of the College Board and participate in the determination of its policies and activities.

This book was prepared and produced by Educational Testing Service (ETS), which develops and administers the tests of the Admissions Testing Program for the College Board.

The College Board and Educational Testing Service are dedicated to the principle of equal opportunity, and their programs, services, and employment policies are guided by that principle.

Contents

Introduction

The College Board has made this book available to help students and teachers become better acquainted with the 14 Achievement Tests that are offered every year through the College Board's Admissions Testing Program. In this book you will find:

- descriptions of each of the 14 Achievement Tests
- discussion of the types of questions used in the tests
- advice on how to prepare for the tests
- a recently administered, full-length edition of each of the 14 tests, which may be used for practice
- instructions on how to score the tests

This book supplements the booklet *Taking the Achievement Tests*, which is free to every student who registers to take an Achievement Test. Copies of *Taking the Achievement Tests* are available at high school guidance offices, or by writing to or calling the College Board Admissions Testing Program (ATP). However, only this book contains recently administered, full-length Achievement Tests. By making these tests and the accompanying information available, the College Board hopes that students and teachers will have a better understanding of what the Achievement Tests are intended to measure, the kinds of questions they contain, how they are scored, and how colleges use the scores.

About the Tests

Each of the College Board Achievement Tests measures your knowledge or skills in a particular subject and your ability to apply that knowledge. The 14 tests fall into five general subject areas:

- English
    - English Composition (two versions:
        all-multiple-choice and
        multiple-choice with essay)
    - Literature
- Foreign Languages
    - French
    - German
    - Hebrew
    - Latin
    - Spanish
- History and Social Studies
    - American History and Social Studies
    - European History and World Cultures
- Mathematics
    - Mathematics Level I
    - Mathematics Level II
- Sciences
    - Biology
    - Chemistry
    - Physics

All the Achievement Tests take one hour of testing time and consist entirely of multiple-choice questions, except the English Composition Test with Essay, which consists of a 20-minute essay and 40 minutes of multiple-choice questions. Detailed descriptions of the contents of each of the tests are included in sections preceding the tests.

Some colleges require Achievement Tests for admission. They know that although your high school record is one measure of how well you will do in your college courses, a better measure is a combination of your high school record and your scores on relevant standardized tests. For this reason, Achievement Test scores, used in combination with your high school record, results of tests such as the Scholastic Aptitude Test (SAT), teacher recommendations, and other background information, provide a reliable measure of your academic achievement. Because past academic achievement is generally a good predictor of future performance, scores on the Achievement Tests can help in assessing how well prepared you are for different programs of college study. The scores are particularly appropriate for use in admissions because they are independent of specific textbooks, grading procedures, and methods of instruction. This independence allows comparison of students whose course preparation and backgrounds vary widely.

In addition to using the scores for predicting whether or not applicants are ready for different kinds of college study, some institutions use the Achievement Tests for placement and guidance. At some colleges, the scores from these tests are used to place new students in particular freshman courses. At others, advisers use the scores in guidance discussions with incoming students to help them select courses.

Planning to Take the Tests

Which Ones Should You Take?

Before deciding which Achievement Tests to take, make a tentative list of all colleges you are thinking of applying to. Check their catalogs or a directory of colleges to determine their Achievement Test requirements. Some will specify which tests you must take; others will allow you to choose.

This list will also be useful as you plan your high school course schedule. You may want to consider adjusting your schedule in light of the colleges' requirements. For example, you may decide to take another year of a foreign language if you learn that a college you might want to attend requires a foreign language Achievement Test for admission, or that the college might exempt you from a freshman requirement if you do well on the test.

A good source of information about colleges' requirements concerning Achievement Tests is *The Col-*

lege Handbook, published by the College Board. The final word on requirements, however, should always be the catalogs and other publications of the institutions to which you are applying.

When Should You Take the Tests?

You probably will do best on an Achievement Test if you take it soon after completing a course (or courses) in the subject being tested, while the material is still fresh in your mind. If you decide to take an Achievement Test in a subject you haven't studied recently, you should plan to review the material thoroughly before taking the test. This review should consist of a careful, methodical study of the course content over several weeks' time. Last-minute cramming is not likely to be of much use.

In deciding when to take the Achievement Tests, you should find out the requirements of the colleges to which you may apply. Colleges that use Achievement Test results as a part of their admissions process often require that the tests be taken no later than December or January of the senior year. (Students who apply under an Early Decision Program are usually required to take the tests no later than June of their junior year.) Other colleges may use Achievement Test results only to help with placement decisions once you decide to enroll. In such cases you might be able to take the tests as late as May or June of your senior year.

Many colleges that do not require Achievement Tests will nevertheless look at these results, if available, to help them learn more about an applicant's academic background as they are making admissions and placement decisions. For example, if you attend a very competitive high school where top grades are seldom given, Achievement Test results may help you demonstrate your academic achievement.

When the Tests Are Offered

Achievement Tests are given on five dates during the academic year: November, December, January, May, and June. Most of the tests are available on all five dates; however, the European History and World Cultures, German, Hebrew, and Latin tests are given only in December and May. The English Composition Test with Essay is administered only during the first hour of the December test session; the all-multiple-choice version of that test is available on the other four dates, but *not* in December. Be sure to consider which tests are available on the various dates in order to meet the requirements of the colleges to which you plan to apply.

The fee for the Achievement Tests entitles you to take one, two, or three tests on any one test date. However, you need not specify in advance which tests you will take.

How to Register

The booklet, *Registration Bulletin for the SAT and the Achievement Tests,* contains a Registration Form and all the information you will need to register for these tests and to have your scores reported to the colleges of your choice. In order to avoid additional fees, you must send in your Registration Form at least five weeks before the test date.

A supply of the *Bulletin* is sent to all high schools each year. High school students should be able to pick up a copy at their school guidance or counseling office. Test candidates who are not currently in high school may obtain a copy at a local high school or by writing to or calling the College Board Admissions Testing Program (ATP).

If you want to write or call. . .	**Address** College Board ATP Box CN 6200 Princeton, NJ 08541-6200	**Phone Numbers (Monday-Friday)**	
		Princeton, NJ **(609) 771-7600** 8:30 a.m. to 9:30 p.m.	Berkeley, CA **(415) 849-0950** 8:15 a.m. to 4:30 p.m.

How to Prepare for the Tests

Know What to Expect

The best way to prepare for the tests is to familiarize yourself with their organization, the types of questions that will appear on them, and what will be expected of you on the test day. To make sure you are prepared for the actual test administration, you should

• *Read this book and Taking the Achievement Tests carefully.* They will help you understand how each test you plan to take is organized and how it will be scored.

• *Study the sample questions and explanations for the tests you plan to take.* The sample questions and explanations will give you a good idea of the kinds of questions that actually appear on the tests. The more familiar you are with the sample questions, the more comfortable you'll feel when you see the questions in your test book on the day of the tests.

• *Study and understand the test directions.* The directions for answering the questions are printed here exactly as they appear in the current test books. Study them now so you will understand them when you take the test. The less time you have to spend reading and interpreting the directions on the test day, the more time you'll have to spend answering the questions.

• *Take the specific tests in this book that you are interested in.* These tests are actual editions of Achievement Tests administered within the last several years. Try to take the tests under conditions as similar as possible to those of the actual test day. (Suggestions for doing so appear on the introductory page for each test.) Make sure that you use one of the answer sheets provided at the back of this book. That way you'll already have been through a "dry run" before you actually take the tests.

• *Score each test after you've taken it.* This will help you understand the scoring procedures that will be used on the actual tests.

Test-Taking Tips

Here are some specific test-taking tips that will help when you take the tests.

• Within each group of questions of the same type, the easier questions usually are at the beginning of the group and the more difficult ones are at the end. Test questions that contain a reading passage or a diagram followed by several questions are an exception. Such questions are ordered according to the logic and organization of the preceding material.

• If you're working on a group of questions of a particular type and find that the questions are getting too difficult for you, quickly read through the rest of the questions in that group and answer only those you think you know. Then go on to the next group of questions. (Again, this advice does not necessarily apply to a set of questions immediately following a reading passage or a diagram. In this case a difficult question might be followed by an easier one.)

• You get just as much credit for correctly answering easy questions as you do for correctly answering difficult ones, so make sure you answer all the questions that seem easy to you before you spend time thinking about the questions that are more difficult.

• You *can* guess. If you know that some of the choices for a question are definitely wrong, then it's to your advantage to guess from the remaining choices. But because of the way the tests are scored, random guessing is unlikely to increase your score and could possibly lower it.

• You *can* omit questions. Many students who do well omit some questions. You can return to the ones you've omitted if you have time left before the test ends.

• You get credit for each question you answer correctly. You lose *partial* credit for each question you answer incorrectly. You neither gain nor lose credit for questions you omit.

• Use the test book for scratchwork and to mark questions you omitted, so you can go back to them if you have time. Do *not* make extra marks on the answer sheet. They may be misread as answers by the scoring machine.

• If the scoring machine reads what looks like two answers for one question, that will be considered an omitted question. So it's in your best interest to keep your answer sheet free of any stray marks.

The Day Before the Tests

Learn as much as you can about the tests well in advance of the day you plan to take them. Then, on the day or evening before the tests, it might help if you

- Take a few minutes to review the sample questions and explanations in this book. Hours of intense study the night before the test day probably will not help your performance on the tests and might even make you more anxious. But a short review of the information you studied earlier will probably make you feel more comfortable and better prepared.
- Get together the materials you need to take to the test center and put them in a place that will be convenient for you in the morning. Use this checklist:
  - ✔ Admission ticket
  - ✔ Positive identification (You won't be admitted to the test center without it. See the *Registration Bulletin for the SAT and Achievement Tests.*)
  - ✔ Two No. 2 pencils with erasers
  - ✔ Directions to the test center, if you need them
  - ✔ All the materials you will need to register as a standby if you have not preregistered. (See the *Registration Bulletin for the SAT and Achievement Tests.*)
- Spend the rest of the evening relaxing. You'll accomplish little by worrying about the next day. Read a book, visit with friends, watch a television program you enjoy, or do anything you find relaxing.
- Get a good night's sleep. You'll want to feel your best when you take the tests, so try to be well rested and refreshed. Get to bed early and set your alarm early enough to avoid having to rush.

After the Tests

Achievement Test Scores

Achievement Test scores are reported on a scale of 200 (lowest) to 800 (highest). The tests have no passing or failing scores, and they are not scored on a curve — that is, the scores of other students who took the test with you had no effect on how you did.

About six weeks after you take the Achievement Tests, you will receive a report that includes your scores and percentile ranks and information that will help you interpret and understand them. You will also receive the booklet, *After the Test.*

How Precise Are Your Scores?

When you consider your scores, keep in mind that no test can measure anyone's abilities with perfect accuracy. If you took a different edition of a test or the same edition on different days, your score would probably be slightly different each time. If you were to take a test an infinite number of times, your scores would tend to cluster about an average value. Testing specialists call this average your "true score," the score you would get if a test could measure your ability with perfect accuracy. To measure the extent to which students' obtained scores vary from their true scores, an index called the Standard Error of Measurement (SEM) is used.

The SEMs for the Achievement Tests are about 30 points above or below your obtained score. You should think of your scores in terms of score bands rather than precise measurements — a 500 Achievement Test score, for example, should be thought of as probably being anywhere between 470 and 530. This will help you realize that a small difference between your score and another student's on the same test may not indicate any real difference in ability. College admissions officers also are advised to look at scores this way.

Will Your Scores Go Up if You Take the Test Again?

As indicated earlier, you are not likely to get exactly the same score on a test twice. Improving your score a great deal is also unlikely. Some students who repeat tests do improve their scores, but, on the average, these increases are small. As could be expected, students who study a subject longer and more thoroughly before retaking an Achievement Test in that field tend to improve their scores more than students who do not.

If you repeat a test, all your scores appear on your score report. Colleges evaluate multiple scores on the same test in different ways. Some look at all the scores on your report; others use just the highest, most recent, or average score.

Who Receives Your Scores?

In addition to the score report you receive, a copy of your report will be sent to your high school if you give your high school code number when you register for the test. Reports will also be sent to any colleges and scholarship programs whose code numbers you give on your Registration Form or on an Additional Report Request Form.

How Do Colleges Use Your Scores?

Colleges use Achievement Tests in making admissions decisions, for academic advising, and for course placement. Although colleges vary in the way they use test scores, few, if any, make admissions decisions based on scores alone. Therefore, low or high scores should neither discourage you nor make you overconfident. Admissions officers often consider the descriptive information on your score report as well as other information sent by you and your school.

Different colleges value different qualities in applicants: one college may be looking for leadership potential, while another may place more weight on various extracurricular activities. Some colleges have open admissions policies and admit almost all applicants. Some will admit students with particular qualities they want, even if the students' grades and scores indicate they will have to make an extra effort. Whatever your scores, remember that there are probably many colleges that could meet your needs and where you would be happy.

How the Tests Are Developed

Many people are involved in the development of each new edition of an Achievement Test. In each subject, the College Board appoints a development committee made up of college faculty and secondary school teachers. These committee members, listed on pages 14 and 15, perform the following functions:

- review and update the content and skills specifications that serve as a blueprint for the new edition of the test (These specifications show the topics to be included in the test and the percentage of the test devoted to each topic.)
- write some of the questions for the test
- evaluate each question for accuracy and appropriateness, suggesting revisions as necessary
- review each new edition of the test twice, once at the draft stage and again just before printing, to ensure that it meets the specifications and contains an appropriate balance of topics and skills

Each test committee may also advise the College Board of special concerns and needs related to the test. It may, for instance, recommend that the Board

undertake certain kinds of research or curriculum surveys.

In the actual work of building a test, the committee has the help of test development staff from Educational Testing Service. The ETS test development staff members, most of whom are former teachers of the subject in which they specialize, provide measurement advice on building the new test. They also arrange for committee members and other teachers to write questions for the test and they review and polish all of the new questions. The ETS staff arrange for these new questions, approved by the committee, to be tried out under standard testing conditions by students with appropriate preparation. This pretesting of new questions provides information about the difficulty of the questions and the number and ability of the students who responded to each of the answer choices. This information may help identify possible ambiguities or other errors in the new questions. Questions with such problems are either revised or eliminated from further consideration. As they assemble a draft test, the test development staff use the information about the difficulty of individual questions to control the overall difficulty of the test.

In examining the draft of a new edition of the test, the committee can do one of two things: it can make minor revisions to questions (major revisions are not permitted unless the questions are pretested again) or it can replace questions in the draft with other pretested questions. After the committee has completed its review, the test is examined by a number of ETS staff members. These staff members include subject matter specialists who evaluate the test's overall integrity and its suitability as a measure of the subject. They also make sure that no errors have been introduced by any revisions. Editors make sure the test conforms to a specified style in spelling, punctuation, format of questions, and wording of directions. Sensitivity reviewers see that the test contains no potentially offensive or disturbing material. After these reviews, the test is prepared for printing. A proof copy of the test is sent to the committee for final approval before the new edition is printed.

After the test has been administered, the statistics from a sample of the students taking the test are checked before scores are reported. The test development staff members respond to any questions or comments received from students who took the test, or from their teachers. Information from these comments is provided to the committee members when they begin work on another edition of the test.

College Board Achievement Test Development Committees, 1983-84

American History and Social Studies

Richard L. McCormick, Rutgers University, *Chairperson*

Estelle Feinstein, University of Connecticut-Stamford

Steven C. Kramer, The Hockaday School, Dallas, Texas

Fay D. Metcalf, Boulder High School, Boulder, Colorado

Nell I. Painter, University of North Carolina at Chapel Hill

Biology

Joann M. Meyer, J. F. Dulles High School, Sugarland, Texas, *Chairperson*

Kendall W. Corbin, University of Minnesota

John W. Kimball, Harvard University

Cherry K. Sprague, Princeton High School, Princeton, New Jersey

Tommy E. Wynn, North Carolina State University

Chemistry

Martin N. Ackermann, Oberlin College, *Chairperson*

Nancy H. Kolodny, Wellesley College

Edward K. Mellon, Florida State University

Michael A. Saltman, Bronxville School System, Bronxville, New York

Bonita K. Williams, Dulaney High School, Timonium, Maryland

English Composition

Roger K. Applebee, University of Illinois at Urbana-Champaign, *Chairperson*

Ann L. Keenan, Braintree Public Schools, Braintree, Massachusetts

Ellen M. Shull, Incarnate Word High School, San Antonio, Texas

Ralph F. Voss, University of Alabama

European History and World Cultures

Paul W. Knoll, University of Southern California, *Chairperson*

Margaret Lavinia Anderson, Swarthmore College

Ann Chapman, Western Reserve Academy, Hudson, Ohio

Rashid K. Silvera, Scarsdale High School, Scarsdale, New York

John O. Voll, University of New Hampshire

French

Jean M. Leblon, Vanderbilt University, *Chairperson*

Lucien R. Boisvert, Hamden High School, Hamden, Connecticut

Isabelle M. Kaplan, Northwestern University

André Maman, Princeton University

Françoise Martinod, The Bishop's School, La Jolla, California

German

Kathy A. Harms, Northwestern University, *Chairperson*

Hans-Dieter Brueckner, Pomona College

D. Victoria Ellis, Princeton High School, Princeton, New Jersey

James R. McIntyre, Colby College

Alan L. Stiegemeier, Quincy Public Schools, Quincy, Illinois

Hebrew

Joshua Bakst, Ramaz Upper School, New York, New York

Edna Grad, Northwestern University

Paula Jacobs, Hebrew College

Samuel Schneider, Yeshiva University

Latin

Glenn M. Knudsvig, The University of Michigan, *Chairperson*

Margaret Brucia, Port Jefferson Public Schools, Port Jefferson, New York

Gloria S. Duclos, University of Southern Maine

Thomas N. Habinek, University of California at Berkeley

Doris L. Kays, MacArthur High School, San Antonio, Texas

Literature

Charles H. Long, Yale University, *Chairperson*

Thomas R. Arp, Southern Methodist University

Ann L. Hayes, Carnegie-Mellon University

Sandra Carter Jackson, Oakland Public Schools, Oakland, California

Deborah S. Wyndham, St. Anne's-Belfield School, Charlottesville, Virginia

Mathematics

George W. Best, Phillips Academy, Andover, Massachusetts, *Chairperson*

Floyd L. Downs, Hillsdale High School, San Mateo, California

Jane Cronin Scanlon, Rutgers University

Richard A. Vandervelde, Hope College

R. O. Wells Jr., Rice University

Physics

Gerald F. Wheeler, Montana State University, *Chairperson*

Judy R. Franz, Indiana University

Manu V. Patel, T. C. Williams High School, Alexandria, Virginia

Arnold A. Strassenburg, State University of New York at Stony Brook

Lora W. Wilhite, Carlinville High School, Carlinville, Illinois

Spanish

Carlos A. Solé, University of Texas at Austin, *Chairperson*

Lourdes M. Cowgill, Pine Crest Preparatory School, Fort Lauderdale, Florida

Alfred Ellis, Hillcrest High School, Jamaica, New York

Carmen Salazar Parr, Los Angeles Valley College

Roberto A. Véguez, Middlebury College

About the English Composition Achievement Test

There are two versions of the English Composition Achievement Test. One, offered on four national test dates, consists of 90 multiple-choice questions. In this version, you are not asked to do any writing. The other version, offered on the December test date only, consists of 70 multiple-choice questions and a 20-minute essay. The all-multiple-choice test is *never* offered on the December test date.

The English Composition Achievement Test differs from other Achievement Tests in that it measures language skills you have acquired throughout your life, rather than knowledge acquired in a particular course. For example, you are not expected to know definitions of grammar or the history of the English language, but you are expected to know the difference between written and spoken language, to know how words fit together to express ideas clearly and logically, and to know about the idioms of the language. Knowledge of this sort is not gained by studying rules; it is gained through extensive experience with the language, especially the written language.

Because the test deals with standard written English, the sentences used in the test are intended to supply a written context for the problems about which you are being asked. The sentences, therefore, usually cover a variety of subjects normally discussed in writing: science, social science, literature, philosophy, history, current affairs. You do not need to be an expert in any subject to work with the sentences in the test. However, you are expected to be familiar enough with common terms such as *disaster relief*, *computer technology*, and *prosecuting attorney* to be able to understand what you read as you answer the questions.

Content of the Test

Common writing problems covered by the English Composition Achievement Test are presented in the chart that follows. Although most of these problems are dealt with in every edition of the test, a few appear only in some editions. This list is used to ensure that a mixture of problems appears in each new edition and that no one problem is overemphasized.

In the list, each kind of problem is accompanied by a sentence illustrating the kind of writing problem mentioned. These sentences are not examples of questions in the test.

Writing Problems	Illustrative sentences
Being consistent	
Sequence of tenses	After he broke his arm, he is home for two weeks.
Shift of pronoun	If one is tense, they should try to relax.
Parallelism	She skis, plays tennis, and flying hang gliders.
Noun agreement	Ann and Sarah want to be a pilot.
Pronoun reference	Several people wanted the job, and he or she filled out the required applications.
Subject-verb agreement	There is eight people on the shore.
Expressing ideas logically	
Coordination and subordination	Nancy has a rash, and she is probably allergic to something.
Logical comparison	Harry grew more vegetables than his neighbor's garden.
Modification and word order	Barking loudly, the tree had the dog's leash wrapped around it.
Being clear and precise	
Ambiguous and vague pronouns	In the newspaper they say that few people voted.
Diction	He circumvented the globe on his trip.
Wordiness	There are many problems in the contemporary world in which we live.
Unclear modification	If your car is parked here while not eating in the restaurant, it will be towed away.

Following conventions

Pronoun case	He sat between you and I at the stadium.
Verb form	She had brung her lunch yesterday.
Idiom	Manuel had a different opinion towards her.
Comparison of modifiers	Of the sixteen executives, Meg makes more money.
Sentence fragment	Jane having to go home early.
Double negative	Natalie has scarcely no free time.
Recognizing correct sentences	The horse is a mammal.

---

90 Questions; Time — 60 minutes

Questions Used in the Test

Three types of multiple-choice questions are currently used in the English Composition Achievement Test. The essay version of the test contains only the first two types.

Type I

The first type of question tests your ability to detect an error in underlined portions of a sentence. The following directions appear in the test:

Directions: The following sentences contain problems in grammar, usage, diction (choice of words), and idiom.

Some sentences are correct.
No sentence contains more than one error.

You will find that the error, if there is one, is underlined and lettered. Assume that all other elements of the sentence are correct and cannot be changed. In choosing answers, follow the requirements of standard written English.

If there is an error, select the <u>one underlined part</u> that must be changed in order to make the sentence correct, and blacken the corresponding space on the answer sheet.

If there is no error, mark answer space E.

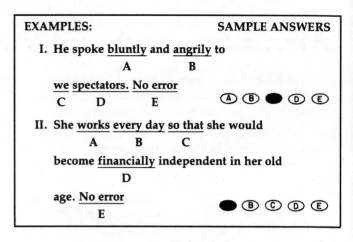

1. Pride <u>alone</u> <u>is usually enough</u> to induce a country
         A   B

   <u>to support</u> <u>their</u> athletes in international competition.
     C   D

   <u>No error</u>
    E

As you read the sentence, you should recognize that the error is at choice (D). *Their* is not the appropriate pronoun to use in referring to *a country*. All of the other choices are acceptable in standard written English. Choice (A), *alone*, is idiomatic; the verb in choice (B), *is*, is correct in number and in tense and the ordering of words in the phrase is idiomatic; in choice (C) the use of the infinitive *to support* is idiomatically acceptable after the verb *induce*.

2. <u>Some</u> genetic research <u>has become</u> <u>highly</u> controversial
    A   B   C

   because the results of the studies suggest that people
   <u>may eventually be able</u> to manipulate the development of
           D

   the human race. <u>No error</u>
               E

The correct response to this question is (E). Each part of the sentence conforms to the requirements of standard written English; no error in grammar, usage, or idiom is present in the sentence.

Type II

Multiple-choice questions of this second type test your ability to identify an error in a sentence and to select the best revision of an unacceptable portion of the sentence (or of the entire sentence). The best revision of an unacceptable part of the sentence will eliminate the original problem and introduce no others. The following directions appear in the test.

Directions: In each of the following sentences, some part of the sentence or the entire sentence is underlined. Beneath each sentence you will find five ways of phrasing the underlined part. The first of these repeats the original; the other four are different. If you think the original is better than any of the alternatives, choose answer A; otherwise choose one of the others. Select the best version and blacken the corresponding space on your answer sheet.

This is a test of correctness and effectiveness of expression. In choosing answers, follow the requirements of standard written English; that is, pay attention to grammar, choice of words, sentence construction and punctuation. Choose the answer that best expresses the meaning of the original sentence. Your choice should produce the most effective sentence — clear and precise, without awkwardness or ambiguity.

EXAMPLE: **SAMPLE ANSWER**

Ms. Rose planning to teach a course in biology next summer.

(A) planning
(B) are planning
(C) have planned
(D) with a plan
(E) plans

---

3. Henry David Thoreau first saw Walden Pond at the age of five years, which was later to become famous as the setting of his experiment in simple living.

(A) Henry David Thoreau first saw Walden Pond at the age of five years, which was later to become famous as the setting of his experiment in simple living.

(B) When he was five years old, Henry David Thoreau first saw Walden Pond, which was later to become famous as the setting of his experiment in simple living.

(C) When he was five years old, Henry David Thoreau first saw Walden Pond, and later this became famous as the setting of his experiment in simple living.

(D) At the age of five years, Henry David Thoreau first saw Walden Pond, and this place was later to become famous as the setting of his experiment in simple living.

(E) Henry David Thoreau, being five years old, first saw Walden Pond, later becoming famous as the setting of his experiment in simple living.

The original sentence presented by this question has a structural problem. Because the clause introduced by the relative pronoun *which* describes Walden Pond, the clause should follow immediately after *Walden Pond.* This basic structural problem is most easily corrected by moving the words *at the age of five years* to the beginning of the sentence. At the same time, the stilted phrasing of *at the age of five years* can also be eliminated. Only choice (B) makes both these changes. Choices (C) and (D) use *and* to connect the two major ideas of the sentence, falsely suggesting that the events happen in sequence: "He saw . . . and it became. . . ." Because *and* does not connect the ideas appropriately, choices (C) and (D) are not acceptable responses. Choice (E) introduces two flaws. The first is the use of *being,* which erroneously suggests a cause-and-effect relationship between ideas. ("He saw . . . being he was five years old. . . .") The second flaw is that in choice (E) the placement of *later becoming* at the end of the sentence suggests that the phrase refers to the subject of the sentence, *Thoreau,* and not to *Walden Pond.*

4. The trachea performs a simple but vital function: it furnishes part of the open passageway that, through it, air can reach the lungs from the outside.

(A) that, through it,
(B) and through it
(C) through which
(D) which, by going through it,
(E) so that through it

This sentence asks you to choose the most appropriate way to connect two related ideas. In all the choices except (C), the word *it* presents a problem. The pronoun should refer to *passageway* but may be interpreted as referring to *part.* In addition, each choice has another problem. (A) is not phrased idiomatically. (B) introduces a change in the relationship between the ideas through the insertion of *and.* (D) is wordy and unidiomatic. The use of *so that* in (E) changes the relationship between the ideas. Only choice (C), the correct answer, avoids all of these problems.

Type III

The third type of question does not ask you to find errors. Instead, you are presented with an acceptable sentence and asked to rephrase that sentence in a specified way. The rephrasing required in questions of this type is the sort you make in your own writing to achieve variety in sentence structure or to change emphasis in a sentence. The following directions appear in the test.

19

Directions: Each of the following sentences is to be rephrased according to the directions that follow it. You should make only those changes that the directions require. Keep the meaning of the revised sentence as close to the meaning of the original sentence as the directions for that sentence permit.

EXAMPLES:

I. Sentence: Coming to the city as a young man, he found a job as a newspaper reporter.

Directions: Change Coming to He came.

(A) and so he found
(B) and found
(C) and there he had found
(D) and then finding
(E) and had found

Your rephrased sentence will probably read: "He came to the city as a young man and found a job as a newspaper reporter." This sentence contains the correct answer: (B) and found. A sentence which used one of the alternate phrases would change the meaning or intention of the original sentence, would be a poorly written sentence, or would be less effective than another possible revision.

II. Sentence: Owing to her political skill, Ms. French had many supporters.

Directions: Begin with Many people supported.

(A) so
(B) while
(C) although
(D) because
(E) and

Your rephrased sentence will probably read: "Many people supported Ms. French because she was politically skillful." This new sentence contains only choice (D), which is the correct answer. None of the other choices will fit into an effective sentence that meets the requirements of standard written English and retains the original meaning.

If you think that more than one good sentence can be made according to the directions, select the sentence that

retains, insofar as possible, the meaning of the original sentence;

is most natural in phrasing and construction;

meets the requirements of standard written English; and

is the best sentence in terms of conciseness, idiom, logic and other qualities found in well-written sentences.

When you have thought out a good rephrasing of the original sentence, find in choices (A) through (E) the word or entire phrase that you have included in your revised sentence and blacken the corresponding space on your answer sheet. Be sure that the choice you select is the fullest expression of your revision available in the choices; that is, for example, if your revised sentence contains was playing and both was playing and playing are offered as choices, playing would not be an acceptable answer.

5. Although it is too costly to use a computer for navigating small pleasure craft, the computer can produce precise measurements of all that happens to any moving vessel.

Begin with Capable of.

(A) but its use
(B) but to use the computer
(C) the cost of the computer
(D) the computer is
(E) it is

In revising this sentence, keep in mind that the revision calls for a beginning modifier that must not be left dangling; that is, the part of the sentence that immediately follows the modifying phrase must begin with the words *the computer*. Only choice (D) permits such a sentence: *Capable of producing precise measurements of all that happens to any moving vessel, the computer is too costly to use for navigating small pleasure craft.*

6. Some elements of fiction appeared in medieval literature; however, not until the eighteenth century did they merge in the modern novel.

Begin with In the eighteenth century.

(A) have been appearing
(B) did appear
(C) had appeared
(D) were to appear
(E) does appear

An acceptable revision of this sentence must maintain proper tense sequence, as this revised sentence does:

In the eighteenth century some elements of fiction that had appeared in medieval literature [finally] were merged in the modern novel.

Although "appeared" can also be considered acceptable in standard written English, only *had appeared* is found among the choices. Choice (C) is the correct response. The other forms of "appear" given in the choices are all inappropriate in tense. (E) is also inappropriate because the verb is singular.

The Essay

At the December administration of the Achievement Tests, the English Composition Achievement Test includes a 20-minute essay on an assigned topic and 40 minutes of multiple-choice questions. Although the essay version of the test is offered at both the Saturday and Sunday administrations, the topics and questions for each day are different.

Because all students at one administration must write on the same topic, the topic must be one that they can react to and begin writing about almost immediately. The faculty committee that selects the topic looks for one that students can respond to readily and in a variety of ways and that allows different students to argue for different points of view.

How the Essays are Scored

Each December, about 150 high school and college English teachers gather for one week to read and score the essays. At this session, each of the approximately 82,000 essays is scored by two different readers. The readers are aware of the quality of writing they can expect from students at the end of high school or at the beginning of college. Therefore, they do not have unrealistic expectations of what you can accomplish in 20 minutes.

The essays written for the English Composition Achievement Test are scored holistically; that is, they are read for the total impression they make on the reader. This total impression is created by every aspect of the essay; spelling, punctuation, organization, choice of words, and the host of other characteristics of writing are all considered. Readers are instructed to read the essays quickly and to score immediately while their impression of the total essay remains fresh. Further, the reader who scores holistically is encouraged to look at what students have done well rather than at what they have failed to do. The scorer does not mark a paper for errors.

Essays are scored on a four-point scale, with four as the highest score and one as the lowest. The total essay score is the sum of the two readers' scores and is weighted to equal one-third of the total English Composition Achievement Test score. Any papers that receive two widely divergent scores are read a third time to resolve the discrepancies.

The English Composition Achievement Test is meant to provide an indication of your total writing ability (when writing ability is defined as the ability to do the kind of writing required in most college classes). That is, the test is not meant to analyze particular strengths or weaknesses in a student's writing ability. Therefore, no subscore for the essay alone is reported. The total score reported is based on both the weighted score on the essay and the score on the multiple-choice questions.

Sample Essays

The following sample essays are actual students' essays set in type from the handwritten texts. The errors in them are the ones the students themselves made. Some of the errors in the papers are, of course, simply the result of haste. As a group, the sample essays suggest the variety of student responses and the range of writing competence shown by the student authors. The discussion that follows each sample essay addresses its specific strengths and weaknesses, but no such analysis occurs during the reading.

The following directions appear in the test book given to students taking the English Composition Achievement Test with Essay.

Directions: You have twenty minutes to plan and write an essay on the topic assigned below. DO NOT WRITE ON ANOTHER TOPIC. AN ESSAY ON ANOTHER TOPIC IS NOT ACCEPTABLE.

The essay is assigned to give you an opportunity to show how well you can write. You should, therefore, take care to express your thoughts on the topic clearly and effectively. How well you write is much more important than how much you write, but to cover the topic adequately you may want to write more than one paragraph. Be specific.

Your essay must be written on the lines provided on your answer sheet. You will receive no other paper on which to write. You will find that you have enough space if you write on every line, avoid wide margins, and keep your handwriting to a reasonable size. It is important to remember that what you write will be read by someone who is not familiar with your handwriting. Try to write or print so that what you are writing is legible.

DO NOT WRITE IN YOUR TEST BOOK. You will receive credit only for what you write on your answer sheet.

The Essay Topic for December 4, 1982

Consider carefully the following quotation and the assignment following it. Then, plan and write your essay as directed.

"People seldom stand up for what they truly believe; instead they merely go along with the popular view."

Assignment: Do you agree or disagree with this statement? Write an essay in which you support your opinion with specific examples from history, contemporary affairs, literature, or personal observation.

Essays with a Total Score of 8 (Each reader gave the essay a score of 4.)

Although essays in this category differ in approach and style and have slight differences in quality, they all have the same characteristics: good organization, good command of the language, and an interesting style. These essays are not perfect, nor are they expected to be, for each is only a first draft written in the 20 minutes allotted. The essay below, which is representative of this category, received the highest possible score.

ESSAY I

Conformity is a necessary part of living in a society. People need one another to survive and must therefore often compromise their individual beliefs for the benefit of the whole. However, I think that the trend to conform is changing in recent decades in our society. People are often unwilling to express their views and stand up for them because they fear criticism. Yet recently, books and politics reflect more and more individual viewpoints and beliefs.

Politically, America has changed radically from the early 1900's. During the 1960's and through the present, people have felt increasingly unafraid to voice their arguments, though they may be against the popularly held view. Rallies against the Vietnam War and against racism began by a few standing out and disagreeing, such as Abbie Hoffman and Martin Luther King, Jr. Though these movements grew in strength and numbers until they became the popular viewpoint, they nevertheless began with people, who wouldn't give into pressure and wouldn't conform.

Non-conforming patterns are evident in late 20th-century literature as well. *Walden Two* by B.F. Skinner is a story of a group of people, headed by one man, who separated themselves from society and built and lived in a community which was the physical expression of their views. They felt that society was too competitive, forcing mankind to strive for unrealistic goals at the expense of happiness. Their society was an experiment in communal living without the pressures from society.

Conformity is a aspect of society which affects these who aren't strong enough to defy their peers. Conformity occurs most often among adolescents, who are the most susceptible to it. However, this trend is rapidly changing in today's society because of an increasing tolerance for different viewpoints.

Essay I has traditional structure: the first paragraph states the topic; the second and third present examples from books and politics, as mentioned in the last sentence of the first paragraph; the fourth concludes the essay, reaffirming what was said in the first paragraph. The essay is a unified statement in which the writer uses pertinent examples to support the opinion expressed. The sentence structure varies; the vocabulary is controlled and effective. Despite a bit of repetition in the last paragraph, the essay must be considered well done, given the 20-minute time limit imposed upon the writer.

Essays with a Total Score of 6 (Each reader gave the essay a score of 3.)

Essays in this category, as in every category, vary in quality. In this group, the essays might be described as ranging from good to merely competent. Although the papers show that the writers have a basic command of the skills needed for good writing, they have the kinds of flaws that keep them out of the highest range. They may lack such qualities as a forceful presentation or adequate development of the basic argument.

ESSAY II

I believe that many people do stand up for what they believe, but the majority of people merely go along with the popular view. This can be seen in everyday situations or can be seen in many examples in History.

I would say that the best example in History of people standing up for what they do believe has to be the early Christians. The early christians were looked down upon and persecuted for their beliefs but this did not stop them. Many of them died because of their beliefs. The christians were so heavily outnumbered that you cannot say that they went along with the popular view.

On the other hand many people do go along with the popular view. I often notice this when observing the teenagers. In certain situations they give in to peer pressure. For instance when other kids are drinking they also drink, in order to be part of the crowd. Some teenagers do this even when they dislike it merely to go along with the popular view.

I believe that this statement can be true of some people while not true of others. It really depends on the type of person you are considering. If he is strong willed and outgoing he will probably do what he believes. If he is unsure of himself or insecure he will probably go along with the popular view.

Essay II is competently written. The writer of the essay takes a middle-of-the-road stance and presents that stance in the first paragraph. Supporting, but generalized, examples are provided and are followed by a conclusion. The essay, however, to some extent lacks force because the writer frequently employs "I believe" and "I would say." The writer relies heavily on the vague "this" and "it" to relate one idea to another. The sentence structure has little variation.

Essays with a Total Score of 4 (Each reader gave the essay a score of 2.)

Essays in this category, in comparison with the other essays being scored, have faults that override whatever merits they may have. Although the essays show that the writers have a fairly good grasp of English sentence structure, they usually have such problems as limited development of the argument, few explicit connections between ideas, and inexactness and ineffectiveness of expression.

ESSAY III

I would agree with this statement, because through my own personal observations I've notice that people will seldom stand up for what they believe, they usually go along with the popular view.

Through my own personal experience I found out that teenagers are always changing their thoughts and going along with the majority. The basic reason for this is "peer pressure". They feel that they will not fit in if they don't agree completely with the majority. Sometimes in my life I've done this, because I did not want to become a standout. I felt that I had to agree with my friends eventhough deep down I knew they were wrong. One example of this was during the past summer when a few of my friends and I went to a party. I really did not want to go, but since my friends went I felt obligated to go. Deep down I knew that if I did not go to the party my friends would desert me for life, but I still wanted to show up an image. If I did not go to the party my image would be

The writer of Essay III has constructed an argument and provided an example to support that argument, but does not express ideas precisely or concisely. This faulty expression of ideas is illustrated in ". . . teenagers are always changing their thoughts" and "One example of this was during the past summer when a few of my friends and I went to a party." In addition, the essay rambles. The organization is not strong; connecting words are not often used; words and ideas are repeated.

Essays with a Total Score of 2 (Each reader gave the essay a score of 1.)

Essays in this category are the poorest of those being scored. They are seriously flawed. No important feature of an essay in this category is well done enough to lift the essay out of the bottom category. Usually, the problems in these essays so interfere with communication that it is difficult to understand exactly what the writer is trying to say.

ESSAY IV

I believe that if a person has an idea about something, but popular opinion disagrees with them, that person will usally change their mind.

Popular opinion is known as the moral way of believing. This is evidenced in peer pressure. Situations where a kid may like or dislike someone, will change if many of the other students disagree with him. The kid doesn't want to appear different from anybody else. He may alienate himself to many other students and he wouldn't like that at all. People don't like to be different because that gives them a radical view, and this would be giving themselves a bad impression.

The language in Essay IV is not exact and the ideas are not clearly presented. Although almost every sentence is syntactically correct, the ideas contained are difficult to understand. The first sentence of the second paragraph, for example, is not explained, and the last sentence is meaningless.

English Composition Achievement Test

The test that follows is an actual edition of an English Composition Achievement Test administered in May 1983. So that you will have an idea of what the actual test administration will be like, try to take this test under conditions as close as possible to those of the actual test. It will probably help if you

- Set aside an hour for the test when you will not be interrupted, so that you can complete all of it in one sitting.

- Sit at a desk with no other papers or books. You can't take a calculator, a dictionary, other books, or notes into the test room.

- Have a kitchen timer or clock in front of you for timing yourself.

- Tear out an answer sheet from the back of this book and fill it in just as you would on the day of the test. You can use one answer sheet for as many as three Achievement Tests.

- Read the instructions that precede the test. When you take the test, you will be asked to read them before you begin answering questions.

- After you finish the test, read the sections on "How to Score the English Composition Achievement Test" and "Reviewing Your Test Performance," which follow the test.

ENGLISH COMPOSITION TEST

The top portion of the section of the answer sheet which you will use in taking the English Composition test must be filled in exactly as shown in the illustration below. Note carefully that you have to do all of the following on your answer sheet:

1. Print ENGLISH COMPOSITION on the line to the right of the words "Achievement Test."
2. Blacken spaces 5 and 7 in the row of spaces immediately under the words "Test Code."
3. Blacken space 1 in the group of five spaces labeled X.
4. Blacken space 4 in the group of five spaces labeled Y.

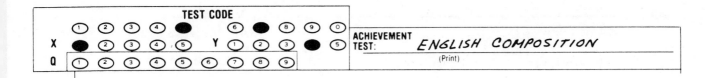

You are to leave blank the nine spaces which are labeled Q.

When the supervisor gives the signal, turn the page and begin the English Composition test. There are 100 numbered spaces on the answer sheet and 90 questions in the English Composition test. Therefore, use only spaces 1 to 90 for recording your answers.

ENGLISH COMPOSITION TEST

Directions: The following sentences contain problems in grammar, usage, diction (choice of words), and idiom.

   Some sentences are correct.
   No sentence contains more than one error.

You will find that the error, if there is one, is underlined and lettered. Assume that all other elements of the sentence are correct and cannot be changed. In choosing answers, follow the requirements of standard written English.

If there is an error, select the one underlined part that must be changed in order to make the sentence correct, and blacken the corresponding space on the answer sheet.

If there is no error, mark answer space E.

EXAMPLES:

  SAMPLE ANSWERS

I. He spoke <u>bluntly</u> and <u>angrily</u> to
     A   B
<u>we</u> <u>spectators</u>. <u>No error</u>
 C D   E

   I. Ⓐ Ⓑ ● Ⓓ Ⓔ

II. She <u>works</u> <u>every day</u> <u>so that</u> she would
     A B   C
become <u>financially</u> independent in her old
     D
age. <u>No error</u>
    E

   II. ● Ⓑ Ⓒ Ⓓ Ⓔ

---

1. In 1977, one week <u>after</u> the Episcopal church
         A
<u>officially decided</u> to accept women <u>into</u>
   B   C
the priesthood, Pauli Murray, a Black woman,

<u>has become</u> that denomination's first female
  D
priest. <u>No error</u>
    E

2. <u>If</u> I am reading the editorial <u>correct</u>, the mayor is
 A   B
deliberately <u>avoiding any</u> discussion of the tax-
      C
reform bill <u>until after</u> the November elections.
       D

<u>No error</u>
  E

3. The report Alexander <u>is discussing</u>, a report
         A
prepared jointly by <u>he and</u> the committee, does
        B
not <u>take into account</u> the socioeconomic status
    C
of those interviewed. <u>No error</u>
    D   E

4. <u>Along</u> the curve of Florida's island keys <u>lies</u>
  A   B
a reef of living coral, <u>the only one</u> of
        C
a kind in the continental United States.
<u>   </u>
D
<u>No error</u>
 E

GO ON TO THE NEXT PAGE ➤

ENGLISH COMPOSITION TEST—*Continued*

5. The Papago Indians of southern Arizona take

   justifiable <u>pride in</u> <u>their</u> traditional craft of
        A   B

   basket-weaving, an art that <u>has brought</u>
             C

   them fame <u>throughout</u> the Southwest.
          D

   <u>No error</u>
     E

6. Austria did not fare <u>well</u> in Third World markets
           A

   <u>because</u> <u>they exported</u> <u>too few</u> of the goods
     B   C   D

   needed for the development of Third World

   nations. <u>No error</u>
         E

7. Driving <u>less</u> frequently is one way to save energy;
        A

   <u>to turn off</u> all appliances <u>when they are</u> not
     B   C

   being used <u>is another.</u> <u>No error</u>
       D   E

8. <u>When</u> rumors of a merger <u>began to spread,</u>
    A   B

   neither of the company presidents <u>were available</u>
              C

   for comment. <u>No error</u>
      D   E

9. After Gertrude Ederle <u>had swam</u> the English
            A

   Channel, she <u>was acclaimed</u> the first woman ever
          B

   <u>to accomplish</u> <u>the feat.</u> <u>No error</u>
     C   D   E

10. The record left by fossils, the ancient remains of

   plants and animals, <u>provide</u> scientists <u>with</u>
            A   B

   their primary <u>source of</u> knowledge <u>about</u>
          C   D

   prehistoric life. <u>No error</u>
         E

11. <u>Being absent</u> the time his enemies <u>voted down</u>
     A   B

   his proposal, Selby <u>is worried</u> about
           C

   <u>missing further</u> meetings of the board of
      D

   directors. <u>No error</u>
       E

12. Apparently <u>convinced by</u> our reasoning, the
         A

   foundation awarded <u>Carlos and I</u> a grant
           B

   <u>to establish</u> a network of community centers
     C

   <u>throughout</u> the city. <u>No error</u>
     D   E

13. Although it is <u>no longer</u> the <u>tallest of</u>
        A   B

   Manhattan's skyscrapers, the Empire State

   Building <u>still</u> <u>dominates</u> the midtown section of
       C   D

   the city. <u>No error</u>
       E

14. <u>Also supported</u> by the commission <u>was</u>
    A   B

   the proposed health clinics and the proposed

   <u>center</u> to distribute information <u>on job-training</u>
     C   D

   opportunities. <u>No error</u>
        E

15. The living conditions of some migrant workers

   <u>having been improved</u> <u>primarily</u>
       A   B

   <u>through the efforts</u> of <u>people like</u> Cesar Chavez.
      C   D

   <u>No error</u>
   E

16. <u>Many of</u> the problems <u>with which</u> modern phi-
    A   B

   losophers have concerned <u>themselves</u> were also
           C

   discussed by Plato and Aristotle. <u>No error</u>
     D   E

GO ON TO THE NEXT PAGE

29

17. The jury <u>took offense</u> at the prosecutor's mocking
    A
    tone, <u>but could deny</u> neither the <u>accuracy of</u>
    B C
    the charges <u>or</u> the seriousness of the crime.
    D
    <u>No error</u>
    E

18. <u>In the opinion</u> of the lecturer, <u>a belief in</u>
    A B
    Christianity is not a condition necessary <u>in</u>
    C
    <u>the enjoyment of</u> medieval literature. <u>No error</u>
    D E

19. <u>Because they</u> painted scenes of life as ordinary
    A
    people <u>lived it</u>, <u>rather than</u> scenes from myths,
    B C
    many nineteenth-century American artists differed
    <u>from prior times</u>. <u>No error</u>
    D E

20. The young fish <u>were</u> very tiny, yet each of
    A
    <u>them ate</u> many times <u>its</u> own <u>weight in</u>
    B C D
    solid food every day. <u>No error</u>
    E

21. Many professional athletes <u>are</u> motivated by
    A
    either personal pride <u>and</u> love of their sport, but
    B
    <u>some seem</u> interested <u>only in money</u>. <u>No error</u>
    C D E

22. How the courts <u>rule on</u> patent procedures
    A
    <u>applicable to</u> laboratory-created microorganisms
    B
    <u>could determine</u> the commercial application of
    C
    such <u>breakthroughs</u>. <u>No error</u>
    D E

23. Intense preoccupation <u>on</u> technique
    A
    <u>appears to be</u> <u>the one</u> trait that great pianists
    B C
    <u>have in</u> common. <u>No error</u>
    D E

24. <u>In 1508</u>, the Spanish explorer Juan Ponce
    A
    De León— <u>the same</u> Ponce de León who
    B
    later <u>would seek</u> the fountain of youth—landed
    C
    on Puerto Rico <u>accompanied</u> by a small force.
    D
    <u>No error</u>
    E

25. Sociologists <u>agree that</u> a status system is
    A
    <u>not only</u> present but also <u>of necessity in</u>
    B C
    <u>any complex</u> social system. <u>No error</u>
    D E

26. The quality of multiple-vitamin tablets
    <u>is determined</u> by <u>how long</u> <u>its</u> potency
    A B C
    <u>can be protected</u> by the manufacturer's coating
    D
    material. <u>No error</u>
    E

27. Each of Beethoven's <u>many acts of</u> ungraciousness
    A
    <u>seems to have been balanced</u> <u>by an act</u> of
    B C D
    kindness. <u>No error</u>
    E

28. Many teachers encourage students <u>to read</u> in
    A
    their spare time on the premise <u>that</u> reading
    B
    <u>increases</u> <u>their</u> minds. <u>No error</u>
    C D E

29. The accidental <u>meeting of</u> the distant cousins
    A
    <u>came about through</u> an <u>incredulous</u> <u>series of</u>
    B C D
    coincidences. <u>No error</u>
    E

30. It is <u>far easier</u> to ride a bicycle <u>than explaining</u>
    A B
    in words <u>exactly how</u> a bicycle <u>is ridden</u>.
    C D
    <u>No error</u>
    E

GO ON TO THE NEXT PAGE

ENGLISH COMPOSITION TEST—*Continued*

<u>Directions:</u>   In each of the following sentences, some part of the sentence or the entire sentence is underlined. Beneath each sentence you will find five ways of phrasing the underlined part. The first of these repeats the original; the other four are different. If you think the original is better than any of the alternatives, choose answer A; otherwise choose one of the others. Select the best version and blacken the corresponding space on your answer sheet.

This is a test of correctness and effectiveness of expression. In choosing answers, follow the requirements of standard written English; that is, pay attention to grammar, choice of words, sentence construction, and punctuation. Choose the answer that best expresses the meaning of the original sentence. Your choice should produce the most effective sentence—clear and precise, without awkwardness or ambiguity.

EXAMPLE:

Ms. Rose <u>planning</u> to teach a course in biology next summer.

SAMPLE ANSWER

Ⓐ Ⓑ Ⓒ Ⓓ ●

(A) planning
(B) are planning
(C) have planned
(D) with a plan
(E) plans

---

31. During the labor dispute, barrels of potatoes were emptied across the <u>highway, and they thereby blocked it to all traffic.</u>

(A) highway, and they thereby blocked it to all traffic
(B) highway and therefore blocking it to all traffic
(C) highway, by which all traffic was therefore blocked
(D) highway, and therefore this had all traffic blocked
(E) highway, thereby blocking all traffic

32. <u>The age of ninety having been reached,</u> the photographer Imogen Cunningham became interested in photographing others who had also achieved that age.

(A) The age of ninety having been reached
(B) The age of ninety being reached
(C) At ninety, when she reached that age
(D) When she reached the age of ninety
(E) When having reached the age of ninety

33. The representatives of the parking-lot operators asserted <u>as to the defensibility of their practices as legal and ethical.</u>

(A) as to the defensibility of their practices as legal and ethical
(B) as to their practices and their defensibility on legal and ethical grounds
(C) that their practices, that is the operators, are defensible in legal terms as well as ethics
(D) that in regards to defensibility their practices are legally and ethically defensible
(E) that the practices of the operators are legally and ethically defensible

34. Many state universities continued to expand during the 1970's <u>despite clear signs of a decline</u> in the number of 18 to 20 year olds.

(A) despite clear signs of a decline
(B) even though clear signs of a decline
(C) with clear signs of a decline
(D) however clearly the declines
(E) when there was clear signs of a decline

GO ON TO THE NEXT PAGE ➡

35. The major reasons students give for failing to participate in the political process is that they have demanding assignments and work at part-time jobs.

    (A) is that they have demanding assignments and work at
    (B) are demanding assignments and they work at
    (C) are that they have demanding assignments and that they have
    (D) is having demanding assignments and having
    (E) are demanding assignments, in addition to working at

36. Although Jonathan is very much interested in Mexican culture, he does not speak Spanish and has never visited Mexico.

    (A) he does not speak Spanish and has never visited Mexico
    (B) it is without being able to speak Spanish or having visited in Mexico
    (C) he does not speak Spanish and has never visited there
    (D) he does not speak Spanish nor has he ever visited there
    (E) it is without speaking Spanish nor having visited there

37. Returning to Dayville after ten years, the small town seemed much livelier to Margo than it had been when she was growing up there.

    (A) Returning to Dayville after ten years, the small town seemed much livelier to Margo
    (B) Having returned to Dayville after ten years, it seemed a much livelier town to Margo
    (C) After Margo returned to Dayville in ten years, the small town had seemed much livelier
    (D) Margo returned to Dayville after ten years, and then she thought the small town much livelier
    (E) When Margo returned to Dayville after ten years, she thought the small town much livelier

38. Many people are alarmed by the recent Supreme Court ruling that gives judges discretionary power to determine about closing trials to the public.

    (A) about closing trials
    (B) whether he or she ought to close trials
    (C) if he or she should close trials
    (D) whether or not trials should be closed
    (E) the closing of trials, if they wish,

39. Archaeologists say that the Pueblo village of Acoma, which is 7,500 feet above sea level and 400 feet above the valley floor, is the oldest continuously inhabited spot in the United States.

    (A) which is 7,500 feet above sea level and 400 feet above
    (B) located 7,500 feet high above sea level while measuring 400 feet above
    (C) with a height 7,500 feet above sea level as well as 400 feet above that of
    (D) 7,500 feet higher than sea level and ascending 400 feet above
    (E) being 7,500 feet above sea level and 400 feet high measured from that of

40. Having command of pathos, tragedy, as well as humor, George Eliot is considered to be a great English novelist.

    (A) Having command of pathos, tragedy, as well as humor
    (B) Having command of pathos, tragedy, and her humorous side
    (C) By being in command of both pathos and tragedy and also humor
    (D) With her command of pathos and tragedy and being humorous
    (E) Because of her command of pathos, tragedy, and humor

41. Journalists should present a balanced view of the news but with their goal to stir discussion, to unsettle complacent thinkers.

    (A) with their goal to stir
    (B) ought also to stir
    (C) aiming at the same time to stir
    (D) also trying to stir
    (E) its goal should also be in stirring

GO ON TO THE NEXT PAGE

42. Separated by the sea from any major population center, the aborigines of Australia <u>have developed a unique culture</u>.

    (A) have developed a unique culture
    (B) have developed into a very unique culture
    (C) have a unique development, their culture
    (D) had developed a very unique culture
    (E) had developed their culture uniquely

43. <u>Whether the ancient Egyptians actually sailed or did not</u> to South America remains uncertain, but that they could have was demonstrated by Heyerdahl's Ra II expedition.

    (A) Whether the ancient Egyptians actually sailed or did not
    (B) Whether in actuality the ancient Egyptians sailed or did not
    (C) The actuality of whether the ancient Egyptians sailed
    (D) That the ancient Egyptians actually did sail
    (E) That the ancient Egyptians may actually have sailed

44. Caution in leadership can <u>sometimes be related more to intelligence than to lack of forcefulness.</u>

    (A) sometimes be related more to intelligence than to lack of forcefulness
    (B) be related often to intelligence, not only to lack of forcefulness
    (C) be related more to intelligence rather than lack of forcefulness
    (D) often be related to intelligence as to lack of forcefulness
    (E) sometimes be related more to intelligence as well as lack of forcefulness

45. Allowed to remain in any warm place, a covered flour mixture will grow the yeast for a sourdough <u>starter, the problem being that the bread</u> may not have the desired taste.

    (A) starter, the problem being that the bread
    (B) starter, but the problem is that using the starter to make the bread
    (C) starter; in using it to make the bread, you
    (D) starter, but bread made from that starter
    (E) starter; the problem is that in making bread from it, it

GO ON TO THE NEXT PAGE

Directions: Each of the following sentences is to be rephrased according to the directions that follow it. You should make only those changes that the directions require. Keep the meaning of the revised sentence as close to the meaning of the original sentence as the directions for that sentence permit.

EXAMPLES:

I. Sentence: Coming to the city as a young man, he found a job as a newspaper reporter.

Directions: Change Coming to He came.

(A) and so he found
(B) and found
(C) and there he had found
(D) and then finding
(E) and had found

Your rephrased sentence will probably read: "He came to the city as a young man and found a job as a newspaper reporter." This sentence contains the correct answer: (B) and found. A sentence which used one of the alternate phrases would change the meaning or intention of the original sentence, would be a poorly written sentence, or would be less effective than another possible revision.

II. Sentence: Owing to her political skill, Ms. French had many supporters.

Directions: Begin with Many people supported.

(A) so
(B) while
(C) although
(D) because
(E) and

Your rephrased sentence will probably read: "Many people supported Ms. French because she was politically skillful." This new sentence contains only choice D, which is the correct answer. None of the other choices will fit into an effective sentence that meets the requirements of standard written English and retains the original meaning.

If you think that more than one good sentence can be made according to the directions, select the sentence that

retains, insofar as possible, the meaning of the original sentence;
is most natural in phrasing and construction;
meets the requirements of standard written English; and
is the best sentence in terms of conciseness, idiom, logic, and other qualities found in
  well-written sentences.

When you have thought out a good rephrasing of the original sentence, find in choices A through E the word or entire phrase that you have included in your revised sentence and blacken the corresponding space on your answer sheet. Be sure that the choice you select is the fullest expression of your revision available in the choices; that is, for example, if your revised sentence contains was playing and both was playing and playing are offered as choices, playing would not be an acceptable answer.

46. Britain applied for membership in the European Economic Community, but that application was vetoed in 1963 by French President Charles de Gaulle.

    Begin with French President Charles de Gaulle.

    (A) found its application vetoed
    (B) to veto Britain's
    (C) vetoed Britain's
    (D) vetoed its
    (E) had vetoed it

47. The supervisor was able, or so he thought, to make the decision himself.

    Change able to capable.

    (A) to be making
    (B) of having made
    (C) of making
    (D) to have made
    (E) to make

GO ON TO THE NEXT PAGE ➤

48. Probably nothing threatens our economy more than our dependence on foreign oil.

    Begin with There is probably.

    (A) no more a threat than
    (B) no greater threat to
    (C) not as much of a threat as
    (D) nothing to threaten
    (E) nothing threatening so much

49. For centuries it was midwives, not doctors, who delivered babies.

    Change who delivered to delivered.

    (A) centuries it was
    (B) centuries midwives were
    (C) centuries midwives
    (D) centuries it was not doctors
    (E) centuries midwives but

50. The immigrant parents who denied a formal education to many second generation Americans did so because they regarded public schools as alien and immoral.

    Begin with Formal education was denied.

    (A) because they regarded them
    (B) by immigrant parents who regarded
    (C) which their immigrant parents regarded
    (D) because of their regard of
    (E) by immigrant parents regarding them

51. In 1978 Mary Clarke became the first woman to achieve the rank of Major General in the United States Army. She was the commander of Fort McClellan, Alabama.

    Combine these two sentences into one.

    (A) Clarke, the commander
    (B) Clarke, the first woman whose
    (C) Clarke, and she was
    (D) Clarke, and so she became
    (E) Clarke, being the commander

52. The creation of Black Studies programs was based on the belief that existing academic offerings did not take the contribution of Black people into account.

    Begin with Those who favored.

    (A) based on believing
    (B) based their belief about
    (C) had a belief
    (D) were believing
    (E) believed

53. The Bank of the United States was easily the largest, the best known, and the most powerful of the privileged monopolies of the nation.

    Begin with Among the.

    Your rewritten sentence will end with which of the following?

    (A) most powerful.
    (B) easily.
    (C) of the nation.
    (D) a privileged monopoly.
    (E) than any of them.

54. Workers with extensive schooling are not necessarily a requirement of advancing technology.

    Change requirement to require.

    Your new sentence will begin with which of the following?

    (A) Workers with extensive schooling
    (B) Extensive schooling for workers
    (C) Advancing technology
    (D) To advance technology
    (E) Technology, when advancing

55. Although the composer Ethel Smyth was famous in England in the early years of this century for her operas and symphonies, she is almost unknown in this country.

    Begin with Almost unknown.

    (A) country, despite being famous for
    (B) country, the composer
    (C) country, the English
    (D) country, although she was famous
    (E) country and famous

56. A great many reforms resulting from the French Revolution were of benefit to the bourgeoisie.

    Begin with The French Revolution.

    (A) resulting benefits
    (B) that benefited
    (C) with a benefit
    (D) a result was the benefit
    (E) and the benefit

GO ON TO THE NEXT PAGE

57. Given the choice of living in the past, the present, or the future, many adventurous individuals doubtless would choose the least certain, most unpredictable future.

    Omit the past.

    (A) less certain, most unpredictable
    (B) less certain and unpredictable
    (C) least certain, unpredictable
    (D) less certain, more unpredictable
    (E) least certain and unpredictable

58. Korat cats, considered by the Thai people to be good-luck charms, had been imported into America in the 1930's, then carefully developed as a pure breed.

    Begin with Considered good-luck charms.

    (A) have been imported
    (B) upon being imported
    (C) were imported
    (D) after importation were
    (E) the importing of

59. The discoveries made by Freud have undermined rationalistic conceptions of mind as effectively as Copernicus' theory undermined classical accounts of the heavens.

    Begin with Just as Copernicus'.

    (A) thus   (B) so   (C) also
    (D) similarly   (E) as well

60. The computer's most profound impact arises less because of its usefulness as a calculating machine than because of its potential for communication.

    Eliminate both occurrences of because.

    (A) not only is it useful
    (B) and it has the potential
    (C) as well as its potential
    (D) more from being useful
    (E) more from its potential

61. The Chilula Indians were the original inhabitants of the Redwood Creek basin; they were dependent for survival on their ability to manage the resources of their land.

    Delete the semicolon.

    (A) basin, depended for survival
    (B) who were dependent on survival
    (C) where they depended on survival
    (D) basin, and depending for survival
    (E) basin, while they were dependent for survival

62. The administrators of the federal agencies that assist education have held long discussions about giving increased support to county colleges.

    Change discussions to discussed.

    (A) at length about giving
    (B) about giving, at length
    (C) the idea that giving
    (D) the idea of giving, at length,
    (E) at length giving

63. These Black artists, wishing like all other artists to communicate, have done so joyously and energetically in the Whitney Museum's current exhibition.

    Begin with These Black artists share.

    (A) as their
    (B) and have
    (C) so they
    (D) but they
    (E) by their

64. Apparently, Greek temples had porches more as a matter of tradition than as a necessary feature.

    Begin with The porch.

    (A) a traditional, if not a necessary, feature of
    (B) a feature that was traditional if it was not necessary for
    (C) featured traditionally but not necessarily in
    (D) not necessarily, if traditionally, featured
    (E) but through tradition, not necessity, a feature

GO ON TO THE NEXT PAGE

ENGLISH COMPOSITION TEST—*Continued*

65. Were they not opposed to all proposals from the current government, the peoples of Subali might have considered the most recent peace offer a major concession to their demands.

Change the peoples of Subali might have considered to the peoples of Subali did not consider.

Your new sentence will begin with which of the following?

(A) Although they were
(B) Despite their
(C) Without having been
(D) Because they were
(E) Due to their being

66. It seems clear that the concept of national honor flourished through the last few centuries not because it satisfied the needs of ordinary soldiers but because it satisfied the needs of rulers and generals.

Place not after the first satisfied.

(A) but those
(B) but because
(C) but that of
(D) but of
(E) but satisfied

67. After overcoming great obstacles, women are finally beginning to win their rightful places in the filmmaking industry.

Begin with Only after.

(A) women did
(B) women, beginning
(C) women are beginning
(D) were women
(E) have women

68. The appreciation of painting, as well as of other forms of art, demands the interplay of judgment and imagination.

Begin with The interplay.

(A) demands
(B) is demanded by
(C) is essential to
(D) are essential to
(E) demand

69. Perhaps to be called an antique an item need only no longer be manufactured.

Begin with Perhaps an antique is.

(A) an item that needs
(B) an item no longer to be
(C) any item no longer needing
(D) any item no longer
(E) any item that is to be

70. Gandhi started out with the normal ambitions of a young Indian student and adopted his nationalist opinions only by degrees.

Begin with Starting.

(A) he only adopted
(B) Gandhi adopted
(C) only adopting
(D) Gandhi had only adopted
(E) and only adopting

GO ON TO THE NEXT PAGE

37

ENGLISH COMPOSITION TEST—*Continued*

Note: These directions are exactly the same as the directions already given. They are <u>repeated</u> for easy reference as you work with the sentences that follow.

Directions: The following sentences contain problems in grammar, usage, diction (choice of words), and idiom.

> Some sentences are correct.
> No sentence contains more than one error.

You will find that the error, if there is one, is underlined and lettered. Assume that all other elements of the sentence are correct and cannot be changed. In choosing answers, follow the requirements of standard written English.

If there is an error, select the <u>one underlined part</u> that must be changed in order to make the sentence correct, and blacken the corresponding space on the answer sheet.

If there is no error, mark answer space E.

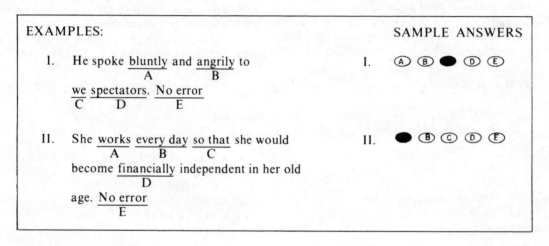

EXAMPLES:

I.   He spoke <u>bluntly</u> and <u>angrily</u> to
              A   B
<u>we</u> <u>spectators</u>. <u>No error</u>
   C   D   E

II.   She <u>works</u> <u>every day</u> <u>so that</u> she would
            A   B   C
become <u>financially</u> independent in her old
               D
age. <u>No error</u>
          E

SAMPLE ANSWERS

I.   Ⓐ Ⓑ ● Ⓓ Ⓔ

II.   ● Ⓑ Ⓒ Ⓓ Ⓔ

71. <u>Studying</u> the language and culture of a foreign
       A
country is highly <u>recommended to</u> the tourist
                        B
<u>who expect</u> <u>to learn from</u> his or her vacation
      C   D
abroad. <u>No error</u>
              E

72. A bottle manufacturer claims <u>to have helped</u>
                                        A
<u>solve</u> the problem of litter by developing <u>one</u>
   B   C
that can be <u>dissolved in</u> water. <u>No error</u>
                  D   E

73. <u>Although</u> malaria <u>has been</u> eradicated <u>from</u>
        A   B   C
the United States, this disease is still a threat

<u>when traveling</u> in some foreign countries.
       D
<u>No error</u>
      E

74. The increase in the number of summer camps

<u>for</u> overweight teen-agers <u>provides</u> a sad
  A   B
<u>commentary of</u> American <u>eating habits</u>.
        C   D
<u>No error</u>
      E

GO ON TO THE NEXT PAGE

ENGLISH COMPOSITION TEST—*Continued*

75. In <u>those cities where</u> public transportation is
            A

   adequate, <u>less</u> traffic problems <u>occur</u> and pedes-
           B   C

   trians are rarely <u>involved in</u> accidents. <u>No error</u>
                D   E

76. There is <u>probably no</u> success story <u>more dramatic</u>
       A   B   C

   <u>than</u> baseball's great hitter and right fielder,
     D

   Hank Aaron. <u>No error</u>
             E

77. The research study <u>reveals</u> startling proof of a
                A

   <u>constant</u> changing seafloor that <u>comprises</u>
      B   C

   the major <u>part of</u> the underwater landscape.
            D

   <u>No error</u>
    E

78. A hospital's <u>ability for supervising</u> the care of
                A

   patients <u>once</u> they <u>have been discharged</u> is
          B   C

   <u>largely determined</u> by the cooperation of those
         D

   patients. <u>No error</u>
          E

79. <u>Even though</u> only parts of clay vessels <u>may be</u>
       A   B

   recovered, pottery is <u>of inestimable</u> value to the
                  C

   archaeologist <u>because</u> it is virtually indestructible.
              D

   <u>No error</u>
     E

80. <u>Since some</u> people are <u>convinced that</u> dowsing,
       A   B

   a method of finding underground water with a

   Y-shaped stick, is effective, but others condemn

   the procedure <u>as</u> <u>mere superstition</u>. <u>No error</u>
             C   D   E

GO ON TO THE NEXT PAGE →

ENGLISH COMPOSITION TEST—*Continued*

<u>Note:</u>   These directions are exactly the same as the directions already given. They are repeated for easy reference as you work with the sentences that follow.

<u>Directions:</u>   In each of the following sentences, some part of the sentence or the entire sentence is underlined. Beneath each sentence you will find five ways of phrasing the underlined part. The first of these repeats the original; the other four are different. If you think the original is better than any of the alternatives, choose answer A; otherwise choose one of the others. Select the best version and blacken the corresponding space on your answer sheet.

This is a test of correctness and effectiveness of expression. In choosing answers, follow the requirements of standard written English; that is, pay attention to grammar, choice of words, sentence construction, and punctuation. Choose the answer that best expresses the meaning of the original sentence. Your choice should produce the most effective sentence—clear and precise, without awkwardness or ambiguity.

EXAMPLE:

Ms. Rose <u>planning</u> to teach a course in biology next summer.

(A) planning
(B) are planning
(C) have planned
(D) with a plan
(E) plans

SAMPLE ANSWER

Ⓐ Ⓑ Ⓒ Ⓓ ●

---

81. Having thought the problem through with some care, <u>that the committee did not understand her solution frustrated her extremely</u>.

    (A) that the committee did not understand her solution frustrated her extremely
    (B) the committee's failing to understand her solution was an extreme frustration
    (C) her frustration at the committee's failing to understand her solution was extreme
    (D) she found the committee's failure to understand her solution extremely frustrating
    (E) she was extremely frustrated about the committee not understanding her solution

82. <u>The more you eat of convenience foods</u>, the more our taste buds will prefer chemical flavors to natural ones.

    (A) The more you eat of convenience foods
    (B) The more we eat convenience foods
    (C) The more convenience foods are eaten
    (D) As the use of convenience foods increases
    (E) As people eat more convenience foods

83. As modern technological civilization advances northward, the Eskimos are losing the skills in hunting, fishing, and survival <u>that once made them self-reliant</u>.

    (A) that once made them self-reliant
    (B) by which they were once self-reliant
    (C) and are less self-reliant as a result of it
    (D) thereby becoming less self-reliant than once
    (E) with the result that of less self-reliance

84. Richard Wright moved many times in his life, <u>moving from the South first he went to the North, then eventually to France from the United States</u>.

    (A) moving from the South first he went to the North, then eventually to France from the United States
    (B) the first move he made was from the South to the North and eventually from the United States to France
    (C) first from the South to the North and eventually from the United States to France
    (D) moving first from the South, he came to the North and eventually to France
    (E) first from the South he moved to the North and ended up in France after leaving the United States

GO ON TO THE NEXT PAGE ▶

85. Because Uranus is nearly three billion kilometers from the Sun and is enveloped by a thick methane cloud layer, this blocks almost all solar radiation.

    (A) layer, this blocks almost all solar radiation
    (B) layer, this accounts for its receiving almost no solar radiation
    (C) layer is the reason why it receives almost no solar radiation
    (D) layer, almost no solar radiation reaches the planet
    (E) layer, it blocks almost all solar radiation from reaching the planet

86. We should be more concerned that a radiation leak will occur in a nuclear power plant and not its exploding like a bomb.

    (A) and not its exploding
    (B) as its exploding
    (C) than about an explosion of it
    (D) than the danger of the plant might explode
    (E) than that the plant will explode

87. Kelp from the sea, fusion, and solar power are energy sources whose future significance far exceeds their present use.

    (A) whose future significance far exceeds their
    (B) whose future significance far exceeds its
    (C) whose future significance more exceeds their
    (D) which future significance far exceeds their
    (E) that future significance far exceeds their

88. Though heavily dependent on the government for business and information, universities supply the space research center with talent, but it is a corporation independent of both.

    (A) information, universities supply the space research center with talent, but it is a corporation
    (B) information, universities supply the space research center with talent, while it remains a corporation
    (C) information while universities supply the space research center with talent, as a corporation it remains
    (D) information and supplied with talent by the universities, the corporation remains as a space research center
    (E) information and supplied with talent by the universities, the space research center is a corporation

89. In dictatorial societies, all information is contrived for a purpose that is as often concealment as it is for enlightenment.

    (A) as often concealment as it is for enlightenment
    (B) as often to conceal as to enlighten
    (C) as often for concealment as for enlightening
    (D) as often concealment as for enlightenment
    (E) often for concealment as for enlightenment

90. Hawaii is populated by people who, although their common language is English, the languages at home range from speaking Japanese to Thai.

    (A) the languages at home range from speaking Japanese to Thai
    (B) speak at home in languages from Japanese to Thai
    (C) the languages range from Japanese to Thai at home
    (D) speak languages at home that range from Japanese to Thai
    (E) they are speaking languages at home ranging from Japanese to Thai

S T O P

IF YOU FINISH BEFORE TIME IS CALLED, YOU MAY CHECK YOUR WORK ON THIS TEST ONLY.
DO NOT WORK ON ANY OTHER TEST IN THIS BOOK.

How to Score the English Composition Achievement Test

When you take the English Composition Achievement Test, your answer sheet will be "read" by a scanning machine that will record your responses to each multiple-choice question. (Essay scoring is described on page 21.) Then a computer will compare your answers with the correct answers and produce your raw score. You get one point for each correct answer. For each wrong answer, you lose one-quarter of a point. Questions you omit (and any for which you mark more than one answer) are not counted. This raw score is converted to a College Board scaled score that is reported to you and to the colleges you specify. After you have taken this test, you can get an idea of what your score might be by following the instructions in the next two sections.

Determining Your Raw Score

Step 1: Table A on the next page lists the correct answers for all the questions on the test.* Compare your answer with the correct answer and
- Put a check in the column marked "Right" if your answer is correct.
- Put a check in the column marked "Wrong" if your answer is incorrect.
- Leave both columns blank if you omitted the question.

Step 2: Count the number of right answers and enter the number here . . . . _____

Step 3: Count the number of wrong answers and enter

the number here . . . . 4)_____

Enter the result of dividing by 4 here . . . . _____

Step 4: Subtract the number you obtained in Step 3 from the number in Step 2; round the result to the nearest whole number (.5 is rounded up) and enter here. . _____

The number you obtained in Step 4 is your raw score. (The correction for guessing — subtraction of a quarter of a point for each incorrect answer — adjusts for the fact that random guessing on a large number of questions will result in some questions being answered correctly by chance.)
Instructions for converting your raw score to a scaled score follow.

*The last column in Table A gives the percentage of students who took the test in May 1983 that answered the question correctly. (See page 45 for further explanation.)

TABLE A

Answers to English Composition Achievement Test, Form 3FBO, and Percentage of Students Answering Each Question Correctly

Question Number	Correct Answer	Right	Wrong	Percentage of Students Answering the Question Correctly	Question Number	Correct Answer	Right	Wrong	Percentage of Students Answering the Question Correctly
1	D			94%	46	C			92%
2	B			75	47	C			81
3	B			69	48	B			80
4	D			83	49	C			83
5	E			89	50	B			80
6	C			23	51	A			69
7	B			68	52	E			76
8	C			35	53	A			62
9	A			74	54	C			50
10	A			56	55	B			63
11	A			40	56	B			59
12	B			59	57	D			47
13	E			80	58	C			68
14	B			55	59	B			25
15	A			89	60	E			44
16	E			49	61	A			26
17	D			75	62	E			24
18	C			62	63	B			41
19	D			38	64	A			34
20	E			46	65	D			40
21	B			90	66	A			32
22	E			53	67	E			30
23	A			59	68	C			40
24	E			51	69	D			48
25	C			73	70	B			69
26	C			46	71	C			78
27	E			33	72	C			68
28	C			36	73	D			38
29	C			24	74	C			35
30	B			68	75	B			31
31	E			87	76	D			26
32	D			81	77	B			40
33	E			69	78	A			39
34	A			92	79	E			30
35	C			43	80	A			66
36	A			81	81	D			62
37	E			49	82	B			67
38	D			86	83	A			60
39	A			64	84	C			53
40	E			73	85	D			52
41	B			31	86	E			35
42	A			73	87	A			49
43	D			26	88	E			16
44	A			49	89	B			23
45	D			65	90	D			46

Note: The percentages are based on the analysis of the answer sheets for a random sample of students who took this test in May 1983 and whose mean score was 501.

Finding Your College Board Scaled Score ▰

When you take Achievement Tests, the scores sent to the colleges you specify will be reported on the College Board scale, ranging from 200 to 800. The raw score that you obtained above (Step 4) can be converted to a scaled score by using Table B.

To find your scaled score on this test, locate your raw score in the left column of Table B; the corresponding score in the right column will be your College Board scaled score. For example, a raw score of 56 on this particular edition of the English Composition Achievement Test corresponds to a College Board scaled score of 580. Raw scores are converted to scaled scores to ensure that a score earned on any one edition of the English Composition Achievement Test is comparable to the same scaled score earned on any other edition of the test.

Because some editions of the English Composition Achievement Test may be slightly easier or more difficult than others, statistical adjustments are made in the scores so that each College Board scaled score indicates the same level of performance, regardless of the edition of the test you take and the ability of the group you take it with. A given raw score will corre-

TABLE B — SCORE CONVERSION TABLE					
English Composition Achievement Test, Form 3FBO					
Raw Score	College Board Scaled Score	Raw Score	College Board Scaled Score	Raw Score	College Board Scaled Score
90	800	55	570	20	360
89	790	54	570	19	360
88	780	53	560	18	350
87	770	52	560	17	350
86	760	51	550	16	340
85	750	50	540	15	330
84	750	49	540	14	330
83	740	48	530	13	320
82	740	47	530	12	320
81	730	46	520	11	310
80	720	45	510	10	300
79	720	44	510	9	300
78	710	43	500	8	290
77	710	42	500	7	290
76	700	41	490	6	280
75	690	40	480	5	280
74	690	39	480	4	270
73	680	38	470	3	260
72	680	37	470	2	260
71	670	36	460	1	250
70	660	35	450	0	250
69	660	34	450	−1	240
68	650	33	440	−2	230
67	650	32	440	−3	230
66	640	31	430	−4	220
65	630	30	420	−5	220
64	630	29	420	−6	210
63	620	28	410	−7 through −22	200
62	620	27	410		
61	610	26	400		
60	600	25	390		
59	600	24	390		
58	590	23	380		
57	590	22	380		
56	580	21	370		

spond to different College Board scores, depending on the edition of the test taken. A raw score of 40, for example, may convert to a College Board score of 480 on one edition of the test, but that raw score might convert to a College Board score of 500 on a slightly more difficult edition. When you take the English Composition Achievement Test on the actual test day, your score is likely to differ somewhat from the score you obtained on this test. People perform at different levels at different times, for reasons unrelated to the test itself. The precision of any test is also limited because it represents only a sample of all the possible questions that could be asked. (See page 12, "How Precise Are Your Scores?" for further information.)

Reviewing Your Test Performance

After you have scored your test, you should take some time to consider the following points in relation to your performance on the test.

- *Did you run out of time before you reached the end of the test?*

  If you did, you may want to consider tactics that will help you pace yourself better. For example, you may have spent too much time working on one or two difficult questions. A better approach might have been to continue the test and return to those questions after you had attempted to answer the remaining questions on the test.

- *Did you take a long time reading the directions for the test?*

  The directions in this test are the same as those in the English Composition Achievement Tests now being administered. You will save time when you read the directions on the test day if you become thoroughly familiar with them in advance.

- *How did you handle questions you were unsure of?*

  If you were able to eliminate one or more of the answer choices and you guessed from the remaining choices, then your approach probably worked to your advantage. On the other hand, omitting questions about which you have some knowledge or guessing answers haphazardly would probably be a mistake.

- *How difficult were the questions for you compared with other students who took the test?*

  By referring to Table A on page 43 you can find out how difficult each question was for the group of students who took the test in May 1983. The right-hand column in the table tells you what percentage of that group of students answered the question correctly. It is important to remember that these percentages are based on only one group of students; had this edition of the test been given to all students in the class of 1983 who took an English Composition Achievement Test, the percentages would probably have been different. A question that was answered correctly by almost everyone in the group, obviously, is an easy question. Question 46, for example, was answered correctly by 92 percent of the students in the sample. On the other hand, question 76 was answered correctly by only 26 percent of the students. If you find that you missed several questions that would be considered easy, you may want to review those questions carefully. They may cover some aspect of the subject that you need to review. Perhaps you misunderstood the directions for one part of the test or you thought the questions were so easy that you did not spend as much time on them as you might have.

About the Literature Achievement Test

For the Literature Achievement Test, you are asked to examine the poems or prose passages on the test using the analytical skills you have developed in your study of literature. The test is designed to measure your skill in reading literature, not your knowledge of the literary background of a period, the life of an author, or the critical opinions about a particular work. There is no prescribed or suggested reading list for this test. You are not expected to have read or studied any of the poems or passages that appear on it. You do not need extensive knowledge of literary terminology for this test, though some knowledge of terminology is useful. You are expected to be familiar with basic terms such as "speaker," "tone," "image," "alliteration," "allegory," "stanza," "blank verse," but not with more obscure terms such as "assonance," "alexandrine," "metonymy," "synaesthesia."

The questions on the test are based on selections from poetry, drama, fiction, and other prose written in English from the Renaissance to the present. Only works originally written in English are included in the test. Close, critical reading in both English and American literature from a variety of historical periods and literary genres is the best way for you to prepare for the test. This reading can be concentrated in a one-year course or spread out over most of your secondary school career. In general, the greater the breadth and depth of your literary study, the better prepared you will be.

Content of the Test

	Approximate Percentage of Test
Sources of Questions	
English Literature	55-65
American Literature	35-45
Other	5-10
Chronology	
Renaissance and 17th Century	33
18th and 19th Centuries	33
20th Century	33
Genre	
Poetry	45
Prose	45
Drama and Other	10

The one-hour Literature Achievement test consists of approximately 60 multiple-choice questions based on six to eight selections, half of which are poetry and half prose. The selections are complete short poems or excerpts from various forms of literature, including longer poems, novels, nonfiction writing, and drama.

The test is designed to measure how well you have learned to interpret literature. Inevitably, many of the questions require a high level of verbal ability, including reading comprehension and general sensitivity to language, but the test focuses on those interpretative skills necessary to read poetry and prose from different periods and cultures. Normally, in each group of questions based on a passage or a poem, several questions ask about meaning, including effect and argument or theme, and about form: structure, generic properties, and method of organization (how one part develops from or differs from another). Where appropriate, the questions may consider the narrative voice (the characterization of the speaker, the possible distinction between the speaker and the author, the speaker's attitude) and the tone (ironic, irate, dispassionate, sympathetic). If a character is represented, several questions may ask about the distinguishing traits of the character and the techniques by which the character is presented and the traits revealed. Still other questions may consider the characteristic use of language in the selection (imagery, figures of speech, diction, allusions). Questions also ask about the meanings of specific words, phrases, and lines in the context of the passage or poem. Some of these questions concern denotation and syntax, but most concern connotations and implications established by the particular literary attributes of the selection.

The Literature Achievement Test included in this book contains 60 questions based on seven selections — a James Thurber fable, William Drummond's "This world a hunting is. . .," Gwendolyn Brooks's "Kitchenette Building," Ezra Pound's "The Garden," Tobias Smollett's *The Adventures of Peregrine Pickle*, Nathaniel Hawthorne's *The Marble Faun*, and John Cheever's *The Wapshot Chronicle*. As frequently happens when tests are composed of lengthy sets of questions based on relatively few selections, the distribution of passages in a particular test differs somewhat from the typical or average content — the one summarized in the chart to the left. The test in this book, for example, contains more passages from American and twentieth century literature than average, and none from plays.

Questions Used in the Test

All of the questions on the Literature Achievement Test are five-choice completion questions, the type of question with which you are probably most familiar. This type of completion question can be posed as a complete statement ("Which of the following best describes the style of the passage?") or as an incomplete statement ("The style of the passage is best described as"). Each question on the Literature Achievement Test can be categorized as one of three types — the regular multiple-choice question, the NOT or EXCEPT question, or the Roman numeral question. Most questions on the test are regular multiple-choice questions that ask you to select the best of the responses offered ("The tone of the poem is best described as") or to evaluate the relevance of the five responses offered, all of which may be at least partly true, and to select the one that is *most precise* or *most suitable* ("In the context of the passage, which of the following statements about character X is most accurate?"). In the NOT or EXCEPT question, you are given four appropriate choices and *one inappropriate* choice and must select the choice that is LEAST applicable to the situation described by the question ("All of the following statements about the diction of this poem are true EXCEPT").

The Roman numeral question is used occasionally to allow for the possibility of combinations of correct statements about a selection. In literary-analysis questions, it is sometimes desirable to phrase questions in a way that acknowledges that words or images have multiple meanings; such questions are meant to test your awareness of the richness and complexity of a poem or passage. In multiple-choice questions of this type, several statements labeled by Roman numerals are printed below the question. The statements are followed by five lettered choices, each of which consists of some combination of the Roman numerals that label the statements. You are asked to select the choice that gives the statement or the combination of statements that best answers the question. For this kind of question, you must evaluate each statement independently of the others in order to select the most appropriate combination. The answer to a question such as "Which of the following statements about the title of the poem is (are) true?" might be expressed by a choice such as "I, II, and IV only."

All of the questions on the Literature Achievement Test are grouped into sets based on poems or prose passages. The number of questions in a set is related to the length and complexity of the passage or poem; a set usually consists of five to ten questions. The questions in a set approach the passage or poem in a logical sequence, but each question is designed to be independent of the others; that is, you do not have to answer one question correctly in order to answer subsequent questions correctly. The questions refer to the passage, not to the other questions. A set of questions often begins by asking about the setting or the speaker's situation, then about specific parts of the passage or poem, and concludes by asking about theme, tone, or structure.

Sample Questions

The James Merrill poem below and many of the six questions that follow it are fairly easy; some of the other passages and questions used in Literature Achievement Tests are likely to be more difficult. James Merrill is a contemporary American poet; therefore, according to the content chart on page 47, all of the questions on this poem would be classified as American Literature, Twentieth Century, Poetry. The directions used in the test book precede the poem.

<u>Directions:</u> **This test consists of selections from literary works and questions on their content, form, and style. After reading each passage or poem, choose the best answer to each question and blacken the corresponding space on the answer sheet.**

<u>Note:</u> **Pay particular attention to the requirement of questions that contain the words NOT, LEAST, or EXCEPT.**

<u>Questions 1-6.</u> **Read the following poem carefully before you choose your answers.**

Kite Poem

"One is reminded of a certain person,"
Continued the parson, settling back in his chair
With a glass of port, "who sought to emulate
The sport of birds (it was something of a chore)
(5) By climbing up on a kite. They found his coat
Two counties away; the man himself was missing."

His daughters tittered: it was meant to be a lesson
To them — they had been caught kissing, or some
    such nonsense,
The night before, under the crescent moon.
(10) So, finishing his pheasant, their father began
This thirty-minute discourse, ending with
A story improbable from the start. He paused for breath,

Having shown but a few of the dangers. However,
   the wind
Blew out the candles and the moon wrought changes
(15) Which the daughters felt along their stockings. Then,
Thus persuaded, they fled to their young men
Waiting in the sweet night by the raspberry bed,
And kissed and kissed, as though to escape on a kite.

1. **The attitude of the parson (line 2) toward the ''certain person'' (lines 1-6) is one of**

   (A) admiration   (B) anxiety   (C) disdain

   (D) curiosity   (E) grief

Choice (C) is the correct response to this question. The parson uses the tale of the person who climbed up on a kite in order to warn his daughters of the danger of imprudent behavior. It is unlikely, given this purpose, that he would feel either ''admiration,'' ''anxiety,'' ''curiosity,'' or ''grief'' for the man, and nothing in the poem suggests that the parson had any of these feelings. His attitude is one of disdain for a person whose behavior he regards as foolish.

2. **The descriptive detail ''settling back in his chair/With a glass of port'' (lines 2-3) underscores the parson's**

   (A) authority   (B) complacency   (C) hypocrisy

   (D) gentleness   (E) indecisiveness

The poem suggests that the parson is a rather rigid, formal man given to lengthy moralizing. It can be inferred from the context that complacency is one element of his character; choice (B) is the correct response. There is no evidence in the poem that the parson is either hypocritical, gentle, or indecisive. Out of context, the quotation from the poem might be interpreted as behavior associated with someone in a position of authority. In context, however, the parson is more notable for his lack of authority — his daughters titter when he lectures and ignore his advice.

3. **The chief reason the parson's daughters ''tittered'' (line 7) is that they**

   (A) were embarrassed to have been caught kissing

   (B) knew where the missing man in their father's story was

   (C) wanted to flatter their father

   (D) did not take their father's lecture seriously

   (E) took cruel pleasure in the kite flyer's disaster

The most plausible explanation of why the daughters ''tittered'' is choice (D) — they did not take their father's lecture seriously. This view is supported by the daughters' actions — as soon as their father paused for breath, they did what his ''thirty-minute discourse'' warned them not to do. There is no indication in the poem that choice (B) or (E) is true, and if the daughters had wanted to flatter their father, as choice (C) claims, they certainly would not have tittered during his serious lecture. If choice (A) were true, it is unlikely that the daughters would have ''fled to their young men'' so quickly a second time.

4. **The speaker's tone suggests that the reader should regard the parson's ''thirty-minute discourse'' (line 11) as**

   (A) scholarly and enlightening

   (B) serious and important

   (C) entertaining and amusing

   (D) verbose and pedantic

   (E) grisly and morbid

The speaker's tone suggests that the reader should regard the parson's ''thirty-minute discourse'' as ''verbose and pedantic,'' choice (D). The parson is presented as one who speaks at length, telling ''improbable'' stories and taking 30 minutes to show ''but a few of the dangers'' he wanted to warn his daughters about. He uses lengthy phrases such as ''emulate/The sport of birds'' when a simple verb such as ''fly'' would have sufficed. The parson might well have intended his discourse to seem ''scholarly and enlightening,'' choice (A), and ''serious and important,'' choice (B), but neither the daughters nor the speaker suggests that the parson succeeded, and the reader has no reason to assess the effectiveness of the discourse differently from the speaker and the daughters. The reader may be entertained and amused by the speaker's account of the discourse, but that response is not the same as being amused by the discourse itself, as choice (C) states. Choice (E) is implausible.

5. **The daughters are ''persuaded'' (line 16) by**

   (A) their own fear of danger

   (B) the fate of the kite flyer

   (C) their own natural impulses

   (D) the parson's authority

   (E) respect for their father

The daughters are ''persuaded'' by ''their own natural impulses,'' choice (C). According to the poem, ''the moon wrought changes/Which the daughters felt along their stockings'' (lines 14-15). These natural impulses were, ironically, more persuasive than the long discourse delivered by their father in an attempt to dissuade them. The daughters, like the kite flyer, are attracted to the possibility of ''escape on a kite'' (line 18) and are not deterred by solemn and tedious warnings of dangers.

6. **All of the following are elements of opposition in the development of the poem EXCEPT**

    (A) indoors..outdoors

    (B) talking..kissing

    (C) caution..adventure

    (D) work..play

    (E) settling back..flying

Choice (D) is the only opposition that is not evident in the poem. Actions such as "climbing up on a kite" and "kissing. . .under the crescent moon" might be regarded as forms of play, but the poem really does not offer any contrasting examples of work. Choices (A), (B), (C), and (E) illustrate the contrasting actions and attitudes of the parson on the one hand and the daughters and/or the kite flyer on the other.

Literature Achievement Test

The test that follows is an edition of the Literature Achievement Test administered in December 1982. So that you will have an idea of what the actual test administration will be like, try to take this test under conditions as close as possible to those of the actual test. It will probably help if you

- Set aside an hour for the test when you will not be interrupted, so that you can complete all of it in one sitting.

- Sit at a desk with no other papers or books. You can't take a calculator, a dictionary, other books, or notes into the test room.

- Have a kitchen timer or clock in front of you for timing yourself.

- Tear out an answer sheet from the back of this book and fill it in just as you would on the day of the test. You can use one answer sheet for as many as three Achievement Tests.

- Read the instructions that precede the test. When you take the test, you will be asked to read them before you begin answering questions.

- After you finish the test, read the sections on "How to Score the Literature Achievement Test" and "Reviewing Your Test Performance," which follow the test.

LITERATURE TEST

The top portion of the section of the answer sheet which you will use in taking the Literature test must be filled in exactly as shown in the illustration below. Note carefully that you have to do all of the following on your answer sheet:

1. Print LITERATURE on the line to the right of the words "Achievement Test."
2. Blacken spaces 3 and 6 in the row of spaces immediately under the words "Test Code."
3. Blacken space 1 in the group of five spaces labeled X.
4. Blacken space 4 in the group of five spaces labeled Y.

You are to leave blank the nine spaces which are labeled Q.

When the supervisor gives the signal, turn the page and begin the Literature test. There are 100 numbered spaces on the answer sheet and 60 questions in the Literature test. Therefore, use only spaces 1 to 60 for recording your answers.

LITERATURE TEST

<u>Directions:</u> This test consists of selections from literary works and questions on their content, form, and style. After read each passage or poem, choose the best answer to each question and blacken the corresponding space on the answer sheet.

<u>Note:</u> Pay particular attention to the requirement of questions that contain the words NOT, LEAST, or EXCEPT.

Questions 1-6. Read the following fable carefully before you choose your answers.

A weaver watched in wide-eyed wonder a silkworm spinning its cocoon in a white mulberry tree.
"Where do you get that stuff?" asked the
(5) admiring weaver.
"Do you want to make something out of it?" inquired the silkworm, eagerly.
Then the weaver and the silkworm went their separate ways, for each thought the other had
(10) insulted him. We live, man and worm, in a time when almost everything can mean almost anything, for this is the age of gobbledygook, doubletalk, and gudda.

MORAL: A word to the wise is not sufficient if it doesn't make any sense.

From *Further Fables for Our Time,* published by Simon & Schuster. © 1956 James Thurber. Originally printed in *The New Yorker.*

1. The central idea of the fable is the

   (A) frequent failure of language as a means of communication
   (B) unstable nature of casual relationships
   (C) richness of language, even in everyday situations
   (D) unwillingness of people to listen to each other
   (E) possibility of misunderstanding in any relationship

2. The silkworm intended "make" (line 6) as a synonym for

   (A) imply (B) arrange (C) start
    (D) draw (E) weave

3. The characters were insulted because the words "stuff" (line 4) and "make something out of it" (line 6) were misinterpreted as

   (A) "nonsense" and "cause a disturbance"
   (B) "material" and "weave a garment from it"
   (C) "junk" and "use it as a reason for a quarrel"
   (D) "garbage" and "make a mountain out of a molehill"
   (E) "rubbish" and "take it for your own use"

GO ON TO THE NEXT PAGE

LITERATURE TEST—*Continued*

4. The effect of the phrase "man and worm" (line 10) is to

   (A) suggest that the narrator is hostile toward the two characters
   (B) demonstrate that human language is appropriate for a wide variety of situations
   (C) emphasize the close relationship among all living creatures
   (D) indicate the narrator's concern for sophisticated and unsophisticated creatures
   (E) suggest the gently satiric attitude of the narrator

5. The primary reason that the misunderstanding between the two is ironic is that

   (A) weavers and silkworms seldom talk to each other in such a way
   (B) neither the weaver nor the silkworm means to be hostile
   (C) the silkworm is a creature that is useful to people
   (D) the weaver and the silkworm are not wise
   (E) the weaver and the silkworm are using language incorrectly

6. The misunderstanding between the two characters might have been prevented if they had paid more attention to

   (A) grammar
   (B) sentence structure
   (C) imagery
   (D) tone
   (E) alliteration

GO ON TO THE NEXT PAGE

LITERATURE TEST—*Continued*

Questions 7-15. Read the following poem carefully before you choose your answers.

> This world a hunting is:
> The prey, poor man; the Nimrod fierce is death;
> His speedy greyhounds are
> Lust, Sickness, Envy, Care,
> (5) Strife that ne'er falls amiss,
> With all those ills which haunt us while we
>   breathe.
> Now if, by chance, we fly
> Of these the eager chase,
> Old Age with stealing pace
> Casts up his nets, and there we panting die.

7. The poem is concerned primarily with the

   (A) gradual coming of old age
   (B) different forms that death can take
   (C) inevitability of death
   (D) cruelty of hunting
   (E) nature of disease

8. In the context of the poem as a whole, the speaker's attitude toward "poor man" (line 2) can best be described as

   (A) condescending
   (B) mocking
   (C) dispassionate
   (D) sympathetic
   (E) deferential

9. From the context we can conclude that "Nimrod" (line 2) refers to a

   (A) predatory animal
   (B) famous hunter
   (C) diabolical old man
   (D) fearless soldier
   (E) dangerous weapon

10. Which of the following changes is introduced in line 6 ?

   (A) The greyhounds become even more threatening.
   (B) Man's chief enemy changes from fierce greyhounds to physical disorders.
   (C) The emphasis is placed on man's struggles to defeat the hunters.
   (D) The multiplicity of man's ills is suggested.
   (E) The impersonal "man" (line 2) becomes the more personal "we."

GO ON TO THE NEXT PAGE

11. What is the effect of "by chance" (line 7) ?

    (A) It stresses man's ineffectualness in influencing his own fate.
    (B) It weakens the speaker's analysis in lines 1-6.
    (C) It marks a shift in the speaker's attitude toward the hunting.
    (D) It introduces the theme of man's good fortune in escaping harm.
    (E) It suggests that man can be the hunter as well as the hunted.

12. Which of the following best describes the relationship between lines 7-8 and the rest of the poem?

    (A) They are even more pessimistic than the rest of the poem.
    (B) They mark a major shift in mood.
    (C) They heighten tension by allowing for a moment of false optimism.
    (D) They echo the gloomy tone of the opening lines.
    (E) They reveal the speaker's complacency.

13. What is the effect of the personification of "Old Age" (lines 9-10) ?

    (A) The essentially human qualities of aging are emphasized.
    (B) A time of life is made especially threatening by depicting it as a determined enemy.
    (C) The identity of "Nimrod" (line 2) becomes clearer.
    (D) Old age fights against the allegorical greyhounds in the series "Lust, Sickness, Envy, Care,/Strife" (lines 4-5).
    (E) Old age is rendered consolingly familiar and comprehensible by making it human.

14. In its context, "stealing" (line 9) suggests that old age is

    (A) sluggish and grasping
    (B) dishonest and mean
    (C) sadistic and vicious
    (D) slow and stealthy
    (E) subtle and complex

15. Which of the following pairs of words does NOT correctly illustrate the contrast in content between the two parts of the poem (lines 1-6 and lines 7-10) ?

    (A) "man" (line 2) and "Old Age" (line 9)
    (B) "Nimrod" (line 2) and "Old Age" (line 9)
    (C) "speedy" (line 3) and "stealing" (line 9)
    (D) "greyhounds" (line 3) and "nets" (line 10)
    (E) "we breathe" (line 6) and "we panting die" (line 10)

GO ON TO THE NEXT PAGE

Questions 16-26. Read the following passage carefully before you choose your answers.

Miss Sally Appleby,

Madam,

    Understanding you have a parcel of heart, warranted sound, to be disposed of, shall be
(5) willing to treat for said commodity, on reasonable terms; doubt not, shall agree for same; shall wait of you for further information, when and where you shall appoint. This the needful from

(10)   Yours etc.

                Gam. Pickle

    This laconic epistle, simple and unadorned as it was, met with as cordial a reception from the person to whom it was addressed, as if it had
(15) been couched in the most elegant terms that delicacy of passion and cultivated genius could supply; nay, I believe, was the more welcome on account of its mercantile plainness; because when an advantageous match is in view, a
(20) sensible woman often considers the flowery professions and rapturous exclamations of love as ensnaring ambiguities, or at best impertinent preliminaries, that retard the treaty they are designed to promote; whereas Mr. Pickle
(25) removed all disagreeable uncertainty by descending at once to the most interesting particular.

16. It can be inferred from his letter that Pickle is

    (A) a cold-hearted exploiter
    (B) a lover too shy to say what he means
    (C) an arrogant snob
    (D) a man too rushed to enjoy life
    (E) a thoroughgoing pragmatist

17. All of the following are true of the letter EXCEPT that its

    (A) opening and closing courtesies suggest that the two people may not be well acquainted
    (B) avoidance of the pronoun "I" makes it seem impersonal
    (C) tone is insincere
    (D) clipped phrases sound hurried
    (E) purpose is practical

18. The narrator's comments (lines 12-27) about the letter are designed to

    (A) dispel any favorable impression the reader might have of Pickle
    (B) confirm the reader's expectation that Sally Appleby would be insulted by the letter
    (C) distract the reader from the letter's offensive tone
    (D) show the superiority of the narrator's taste to that of Pickle or Sally Appleby
    (E) indicate that the letter is more appropriate than it might seem

GO ON TO THE NEXT PAGE

19. According to the narrator, Miss Appleby's reaction to the letter makes clear that she values

    (A) success over happiness
    (B) directness over decoration
    (C) humility over assertiveness
    (D) style over substance
    (E) her welfare over that of others

20. The phrase "delicacy of passion" (line 16) means

    (A) refinement of feeling
    (B) concealment of emotion
    (C) shyness and coyness
    (D) feeble affection
    (E) witty expression

21. The statement made in lines 18-24 is presented in which of the following ways?

    (A) As a general truth that helps the reader understand the incident
    (B) As a controversial statement requiring closer examination
    (C) As an excuse made up by Pickle for his unconventional behavior
    (D) As a cynical observation made by the narrator
    (E) As a belief held by the rich, but not by the poor

22. As used by the narrator, the effect of such phrases as "elegant terms" (line 15), "delicacy of passion" (line 16), "flowery professions" (lines 20-21), and "rapturous exclamations" (line 21) is to

    (A) indicate the narrator's appreciation of true love letters
    (B) stress the narrator's contempt for emotion
    (C) satirize the language of conventional love
    (D) reveal the deeply sentimental nature of language
    (E) mock Pickle's futile attempt at fine language

23. Which of the following best describes the effect of the words "advantageous" (line 19), "match" (line 19), "treaty" (line 23), and "promote" (line 24) ?

    (A) They imply that the commercialism of marriage is degrading.
    (B) They provide a contrast to the phrase "mercantile plainness" (line 18).
    (C) They suggest that marriage is like a sporting contest.
    (D) They echo the commercial and legal metaphors of Pickle's letter.
    (E) They elaborate on the analogy between marital and international strife.

24. As it is used in the passage, the word "impertinent" (line 22) means

    (A) distressing   (B) rude   (C) exaggerated
      (D) critical   (E) irrelevant

25. The "most interesting particular" (lines 26-27) is best understood as a

    (A) consummation of the marriage
    (B) proposed marriage settlement
    (C) date for the marriage
    (D) token of eternal love
    (E) reconciliation of the two lovers

26. The narrator's attitude toward a sensible woman's considerations in regard to marriage is best described as

    (A) heavily ironic
    (B) bitterly disapproving
    (C) strongly defensive
    (D) gently satirical
    (E) somewhat shocked

GO ON TO THE NEXT PAGE

<u>Questions 27-35</u>. Read the following poem carefully before you choose your answers.

Kitchenette Building

We are things of dry hours and the involuntary plan,
Grayed in, and gray. "Dream" makes a giddy sound, not strong
Like "rent," "feeding a wife," "satisfying a man."

But could a dream send up through onion fumes
(5) Its white and violet, fight with fried potatoes
And yesterday's garbage ripening in the hall,
Flutter, or sing an aria down these rooms

Even if we were willing to let it in,
Had time to warm it, keep it very clean,
(10) Anticipate a message, let it begin?

We wonder. But not well! not for a minute!
Since Number Five is out of the bathroom now,
We think of lukewarm water, hope to get in it.

"Kitchenette Building," *The World
of Gwendolyn Brooks*. Copyright,
1945 by Gwendolyn Brooks
Blakely. By permission of Harper
& Row, Publishers, Inc.

27. The best paraphrase of "dry hours" (line 1) is

(A) summer drought
(B) fruitless existence
(C) chronic fatigue
(D) sudden misfortune
(E) orderly lives

28. The kind of paradox in the phrase "involuntary plan" (line 1) most closely resembles that in which of the following?

(A) Careful disorder
(B) Spontaneous combustion
(C) Dangerous hobby
(D) Secret agreement
(E) Irrelevant information

29. As it is used in the poem, "giddy" (line 2) can be understood in all of the following senses EXCEPT

(A) dizzy   (B) flighty   (C) ephemeral
  (D) impractical   (E) raucous

30. In the context of the poem, the opposition of "white and violet" (line 5) to "Grayed in, and gray" (line 2) suggests all of the following contrasts EXCEPT the

(A) attractiveness of dreams and the dullness of reality
(B) varied nature of dreams and the monotonous nature of routine duties
(C) purity and intensity of abstractions and the dinginess of concreteness
(D) beauty of the outside world and the drabness of the apartment
(E) poetic and the prosaic

GO ON TO THE NEXT PAGE

31. An aria (line 7) is unlikely to be heard because

    (A) the speaker is too poor to attend the opera
    (B) the speaker does not like loud or giddy
        noises
    (C) the speaker is too tired to listen to music
    (D) it would not be a pleasant diversion from
        the daily routine
    (E) it would be too weak to compete with the
        sordidness of daily life

32. Lines 8-9 refer to the dream as though it were a

    (A) dangerous vagrant
    (B) valuable possession
    (C) distant relative
    (D) young creature requiring care
    (E) mysterious but beneficent force

33. The primary effect of the change of tempo in
    line 11 is to suggest that the speaker

    (A) is putting aside the temptation to dream
        and returning to the reality at hand
    (B) is excited by the possibilities she has just
        imagined
    (C) is unaccustomed to sustaining a pessimistic
        mood for any length of time
    (D) is angry because she has missed the
        opportunity to get hot water
    (E) recognizes the need for haste in finishing
        the chores so that important decisions can
        be made

34. The "onion fumes" (line 4), "garbage" (line 6),
    and "lukewarm water" (line 13) help to indicate
    that the

    (A) speaker is indifferent to housekeeping
    (B) speaker does not like the finer things in life
    (C) speaker's life is ruled by necessities
    (D) speaker's senses are very acute
    (E) speaker is afraid of change and excitement

35. In this poem, the sequence "dream" (line 2) to
    "wonder" (line 11) to "hope" (line 13)
    emphasizes a progression from the

    (A) divine to the profane
    (B) improbable to the attainable
    (C) permanent to the transient
    (D) unpleasant to the pleasant
    (E) present to the future

GO ON TO THE NEXT PAGE

Questions 36-44. Read the following passage
carefully before you choose your answers.

    Other faces there were, too, of men who (if
the brevity of their remembrance, after death,
can be augured from their little value in life)
should have been represented in snow rather
(5) than marble. Posterity will be puzzled what to
do with busts like these, the concretions and
petrifactions of a vain self-estimate; but will
find, no doubt, that they serve to build into
stone walls, or burn into quicklime, as well as if
(10) the marble had never been blocked into the
guise of human heads.
    But it is an awful thing, indeed, this endless
endurance, this almost indestructibility, of a
marble bust! Whether in our own case, or that
(15) of other men, it bids us sadly measure the little,
little time during which our lineaments are likely
to be of interest to any human being. It is
especially singular that Americans should care
about perpetuating themselves in this mode. The
(20) brief duration of our families, as a hereditary
household, renders it next to a certainty that the
great-grandchildren will not know their father's
grandfather, and that half a century hence, at
furthest, the hammer of the auctioneer will
(25) thump its knockdown blow against his
blockhead, sold at so much for the pound of
stone! And it ought to make us shiver, the idea
of leaving our features to be a dusty-white ghost
among strangers of another generation, who will
(30) take our nose between their thumb and fingers
(as we have seen men do by Caesar's), and
infallibly break it off if they can do so without
detection!

36. In this passage, marble busts become sym-
bolic of

(A) man's foolish attempts to transcend time
(B) the extravagant aspirations of the artist
(C) the loneliness of man in his own time
(D) the hardness of man's heart
(E) nature's triumph over civilization

37. The "other faces" mentioned in line 1 should
have been represented in snow because they

(A) were cold-hearted and arrogant
(B) did not wish to be remembered
(C) failed to remember their friends
(D) did not merit a permanent memorial
(E) were not respected by their friends

38. The speaker's tone in lines 7-11 is best
described as

(A) arrogant and patronizing
(B) shocked and indignant
(C) mildly disappointed
(D) reluctantly approving
(E) contemptuously ironic

GO ON TO THE NEXT PAGE

39. As it is used in line 26, the word "blockhead" functions as a

    (A) play on words
    (B) literary allusion
    (C) reference to the sculptor
    (D) nonsense word
    (E) paradoxical term

40. In the second paragraph, the speaker implies that American families are characterized by their

    (A) contempt for foreigners
    (B) lack of interest in their own past
    (C) indifference to fine works of art
    (D) overindulgence of their children and grandchildren
    (E) eagerness to acquire and exhibit wealth

41. The "shiver" described in line 27 is occasioned by

    (A) the coldness of our graves
    (B) fear of the disrespect of those who come after us
    (C) apprehension about what our ghosts will do
    (D) horror at the corruption of our bodies
    (E) the knowlege that we must come to dust

42. As it is used in line 28, the image of the ghost suggests something that is

    (A) pitiful (B) ominous (C) vindictive
    (D) restless (E) ageless

43. In the second paragraph, the speaker characterizes posterity as

    (A) pious (B) resentful (C) frugal
    (D) impudent (E) industrious

44. According to the passage, which of the following properties of marble is most important to those who have busts of themselves made?

    (A) Beauty (B) Translucence (C) Usefulness
    (D) Coldness (E) Durability

GO ON TO THE NEXT PAGE ➤

Questions 45-52. Read the following poem carefully before you choose your answers.

The Garden

En robe de parade.

Samain

Like a skein of loose silk blown against a wall
She walks by the railing of a path in Kensington Gardens,
And she is dying piece-meal
        of a sort of emotional anaemia.

(5) And round about there is a rabble
Of the filthy, sturdy, unkillable infants of the very poor.
They shall inherit the earth.

In her is the end of breeding.
Her boredom is exquisite and excessive.
(10) She would like some one to speak to her,
And is almost afraid that I
        will commit that indiscretion.

Ezra Pound, *Personae,* © 1926.
Reprinted by permission of New
Directions Publishing Corporation.

45. The woman in the poem is best described as a

    (A) lonely social outcast
    (B) feeble but kindly elderly woman
    (C) devitalized aristocrat
    (D) determined and ambitious social climber
    (E) person who has lost her inherited money

46. Which of the following best represents the relationship between "she" in lines 1-4 and "infants" in lines 5-7 ?

    (A) "skein" (line 1) and "poor" (line 6)
    (B) "walks" (line 2) and "inherit" (line 7)
    (C) "Kensington Gardens" (line 2) and "the earth" (line 7)
    (D) "dying" (line 3) and "unkillable" (line 6)
    (E) "piece-meal" (line 3) and "filthy" (line 6)

47. What is the effect of using the word "infants" (line 6) rather than "children" or simply "the very poor"?

    (A) To suggest that "They" (line 7) seem particularly vulnerable and pathetic to "her" (line 8)
    (B) To stress "her" (line 8) maternal sympathies
    (C) To indicate that "They" (line 7) will be irresponsible in governing the earth they will eventually inherit
    (D) To symbolize the universality of the problem of poverty
    (E) To link the word to "inherit" (line 7) by alliteration

GO ON TO THE NEXT PAGE ➤

48. Given the context of the poem, the poor are most likely to inherit the earth because they

    (A) have been promised it
    (B) are determined to have it
    (C) are the only ones willing to accept it
    (D) are stronger than those who control it now
    (E) are the legal heirs of the present owners

49. In its context, the phrase "end of breeding" (line 8) conveys which of the following ideas?

    I. Result of centuries of privilege
    II. Epitome of refined manners
    III. Termination of reproduction

    (A) I only   (B) II only   (C) III only
       (D) I and II only   (E) I, II, and III

50. "I" (line 11) can best be described as

    (A) the critical observer
    (B) a sympathetic friend
    (C) her would-be lover
    (D) a social activist
    (E) a social snob

51. The attitude of "She" (line 10) toward "I" (line 11) is best described as

    (A) hostile   (B) ambivalent   (C) indifferent
       (D) curious   (E) receptive

52. In this poem, the woman functions as which of the following?

    I. A symbol of the emptiness of modern life
    II. The representative of a social class
    III. The personification of the power of love

    (A) I only   (B) II only   (C) I and III only
       (D) II and III only   (E) I, II, and III

GO ON TO THE NEXT PAGE

Questions 53-60. Read the following passage carefully before you choose your answers.

But Leander got the last word. Opening Aaron's copy of Shakespeare, after it had begun to rain, Coverly found the place marked with a note in his father's hand. "Advice to my sons,"
(5) it read. "Never put whisky into hot water bottle crossing borders of dry states or countries. Rubber will spoil taste. Never make love with pants on. Beer on whisky, very risky. Whisky on beer, never fear. Never eat apples, peaches,
(10) pears, etc., while drinking whisky except long French-style dinners, terminating with fruit. Other viands have mollifying effect. Never sleep in moonlight. Known by scientists to induce madness. Should bed stand beside window on
(15) clear night draw shades before retiring. Never hold cigar at right angles to fingers. Hayseed. Hold cigar at diagonal. Remove band or not as you prefer. Never wear red necktie. Provide light snorts for ladies if entertaining. Effects of
(20) harder stuff on frail sex sometimes disastrous. Bathe in cold water every morning. Painful but exhilarating. Also reduces horniness. Have haircut once a week. Wear dark clothes after 6 p.m. Eat fresh fish for breakfast when
(25) available. Avoid kneeling in unheated stone churches. Ecclesiastical dampness causes prematurely gray hair. Fear tastes like a rusty knife and do not let her into your house. Courage tastes of blood. Stand up straight. Admire the world. Relish the love of a gentle woman. Trust in the Lord."

53. With which of the following is Leander's advice most concerned?

(A) Practical knowledge and sensible living
(B) Fortitude and salvation
(C) Accomplishment and material success
(D) Determination and moral rectitude
(E) Wit and serenity

54. The first sentence suggests that the

(A) sons tried to be unlike their father in every way they could
(B) father was never able to communicate with his sons
(C) father was never more profound than in his note
(D) sons exercised great control over their own lives
(E) sons and father debated about the conduct of the sons' lives

55. The humor of the advice given in lines 5-7 ("Never...taste") depends primarily on the fact that Leander

(A) is aware that his sons enjoy whisky
(B) thinks it likely that his sons have hot water bottles
(C) assumes that his sons will be traveling
(D) assumes that his sons' cars will be searched
(E) is unconcerned about his sons' breaking the law

GO ON TO THE NEXT PAGE

56. Which of the following pieces of advice is most probably based on superstition?

    (A) "Never make love with pants on."
        (lines 7-8)
    (B) "Never eat [fruit] while drinking whisky."
        (lines 9-10)
    (C) "Never sleep in moonlight." (lines 12-13)
    (D) "Never hold cigar at right angles to
        fingers." (lines 15-16)
    (E) "Bathe in cold water every morning."
        (line 21)

57. Which of the following pairs best points up the contrast in levels of diction in the passage?

    (A) "viands" (line 12). ."snorts" (line 19)
    (B) "mollifying" (line 12). ."entertaining"
        (line 19)
    (C) "sleep" (line 12). ."retiring" (line 15)
    (D) "Painful" (line 21). ."exhilarating" (line 22)
    (E) "Fear" (line 27). ."Courage" (line 29)

58. Leander's comment "Hayseed" (line 16) suggests that

    (A) Leander has a favorite brand of cigar
    (B) Leander thinks it undignified for gentlemen
        to smoke
    (C) holding a cigar at right angles is a hazard
    (D) holding a cigar at right angles is unrefined
    (E) holding a cigar at right angles indicates
        aggressiveness

59. Leander writes, "Fear tastes like a rusty knife and do not let her into your house. Courage tastes of blood" (lines 27-29). All of the following are true of these sentences EXCEPT:

    (A) They are metaphorical.
    (B) They summarize the rest of the passage.
    (C) They are aphoristic.
    (D) They are abstractions following many
        specific and concrete statements.
    (E) They serve as a transition to the serious
        closing statements.

60. Which of the following best characterizes the language in which Leander's advice is conveyed?

    (A) Concise syntax
    (B) Abundance of metaphors
    (C) Florid diction
    (D) Coherent organization
    (E) Regular rhythm

S T O P

IF YOU FINISH BEFORE TIME IS CALLED, YOU MAY CHECK YOUR WORK ON THIS TEST ONLY.
DO NOT WORK ON ANY OTHER TEST IN THIS BOOK.

How to Score the Literature Achievement Test

When you take the Literature Achievement Test, your answer sheet will be "read" by a scanning machine that will record your responses to each question. Then a computer will compare your answers with the correct answers and produce your raw score. You get one point for each correct answer. For each wrong answer, you lose one-fourth of a point. Questions you omit (and any for which you mark more than one answer) are not counted. This raw score is converted to a College Board scaled score that is reported to you and to the colleges you specify. After you have taken this test, you can get an idea of what your score might be by following the instructions in the next two sections.

Determining Your Raw Score

Step 1: Table A on the next page lists the correct answers for all the questions on the test.* Compare your answer with the correct answer and
- Put a check in the column marked "Right" if your answer is correct.
- Put a check in the column marked "Wrong" if your answer is incorrect.
- Leave both columns blank if you omitted the question.

Step 2: Count the number of right answers and enter the number here . . . . _____

Step 3: Count the number of wrong answers and enter

the number here . . . . 4)‾‾‾‾‾‾‾‾‾

Enter the result of dividing by 4 here . . . . _____

Step 4: Subtract the number you obtained in Step 3 from the number in Step 2; round the result to the nearest whole number (.5 is rounded up) and enter here. . _____

The number you obtained in Step 4 is your raw score. (The correction for guessing — subtraction of a quarter of a point for each incorrect answer — adjusts for the fact that random guessing on a large number of questions will result in some questions being answered correctly by chance.) Instructions for converting your raw score to a scaled score follow.

*The last column in Table A gives the percentage of students who took the test in December 1982 that answered the question correctly. (See page 71 for further explanation.)

TABLE A

Answers to Literature Achievement Test, Form 3EAC, and Percentage of Students Answering Each Question Correctly

Question Number	Correct Answer	Right	Wrong	Percentage of Students Answering the Question Correctly	Question Number	Correct Answer	Right	Wrong	Percentage of Students Answering the Question Correctly
1	A			66%	31	E			73%
2	E			76	32	D			70
3	C			84	33	A			86
4	E			51	34	C			65
5	B			86	35	B			69
6	D			51	36	A			80
7	C			73	37	D			78
8	D			66	38	E			51
9	B			50	39	A			70
10	E			68	40	B			83
11	A			57	41	B			77
12	C			78	42	A			47
13	B			54	43	D			37
14	D			59	44	E			73
15	A			40	45	C			50
16	E			37	46	D			67
17	C			51	47	E			11
18	E			81	48	D			46
19	B			76	49	E			23
20	A			53	50	A			63
21	A			56	51	B			40
22	C			63	52	B			42
23	D			49	53	A			59
24	E			72	54	E			54
25	B			55	55	E			40
26	D			56	56	C			85
27	B			61	57	A			48
28	A			50	58	D			48
29	E			56	59	B			51
30	D			33	60	A			33

Note: The percentages are based on the analysis of the answer sheets for a random sample of students who took this test in December 1982 and whose mean score was 523.

Finding Your College Board Scaled Score ▬

When you take Achievement Tests, the scores sent to the colleges you specify will be reported on the College Board scale, ranging from 200 to 800. The raw score that you obtained above (Step 4) can be converted to a scaled score by using Table B.

To find your scaled score on this test, locate your raw score in the left column of Table B; the corresponding score in the right column will be your College Board scaled score. For example, a raw score of 37 on this particular edition of the Literature Achievement Test corresponds to a College Board scaled score of 580. Raw scores are converted to scaled scores to ensure that a score earned on any one edition of the Literature Achievement Test is comparable to the same scaled score earned on any other edition of the test.

TABLE B — SCORE CONVERSION TABLE			
Literature Achievement Test, Form 3EAC			
Raw Score	College Board Scaled Score	Raw Score	College Board Scaled Score
60	800	25	480
59	780	24	470
58	770	23	470
57	760	22	460
56	750	21	450
55	740	20	440
54	730	19	430
53	720	18	420
52	710	17	420
51	700	16	410
50	690	15	400
49	680	14	390
48	670	13	380
47	660	12	370
46	660	11	370
45	650	10	360
44	640	9	350
43	630	8	340
42	620	7	330
41	620	6	320
40	610	5	320
39	600	4	310
38	590	3	300
37	580	2	290
36	570	1	280
35	570	0	270
34	560	−1	270
33	550	−2	260
32	540	−3	250
31	530	−4	240
30	520	−5	230
29	520	−6	220
28	510	−7	220
27	500	−8	210
26	490	−9 through −15	200

Because some editions of the Literature Achievement Test may be slightly easier or more difficult than others, statistical adjustments are made in the scores so that each College Board scaled score indicates the same level of performance, regardless of the edition of the test you take and the ability of the group you take it with. A given raw score will correspond to different College Board scores, depending on the edition of the test taken. A raw score of 40, for example, may convert to a College Board score of 610 on one edition of the test, but that raw score might convert to a College Board score of 630 on a slightly more difficult edition. When you take the Literature Achievement Test on the actual test day, your score is likely to differ somewhat from the score you obtained on this test. People perform at different levels at different times, for reasons unrelated to the test itself. The precision of any test is also limited because it represents only a sample of all the possible questions that could be asked. (See page 12, "How Precise Are Your Scores?" for further information.)

Reviewing Your Test Performance

After you have scored your test, you should take some time to consider the following points in relation to your performance on the test.

- *Did you run out of time before you reached the end of the test?*

  If you did, you may want to consider tactics that will help you pace yourself better. For example, you may have spent too much time working on one or two difficult questions. A better approach might have been to continue the test and return to those questions after you had attempted to answer the remaining questions on the test.

- *Did you take a long time reading the directions for the test?*

  The directions in this test are the same as those in the Literature Achievement Tests now being administered. You will save time when you take the test if you become thoroughly familiar with them in advance.

- *How did you handle questions you were unsure of?*

  If you were able to eliminate one or more of the answer choices and you guessed from the remaining choices, then your approach probably worked to your advantage. On the other hand, omitting questions about which you have some knowledge or guessing answers haphazardly would probably be a mistake.

• *How difficult were the questions for you compared with other students who took the test?*

By referring to Table A on page 69 you can find out how difficult each question was for the group of students who took the test in December 1982. The right-hand column in the table tells you what percentage of that group of students answered the question correctly. It is important to remember that these percentages are based on only one group of students; had this edition of the test been given to all students in the class of 1983 who took a Literature Achievement Test, the percentages would probably have been different. A question that was answered correctly by almost everyone in the group, obviously, is an easy question. Question 5, for example, was answered correctly by 86 percent of the students in the sample. On the other hand, question 16 was answered correctly by only 37 percent of the students. If you find that you missed several questions that would be considered easy, you may want to review those questions carefully. They may cover some aspect of the subject that you need to review. Perhaps you misunderstood the directions for one part of the test or you thought the questions were so easy that you did not spend as much time on them as you might have.

About the French Achievement Test

The French Achievement Test is not based on a particular textbook or teaching methodology, but is designed to allow for variation in language preparation. You will not be penalized or favored for having followed any one method of preparation. The best preparation for the test is the gradual development of competence in French over a period of years. The test evaluates your reading ability in three areas essential for mastery of a language: vocabulary, structure, and reading comprehension. There is no writing, listening, or speaking component. Your previous course of study should prepare you to use appropriate vocabulary in a particular context, identify the correctness of grammatical forms in a given linguistic environment, and recognize the main and supporting ideas in reading passages of differing genres and styles.

The test questions vary greatly in level of difficulty to accommodate the different language backgrounds of the students who take the test. Some students who take the test have completed only two years of French in secondary school; others have had varying amounts of secondary school study preceded by study at the elementary or junior high school level. Most students who take the French Achievement Test have studied the language for three or four years in secondary school. Only unusually proficient students should take the French Achievement Test before having completed two full years of secondary school study or the equivalent.

Colleges that require their applicants to take the French Achievement Test may use the scores for course placement. Because scores are not adjusted on the basis of years of study, colleges are advised to consider the preparation of students when evaluating their scores.

Content of the Test

The French Achievement Test measures your knowledge and ability in three areas of reading skill. A certain percentage of each test is devoted to questions testing skill in these areas (see chart below).

Skills Measured	Approximate Percentage of Test
Vocabulary in Context	30
Structure	40
Reading Comprehension	30

85-90 Questions; Time — 60 minutes

Within each of the three sections of the test, a variety of questions requiring a wide-ranging knowledge of the language is included. In the vocabulary-in-context section, various parts of speech and idiomatic expressions are tested (nouns, verbs, adjectives, etc.). Structure is tested through various language patterns, such as prepositions, gender and number agreement, and expressions or conjunctions that require the use of the subjunctive. In the reading comprehension section, questions are designed to test your ability to understand the passages selected. The questions are diversified and test points such as main and supporting ideas and themes and the passage's spatial and temporal setting. The nature of the passages also varies; prose fiction, interviews, historical selections, and social commentaries are used in order to include writings from as varied sources as possible.

Questions Used in the Test

All questions in the French Achievement Test are multiple-choice questions in which you must choose the best response from the four choices offered. The types of questions used to test the three components of reading skill are discussed in greater detail below.

Vocabulary in Context

Vocabulary-in-context questions test vocabulary in the context of a sentence reflecting spoken or written language. Since you are presented with a full sentence, a given question can test knowledge of more than one word. This type of question consists of a sentence containing a blank space. Four choices are listed below the sentence, from which you are to select the best response. To ensure that only your knowledge of vocabulary is tested in this section, all of the suggested answers are grammatically correct.

In all multiple-choice questions the wrong answers are chosen carefully. In the vocabulary-in-context section of the test, they are often related either in terms of meaning (semantically) or in terms of sound (phonologically) to the correct answer. If you are sure of the correct answer, you will not be attracted by the wrong answers; however, if you are in doubt you may find yourself debating among several choices. If you have difficulty, you will have to rely on your knowledge and analytical skills to eliminate all the choices except the correct answer.

Directions: This part consists of a number of incomplete statements, each having four suggested completions. Select the most appropriate completion and blacken the corresponding space on the answer sheet.

1. Elle était si triste qu'elle s'est mise à . . . tout doucement.

   (A) pleuvoir

   (B) pleurer

   (C) crier

   (D) croire

The correct answer is (B). In order to pick (B), you must understand both *triste* and *tout doucement.* None of the wrong answers makes sense when inserted in the sentence. *Pleuvoir* was included as an answer choice because of the resemblance to *pleurer,* which often leads to confusion between the two words. The word *crier* appears because of its similarity to the English verb for *pleurer:* "to cry." *Tout doucement* was added to the end of the sentence in order to make it absolutely impossible for *crier* to be a correct answer. *Croire* was also chosen because of its resemblance to "to cry" but lacks the semantic attraction of *crier.*

2. Ajoutez du sel si vous trouvez que c'est trop . . .

   (A) froid

   (B) fade

   (C) fondu

   (D) faux

The correct answer is (B). All the answer choices are phonetically similar to the correct answer, since they all begin with "f." The attraction of *fondu* lies in its use as a cooking term; *froid,* too, is often heard in speaking about food. Both *froid* and *faux* pick up on the idea that there is something wrong with the dish.

Situations

This type of question, which also tests vocabulary, appears in some French Achievement Tests, but will not be included in any tests after 1984. A conversational situation or scene is described, and four responses are suggested. You must choose the most appropriate response.

Directions: In each of the following questions a certain situation is suggested. From the four choices given, select the remark which is most likely to be made in the situation and blacken the corresponding space on the answer sheet.

3. Quand Jean a bu en l'honneur de son meilleur ami, que lui a-t-il dit?

   (A) A bientôt!

   (B) A ta santé!

   (C) Mille regrets!

   (D) A la bonne heure!

The most likely response in this situation, toasting one's host, is (B). Since this question deals with a courtesy formula, other formulas that are inappropriate in this context are given in the answer choices. (A) and (D) are used when saying goodbye to someone, and (C) expresses polite refusal.

Structure – One Correct

This type of question includes a sentence with an underlined word or words. You are to select from the possible answers the one choice that will be grammatically correct in the context of the sentence when substituted for the underlined portion. Although all of the choices contain appropriate vocabulary and are forms that exist in French, only one will result in a grammatically correct sentence. The correct answer and the other choices need not be synonyms of the underlined word, since this type of question tests structure, not vocabulary. A wide variety of grammatical structures is included. Knowledge of grammatical terms themselves is not tested.

Directions: Each of the following sentences contains one or more underlined words. From the choices given select the one which, when substituted for the underlined word or words, fits grammatically into the original sentence.

4. Tu vois cet <u>homme</u> devant la maison?

   (A) agents

   (B) femme

   (C) voiture

   (D) arbre

The correct answer is (D) *arbre.* This question tests the demonstrative adjective *cet,* which precedes a masculine singular noun beginning with a vowel or "h." (A), *agents,* is wrong because it is plural, and (B) and (C) are incorrect because they are feminine.

74

5. Ce cahier est à <u>moi.</u>

   (A) il

   (B) elle

   (C) tu

   (D) nôtre

The correct answer is (B), *elle*. In order to answer the question correctly, you have to know that disjunctive pronouns are used after prepositions in French. *Elle* functions as both a subject and a disjunctive pronoun, while (A) *il* and (C) *tu* are used only as subject pronouns. (D), *nôtre*, must be used with an article (*le, la*).

Structure – One Incorrect ■■■■■■■

This type of question consists of a sentence containing one or more underlined words. The sentence is followed by four choices from which you are to choose the one that does *not* result in a grammatically correct sentence when substituted for the underlined word. This type of question will not appear on the French Achievement Test after 1984.

<u>Directions</u>: **In each of the sentences in this part of the test, one or more words are underlined. Three of the four choices which follow each sentence can be substituted for the underlined words to form sentences which are grammatically correct though usually different in meaning from the original sentence. You are to select the one choice which does NOT fit grammatically into the original sentence. Please note that in this one part of the test you are asked to identify not a correct choice, but a form which would be <u>wrong</u> if used in the given sentence.**

  6. <u>Ce livre-ci</u> me plaît énormément.

    (A) Tout

    (B) Cela

    (C) Il

    (D) Chaque

The correct answer (that is, the choice that does *not* fit grammatically into the sentence) is (D) *Chaque*, which must be used with a noun.

Structure in Paragraph ■■■■■■■

This type of question is also called "paragraph with blanks." You are given a printed sentence or sentences containing blank spaces. From the four choices beneath each blank, you must select the one that will result in a grammatically correct sentence. Sometimes choice (A) appears as a blank; only in a sentence in which nothing need be added would that choice be

the correct answer. The structure-in-paragraph question tests structures that cannot be tested in either of the other structure types of questions, such as the sequence of tenses in narration and in "if" clauses.

<u>Directions</u>: **The paragraphs below contain blank spaces indicating omissions in the text. Below each blank are four choices. Select the choice that is grammatically correct in the context and blacken the corresponding space on the answer sheet. You will note that in some instances choice A consists of dashes which indicate that no insertion is required at that point.**

Après ce coup de téléphone, vois-tu, mon plus gros travail a été de ------- empêcher ------- penser.

  7. (A) me   8. (A) - - -

    (B) lui   (B) de

    (C) m'   (C) pour

    (D) moi   (D) à

The correct answer to question 7 is (C). To answer the question correctly, you must know that *empêcher* takes a direct object and that the "e" of *me* is elided because *empêcher* begins with a vowel. The correct answer for question 8 is (B), as *empêcher* takes the preposition *de* before an infinitive.

Reading Comprehension ■■■■■■■

This section of the French Achievement Test consists of passages followed by several questions that test your understanding of the literal meaning of the passage. The passages are generally one or more paragraphs in length, and most of them are taken from novels, short stories, essays, and newspaper or magazine articles. Since the French Achievement Test is not a literature test, an effort is made to include journalistic prose, historical writing, and passages taken from the social sciences. Any unusual terms are explained in the context of the passage or in a glossary. Most of the questions focus on main and supporting ideas as well as specific details such as the passage's setting in place or time. A few questions test understanding of the author's point of view, the feelings of the characters, or the mood and tone of the passage. All of the questions test your understanding of the passage on a literal or factual level.

A typical example of a reading comprehension passage and questions is given on page 76.

Directions: Read the following passages carefully for comprehension. Each passage is followed by a number of questions or incomplete statements. Select the completion or answer that is best according to the passage and blacken the corresponding space on the answer sheet.

Je voyageais en Afrique et avant de regagner l'Europe, je résolus de passer par un des Parcs Royaux du Kenya où des lois très sévères protègent les bêtes sauvages. Là, m'avait-on dit,
(5) antilopes, girafes, rhinocéros, éléphants par centaines et centaines erraient, s'arrêtaient ou se déplaçaient au pas du loisir, au gré de la soif. J'en avais aperçu beaucoup le long des routes et des pistes au cours du voyage que je
(10) venais d'achever. Mais ce n'étaient que des visions incertaines et fugitives: troupeaux que le bruit de la voiture dispersait, silhouettes rapides, effrayées, évanouies.

Lorsque, parfois, j'avais eu la chance d'épier
(15) quelque temps un animal sauvage à son insu, je n'avais pu le faire que de très loin ou en cachette.

J'arrivai donc un soir au pied du Kilimandjaro épuisé, à la nuit tombante. Dès l'aube, le
(20) lendemain matin, je quittai ma hutte et me mis en marche. Les bêtes par centaines étaient là. J'avançai sur le sentier le long d'un rideau formé par les arbres et les buissons. Tout à coup, un léger bruit m'arrêta. J'entendis alors
(25) ces mots, en anglais: "Vous ne devez pas aller plus loin." J'avais en face de moi un enfant d'une dizaine d'années, tête nue. Une frange de cheveux noirs et coupés en boule couvrait le front. De grands yeux bruns qui semblaient ne pas me voir étaient fixés sur les bêtes.

9. Le narrateur de cette histoire indique qu'il

   (A) s'intéresse aux bêtes sauvages
   (B) a peur des habitants du pays
   (C) a l'habitude de vivre dans la jungle
   (D) n'a vu aucun animal

10. D'après cette histoire, il est clair que dans les Parcs Royaux du Kenya

   (A) on peut faire ce que l'on veut
   (B) il n'y a que de rares animaux
   (C) les bêtes sont en captivité
   (D) il est défendu de chasser

11. Que peut-on dire des animaux aperçus le long des routes?

   (A) Ils ne se laissent guère observer.
   (B) Ils n'ont pas peur des voyageurs.
   (C) Ils font beaucoup de bruit.
   (D) Ils sont imaginaires.

12. Comment le voyageur réagit-il quand il rencontre l'enfant?

   (A) Il se fâche.
   (B) Il est rassuré.
   (C) Il s'enfuit.
   (D) Il est surpris.

Question 9 tests your comprehension of a main idea found in the passage. The correct answer is (A). To answer this question correctly you must infer information from the passage as a whole. In the first paragraph the narrator mentions his resolve to visit a Royal Park in Kenya, and the rest of the passage reveals his interest in the animals by the attention focused on them.

Questions 10 and 11 test your understanding of supporting ideas. The correct answer to question 10 is (D). Several points mentioned in the passage lead to the correct answer. First, the text states that the animals are protected by strict laws. Second, emphasis is placed on the sheer number of animals found in the park. Third, the child orders the narrator not to proceed any further.

The correct answer to question 11 is (A). To answer this question correctly, you must comprehend the detailed description of the animals found at the end of the first paragraph, as well as the narrator's efforts to catch a glimpse of them.

Question 12 asks you to make inferences. The correct answer is (D). The circumstances surrounding the meeting of the narrator and the child give you the necessary clues to answer the question correctly.

French Achievement Test

The test that follows is an edition of a French Achievement Test administered in November 1982. So that you will have an idea of what the actual test administration will be like, try to take this test under conditions as close as possible to those of the actual test. It will probably help if you

- Set aside an hour for the test when you will not be interrupted, so that you can complete all of it in one sitting.

- Sit at a desk with no other papers or books. You can't take a calculator, a dictionary, other books, or notes into the test room.

- Have a kitchen timer or clock in front of you for timing yourself.

- Tear out an answer sheet from the back of this book and fill it in just as you would on the day of the test. You can use one answer sheet for as many as three Achievement Tests.

- Read the instructions that precede the test. When you take the test, you will be asked to read them before you begin answering questions.

- After you finish the test, read the sections on "How to Score the French Achievement Test" and "Reviewing Your Test Performance," which follow the test.

FRENCH TEST

The top portion of the section of the answer sheet which you will use in taking the French test must be filled in exactly as shown in the illustration below. Note carefully that you have to do all of the following on your answer sheet:

1. Print FRENCH on the line to the right of the words "Achievement Test."
2. Blacken spaces 3 and 8 in the row of spaces immediately under the words "Test Code."
3. Blacken space 1 in the group of five spaces labeled X.
4. Blacken space 2 in the group of five spaces labeled Y.

In the group of nine spaces labeled Q, you are to blacken ONE and ONLY ONE space, as described below, to indicate how you obtained your knowledge of French. The information that you provide is for statistical purposes only and will not influence your score on the test.

If your knowledge of French does not come primarily from courses taken in grades 9 through 12, blacken space 9 and leave the remaining spaces blank, regardless of how long you studied the subject in school. For example, you are to blacken space 9 if your knowledge of French comes primarily from any of the following sources: study prior to the ninth grade, courses taken at a college, special study, residence abroad, or living in a home in which French is spoken.

If your knowledge of French does come primarily from courses taken in grades 9 through 12, blacken the space that indicates the level of the French course in which you are currently enrolled. If you are not now enrolled in a French course, blacken the space that indicates the level of the most advanced course in French that you have completed.

Level I:	first or second half	— blacken space 1
Level II:	first half	— blacken space 2
	second half	— blacken space 3
Level III:	first half	— blacken space 4
	second half	— blacken space 5
Level IV:	first half	— blacken space 6
	second half	— blacken space 7
Advanced Placement or course that represents a level of study higher than Level IV: second half		— blacken space 8

If you are in doubt about whether to mark space 9 rather than one of the spaces 1-8, mark space 9.

When the supervisor gives the signal, turn the page and begin the French test. There are 100 numbered spaces on the answer sheet and 90 questions in the French test. Therefore, use only spaces 1 to 90 for recording your answers.

FRENCH TEST

PLEASE NOTE THAT YOUR ANSWER SHEET HAS FIVE ANSWER POSITIONS MARKED A, B, C, D, E, WHILE THE QUESTIONS THROUGHOUT THIS TEST CONTAIN ONLY FOUR CHOICES. BE SURE <u>NOT</u> TO MAKE ANY MARKS IN COLUMN E.

Part A

<u>Directions:</u> In each of the following questions a certain situation is suggested. From the four choices given, select the remark that is most likely to be made in the situation and blacken the corresponding space on the answer sheet.

1. Martin arrive à l'hôtel. Le concierge fait le geste de prendre sa valise. Martin, qui ne veut pas s'en séparer, lui dit:

   (A) Je resterai ici jusqu'à mardi.
   (B) Vous pouvez la prendre.
   (C) L'avez-vous louée?
   (D) Laissez-la! Je la porterai moi-même.

2. Un client est assis dans un restaurant chic. Le garçon maladroit lui renverse le potage sur les genoux. Le client s'exclame:

   (A) Vous ne pourriez pas faire attention, non?
   (B) La soupe est délicieuse!
   (C) Quel beau service de table!
   (D) Je voudrais une cuiller!

3. Marie est dans le salon. Elle attend avec impatience son amie qui est en retard. Elle se dit:

   (A) Comme on est bien à la maison.
   (B) J'écris depuis trois heures.
   (C) C'est dommage qu'il pleuve.
   (D) Elle pourrait au moins me téléphoner.

4. En arrivant à la plage, Jean dit à Pierre:

   (A) Mettons-nous à l'eau tout de suite.
   (B) J'adore la neige.
   (C) La baignoire est vide.
   (D) Je vais patiner.

5. D'un coup d'oeil nous avons vu en entrant que le cinéma était plein. J'ai dit à mon ami:

   (A) Evidemment ce film attire du monde.
   (B) Ce n'est pas les bonnes places qui manquent.
   (C) Nous serons presque seuls ce soir.
   (D) Tous les fauteuils sont couverts de poussière.

6. Comme sa voiture venait de s'arrêter en pleine campagne sans raison apparente, Pierre dit à son camarade:

   (A) Je n'aime pas rouler trop vite.
   (B) J'aime bien travailler à la campagne.
   (C) Je crois que c'est une panne d'essence.
   (D) Je crois que je vais ralentir un peu.

7. Jacques constate que sa montre ne marche plus. Il demande donc à un passant:

   (A) Pourquoi marchez-vous si vite?
   (B) Quelle heure est-il, s'il vous plaît?
   (C) Y a-t-il un médecin pas trop loin d'ici?
   (D) Pourriez-vous me la montrer?

8. La visite de la cathédrale terminée, le guide, dont le salaire est très bas, tend la main en nous disant:

   (A) Je voudrais me laver les mains.
   (B) Je tiens à vous signaler les beautés de la façade.
   (C) N'oubliez pas le guide, s'il vous plaît.
   (D) Permettez-moi de vous indiquer le magasin.

9. L'avion avait deux heures de retard. Un voyageur s'adressa à l'hôtesse:

   (A) Est-ce parce qu'il coûte trop cher?
   (B) Est-ce que les bureaux sont toujours fermés?
   (C) C'est extrêmement ennuyeux!
   (D) C'est certainement notre faute à tous!

GO ON TO THE NEXT PAGE ➡

10. L'automobiliste s'arrêta devant l'auberge,
    y entra et demanda:

    (A) Auriez-vous une chambre?
    (B) Etes-vous le curé?
    (C) Combien êtes-vous?
    (D) Avez-vous sommeil?

11. Bernard s'est moqué de son ami Alain. Il
    reconnaît qu'il a eu tort et lui dit:

    (A) Oublions tout ça, veux-tu?
    (B) Allons lui faire nos excuses.
    (C) Tu n'es pas gentil toi!
    (D) Est-ce que tu t'amuses?

12. Suite à une imprudence je dus garder le lit deux
    jours. Juliette me soigna avec un dévouement
    admirable. Quand je m'accusais de la déranger,
    elle m'apaisait, disant:

    (A) C'est un vrai plaisir d'être auprès
        de vous.
    (B) Cela m'ennuie beaucoup de m'occuper
        de vous.
    (C) Vous n'auriez jamais dû m'appeler ici!
    (D) A quelle heure voulez-vous sortir ensemble?

13. Au sortir de la présentation de la collection
    d'hiver, qui lui a beaucoup plu, Marie dit à
    Monsieur Alphonse, son couturier préféré:

    (A) C'est vraiment un très beau choix de
        tableaux.
    (B) L'hiver à Paris est bien trop humide
        pour moi.
    (C) On n'a jamais vu de couleurs aussi laides.
    (D) Quel talent vous avez pour plaire à vos
        clientes!

14. Le coiffeur a pitié d'une cliente ridée et
    courbée par l'âge. En la voyant, il se dit:

    (A) Madame a l'air rajeuni.
    (B) Elle arrive toujours en retard.
    (C) La vieillesse est souvent cruelle.
    (D) Elle mérite bien ce qui lui arrive.

GO ON TO THE NEXT PAGE

FRENCH TEST—*Continued*

Part B

Directions: This part consists of a number of incomplete statements, each having four suggested completions. Select the most appropriate completion and blacken the corresponding space on the answer sheet.

15. Si vous avez trop chaud, ouvrez la . . .

    (A) fenêtre
    (B) valise
    (C) pomme
    (D) bouche

16. La salle de bains est libre; tu peux te . . .

    (A) laver
    (B) promener
    (C) coucher
    (D) sauver

17. Pour prendre le train, Monsieur et Madame Dupont vont à . . .

    (A) la station-service
    (B) la guerre
    (C) la gare
    (D) l'atelier

18. J'ai perdu mon argent parce qu'il y avait un trou dans la . . . de mon pantalon.

    (A) manche
    (B) jambe
    (C) poche
    (D) ceinture

19. Paul ne se sent pas bien parce qu'il a un gros . . .

    (A) rhume
    (B) fauteuil
    (C) rôti
    (D) cadeau

20. La . . . dans cette boucherie est appétissante.

    (A) bouche
    (B) tarte
    (C) bière
    (D) viande

21. Il fera son cours s'il y a un . . . suffisant d'étudiants.

    (A) numéro
    (B) nombre
    (C) nom
    (D) conte

22. Quels sont les . . . de la semaine?

    (A) mois
    (B) ans
    (C) jours
    (D) temps

23. Il n'y a pas assez de chaises pour . . . tout le monde.

    (A) assommer
    (B) asseoir
    (C) assurer
    (D) associer

24. De quoi a-t-on . . . pour faire de l'alpinisme?

    (A) honte
    (B) besoin
    (C) hâte
    (D) raison

25. Je suis tombé lorsque la branche s'est . . .

    (A) envolée
    (B) échappée
    (C) cassée
    (D) attrapée

GO ON TO THE NEXT PAGE

26. Avez-vous beaucoup de légumes dans votre . . . ?

    (A) cheminée
    (B) jardin
    (C) gazon
    (D) quartier

27. On a mal aux . . . quand on porte des souliers trop petits.

    (A) poumons
    (B) oreilles
    (C) pieds
    (D) yeux

28. Mon père travaille dans une . . . de produits chimiques.

    (A) facture
    (B) plante
    (C) fabrication
    (D) usine

29. Pour aller en Espagne, les Français doivent . . . une frontière.

    (A) transformer
    (B) traverser
    (C) transférer
    (D) transporter

30. Les explorateurs n'ont pas pu . . . tous les dangers.

    (A) atteindre
    (B) attraper
    (C) ramasser
    (D) éviter

31. J'ai si peu confiance en lui que je me . . . de tout ce qu'il dit.

    (A) méfie
    (B) contente
    (C) débarrasse
    (D) sers

32. Pendant tout le voyage, la voiture a roulé très . . .

    (A) bassement
    (B) prochainement
    (C) couramment
    (D) régulièrement

33. Je viens de . . . ce livre qui m'a l'air très intéressant.

    (A) frotter
    (B) feuilleter
    (C) fréquenter
    (D) secourir

34. Après avoir reconnu sa femme dans la foule, le soldat s'est . . . vers elle.

    (A) étendu
    (B) précipité
    (C) entraîné
    (D) enlevé

35. Il avait tant mangé qu'il ne pouvait plus . . . une bouchée.

    (A) soutenir
    (B) emporter
    (C) avaler
    (D) évaluer

36. Nous devons faire réparer . . . parce qu'il pleut dans le grenier.

    (A) le parapluie
    (B) le trottoir
    (C) la baignoire
    (D) le toit

37. J'étais bloqué dans la file de voitures. Pas moyen d'avancer ni de . . .

    (A) repasser
    (B) retarder
    (C) repousser
    (D) reculer

GO ON TO THE NEXT PAGE

FRENCH TEST—*Continued*

Part C

<u>Directions</u>: In each of the sentences in this part of the test, one or more words are underlined. Three of the four choices that follow each sentence can be substituted for the underlined words to form sentences that are grammatically correct though usually different in meaning from the original sentence. You are to select the one choice that does NOT fit grammatically into the original sentence. Please note that in this one part of the test you are asked to identify not a correct choice, but a form that would be <u>wrong</u> if used in the given sentence.

<u>Example:</u>

J'ai <u>tant</u> à vous raconter!

(A) quelque chose
(B) si peu
(C) un tas de choses
(D) mal

<u>Sample Answer</u>

38. On vous a dit de venir <u>bientôt</u>.

(A) jamais
(B) tout à l'heure
(C) avant de manger
(D) mardi

39. C'est une offre que notre gouvernement va <u>accepter</u>.

(A) refuser
(B) faire
(C) approuver
(D) réfléchir

40. Qui a sonné? <u>Personne</u>.

(A) Quelqu'un
(B) Moi
(C) Aucun
(D) Le laitier

41. Je n'ai jamais vu de robe <u>si</u> belle.

(A) plus
(B) mieux
(C) trop
(D) moins

42. André <u>veut</u> venir ce soir.

(A) peut
(B) refuse
(C) espère
(D) va

43. Voilà une personne <u>avec qui</u> je ne peux pas travailler.

(A) chez qui
(B) sans laquelle
(C) dont
(D) pour qui

44. Il est temps de <u>me</u> lever.

(A) te
(B) lui
(C) nous
(D) se

45. François peut aller avec <u>Pierre</u>.

(A) moi
(B) elle
(C) leur
(D) lui

46. Un mariage entre Jean et cette fille est <u>impossible</u>.

(A) probable
(B) douteux
(C) difficilement
(D) certain

GO ON TO THE NEXT PAGE

47. Marie est contente <u>que vous veniez</u> chez nous.

    (A) qu'il vient
    (B) quand vous venez
    (C) que vous soyez venu
    (D) d'être venue

48. <u>A quoi</u> pensez-vous?

    (A) A qui
    (B) Y
    (C) Qu'en
    (D) Dont

49. Je n'avais pas <u>envie</u> de le faire.

    (A) peur
    (B) voulu
    (C) oublié
    (D) le temps

50. <u>Si tu en avais envie</u>, nous nous en irions.

    (A) Si tu le pouvais
    (B) Si elle le permet
    (C) Si tu avais fini
    (D) S'il s'endormait

51. Est-ce <u>qu'il n'y a personne</u> qui puisse nous aider?

    (A) Avez-vous quelque chose
    (B) Ne trouvez-vous rien
    (C) Est-ce le seul
    (D) Est-ce que c'est ce monsieur

52. Il est resté optimiste <u>malgré</u> sa longue maladie.

    (A) en dépit de
    (B) après
    (C) afin de
    (D) durant

GO ON TO THE NEXT PAGE

FRENCH TEST—*Continued*

Part D

<u>Directions:</u> The paragraphs below contain blank spaces indicating omissions in the text. Below each blank are four choices. Select the choice that is grammatically correct in the context and blacken the corresponding space on the answer sheet. You will note that in some instances choice A consists of dashes, which indicate that no insertion is required at that point.

Francois et ------- amie Lucie ont énormément ------- à la réussite de

53. (A) s'
    (B) son
    (C) sa
    (D) ses

54. (A) contribué
    (B) contribuée
    (C) contribués
    (D) contribuées

notre projet. Sans -------, il y a longtemps que nous nous serions -------.

55. (A) ils
    (B) les
    (C) leur
    (D) eux

56. (A) découragé
    (B) découragée
    (C) découragés
    (D) décourager

Dès que vous ------- le temps ------- prendre contact avec elle, donnez- ------- un

57. (A) auriez
    (B) ayez
    (C) aurez
    (D) aviez

58. (A) ---
    (B) à
    (C) de
    (D) pour

59. (A) lui
    (B) elle
    (C) vous
    (D) la

coup de téléphone. Il faut l'avertir que tout ------- arrangé et que j'arriverai -------

60. (A) a
    (B) est
    (C) ait
    (D) soit

61. (A) le
    (B) au
    (C) sur le
    (D) dans le

vingt.

Avant d'entrer dans la pâtisserie, j'ai compté ma monnaie ------- m'assurer que

62. (A) ---
    (B) à
    (C) de
    (D) pour

j'------- de quoi payer la friandise ------- j'allais m'acheter.

63. (A) ai
    (B) aie
    (C) avais
    (D) aurai

64. (A) qui
    (B) que
    (C) dont
    (D) quelle

GO ON TO THE NEXT PAGE

FRENCH TEST—*Continued*

Part E

<u>Directions:</u> Read the following passages carefully for comprehension. Each passage is followed by a number of questions or incomplete statements. Select the completion or answer that is best according to the passage and blacken the corresponding space on the answer sheet.

Le choc fut tel que je ne pus rester en selle et je tombai de cheval. C'est tout ce dont je me souviens. Quand je revins à moi, j'étais dans mon lit. De violents maux de tête et des douleurs dans tous les membres signalèrent mon retour à la vie. Bientôt je regrettai ma défaillance pendant laquelle j'avais été maintenu dans un état cotonneux d' où la souffrance était exclue.

65. L'auteur a été victime

    (A) d' une maladie
    (B) d' un accident
    (C) d' un oubli
    (D) d' une hallucination

66. On comprend que l'auteur s'est

    (A) évadé
    (B) évanoui
    (C) tué
    (D) endormi

67. L'auteur est conscient d'avoir

    (A) enfin raison
    (B) peur de la mort
    (C) honte de sa sottise
    (D) mal partout

68. A la fin du passage l'auteur regrette

    (A) d'avoir trop dormi
    (B) d'avoir abandonné son cheval
    (C) de ne pas pouvoir sortir
    (D) d'être revenu à lui

A deux kilomètres de la gare, quand j'atteignis d'un pas prudent la villa d'Almaro, je ne vis aucune lumière aux fenêtres. La salle à manger devait donner sur le côté de la maison tourné vers la mer. La lune n'était pas encore levée et dans l'ombre, les arbres du jardin arrondissaient leurs grosses masses noires. Je me souvins de mon rêve, des fontaines qui devenaient vivantes sous le soleil éclatant. Impossible maintenant de distinguer si quelqu'un se trouvait à l'affût sous les feuillages alors que j'étais moi-même bien visible, éclairé faiblement mais suffisamment par un lampadaire. Cette idée m'alarma, mais ne m'empêcha pas de considérer la conduite à suivre. Fuir vers la ville serait une mauvaise tactique. Trop de monde à cette heure encore. Mieux vaudrait gagner les hauteurs, l'abri des pins sous le fort. Toute cette zone était peu fréquentée, sans lumière, et je la connaissais bien.

69. Comment le narrateur est-il arrivé à cet endroit?

    (A) A pied
    (B) En voiture
    (C) En bateau
    (D) Par le train

70. De quoi le narrateur a-t-il peur?

    (A) Des fontaines
    (B) De faiblir
    (C) De l'obscurité
    (D) D'être observé

71. Comment le narrateur réagit-il à sa peur?

    (A) Il perd la tête.
    (B) Il s'enfuit.
    (C) Il réfléchit.
    (D) Il cherche de la lumière.

GO ON TO THE NEXT PAGE

La guerre finie, Bertrand se rongea d'impatience dans la Sarre et, sitôt libéré, il prit le train pour la capitale où Barbara attendait sa visite.

Que se passa-t-il entre eux? Personne ne le sut. Au bout de quelques jours, Bertrand revint parmi les siens, plus renfermé que jamais. On le sentait l'esprit ailleurs. Les gens du pays qui le rencontraient sur la côte où il errait, désoeuvré, ne s'intéressant plus aux distractions de la mer, aux plaisirs des anciennes vacances, pensaient qu'il avait "un air à faire peur". Si la guerre n'avait pas été terminée, ceux qui ne le connaissaient pas l'eussent traité d'espion.

Il ne pouvait plus dormir. Il se laissait vivre, l'âme absente, la volonté brisée. Il ne songeait pas à choisir une carrière. La pensée de partir aux colonies lui vint, mais cela eût exigé un effort. Sa mère tremblait à le regarder nettoyer, de temps en temps, son revolver.

72. Bertrand était impatient d'aller à Paris

   (A) parce qu'il y trouverait du travail
   (B) afin d'être libéré plus tôt
   (C) pour y attendre la fin de la guerre
   (D) pour rendre visite à une femme

73. Bertrand est rentré dans son village

   (A) parce qu'il était impatient de revoir les siens
   (B) après avoir fait un long séjour à Paris
   (C) après un chagrin dont il ne parlait pas
   (D) car son amie Barbara voulait le faire enfermer

74. La famille de Bertrand trouvait

   (A) qu'il était plus gai qu'avant la guerre
   (B) qu'il vivait constamment dans un rêve
   (C) qu'il était allé sur la côte par erreur
   (D) que seule la mer pourrait le distraire

75. Ceux qui ne le connaissaient pas pensaient que Bertrand

   (A) avait peur de quelque chose
   (B) agissait un peu comme un espion
   (C) regrettait que la guerre fût terminée
   (D) était content d'être de retour au pays

76. A la fin du passage, Bertrand souffrait tant qu'il

   (A) résolut d'aller voir Barbara une dernière fois
   (B) décida de se trouver un emploi n'importe où
   (C) passait des nuits entières sans fermer l'oeil
   (D) voulait vendre son revolver

77. La mère de Bertrand craignait que son fils ne

   (A) se tue d'un coup de revolver
   (B) parte aux colonies
   (C) choisisse une carrière dans l'armée
   (D) s'absente sans lui dire où il allait

GO ON TO THE NEXT PAGE

Lorsque j'étais en classe de cinquième, je pleurais doucement sur mon cahier en pensant à la campagne où nous passions nos vacances. Je me disais que, à cette heure même, les prairies
(5) étaient belles, là-bas, et que les oiseaux chantaient dans les bois, mais je n'y étais pas. Un coup d'oeil jeté dans la cour du lycée me montrait le soleil brillant sur le gravier et le sombre préau où les garçons jouaient à la
(10) balle au mur. Je n'en pouvais plus de tristesse. Déjà nos rangs se clairsemaient et dès les premiers jours de juillet, les classes étaient presque vides. Les vacances n'allaient pas tarder mais avant il y avait la distribution des prix.
(15) Dans l'immense salle d'honneur, le corps professoral se réunissait pour la dernière fois de l'année scolaire.

78. Ce passage nous décrit

    (A) les premiers jours d'une année scolaire
    (B) les journées qui précèdent les grandes vacances
    (C) la joie du travail
    (D) la distribution des prix

79. Lorsqu'il était en classe, le narrateur regardait

    (A) la cour longuement
    (B) la cour brièvement
    (C) le calendrier sans cesse
    (D) la verdure de la cour

80. A la ligne 11, les "rangs se clairsemaient" veut dire

    (A) que rien ne changeait
    (B) qu'il y avait de plus en plus d'absents
    (C) que tout le monde était parti
    (D) que les rangs plaisaient au narrateur

81. Qu'est-ce que le narrateur pensait des vacances?

    (A) Elles seraient longues à venir.
    (B) Elles allaient interrompre la distribution des prix.
    (C) Elles n'intéressaient pas le narrateur.
    (D) Elles n'allaient pas se faire attendre longtemps.

A la clinique, maman commençait à aller mieux. Toute la journée nous l'avons étourdie de projets. Elle écoutait, les yeux fermés. Ma soeur Jeanne et son mari venaient d'acheter en Alsace une vieille ferme qu'ils allaient faire aménager. Maman y occuperait une grande chambre, indépendante, où elle achèverait de se rétablir.
—Mais ça n'ennuiera pas Lionel que je reste longtemps?
—Bien sûr que non.
—Tu as raison, à la campagne je ne vous dérangerai pas. A Paris c'était trop petit, je vous gênais.

82. La raison pour laquelle Jeanne et son mari invitent la mère à venir habiter avec eux c'est qu'ils

    (A) ont fait construire une maison
    (B) ont acheté un château
    (C) ont loué un appartement
    (D) vont s'installer en province

83. D'après ce texte, on peut dire que la vieille dame est

    (A) aveugle
    (B) en convalescence
    (C) sur le point de mourir
    (D) en bonne santé

84. Ce passage indique que la famille de la vieille dame

    (A) vient rarement la voir
    (B) pense qu'elle est ennuyeuse
    (C) croit qu'elle va mourir
    (D) a de l'affection pour elle

85. Quelle est l'attitude de la vieille dame au cours de cette scène?

    (A) Elle fait semblant de ne pas entendre.
    (B) Elle craint d'être à la charge de ses enfants.
    (C) Elle est incapable de comprendre ses enfants.
    (D) Elle se plaint amèrement de son sort.

GO ON TO THE NEXT PAGE

Le métier de marin de son mari avait habitué Mme de Séryeuse au veuvage longtemps avant la mort de celui-ci. Tant par une sauvagerie naturelle, que par respect pour lui, elle montrait, alors déjà, peu d'empressement envers les familles nobles qui l'eussent accueillie comme leur enfant. Puis son chagrin l'enfonça dans cette paresse. Elle s'en tint au commerce des parents de M. de Séryeuse. Cette famille, composée surtout de vieilles filles, de femmes âgées, jugeait de tout assez petitement. En leur unique compagnie, Mme de Séryeuse finit par prendre les préjugés de l'ancienne bourgeoisie contre l'aristocratie, sans se douter que c'était les siens qu'elle condamnait. Cela ne l'empêchait pas d'ailleurs d'agir sans cesse d'une façon qui prouvait sa naissance. Ces manières surprenaient sa belle-famille. On les mettait sur le compte d'un caractère singulier, d'un manque d'expérience.

86. Le mari de Mme de Séryeuse avait probablement été

    (A) exportateur
    (B) ministre de la Marine
    (C) capitaine de vaisseau
    (D) professeur à la faculté des arts

87. Dans la première phrase du texte, l'auteur donne à entendre

    (A) que le mari était très souvent absent
    (B) que les époux ne s'aimaient pas
    (C) que Mme de Séryeuse avait chassé son mari
    (D) qu'elle restait, au fond du coeur, vieille fille

88. La famille du mari se caractérisait par

    (A) l'étroitesse de ses vues
    (B) son peu d'expérience de la vie
    (C) ses préoccupations financières
    (D) sa conduite singulière

89. Si l'on compare la conduite et les idées de Mme de Séryeuse, on peut dire

    (A) qu'elles sont en contradiction
    (B) qu'elles sont en parfaite harmonie
    (C) que ses idées sont plus généreuses que ses actes
    (D) que ses préjugés remontent à sa naissance

90. La belle-famille attribuait en partie les manières de Mme de Séryeuse à

    (A) son snobisme incurable
    (B) la douceur de son caractère
    (C) l'ignorance des moeurs bourgeoises
    (D) la banalité de ses sentiments

S T O P

IF YOU FINISH BEFORE TIME IS CALLED, YOU MAY CHECK YOUR WORK ON THIS TEST ONLY. DO NOT WORK ON ANY OTHER TEST IN THIS BOOK.

How to Score the French Achievement Test

When you take the French Achievement Test, your answer sheet will be "read" by a scanning machine that will record your responses to each question. Then a computer will compare your answers with the correct answers and produce your raw score. You get one point for each correct answer. For each wrong answer, you lose one-third of a point. Questions you omit (and any for which you mark more than one answer) are not counted. This raw score is converted to a College Board scaled score that is reported to you and to the colleges you specify. After you have taken this test, you can get an idea of what your score might be by following the instructions in the next two sections.

Determining Your Raw Score

Step 1: Table A on the next page lists the correct answers for all the questions on the test.* Compare your answer with the correct answer and
- Put a check in the column marked "Right" if your answer is correct.
- Put a check in the column marked "Wrong" if your answer is incorrect.
- Leave both columns blank if you omitted the question.

Step 2: Count the number of right answers and enter the number here . . . . _____

Step 3: Count the number of wrong answers and enter

the number here . . . . 3)‾‾‾‾‾‾‾‾‾‾

Enter the result of dividing by 3 here . . . . _____

Step 4: Subtract the number you obtained in Step 3 from the number in Step 2; round the result to the nearest whole number and enter here . . . . _____

The number you obtained in Step 4 is your raw score. (The correction for guessing — subtraction of a third of a point for each incorrect answer — adjusts for the fact that random guessing on a large number of questions will result in some questions being answered correctly by chance.) Instructions for converting your raw score to a scaled score follow.

*The last column in Table A gives the percentage of a selected sample of students who took the test in November 1982 that answered the question correctly. (See page 94 for further explanation.)

TABLE A

Answers to French Achievement Test, Form 3EAC2, and Percentage of Students Answering Each Question Correctly

Question Number	Correct Answer	Right	Wrong	Percentage of Students Answering the Question Correctly	Question Number	Correct Answer	Right	Wrong	Percentage of Students Answering the Question Correctly
1	D			88%	46	C			72%
2	A			76	47	A			21
3	D			87	48	D			34
4	A			86	49	B			38
5	A			66	50	B			37
6	C			71	51	D			12
7	B			76	52	C			25
8	C			59	53	B			75
9	C			84	54	A			51
10	A			68	55	D			76
11	A			44	56	C			72
12	A			41	57	C			39
13	D			54	58	C			42
14	C			40	59	A			44
15	A			99	60	B			36
16	A			93	61	A			54
17	C			88	62	D			67
18	C			93	63	C			60
19	A			68	64	B			65
20	D			68	65	B			76
21	B			63	66	B			30
22	C			99	67	D			40
23	B			84	68	D			30
24	B			67	69	A			33
25	C			75	70	D			56
26	B			96	71	C			39
27	C			77	72	D			71
28	D			63	73	C			30
29	B			87	74	B			46
30	D			53	75	B			39
31	A			32	76	C			48
32	D			67	77	A			59
33	B			35	78	B			56
34	B			25	79	B			32
35	C			32	80	B			27
36	D			33	81	D			29
37	D			25	82	D			31
38	A			64	83	B			52
39	D			49	84	D			64
40	C			65	85	B			28
41	B			63	86	C			37
42	B			46	87	A			43
43	C			56	88	A			18
44	B			76	89	A			23
45	C			72	90	C			28

Note: The percentages are based on the analysis of the answer sheets for a sample of students who took this test in November 1982 and whose mean score was 539. The analysis sample was selected to represent students for whom the test is intended. Students whose knowledge of the language does not come almost entirely from high school courses were excluded, and only those students who had at least four semesters of language study were included.

Finding Your College Board Scaled Score ■■■

When you take Achievement Tests, the scores sent to the colleges you specify will be reported on the College Board scale, ranging from 200 to 800. The raw score that you obtained above (Step 4) can be converted to a scaled score by using Table B.

To find your scaled score on the practice test, locate your raw score in the left column of Table B; the corresponding score in the right column will be your College Board scaled score. For example, a raw score of 39 on this particular edition of the French Achievement Test corresponds to a College Board scaled score of 540. Raw scores are converted to scaled scores to ensure that a score earned on any one edition of the French Achievement Test is comparable to the same scaled score earned on any other edition of the test.

Because some editions of the French Achievement Test may be slightly easier or more difficult than others, statistical adjustments are made in the scores so that each College Board scaled score indicates the same level of performance, regardless of the edition of the test you take and the ability of the group you

TABLE B — SCORE CONVERSION TABLE					
French Achievement Test, Form 3EAC2					
Raw Score	College Board Scaled Score	Raw Score	College Board Scaled Score	Raw Score	College Board Scaled Score
90	800	50	600	10	390
89	790	49	590	9	380
88	790	48	590	8	380
87	780	47	580	7	370
86	780	46	580	6	370
85	770	45	570	5	360
84	770	44	570	4	350
83	760	43	560	3	350
82	760	42	560	2	340
81	750	41	550	1	340
80	750	40	550	0	330
79	740	39	540	−1	330
78	740	38	530	−2	320
77	730	37	530	−3	320
76	730	36	520	−4	310
75	720	35	520	−5	310
74	720	34	510	−6	300
73	710	33	510	−7	300
72	710	32	500	−8	290
71	700	31	500	−9	290
70	700	30	490	−10	280
69	690	29	490	−11	280
68	690	28	480	−12	270
67	680	27	480	−13	260
66	680	26	470	−14	260
65	680	25	470	−15	250
64	670	24	460	−16	250
63	670	23	460	−17	240
62	660	22	450	−18	240
61	660	21	440	−19	230
60	650	20	440	−20	230
59	650	19	430	−21	220
58	640	18	430	−22	220
57	640	17	420	−23	210
56	630	16	420	−24	210
55	620	15	410	−25 through −30	200
54	620	14	410		
53	610	13	400		
52	610	12	400		
51	600	11	390		

take it with. A given raw score will correspond to different College Board scores, depending on the edition of the test taken. A raw score of 40, for example, may convert to a College Board score of 550 on one edition of the test, but that raw score might convert to a College Board score of 570 on a slightly more difficult edition. When you take the French Achievement Test on the actual test day, your score is likely to differ somewhat from the score you obtained on this test. People perform at different levels at different times, for reasons unrelated to the test itself. The precision of any test is also limited because it represents only a sample of all the possible questions that could be asked. (See page 12, "How Precise Are Your Scores?" for further information.)

Reviewing Your Test Performance

After you have scored your test, you should take some time to consider the following points in relation to your performance on the test.

- *Did you run out of time before you reached the end of the test?*

  If you did, you may want to consider tactics that will help you pace yourself better. For example, you may have spent too much time working on one or two difficult questions. A better approach might have been to continue the test and return to those questions after you had attempted to answer the remaining questions on the test.

- *Did you take a long time reading the directions for the test?*

  The directions in this test are the same as those in the French Achievement Tests now being administered. You will save time when you read the directions on the test day if you become thoroughly familiar with them in advance.

- *How did you handle questions you were unsure of?*

  If you were able to eliminate one or more of the answer choices and you guessed from the remaining choices, then your approach probably worked to your advantage. On the other hand, omitting questions about which you have some knowledge or guessing answers haphazardly would probably be a mistake.

- *How difficult were the questions for you compared with other students who took the test?*

  By referring to Table A on page 92 you can find out how difficult each question was for a selected sample of the students who took the test in November 1982. The right-hand column in the table tells you what percentage of that group of students answered the question correctly. It is important to remember that these percentages are based on only one group of students; had this edition of the test been given to all students in the class of 1983 who took a French Achievement Test, the percentages would probably have been different. A question that was answered correctly by almost everyone in the group, obviously, is an easy question. Question 22, for example, was answered correctly by 99 percent of the students in the sample. On the other hand, question 51 was answered correctly by only 12 percent of the students. If you find that you missed several questions that would be considered easy, you may want to review those questions carefully. They may cover some aspect of the subject that you need to review. Perhaps you misunderstood the directions for one part of the test or you thought the questions were so easy that you did not spend as much time on them as you might have.

About the German Achievement Test

The German Achievement Test is a one-hour test consisting of 80 to 90 multiple-choice questions. It is designed to allow for variation in language preparation; you are neither favored nor penalized for having followed a specific method. The best preparation is the gradual development of competence in German over a period of years. Reading comprehension, knowledge of vocabulary, and structure (grammar) are tested; listening, writing, and speaking are not. Some students who take the test have completed only two years of German in secondary schools; others have had varying amounts of secondary school study preceded by study at the elementary or junior high school level. Most students who take the German Achievement Test have studied the language for three or four years in secondary school.

Colleges that require their applicants to take the German Achievement Test may use the scores for course placement. Because scores are not adjusted to take into consideration years of study, colleges are advised to consider students' preparation when evaluating their scores.

Content of the Test

The German Achievement Test contains four types of questions that are used in certain percentages within each test.

Skills Measured	Approximate Percentage of Test
Vocabulary in Context	25
Structure in Context (grammar)	25
Paragraph Completion	25
Reading Comprehension	25

80-90 Questions; Time — 60 minutes

Questions Used in the Test

Four types of questions are used in the German Achievement Test: vocabulary, grammar, paragraph completion, and reading comprehension. All test questions are multiple-choice questions in which you must choose the best response from the four choices offered.

Vocabulary and Grammar

Questions that test vocabulary mastery require you to know the meaning of words and idiomatic expressions in context. Questions that test your mastery of grammar require you to identify usage that is structurally correct and appropriate. Examples of questions in this first category are as follows:

Directions: Each of the sentences in this part has a blank space indicating that a word or phrase has been omitted. From the four choices select the ONE that when inserted in the sentence fits grammatically and logically with the sentence as a whole. Then blacken the corresponding space on the answer sheet.

1. Der Präsident hat gestern abend eine . . . gehalten.

    (A) Rede

    (B) Sprache

    (C) Nachricht

    (D) Erklärung

2. Das muß ich mit eigenen Augen sehen, sonst . . .

    (A) gefällt es mir nicht

    (B) gehört es mir

    (C) glaube ich es nicht

    (D) verstehe ich es besser

Question 1 is an example of a question that tests how well you have mastered vocabulary. Choice (A) *Rede* is the best answer. In order to arrive at the correct answer, you need to know that "eine Rede halten" means "to give a speech" or "to deliver an address," and that the verb "halten" cannot be used idiomatically with any of the other choices offered. The wrong answers all have something to do with communication but are inappropriate in this particular context.

Question 2 is an example of a question that tests your command of grammar. To answer question 2, you need to know, above all, that *sonst* means "or else" or "otherwise." Choice (C) is the best answer because it is the only choice that describes a situation that could be verified by taking a look at something.

Paragraph Completion

In this kind of question you are presented with sentences from which words have been omitted. You must select the choice that best fits each sentence. Examples are as follows:

Directions: The sentences below contain blank spaces indicating omissions in the text. Below each blank are four choices. Select the choice that is grammatically correct in the context and blacken the corresponding space on the answer sheet. Be sure to read the sentences first.

3. Gerda ist meine . . . Freundin. Sie kommt

   (A) gut

   (B) lieben

   (C) beste

   (D) besser

4. jeden Tag . . . mir, und wir machen unsere

   (A) zu

   (B) bei

   (C) nach

   (E) an

5. Schularbeiten . . .

   (A) eīnander

   (B) mit

   (C) auf

   (D) zusammen

Choice (C) is the best answer to question 3. You are asked to find the correct ending for an adjective following an "ein" word. The case required is the nominative, as the modified noun is a predicate nominative. Gender and number must agree with the gender and number of the modified noun, which is feminine singular. The adjective ending in this situation is "-e." The only choice providing an adjective with this ending is (C). (B) would be correct if the modified noun were in the plural and if the sentence had a plural subject. (D) would be correct if "mein" did not have an "-e" ending, if the choice read "bester", and if the modified noun were masculine. (A) may be attractive to you if you merely associate *gut* with the English "good."

In question 4 you are asked to choose the correct preposition in the idiomatic phrase for the German equivalent of "to my place," which is *zu mir.* Hence the best choice is (A). Choice (B) would be best if the context of the sentence called for the equivalent of the phrase "*at* my place" and the verb were "ist." In order to eliminate (C), you must distinguish between the related ideas of going to somebody's place "Ich komme zu dir," and of going home "Ich gehe nach Hause." Choice (D) may attract you if you vaguely recall that the German preposition "an" is used in certain situations describing movement toward a goal (in which case, however, the noun following it would have to be in the accusative case), or that "an" plus the dative is used in certain situations where the action does not express or imply motion toward a goal.

In question 5, the best choice is (D) because it is the only choice that provides the correct adverbial complement for the verb "machen," and thus completes the sentence meaningfully; that is, to do together. (A) may seem correct by association with the English phrase "to do for each other," which in German is used with a different verb, "einander helfen." (B) may appeal to you if you think of the idea "to bring along," "mitbringen" or "to participate in" as in "mitmachen." If you select (C), you are probably simply recalling that *Schularbeiten* may also be called "Schulaufgaben," or you associate it with "Schularbeiten aufhaben."

Reading Comprehension

This type of question examines your ability to read passages representative of various styles and levels of difficulty. Each of the German Achievement Tests contains several prose passages followed by questions that test understanding of the passage. The passages are generally one or two paragraphs in length, and most of them are adapted from literary sources and newspaper or magazine articles. The questions test whether or not you comprehend the main idea and facts or details contained in the text. The passage and questions that follow are a sample of the material that appears in the German Achievement Test.

Directions: Read the following passage carefully for comprehension. The passage is followed by a number of incomplete statements or questions. Select the completion or answer that is best according to the passage and blacken the corresponding space on the answer sheet.

Eine Dame in London, die eine Ferienreise nach Deutschland machen wollte, fragte bei dem Besitzer eines Hotels an, ob sie ihren Hund mitbringen dürfe. Die Antwort lautete ungefähr wie folgt:

". . . Auf Ihre Anfrage wegen Ihres Hundes möchte ich Ihnen folgende Auskunft erteilen: ich bin seit dreißig Jahren Hotelbesitzer und hatte während dieser Zeit Gelegenheit, viele Erfahrungen zu sammeln. Niemals habe ich in meinem Hotel einen Hund gehabt, der seine Bettdecke verbrannte, weil er im Bett rauchte. Kein Hund hat jemals Aschenbecher, Messer oder Handtücher als Andenken mitgenommen. Niemals habe ich von einem Hund eine Beschwerde über das Essen oder meine Angestellten zu hören bekommen.

Um es kurz zu fassen: ich habe absolut nichts dagegen, Hunde in meinem Hotel zu empfangen; sie sind mir im Gegenteil äußerst willkommen. Wenn sich darüber hinaus Ihr Hund auch für Sie verbürgt, sehr verehrte gnädige Frau, so kann ich nicht umhin, sie beide in meinem Haus aufs herzlichste willkommen zu heißen."

6. Aus dem Brief des Hotelbesitzers kann man schließen, daß er viele schlechte Erfahrungen mit

   (A) seinen Gästen gemacht hat

   (B) Hunden gemacht hat

   (C) Engländerinnen gemacht hat

   (D) seinen Angestellten gemacht hat

7. Die Dame aus London ist dem Hotelbesitzer willkommen, wenn

   (A) sie ihren Hund zu Hause läßt

   (B) sie verspricht, nicht im Bett zu rauchen

   (C) ihr das Essen in Deutschland schmeckt

   (D) ihr Hund sie empfiehlt

8. Der Hotelbesitzer hat offenbar

   (A) noch nie Hunde in seinem Hotel gehabt

   (B) eine Vorliebe für Hunde

   (C) kein Vertrauen zu Hunden

   (D) keinen Sinn für Humor

Question 6 tests your comprehension of a main idea found in the passage. The correct answer is (A). In reply to the English woman's request that her dog be permitted to stay with her in a hotel in Germany, the hotel owner provides a detailed list of sins committed by human guests in his hotel over the past several years — bedding burned by cigarette smokers; ashtrays, knives, and towels stolen as souvenirs; and complaints about the quality of the food. To answer this question, you must understand the specific series of complaints mentioned in the text; then you must recognize these complaints in the question, where they are contained in a general statement about the unpleasant experiences the hotel owner has had with guests at his hotel.

To answer question 7, you must read the final paragraph in the passage very carefully. The correct answer is (D). This section is written "tongue in cheek"; you must comprehend that the hotel owner is telling the woman that if her dog can vouch for her behavior, the hotel owner will be glad to have her register, with her dog, as a guest at the hotel. The last paragraph contains an unusual twist near the end, where you have to integrate information from the first paragraph with a humorous concluding statement in order to answer the question correctly.

Question 8 asks you to make an inference. The correct answer is (B). Nowhere in the passage is it directly stated that the hotel owner is fond of dogs. You must infer this from the indirect references made to dogs and their human masters throughout the passage.

German Achievement Test

The test that follows is an edition of the German Achievement Test administered in May 1983. So that you will have an idea of what the actual test administration will be like, try to take this test under conditions as close as possible to those of the actual test. It will probably help if you

- Set aside an hour for the test when you will not be interrupted, so that you can complete all of it in one sitting.

- Sit at a desk with no other papers or books. You can't take a calculator, a dictionary, other books, or notes into the test room.

- Have a kitchen timer or clock in front of you for timing yourself.

- Tear out an answer sheet from the back of this book and fill it in just as you would on the day of the test. You can use one answer sheet for as many as three Achievement Tests.

- Read the instructions that precede the test. When you take the test, you will be asked to read them before you begin answering questions.

- After you finish the test, read the sections on "How to Score the German Achievement Test" and "Reviewing Your Test Performance," which follow the test.

GERMAN TEST

The top portion of the section of the answer sheet which you will use in taking the German test must be filled in exactly as shown in the illustration below. Note carefully that you have to do all of the following on your answer sheet:

1. Print GERMAN on the line to the right of the words "Achievement Test."
2. Blacken spaces 3 and 9 in the row of spaces immediately under the words "Test Code."
3. Blacken space 2 in the group of five spaces labeled X.
4. Blacken space 4 in the group of five spaces labeled Y.

In the group of nine spaces labeled Q, you are to blacken ONE and ONLY ONE space, as described below, to indicate how you obtained your knowledge of German. The information that you provide is for statistical purposes only and will not influence your score on the test.

If your knowledge of German does not come primarily from courses taken in grades 9 through 12, blacken space 9 and leave the remaining spaces blank, regardless of how long you studied the subject in school. For example, you are to blacken space 9 if your knowledge of German comes primarily from any of the following sources: study prior to the ninth grade, courses taken at a college, special study, residence abroad, or living in a home in which German is spoken.

If your knowledge of German does come primarily from courses taken in grades 9 through 12, blacken the space that indicates the level of the German course in which you are currently enrolled. If you are not now enrolled in a German course, blacken the space that indicates the level of the most advanced course in German that you have completed.

Level I:	first or second half	—	blacken space 1
Level II:	first half	—	blacken space 2
	second half	—	blacken space 3
Level III:	first half	—	blacken space 4
	second half	—	blacken space 5
Level IV:	first half	—	blacken space 6
	second half	—	blacken space 7
Advanced Placement or course that represents a level of study higher than Level IV: second half		—	blacken space 8

If you are in doubt about whether to mark space 9 rather than one of the spaces 1-8, mark space 9.

When the supervisor gives the signal, turn the page and begin the German test. There are 100 numbered spaces on the answer sheet and 80 questions in the German test. Therefore, use only spaces 1 to 80 for recording your answers.

GERMAN TEST

PLEASE NOTE THAT YOUR ANSWER SHEET HAS FIVE ANSWER POSITIONS MARKED A, B, C, D, E, WHILE THE QUESTIONS THROUGHOUT THIS TEST CONTAIN ONLY FOUR CHOICES. BE SURE <u>NOT</u> TO MAKE ANY MARKS IN COLUMN E.

Part A

<u>Directions:</u> Each of the sentences in this part has a blank space indicating that a word or phrase has been omitted. From the four choices select the ONE that when inserted in the sentence fits <u>grammatically and logically</u> with the sentence as a whole. Then blacken the corresponding space on the answer sheet.

1. Wer will mit ins Kino . . . ?

   (A) geht
   (B) gehen
   (C) gegangen
   (D) gingen

2. Frau Jakobs . . . jeden Tag die Zeitung.

   (A) lese
   (B) liest
   (C) lies
   (D) lest

3. . . . du jemand?

   (A) Suchtet
   (B) Suchten
   (C) Suchst
   (D) Sucht

4. Nein, Hamburg kenne ich gar nicht. Ich war . . . dort.

   (A) noch nie
   (B) schon oft
   (C) immer wieder
   (D) mehrmals

5. . . . Sie morgen um zehn Uhr hier sind, kann Doktor Müller Sie sprechen.

   (A) Wenn
   (B) Als
   (C) Ob
   (D) Wann

6. Ich würde gerne kommen, aber leider habe ich . . . Zeit.

   (A) mehr
   (B) viel
   (C) keine
   (D) lange

7. Ich möchte meine Kusine in Berlin . . .

   (A) aussehen
   (B) laufen
   (C) besuchen
   (D) bestellen

8. Unsere Gäste sind gestern . . .

   (A) kommend
   (B) zu kommen
   (C) kommen
   (D) gekommen

9. . . . Zeit hat, wird kommen.

   (A) Wer
   (B) Der
   (C) Wem
   (D) Er

10. Als ich zu spät kam, sagte der Lehrer: "Bitte, kommen Sie . . . oder gar nicht!"

    (A) sofort
    (B) pünktlich
    (C) genau
    (D) bald

11. Johanna saß am Schreibtisch und schrieb . . . Morgen.

    (A) all
    (B) allen
    (C) des ganzen
    (D) den ganzen

GO ON TO THE NEXT PAGE

12. Stell dir vor, . . . Bücher sind ins Wasser gefallen!

    (A) allen meinen
    (B) aller meiner
    (C) alle meine
    (D) alle meinen

13. Weder Hunde . . . Katzen können fliegen.

    (A) anderseits
    (B) oder
    (C) als auch
    (D) noch

14. Bist du mit deinem neuen Wagen . . . ?

    (A) besetzt
    (B) bestimmt
    (C) zeitig
    (D) zufrieden

15. Danke, ich will . . . Frühstück; ich habe heute gar keinen Appetit.

    (A) nicht
    (B) kein
    (C) nein
    (D) nie

16. Das Haus dort drüben ist . . .

    (A) schönes
    (B) schön
    (C) schönste
    (D) schöne

17. Wir sind gestern nicht schwimmen gegangen, . . . es regnete.

    (A) weil
    (B) seit
    (C) für
    (D) darum

18. Das ging viel . . . als vorher.

    (A) mehr
    (B) lieber
    (C) besser
    (D) größer

19. Herr Ober, bringen Sie . . . die Speisekarte, bitte!

    (A) uns
    (B) mich
    (C) ihn
    (D) sie

20. Das Stück hat uns so gut gefallen, daß wir es uns . . . angesehen haben.

    (A) zweifach
    (B) zweitens
    (C) zweimal
    (D) doppelt

21. Wir konnten leider nicht . . .

    (A) mitzukommen
    (B) kommen mit
    (C) mitkommen
    (D) mitgekommen

22. Wir haben noch nichts . . . gehört.

    (A) dadurch
    (B) dafür
    (C) davon
    (D) darum

23. Sie kommt erst am 21. Dezember zurück, also kurz . . . Weihnachten.

    (A) zu
    (B) für
    (C) bei
    (D) vor

24. Die Bank ist jetzt zu. Sie . . . pünktlich um fünf Uhr.

    (A) endet
    (B) schließt
    (C) dauert
    (D) bleibt

25. Inge war im Theater, aber ich weiß nicht, wie . . . gefallen hat.

    (A) ihr sie
    (B) sie es
    (C) es sie
    (D) es ihr

GO ON TO THE NEXT PAGE

26. Kurt hat mich zu seinem Geburtstag . . .

    (A) gefragt
    (B) gerufen
    (C) geschenkt
    (D) eingeladen

27. Industrieabgase . . . die Umwelt.

    (A) verlieren
    (B) verschmutzen
    (C) verschönern
    (D) bereichern

28. Wir gingen ins Gasthaus, um ein Bier . . .

    (A) zu trinken
    (B) trinken
    (C) trinkend
    (D) getrunken

29. Auch gesunde Zähne soll man regelmäßig . . .

    (A) schlucken
    (B) essen
    (C) putzen
    (D) beißen

30. Er . . . , weil er einen roten Hut trägt.

    (A) wacht auf
    (B) fällt auf
    (C) nimmt an
    (D) sieht aus

31. Die Jungen beschlossen, einen Fußballklub zu . . .

    (A) machen
    (B) bauen
    (C) errichten
    (D) gründen

32. Wissen Sie darüber . . . ?

    (A) Bedauern
    (B) Entscheidung
    (C) Bescheid
    (D) Rücksicht

33. Meiner Meinung . . . kostet das zuviel.

    (A) nach
    (B) wegen
    (C) trotz
    (D) auf

34. Wenn Monika zu uns gekommen . . . , hätten wir uns gefreut.

    (A) hätte
    (B) würde
    (C) wäre
    (D) seid

35. Der Dieb kam ins Haus, ohne gesehen zu . . .

    (A) wollen
    (B) tun
    (C) werden
    (D) sein

36. Es gibt nichts, . . . ich nicht essen mag.

    (A) was
    (B) daß
    (C) denn
    (D) dieses

37. Wie adressiert man einen Brief an eine Frau, . . . Beruf Ärztin ist?

    (A) deren
    (B) dessen
    (C) denen
    (D) der

38. . . . eine Überraschung!

    (A) Welche
    (B) Was
    (C) Wo
    (D) Welch

GO ON TO THE NEXT PAGE

GERMAN TEST—*Continued*

Part B

Directions: Read the following passages carefully for comprehension. Each passage is followed by a number of incomplete statements or questions. Select the completion or answer that is best according to the passage and blacken the corresponding space on the answer sheet.

In einer Bar in Hamburg erschien eines Tages ein Mann mit einem Schäferhund. Beim Anblick des großen Hundes wurden einige der Gäste etwas unruhig, aber der Fremde ging mit dem Hund direkt zur Theke und bestellte zwei Bier. Der Wirt machte große Augen, als er sah, wie der Fremde das eine Glas auf den Boden stellte, damit der Hund trinken konnte. In kurzer Zeit leerte der Hund das Glas, und sofort bestellte der Fremde noch eine Runde.

Die Gäste wurden aufmerksam. Ein paar Leute standen sogar auf, um den merkwürdigen Hund näher zu betrachten, der auch das zweite Glas schnell leerte. Der Wirt wollte noch zwei Bier holen, denn ein begeisterter Gast hatte ihm schon gesagt, daß er das nächste Bier bezahlen wollte. Aber der Fremde hob langsam die Hand.

"Vielen Dank, meine Herrschaften", sagte er höflich, "aber Tyras trinkt abends nur zwei Bier, sonst wird ihm schlecht."

39. Was geschah, als der Mann mit dem Schäferhund in die Bar kam?

   (A) Die Gäste grüßten den Mann freundlich.
   (B) Einige der Gäste wurden nervös.
   (C) Der Hund bestellte zwei Bier.
   (D) Der Wirt wollte gerade zumachen.

40. Was machte der Hund mit dem Bier?

   (A) Er stellte es auf den Boden.
   (B) Er trank es mit Mühe.
   (C) Er schaute es nur an.
   (D) Er trank es schnell aus.

41. Wie reagierten die Leute in der Bar auf den Hund?

   (A) Sie waren böse auf ihn.
   (B) Sie achteten nicht auf ihn.
   (C) Sie interessierten sich für ihn.
   (D) Sie hatten Mitleid mit ihm.

42. Was geschah, als das erste Glas leer war?

   (A) Der Hund bekam ein zweites Bier.
   (B) Der Hund mußte die Bar sofort verlassen.
   (C) Der Hund wollte kein Bier mehr.
   (D) Dem Hund wurde schlecht.

43. Der Wirt wollte noch mehr Bier bringen, weil

   (A) er Angst vor dem Hund hatte
   (B) ein Gast dafür bezahlen wollte
   (C) die Sache ihm unglaublich schien
   (D) es spät war und er nach Hause gehen wollte

44. Der Hund bekam kein drittes Glas, weil

   (A) der Mann kein Geld mehr hatte
   (B) die Gäste dagegen waren
   (C) er schon betrunken war
   (D) es nicht gut für ihn gewesen wäre

GO ON TO THE NEXT PAGE

Der Komponist Richard Strauss stand auf der Höhe seines Ruhms, als ihn eines Tages ein junger Musiker bat, ihm einige seiner eigenen Stücke vorspielen zu dürfen. Er wollte von dem großen Komponisten hören, daß er Talent habe. Richard Strauss zögerte zunächst, da er mit den Proben zu seiner Oper "Ariadne auf Naxos" sehr beschäftigt war, erklärte sich aber schließlich bereit, den jungen Mann zu empfangen.

Strauss saß im Hintergrund des Musikzimmers und hörte aufmerksam zu, als der junge Musiker seine Stücke vortrug. Der Meister saß noch schweigend da, als der junge Mann geendet hatte und jetzt gespannt auf Strauss' Urteil wartete. "Mein Lieber", meinte Strauss endlich, "ich möchte Ihnen einen sehr guten Rat geben. Geben Sie das Komponieren auf." Der junge Mann sprang erregt und ärgerlich auf, lief aus dem Zimmer und den langen Korridor hinunter. Strauss, dem sein abrupter Bescheid leid tat, lief dem jungen Mann nach. "Hören Sie", rief er hinter ihm her. "Nehmen Sie das nicht so ernst. Das hat man mir auch einmal gesagt!"

45. Strauss wollte den jungen Mann zuerst nicht empfangen, weil Strauss

   (A) zuviel zu tun hatte
   (B) selber besser komponierte
   (C) nicht an dessen Talent glaubte
   (D) selbst noch unbekannt war

46. Der junge Musiker spielte Strauss einige seiner eigenen Kompositionen vor, weil er hören wollte, ob er

   (A) gut Klavier spiele
   (B) begabt sei
   (C) aufhören solle
   (D) an Strauss' Oper mitarbeiten könne

47. Die Antwort des Meisters machte den jungen Mann

   (A) unbeliebt
   (B) böse
   (C) gespannt
   (D) ängstlich

48. Strauss lief dem jungen Musiker nach, denn er wollte

   (A) die Komposition erklärt haben
   (B) das Stück noch einmal hören
   (C) den jungen Mann gern beruhigen
   (D) ihm seine Begabung bestätigen

49. Am Ende riet Strauss dem jungen Mann, er solle

   (A) ernster sein
   (B) auf ihn hören
   (C) sich mit Opern beschäftigen
   (D) die Hoffnung nicht ganz aufgeben

GO ON TO THE NEXT PAGE →

Wir waren gerade mit dem Abendessen fertig, als es klingelte. Wir standen schnell vom Tisch auf und liefen ans Fenster. Mutter räumte das Geschirr ab und stellte es in das Spülbecken. Da es draußen schon dunkel war, sahen wir nur einen Schatten auf der Treppe.

"Hans, alter Freund", rief Vater voller Freude, als er die Tür aufmachte, "wie es mich freut, dich nach so langer Zeit wiederzusehen." Vater nahm dem Besucher den nassen Schirm ab und stellte ihn vor den Kamin.

"Hans", sagte er, "jetzt mußt du etwas essen. Wie wäre es mit einem Stück Braten?"

"Das wäre gerade richtig. Im Zug gab es nichts Warmes mehr zu essen."

Wir wollten länger aufbleiben, um uns mit diesem netten Mann zu unterhalten, aber leider schickte uns die Mutter ins Bett.

50. Was erfahren wir über die Familie am Anfang der Geschichte?

   (A) Sie gehen gerade in die Kirche.
   (B) Sie haben gerade zu Abend gegessen.
   (C) Sie sind gerade morgens aufgestanden.
   (D) Sie sind gerade nach Hause gekommen.

51. Am Benehmen des Vaters merkt man, daß er den Besucher

   (A) sofort erkennt
   (B) zum ersten Mal im Leben sieht
   (C) nicht hereinlassen will
   (D) täglich im Büro sieht

52. Wie ist das Wetter, als der Besucher ankommt?

   (A) Es ist neblig.
   (B) Die Sonne scheint.
   (C) Es regnet.
   (D) Es ist windig.

53. Als der Vater dem Besucher etwas zu essen geben will, sagt ihm Hans, daß er

   (A) gerne etwas Braten haben würde
   (B) nie Fleisch ißt
   (C) das Essen zu warm findet
   (D) schon im Zug gegessen hat

54. An der Reaktion der Kinder kann man sehen, daß sie·

   (A) Angst vor dem Besucher haben
   (B) schläfrig sind
   (C) noch Hunger haben
   (D) neugierig sind

GO ON TO THE NEXT PAGE

GERMAN TEST—*Continued*

Part C

Directions: The sentences below contain blank spaces indicating omissions in the text. Below each blank are four choices. Select the choice that is grammatically correct in the context and blacken the corresponding space on the answer sheet. Be sure to read the sentences first.

Nicht ------- Tag hat man Gelegenheit, in ------- Stadt zu fahren. Oft muß man

55. (A) jeder
    (B) jede
    (C) jeden
    (D) jedem

56. (A) der
    (B) die
    (C) dem
    (D) den

zu Hause ------- und Schularbeiten machen.

57. (A) setzen
    (B) bleiben
    (C) spenden
    (D) laufen

------- man eine Auslandsreise plant, ------- man zuerst ein Buch ------- lesen,

58. (A) Wo
    (B) Wann
    (C) Wie
    (D) Wenn

59. (A) sollte
    (B) hat
    (C) darf
    (D) braucht

60. (A) wovon
    (B) über dem Land
    (C) davon
    (D) über das Land

------- man zu besuchen vorhat. Sonst ist man nicht informiert.

61. (A) das
    (B) was
    (C) des
    (D) dessen

GO ON TO THE NEXT PAGE →

GERMAN TEST—*Continued*

Hildegard wird achtzehn, und Walter möchte ------- gern eine Freude -------

62. (A) ihn
    (B) sie
    (C) ihr
    (D) er

63. (A) für
    (B) zum
    (C) als
    (D) wie

Geburtstag machen.

Der Reisende war ------- drei Tage unterwegs, als er seine Fahrt -------.

64. (A) noch
    (B) seit
    (C) bis
    (D) erst

65. (A) zu unterbrechen mußte
    (B) unterbrechen mußte
    (C) mußte unterbrechen
    (D) mußte unterzubrechen

------- Wagen hatte nämlich Motorschaden und -------.

66. (A) Seiner
    (B) Seinen
    (C) Seinem
    (D) Sein

67. (A) wird abgeschleppt sein
    (B) abgeschleppt war
    (C) mußte abgeschleppt werden
    (D) abgeschleppt wurde

Mein Nachbar ist ein Mensch, ------- immer zuviel ißt, ------- er zu dick ist

68. (A) wo
    (B) wer
    (C) was
    (D) der

69. (A) obwohl
    (B) wenn auch
    (C) ungleich
    (D) ebenso

und seine Ärztin ------- schon lange streng -------.

70. (A) es ihm
    (B) ihn es
    (C) ihr ihn
    (D) er es

71. (A) verboten wurde
    (B) verboten hat
    (C) ist verboten
    (D) verboten worden

GO ON TO THE NEXT PAGE

GERMAN TEST—*Continued*

Part D

Directions: Read the following passages carefully for comprehension. Each passage is followed by a number of incomplete statements or questions. Select the completion or answer that is best according to the passage and blacken the corresponding space on the answer sheet.

Wenn der Dichter und Staatsminister Goethe sich von seiner anstrengenden Arbeit erholen wollte, fuhr er gern nach dem stillen Ilmenau, einem kleinen Städtchen in der Nähe von Weimar. Dort genoß er die Ruhe und Einsamkeit des Waldes. Er wohnte oben auf einem Berg in einem kleinen Sommerhäuschen, und an einem besonders schönen Abend im Jahre 1783 entstand dort sein Gedicht "Über allen Gipfeln ist Ruh". Goethe schrieb es mit Bleistift an die hölzerne Wand des Häuschens. Erst 1815 gab er einen Lyrikband heraus, der auch dieses Gedicht enthielt.

Im Jahre 1831 fuhr Goethe zum letztenmal nach Ilmenau. Er wollte die herrliche Landschaft und das Sommerhäuschen noch einmal sehen. Für seine 81 Jahre war Goethe immer noch jung, und das letzte Stück der Reise wollte er zu Fuß gehen. Bald hatte er das Häuschen erreicht und stieg die Treppe hinauf zu dem Zimmer, in dem er so oft gewohnt hatte. "Ich habe hier früher einmal ein kleines Gedicht an die Wand geschrieben", sagte er zu seinem Begleiter. "Vielleicht finden wir es noch." Sie fanden das Gedicht und das Datum seiner Entstehung: 7. September 1783.

Im Jahre 1870 brannte das Haus nieder. Aber ein paar Jahre später wurde es wieder aufgebaut. Und das Gedicht Goethes, das man schon vorher fotografiert hatte, kam wieder an dieselbe Stelle.

72. Goethe reiste manchmal nach Ilmenau, weil er

(A) dort arbeiten mußte
(B) sich ausruhen wollte
(C) nicht mehr sehr jung war
(D) jemanden dort besuchen wollte

73. An dem Gedicht "Über allen Gipfeln ist Ruh" arbeitete Goethe höchstens

(A) ein paar Stunden
(B) acht Tage
(C) einige Wochen
(D) ein Jahr lang

74. Was erfahren wir aus der Beschreibung der Rückkehr des alten Goethe nach dem Sommerhäuschen?

(A) Er hatte das Gedicht vergessen.
(B) Das Gedicht auf der Holzwand war nicht mehr zu lesen.
(C) Sein Gedicht gefiel ihm nicht mehr.
(D) Er erinnerte sich sofort an das Gedicht.

75. Dem Lesepublikum ist "Über allen Gipfeln ist Ruh" bekannt seit

(A) 1783
(B) 1815
(C) 1831
(D) 1870

76. Nach dem Wiederaufbau des Hauses konnte man das Gedicht wieder genau wie im Original an die Wand schreiben, weil

(A) man ein Bild davon hatte
(B) man es in einer Sammlung fand
(C) Freunde es mit Bleistift kopiert hatten
(D) Goethes Begleiter es kannte

GO ON TO THE NEXT PAGE

Die vielen Jugendlichen, die abends in den Frankfurter Sinkkasten kommen, fühlen sich sehr wohl: Langeweile kennt man hier überhaupt nicht. Die Abende bei Pop, Jazz, Folk, Theater und Filmen vergehen für sie wie im Fluge.

Der Sinkkasten ist ein Verein, der 1971 von drei jungen Leuten—Aina, Wolfgang und Werner—in einem Kellergewölbe am Main gegründet wurde, nachdem sie sich eines Tages entschlossen hatten, ihren Feierabend nicht weiter in Kneipen zu verbringen.

Der Sinkkasten verlangt einen Mitgliedsbeitrag von fünf Mark monatlich, obgleich es ihm gar nicht um Gewinne geht. Hier können aber endlich jeden Abend Jugendliche zusammenkommen und fröhlich sein. Im Sinkkasten treten außerdem viele prominente Musiker und Gruppen auf. Dazu kommen dann noch interessante Theateraufführungen. Oft werden den Gästen auch sehr gute Filme gezeigt. Junge Maler können hier ihre ersten Werke ausstellen, und regelmäßig dürfen die jungen Gäste selbst auch mal Künstler spielen: sie können beim freien Malen ihre bisher verborgenen Talente entdecken. Die schönsten Werke werden anschließend ausgestellt.

Das Programm ersetzt den Jugendlichen Theater, Kino und Kneipe zugleich. Deshalb kommen sie auch in Scharen! Längst hat es sich herumgesprochen, daß man im Sinkkasten ganz nette Leute kennenlernen kann. Die Stadtverwaltung von Frankfurt am Main hat inzwischen den Sinkkasten schätzen gelernt: seit Anfang 1975 wird der Klub vom Kulturamt mit Geld unterstützt.

77. Die Abende im Sinkkasten vergehen den Jugendlichen im allgemeinen

(A) aus lauter Langeweile viel zu schnell
(B) wegen der vielen Unterhaltungs-möglichkeiten sehr rasch
(C) ziemlich langsam, weil das Programm zu lange dauert
(D) sehr angenehm, denn sie machen große Gewinne

78. Wo ist der Sinkkasten untergebracht?

(A) In einem alten Theater
(B) Gleich neben der Konzerthalle
(C) In der Kneipe eines Kinos
(D) Ganz unten in einem Gebäude

79. Was können die Gäste in diesem Klub tun?

(A) Ihre eigenen Schöpfungen ausstellen
(B) Endlich ihre Kochkunst zeigen
(C) Ohne monatlichen Beitrag alles mitmachen
(D) Die täglichen Hausaufgaben erledigen

80. Was kann man im allgemeinen über den Klub sagen?

(A) Er ist das Kulturzentrum der Stadt Frankfurt.
(B) Er ist finanzieller Mittelpunkt für die Stadtväter.
(C) Er ist Anziehungspunkt für viele junge Leute.
(D) Er ist als kultureller Treffpunkt nicht erfolgreich.

S T O P

IF YOU FINISH BEFORE TIME IS CALLED, YOU MAY CHECK YOUR WORK ON THIS TEST ONLY. DO NOT WORK ON ANY OTHER TEST IN THIS BOOK.

How to Score the German Achievement Test

When you take the German Achievement Test, your answer sheet will be "read" by a scanning machine that will record your responses to each question. Then a computer will compare your answers with the correct answers and produce your raw score. You get one point for each correct answer. For each wrong answer, you lose one-third of a point. Questions you omit (and any for which you mark more than one answer) are not counted. This raw score is converted to a College Board scaled score that is reported to you and to the colleges you specify. After you have taken this test, you can get an idea of what your score might be by following the instructions in the next two sections.

Determining Your Raw Score

Step 1:	Table A on the next page lists the correct answers for all the questions on the test.* Compare your answer with the correct answer and • Put a check in the column marked "Right" if your answer is correct. • Put a check in the column marked "Wrong" if your answer is incorrect. • Leave both columns blank if you omitted the question.
Step 2:	Count the number of right answers and enter the number here . . . . _____
Step 3:	Count the number of wrong answers and enter the number here . . . . 3)‾‾‾‾‾‾‾‾‾‾ Enter the result of dividing by 3 here . . . . _____
Step 4:	Subtract the number you obtained in Step 3 from the number in Step 2; round the result to the nearest whole number and enter here . . . . _____
	The number you obtained in Step 4 is your raw score. (The correction for guessing — subtraction of a third of a point for each incorrect answer — adjusts for the fact that random guessing on a large number of questions will result in some questions being answered correctly by chance.) Instructions for converting your raw score to a scaled score follow.

*The last column in Table A gives the percentage of a selected sample of students who took the test in May 1983 that answered the question correctly. (See page 115 for further explanation.)

Answers to German Achievement Test, Form 3FAC, and Percentage of Students Answering Each Question Correctly

Question Number	Correct Answer	Right	Wrong	Percentage of Students Answering the Question Correctly	Question Number	Correct Answer	Right	Wrong	Percentage of Students Answering the Question Correctly
1	B			93%	41	C			87%
2	B			84	42	A			85
3	C			98	43	B			78
4	A			89	44	D			81
5	A			59	45	A			45
6	C			91	46	B			29
7	C			85	47	B			63
8	D			94	48	C			45
9	A			65	49	D			56
10	B			92	50	B			83
11	D			86	51	A			76
12	C			52	52	C			56
13	D			30	53	A			77
14	D			61	54	D			68
15	B			90	55	C			63
16	B			87	56	B			53
17	A			89	57	B			88
18	C			83	58	D			67
19	A			67	59	A			63
20	C			90	60	D			35
21	C			63	61	A			48
22	C			72	62	C			51
23	D			66	63	B			63
24	B			75	64	D			14
25	D			58	65	B			72
26	D			80	66	D			57
27	B			69	67	C			53
28	A			77	68	D			57
29	C			70	69	A			48
30	B			27	70	A			58
31	D			35	71	B			66
32	C			22	72	B			66
33	A			38	73	A			68
34	C			57	74	D			67
35	C			26	75	B			49
36	A			32	76	A			60
37	A			49	77	B			34
38	D			10	78	D			51
39	B			68	79	A			44
40	D			90	80	C			53

Note: The percentages are based on the analysis of the answer sheets for a random sample of students who took this test in May 1983 and whose mean score was 533. The analysis sample was selected to represent students for whom the test is intended. Students whose knowledge of the language does not come almost entirely from high school courses were excluded, and only those students who had at least four semesters of language study were included.

Finding Your College Board Scaled Score ■

When you take Achievement Tests, the scores sent to the colleges you specify will be reported on the College Board scale, ranging from 200 to 800. The raw score that you obtained above (Step 4) can be converted to a scaled score by using Table B.

To find your scaled score on this test, locate your raw score in the left column of Table B; the corresponding score in the right column will be your College Board scaled score. For example, a raw score of 38 on this particular edition of the German Achievement Test corresponds to a College Board scaled score of 510. Raw scores are converted to scaled scores to ensure that a score earned on any one edition of the German Achievement Test is comparable to the same scaled score earned on any other edition of the test.

Because some editions of the German Achievement Test may be slightly easier or more difficult than others, statistical adjustments are made in the scores so that each College Board scaled score indicates the same level of performance, regardless of the edition of the test you take and the ability of the group you take it with. A given raw score will correspond to different College Board scores, depending on the edition of the test taken. A raw score of 40, for example, may convert to a College Board score of 520 on one edition of the test, but that raw score might convert to a College Board score of 540 on a slightly more difficult edition. When you take the German Achievement Test on the actual test day, your score is likely to differ somewhat from the score you obtained on this test. People perform at different levels at dif-

TABLE B — SCORE CONVERSION TABLE					
German Achievement Test, Form 3FAC					
Raw Score	College Board Scaled Score	Raw Score	College Board Scaled Score	Raw Score	College Board Scaled Score
80	780	45	550	10	360
79	770	44	540	9	360
78	760	43	540	8	350
77	750	42	530	7	350
76	740	41	530	6	340
75	730	40	520	5	340
74	720	39	520	4	330
73	710	38	510	3	320
72	700	37	500	2	320
71	690	36	500	1	310
70	680	35	490	0	310
69	670	34	490	−1	300
68	670	33	480	−2	300
67	660	32	480	−3	290
66	660	31	470	−4	290
65	650	30	470	−5	280
64	650	29	460	−6	280
63	640	28	460	−7	270
62	640	27	450	−8	270
61	630	26	450	−9	260
60	630	25	440	−10	260
59	620	24	440	−11	250
58	620	23	430	−12	250
57	610	22	430	−13	240
56	610	21	420	−14	230
55	600	20	410	−15	230
54	590	19	410	−16	220
53	590	18	400	−17	220
52	580	17	400	−18	210
51	580	16	390	−19	210
50	570	15	390	−20 through −27	200
49	570	14	380		
48	560	13	380		
47	560	12	370		
46	550	11	370		

ferent times, for reasons unrelated to the test itself. The precision of any test is also limited because it represents only a sample of all the possible questions that could be asked. (See page 12, "How Precise Are Your Scores?" for further information.)

Reviewing Your Test Performance

After you have scored your test, you should take some time to consider the following points in relation to your performance on the test.

- *Did you run out of time before you reached the end of the test?*

  If you did, you may want to consider tactics that will help you pace yourself better. For example, you may have spent too much time working on one or two difficult questions. A better approach might have been to continue the test and return to those questions after you had attempted to answer the remaining questions on the test.

- *Did you take a long time reading the directions for the test?*

  The directions in this test are the same as those in the German Achievement Tests now being administered. You will save time when you read the directions on the test day if you become thoroughly familiar with them in advance.

- *How did you handle questions you were unsure of?*

  If you were able to eliminate one or more of the answer choices and you guessed from the remaining choices, then your approach probably worked to your advantage. On the other hand, omitting questions about which you have some knowledge or guessing answers haphazardly would probably be a mistake.

- *How difficult were the questions for you compared with other students who took the test?*

  By referring to Table A on page 113 you can find out how difficult each question was for a selected sample of the students who took the test in May 1983. The right-hand column in the table tells you what percentage of that group of students answered the question correctly. It is important to remember that these percentages are based on only one group of students; had this edition of the test been given to all students in the class of 1983 who took a German Achievement Test, the percentages would probably have been different. A question that was answered correctly by almost everyone in the group, obviously, is an easy question. Question 3, for example, was answered correctly by 98 percent of the students in the sample. On the other hand, question 38 was answered correctly by only 10 percent of the students. If you find that you missed several questions that would be considered easy, you may want to review those questions carefully. They may cover some aspect of the subject that you need to review. Perhaps you misunderstood the directions for one part of the test or you thought the questions were so easy that you did not spend as much time on them as you might have.

About the Hebrew Achievement Test

The Hebrew Achievement Test is written to reflect general trends in secondary school curriculums and is independent of particular textbooks or methods of instruction. Students who take the Hebrew Achievement Test have studied two or more years of Hebrew in high school. Approximately half of the students taking the test have studied Hebrew for 10 or more years. The best preparation for the test is the gradual development of competence in Hebrew over a period of years. You may also prepare for the Hebrew Achievement Test as you would for any comprehensive examination that requires knowledge of facts and concepts and the ability to apply them. Reading the explanations and descriptions in this book should give you an indication of what to expect.

Since the Hebrew Achievement Test is intended to measure the Hebrew reading skills of secondary school students who have studied Hebrew for different amounts of time, the difficulty level of the questions varies. Some questions are directed toward students who have had only two years of study and some to students who have had more. The questions range from very easy ones that can be answered correctly by almost all of the students to difficult ones that only 15 percent to 20 percent can answer.

Colleges that require their applicants to take the Hebrew Achievement Test may use the scores for course placement. Because scores are not adjusted on the basis of years of study, colleges should consider the preparation of students in evaluating their scores.

Content of the Test

The Hebrew Achievement Test measures knowledge and ability in the following areas of reading skill: grammar and reading comprehension. These skills are tested by four different types of questions. (See the discussion of question types below.) Each type of question represents a different means of testing either or both of these skills.

Skills Measured	Approximate Percentage of Test
Grammar	33
Reading Comprehension	67

90 Questions; Time — 60 minutes

Questions Used in the Test

The Hebrew Achievement Test measures your knowledge of Hebrew grammar and the ability to read and understand modern and classical Hebrew. The test consists of 90 multiple-choice questions. Each question is followed by five choices from which you must select one as the best answer to the question. The 90 questions are divided into four major parts, each of which tests different skills of language mastery and places emphasis on modern Hebrew.

Except for the directions, the whole test is in Hebrew; there are no questions requiring you to translate from English to Hebrew or from Hebrew to English.

Modern Conversational Hebrew ▪▪▪

This type of question tests your mastery of modern conversational vocabulary. In each item a situation is suggested by a statement. The statement is followed by five lettered choices (A), (B), (C), (D), and (E). You are asked to select the choice that is most appropriate to the situation suggested in the preceding statement.

Directions: In each of the following questions, a situation is suggested by a statement and each statement is followed by five lettered choices. Select the choice that is most applicable to the situation and blacken the corresponding space on the answer sheet. Be sure to note that the questions are numbered on the RIGHT side of each column and begin on the RIGHT side of the page.

1.

הַשּׁוֹטֵר שֶׁעָמַד בְּאֶמְצַע הָרְחוֹב הֵרִים אֶת יָדוֹ, עָצַר אֶת הַמְּכוֹנִית וְנָזַף בַּנֶּהָג:

(A) בֵּינְתַיִם תּוּכַל לְעַשֵּׁן סִגַרְיָה.

(B) אָסוּר לְהַחֲזִיק אֶת הַהֶגֶה בְּיָד אַחַת.

(C) פְּרָצָה שְׁבִיתָה בָּעִיר; שׁוּב לְבֵיתְךָ!

(D) מַדּוּעַ עָצַרְתָּ אֶת הַמְּכוֹנִית?

(E) הֲתִרְצֶה לָלֶכֶת עִמִּי אֶל בֵּית הַמִּשְׁפָּט?

The situation is suggested by the statement: "The policeman, who stood in the middle of the street, lifted his hand, stopped the car, and scolded the driver." The five choices:

(A) In the meantime you can smoke a cigarette.

(B) It is forbidden to hold the steering wheel with one hand.

(C) A strike broke out in the city; go back home!

(D) Why did you stop the car?

(E) Do you want to go with me to the court house?

The choice that is most appropriate to the suggested situation is (B). Since the policeman *scolded* the driver, the driver must have done something wrong. This eliminates choices (A) and (C). Since the policeman made the driver stop his car, choice (D) is eliminated. No reason is given why the driver would want (or would have) to go to the court house with the policeman. Besides, since the policeman was standing in the middle of the street — and obviously assigned to direct the traffic there — it is unlikely that he would leave his post and go to the court house. So, choice (E) is eliminated. This leaves choice (B) as the only logical choice.

Grammar ▬▬▬▬▬▬

This type of question tests your mastery of Hebrew grammar, with special emphasis on prepositions as they are required by certain verbs. Each question consists of a single sentence in which one or more words are underlined. Four of the five choices that follow each sentence can be substituted for the underlined word(s) *to form sentences that are grammatically correct, though they may differ in meaning from the original sentence.* You are asked to select the one choice that does *not* fit *grammatically* into the original sentence; that is, you are asked to identify the one choice that would be *wrong* if used in the given sentence.

Directions: One or more words are underlined in each of the sentences in this part of the test. Four of the five choices which follow each sentence can be substituted for the underlined words to form sentences which are grammatically correct though they may differ in meaning from the original sentence. You are to select the one choice which does NOT fit grammatically into the original sentence. Please note that in this part of the test you are asked to identify not a correct form, but one which would be **wrong** if used in the given sentence.

The meaning of the sentence is: I wanted him *to remain* in my house. Choices (A), (C), (D), and (E) would lead to the following grammatically correct sentences:

(A) I wanted him to stay overnight in my house.

(C) I wanted him to eat in my house.

(D) I wanted him to wait in my house.

(E) I wanted him to be happy in my house.

If choice (B) were used without any other change in the sentence, it would read:

(B) I wanted him to be entered in my house (passive voice). In addition, the word בְּבֵיתִי would have to be changed to לְבֵיתִי

Text Comprehension ▬▬▬▬▬▬

This part consists of a Biblical passage and several narratives (some vocalized, some not) that reflect varied styles of modern Hebrew prose. The Biblical passage and each of the narratives is followed by a number of incomplete statements. You are asked to complete each statement by selecting the most appropriate choice from the five choices following each incomplete statement.

Directions: Read the following passages carefully for comprehension. Each passage is followed by a number of incomplete statements or questions. Select the completion or answer that is best according to the passage.

2.

הָיִיתִי רוֹצֶה שֶׁיִשָּׁאֵר בְּבֵיתִי.

(A) שֶׁיָלוּן

(B) שֶׁיִכָּנֵס

(C) שֶׁיֹאכַל

(D) שֶׁיְחַכֶּה

(E) שֶׁיִשְׂמַח

118

בקצה השכונה, לא רחוק מבתיה האחרונים, עומדת סוכה בודדת
ורעועה ובה גר זקן גלמוד. על יד הסוכה מגרש ריק המשמש מקום
משחק לילדי הסביבה. בימי החופש, משעות הבוקר המוקדמות ועד
שעות הערב המאוחרות מלא המגרש שאון והמולה. נשמעים קולות
חזקים וצחוק בריא של ילדים. לפעמים פורץ ריב בין המשחקים
הנגמר לרוב בכי טוב. המשחק נמשך והשמחה רבה. בעברי על יד
המגרש עלה בדעתי, כי הקטנים האלה בודאי מפריעים לזקן, גוזלים
ממנו את מנוחתו ואת שנתו. יום אחד מצאתי אותו יושב על כסא
נוח, כשהוא מסתכל במשחקי הילדים. נגשתי אליו ונכנסתי עמו
בשיחה.

„הגד נא לי, סבא, המפריעים לך הילדים במשחקיהם?"
„חס וחלילה! להפך. הם מנעימים לי את חיי. קולותיהם, ואפילו
צעקותיהם, נשמעים באזני כרננת צפרים. יודע אני כי רבים האנשים
המתאוננים על ילדינו כי מרבים רעש הם, כי אינם מתנהגים יפה.
אבל אני אומר לך שכדאי לנו למבוגרים לסבול קצת מרעש ובלבד
שלא יסתובבו ברחובות העיר. הרחוב הוא חבר רע ומזיק בהרבה
מובנים. המבוגרים צריכים להבין זאת ואז לא יתאוננו כל כך.
ילדינו טובים הם. שמע על מעשיהם הטובים. כפי שעיניך רואות
אינני צעיר ביותר. יום אחד הרגשתי חולשה נוראה. פחדתי ללכת
לבדי לבית המדרש. מה לעשות? נגשתי אל חבורת הילדים ובקשתי
שאחד מהם ילוה אותי לבית המדרש. ובקשתי נתנה לי מיד. שלשה
ימים הוליכו אותי שמה, ומשם אל סוכתי הקטנה עד ששבתי
לאיתני. היו מביאים לי גם את ארוחותי וקונים צרכי אוכל בשבילי.
האם לא כדאי לסלוח להם על הרעש שהם מקימים לפעמים?
חביבים הם עלי. מתוקים הם."

3.

הזקן גר

(A) בבית גדול (B) בצריף מט לנפול
(C) בדירה נאה (D) בבית זקנים
(E) בבית משותף

The old man lived in

(A) a big house
(B) a hut about to fall
(C) a beautiful apartment
(D) an Old Age Home
(E) a shared house

The answer is (B), since lines 1 and 2 of the narrative say that the man lived in a solitary, dilapidated hut.

4.

הילדים נוהגים לבוא ולשחק

(A) בבית הזקן
(B) בגן המשחקים
(C) בשטח העזוב
(D) ברחוב הסמוך
(E) בשעות הבוקר

The children would come and play

(A) in the house of the old man
(B) in the playground
(C) in the deserted lot
(D) in the nearby street
(E) during the morning hours

The correct answer is (C), since lines 2 and 3 of the narrative say that near the hut there was a deserted lot which served as a playground for the children.

5.

על פי רוב הם משחקים

(A) ברעש
(B) בשקט
(C) בצחוק קל
(D) באדישות
(E) בצעצועי הזקן

Usually they would play

(A) noisily
(B) silently
(C) with light laughter
(D) with indifference
(E) with the toys of the old man

The answer is (A), since lines 4 and 5 of the narrative say: "strong voices and healthy laughter of children are heard."

6.

הם נוהגים לשחק שם כמעט
(A) כל הבוקר (B) כל היום
(C) מדי פעם (D) כל אחר הצהרים
(E) אף־פעם

They usually played there nearly

(A) all morning

(B) all day

(C) sometimes

(D) all afternoon

(E) even once

The answer is (B), since lines 3 and 4 of the narrative say that during vacations, from the earliest hours in the morning to the latest hours at night, the lot was filled with noise and tumult.

7.

המחבר רצה לדעת אם הזקן
(A) אוהב את הילדים
(B) סובל מרעש משחקיהם
(C) מסתכל במשחקיהם
(D) משוחח עם הילדים
(E) מתלהב ממשחקיהם

The author wanted to know whether the old man

(A) loves the children

(B) suffers from the noise of their games

(C) watches their games

(D) talks with the children

(E) gets enthusiastic about their games

The answer is (B), since according to line 11 (second paragraph) of the narrative, the author asks: "Tell me, old timer, do the children disturb you with their games?"

8.

הזקן פחד ללכת לבדו לבית המדרש כי
(A) הרחובות היו מלאים מכוניות
(B) הילדים פצעו אותו
(C) לא הרגיש בטוב
(D) רעש הרחובות הפחיד אותו
(E) הילדים נהגו בו כבוד

The old man was afraid to walk alone to the synagogue because

(A) the streets were full of cars

(B) the children injured him

(C) he did not feel well

(D) the noise of the streets frightened him

(E) the children treated him with respect

The answer is (C), since it is said in lines 7 and 6 from the bottom: "One day I felt weak and I was afraid to go alone to the synagogue."

Idioms and Common Word Combinations ▰

Questions of this type test your knowledge of common word combinations and idioms. They consist of a number of incomplete statements, each followed by five suggested completions consisting of a word or phrase. You are to select the completion that best fits the statement logically and structurally.

Directions: In this part, each of the sentences contains a blank space indicating that a word or phrase has been omitted. Following each sentence are five words or phrases. Select the word or phrase that best completes the sentence logically and structurally, and then blacken the corresponding space on the answer sheet.

9.

קָשֶׁה לַיֶּלֶד...בֵּין טוֹב לְרָע
(A) לְהָבִין
(B) לְהִתְבּוֹנֵן
(C) לִרְאוֹת
(D) לְהַבְחִין
(E) לָדַעַת

It is hard for the child . . . between good and bad.

(A) to understand

(B) to observe

(C) to see

(D) to distinguish

(E) to know

The best choice is clearly (D), since the word בֵּין (between) fits only with "distinguish."

Hebrew Achievement Test

The test that follows is an edition of a Hebrew Achievement Test administered in December 1982. So that you will have an idea of what the actual test administration will be like, try to take this test under conditions as close as possible to those of the actual test. It will probably help if you

- Set aside an hour for the test when you will not be interrupted, so that you can complete all of it in one sitting.

- Sit at a desk with no other papers or books. You can't take a calculator, a dictionary, other books, or notes into the test room.

- Have a kitchen timer or clock in front of you for timing yourself.

- Tear out an answer sheet from the back of this book and fill it in just as you would on the day of the test. You can use one answer sheet for as many as three Achievement Tests.

- Read the instructions that precede the test. When you take the test, you will be asked to read them before you begin answering questions.

- After you finish the test, read the sections on "How to Score the Hebrew Achievement Test" and "Reviewing Your Test Performance," which follow the test.

HEBREW TEST

The top portion of this section of the answer sheet which you will use in taking the Hebrew test must be filled in exactly as shown in the illustration below. Note carefully that you have to do all of the following on your answer sheet:

1. Print HEBREW on the line to the right of the words "Achievement Test."
2. Blacken spaces 4 and 9 in the row of spaces immediately under the words "Test Code."
3. Blacken space 2 in the group of five spaces labeled X.
4. Blacken space 1 in the group of five spaces labeled Y.

To provide information on your training in Hebrew, please answer the two questions below. For each question, indicate your answer by blackening one of the spaces labeled Q on the answer sheet. (You will blacken a total of TWO of the spaces labeled Q.) The information that you provide will not influence your score on the test.

I. Which of the following patterns of Hebrew education has contributed most to your knowledge of Hebrew?

Blacken one of the following spaces:

Space 1. Public high school courses

Space 2. Public high school courses and supplementary Hebrew education

Space 3. All-day school

Space 4. All-day school and public high school courses, with or without supplementary Hebrew education

Space 5. Hebrew spoken at home, residence or stay in Israel, Hebrew summer camp, or independent study

II. Which of the following represents the total number of years of your study of Hebrew?

Blacken one of the following spaces:

Space 6. Three or less

Space 7. Four to six

Space 8. Seven to nine

Space 9. Ten or more

When the supervisor gives the signal, turn the page and begin the Hebrew test. There are 100 numbered spaces on the answer sheet and 90 questions in the Hebrew Test. Therefore, use only spaces 1 to 90 for recording your answers.

HEBREW TEST

Part A

Directions: In each of the following questions, a situation is suggested by a statement and each statement is followed by five lettered choices. Select the choice that is most applicable to the situation and blacken the corresponding space on the answer sheet.

Be sure to note that the questions are numbered on the RIGHT side of each column and begin on the RIGHT side of the page.

1. דָּן עָמַד בֶּחָצֵר וְנִקָּה אֶת הַשֶּׁלֶג, כְּשֶׁהוּא לָבוּשׁ בִּגְדִים קַלִּים. קָרְאָה אַחֲרָיו אִמּוֹ:

   (A) חֲבָל עַל עֲבוֹדָתְךָ; מָחָר שׁוּב יֵרֵד שֶׁלֶג.
   (B) הִכָּנֵס וּלְבַשׁ אֶת מְעִיל הַחֹרֶף, פֶּן תִּצְטַנֵּן.
   (C) גְּרֹף אֶת הַשֶּׁלֶג גַּם מִן הַמַּדְרֵגוֹת.
   (D) הִזְדָּרֵז בַּעֲבוֹדָתְךָ, כְּדֵי שֶׁלֹּא תְּאַחֵר לְבֵית הַסֵּפֶר.
   (E) אַל תִּשְׁכַּח לְהַחֲזִיר אֶת כְּלֵי הָעֲבוֹדָה לִמְקוֹמָם.

2. בַּגַּן הָיוּ עֲרוּגוֹת פְּרָחִים נֶהְדָּרִים. אֵם וְיַלְדָּהּ טִיְּלוּ בֵּין הָעֲרוּגוֹת. הַיֶּלֶד הִתְרוֹצֵץ בֵּין הָעֲרוּגוֹת וּמִפַּעַם לְפַעַם נָגַע בַּפְּרָחִים. הָאֵם הִסְבִּירָה לוֹ כִּי:

   (A) תָּמִיד צוֹמְחִים הַפְּרָחִים כָּךְ.
   (B) צֶבַע הַפְּרָחִים כְּצֶבַע עֵינָיו.
   (C) אָסוּר לִנְגֹּעַ בְּפִרְחֵי הַגָּן.
   (D) צָרִיךְ לִקְטֹף אֶת הַפְּרָחִים.
   (E) הַפְּרָחִים טוֹבִים גַּם לְמַאֲכָל.

3. שִׁמְעוֹן הִדְלִיק אֶת הַסִּיגַרְיָה הַשְּׁלִישִׁית שֶׁלּוֹ. אָמַר לוֹ יַעֲקֹב:

   (A) אַל תְּעַשֵּׁן כָּל כָּךְ הַרְבֵּה!
   (B) אֵיזוֹ לֶהָבָה יָפָה!
   (C) תֵּן לִי גַּפְרוּר, בְּבַקָּשָׁה!
   (D) אָסוּר לְעַשֵּׁן כָּאן.
   (E) הַטַּבָּק הַטּוֹב בְּיוֹתֵר בָּא מְוּרג׳ינְיָה.

4. דָּן לֹא רָאָה שֶׁלֶג מֵעוֹלָם, וּכְשֶׁהִסְתַּכֵּל בַּפְּתִיתִים הַיּוֹרְדִים מִן הַשָּׁמַיִם קָרָא:

   (A) גֶּשֶׁם, גֶּשֶׁם, רֵד!
   (B) מַה נִּפְלָא הַמַּרְאֶה!
   (C) טוֹב שֶׁיֵּשׁ גַּם קַיִץ.
   (D) חֲבָל שֶׁהַזְּמַן עוֹבֵר!
   (E) הָעִתּוֹן יוֹדִיעַ עַל כָּךְ.

5. מִרְיָם אוֹהֶבֶת מְאֹד בַּעֲלֵי חַיִּים וְדוֹאֶגֶת לָהֶם תָּמִיד. כְּשֶׁעָבַרְנוּ לְיַד חָתוּל צָנוּם וְצוֹלֵעַ הֶעִירָהּ בְּרַחֲמִים:

   (A) חָתוּל שָׁחֹר הוּא סִמָּן רָע.
   (B) חָתוּל וְעַכְבָּר הֵם אוֹיְבִים בְּנֶפֶשׁ.
   (C) עָלֵינוּ לְהוֹשִׁיט עֶזְרָה לֶחָתוּל זֶה.
   (D) חָתוּל אוֹהֵב מַאַכְלֵי חָלָב.
   (E) אַל תִּתֵּן אֵמוּן בֶּחָתוּל.

6. חַנָּה בַּת הַשֶּׁבַע בִּקְשָׁה שֶׁיַּרְשׁוּ לָהּ לְהִסְתַּכֵּל בַּטֶּלֶוִיזְיָה בְּתָכְנִית הָעֶרֶב הַמְאֻחֶרֶת. אָמְרוּ לָהּ הוֹרֶיהָ:

   (A) הַתָּכְנִית הַזֹּאת מְשַׁעֲמֶמֶת מְאֹד.
   (B) הַטֶּכְנַאי לֹא בָּא עֲדַיִן לְתַקֵּן אֶת הַטֶּלֶוִיזְיָה.
   (C) רַעַשׁ הַטֶּלֶוִיזְיָה מַפְרִיעַ לַשְּׁכֵנִים בִּשְׁעוֹת הָעֶרֶב.
   (D) עָלַיִךְ לָלֶכֶת לִישֹׁן מִיָּד, כְּדֵי שֶׁלֹּא תְּאַחֲרִי לָקוּם בַּבֹּקֶר.
   (E) הִסְתַּכְּלוּת רַבָּה בַּטֶּלֶוִיזְיָה מַזִּיקָה לָעֵינַיִם.

GO ON TO THE NEXT PAGE ▶

7. אָב וּבְנוֹ הָלְכוּ לָדוּג. חָזְרוּ וּבְסַלָּם דָּגִים לָרֹב. פָּגְשָׁה אוֹתָם הָאֵם, הִסְתַּכְּלָה בַּסַּל הַמָּלֵא וְאָמְרָה:

(A) קִוִּיתִי שֶׁתַּעַזְרוּ לִי בַּעֲבוֹדָתִי.

(B) טִיּוּל יָפֶה עֲרַכְתֶּם לָכֶם !

(C) הָיְתָה סְעָרָה גְדוֹלָה כַּנִּרְאָה.

(D) תִּהְיֶה לָנוּ אֲרוּחָה נִפְלָאָה !

(E) מַה יָּפִים הָעוֹפוֹת הָאֵלֶּה !

8. הַשָּׁעָה עֶשֶׂר, עֶשֶׂר וָרֶבַע, עֶשֶׂר וָחֵצִי, וְהָאוֹטוֹבּוּס אֵינֶנּוּ. זֶה שָׁעָה שֶׁאֲנַחְנוּ עוֹמְדִים פֹּה, הַשֶּׁמֶשׁ מַכָּה עַל רָאשֵׁינוּ וְאֵין כָּל סִמָּן שֶׁהוּא עוֹמֵד לָבוֹא. כֻּלָּנוּ מִתְאוֹנְנִים וְקוֹרְאִים:

(A) הַחֹם יַהֲרֹג אוֹתָנוּ.

(B) הַצְּפִיפוּת פֹּה נוֹרָאָה.

(C) צָרִיךְ הָיָה לְהַגִּיעַ בְּאַחַת עֶשְׂרֵה.

(D) דּוֹאֲגִים אָנוּ לְבָתֵּינוּ.

(E) אֵין דָּבָר, בְּוַדַּאי יָבוֹא.

9. דָּוִד, שֶׁהִשְׁכִּים לָקוּם כְּדֵי לְהַקְדִּים לְהַגִּיעַ לְמִשְׂרָדוֹ, לֹא יָכֹל לְהַתְנִיעַ אֶת הַמְּכוֹנִית. רָטַן בְּכַעַס לְעַצְמוֹ:

(A) דַּוְקָא הַיּוֹם מִכָּל הַיָּמִים צָרִיךְ דָּבָר זֶה לִקְרוֹת.

(B) הַשָּׁעָה כְּבָר מְאֻחֶרֶת מְאֹד וְעָלַי לְהִזְדָּרֵז.

(C) חֲצִי נֶחָמָה; גַּם שְׁכֵנִי אֵינוֹ יָכֹל לְהַתְנִיעַ אֶת מְכוֹנִיתוֹ.

(D) אֲצַלְצֵל לַמִּשְׂרָד וַאֲבַקֵּשׁ אֶת עֶזְרָתָם.

(E) אָמַרְתִּי לְאִשְׁתִּי לֹא לְהַחֲנוֹת אֶת הַמְּכוֹנִית בְּמָקוֹם זֶה.

10. אוּרִי חָזַר לְתֵל-אָבִיב מִנְּיוּ יוֹרְק. בִּשְׂדֵה הַתְּעוּפָה פָּגַשׁ אוֹתוֹ אָחִיו וְשָׁאַל:

(A) מֶה חָדָשׁ בִּירוּשָׁלַיִם ?

(B) כַּמָּה זְמַן אָרְכָה הַטִּיסָה ?

(C) הַאִם קִבַּלְתָּ אֶת הַמִּכְתָּב שֶׁשָּׁלַחְתִּי הַבֹּקֶר ?

(D) כַּמָּה זְמַן הָיִיתָ בָּאָרֶץ ?

(E) מִי סִפֵּר לְךָ שֶׁאֲנִי גָּר בְּתֵל-אָבִיב ?

11. אֲבִיבָה מָסְרָה אֶת הַבַּד לַתּוֹפֶרֶת וְאָמְרָה:

(A) הַבַּד הַזֶּה מְכֹעָר מְאֹד.

(B) עֲשִׂי לִי שִׂמְלַת קַיִץ, בְּבַקָּשָׁה.

(C) אַתְּ הִשְׁמַנְתְּ מְאֹד בַּשָּׁנָה הָאַחֲרוֹנָה.

(D) תִּפְרִי לִי זוּג נַעֲלַיִם, בְּבַקָּשָׁה.

(E) הַאִם אַתְּ יוֹדַעַת לִתְפֹּר ?

12. בָּאנוּ הַבַּיְתָה בְּשָׁעָה מְאֻחֶרֶת בַּלַּיְלָה, וְלֹא יָכֹלְנוּ לִמְצֹא אֶת הַמַּפְתֵּחַ. אָמַר אַבָּא:

(A) טִיּוּל לְאוֹר הַכּוֹכָבִים מוֹשֵׁךְ אֶת לִבִּי.

(B) אֵין דָּבָר; יֵשׁ הַרְבֵּה בָּתֵּי מָלוֹן בַּשְּׁכוּנָה הַזֹּאת.

(C) נִצְטָרֵךְ לָעִיר אֶת הַשּׁוֹעֵר כְּדֵי לְהִכָּנֵס.

(D) לוּ גַּרְנוּ בְּמָלוֹן, לֹא הָיָה זֶה קוֹרֶה לָנוּ.

(E) עָלַי לְהַשְׁכִּים מָחָר כְּדֵי לָטוּס לְיִשְׂרָאֵל.

13. הַמַּדְרִיךְ שֶׁל קְבוּצַת הַצּוֹפִים נִהֵל אֶת הַמִּשְׂחָק "סִמָּנֵי דֶרֶךְ". הַצּוֹפִים הִתְפַּזְּרוּ לְכָל עֵבֶר. יֶלֶד אֶחָד, לְפִי הַסִּמָּנִים, קָרָא אֶת הַהוֹדָעָה הַבָּאָה:

(A) מָה אַתָּה עוֹשֶׂה כָּאן בְּתוֹךְ הַיַּעַר ?

(B) מְגִלּוֹת יָם הַמֶּלַח נִמְצְאוּ בַּמְּעָרוֹת.

(C) קַבֵּל רְשׁוּת לִקְרֹא אֶת הַפִּתְקָה הַזֹּאת.

(D) אֲנַחְנוּ נִמְצָאִים בְּמֶרְחָק מֵאָה צְעָדִים וּמְכִינִים מְדוּרָה.

(E) אִם אֵינְךָ יָכוֹל לִקְרֹא אֶת הַהוֹדָעָה שְׁאַל אֶת הַמַּדְרִיךְ.

GO ON TO THE NEXT PAGE

14. יָשַׁבְנוּ וְהִתְוַכַּחְנוּ עַל הַשִּׁדּוּר שֶׁל שְׁלֹשֶׁת הַמֻּעֲמָדִים. לְבַסּוֹף לֹא יָכֹלְתִּי לְהִתְאַפֵּק עוֹד וְאָמַרְתִּי לִידִידִי:

    (A) דְּבָרֶיךָ סוֹתְרִים אֵלּוּ אֶת אֵלּוּ.

    (B) אֲנִי מְכַבֵּד מְאֹד אֶת פִּקְחוּתְךָ.

    (C) גַּם מוֹרִי הִתְבַּטֵּא כָּמוֹךָ.

    (D) מִי יוֹדֵעַ? אוּלַי יִתְקַיְּמוּ דְּבָרֶיךָ.

    (E) אֲנִי מַסְכִּים לְכָל מַה שֶּׁאָמַרְתָּ.

15. גִּשְׁמֵי זַעַף יָרְדוּ בָּאָרֶץ וְהַכְּבִישִׁים הָיוּ מוּצָפִים מַיִם. קַרְיָן הָרַדְיוֹ הִזְהִיר אֶת הַשּׁוֹמְעִים וְאָמַר:

    (A) יֵשׁ חֲשָׁשׁ לְבַצֹּרֶת.

    (B) רָצוּי לְהִמָּנַע מִנְּהִיגָה.

    (C) יוֹרְדִים גִּשְׁמֵי בְרָכָה.

    (D) אַל תַּעַבְרוּ אֶת הָרְחוֹב!

    (E) לֹא כְדַאי לְהִשָּׁאֵר בַּבַּיִת.

16. מֵחֲמַת עֲלִיַּת הַמְּחִירִים אָמְרָה הַמַּזְכִּירָה לַמְּנַהֵל:

    (A) אֲנִי מְבַקֶּשֶׁת הַעֲלָאָה בְּמַשְׂכֻּרְתִּי.

    (B) אֲנִי מִתְפַּטֶּרֶת מִמִּשְׂרָתִי תֵּכֶף וּמִיָּד.

    (C) הָעֲבוֹדָה הַזֹּאת אֵינָה מוֹצֵאת חֵן בְּעֵינַי.

    (D) הִצִּיעוּ לִי מִשְׂרָה בְּמִשְׂרָד אַחֵר.

    (E) אַתָּה מַעֲבִיד אוֹתִי קָשֶׁה מִדַּי.

17. בָּרַדְיוֹ הוֹדִיעוּ שֶׁמֶזֶג הָאֲוִיר בִּצְפוֹן הָאָרֶץ וּבְמֶרְכָּזָהּ יִהְיֶה חַם מְאֹד. דָּן הֶחְלִיט לַעֲרֹךְ אֶת טִיּוּלוֹ לַמְרוֹת הַחוֹם הַכָּבֵד, וְאָמַר לְהוֹרָיו:

    (A) לֹא חָלוּ כָּל שִׁנּוּיִים בְּתָכְנִיּוֹתַי.

    (B) הַשָּׁרָב יִפָּסֵק בְּעוֹד יוֹמַיִם.

    (C) אֵין סִכּוּי לְשִׁנּוּי מֶזֶג הָאֲוִיר בְּמֶרְכַּז הָאָרֶץ.

    (D) יֵשׁ מַעְיָנוֹת רַבִּים בְּאֵזוֹר הַצָּפוֹן.

    (E) אֵין אִישׁ מְטַיֵּל בְּעוֹנָה זוֹ.

GO ON TO THE NEXT PAGE ➡

HEBREW TEST—Continued

Part B

Directions: One or more words are underlined in each of the sentences in this part of the test. Four of the five choices that follow each sentence can be substituted for the underlined words to form sentences that are grammatically correct though they may be different in meaning from the original sentence. You are to select the one choice that does NOT fit grammatically into the original sentence. Please note that in this part of the test you are asked to identify not a correct form, but a form that would be wrong if used in the given sentence.

Be sure to note that the questions are numbered on the RIGHT side of each column and begin on the RIGHT side of the page.

Example:

Ⓐ Ⓑ Ⓒ Ⓓ ⬤

18. הֵם הִגִּיעוּ הַבַּיְתָה בְּשָׁעָה מְאֻחֶרֶת.

    (A) עֲלִיזִים
    (B) בָּרֶגֶל
    (C) עֲיֵפִים
    (D) מָחָר
    (E) בְּשָׁלוֹם

19. אֱמֹר לָנוּ לְשֵׁם מָה בָּאתָ הֵנָּה.

    (A) מַדּוּעַ
    (B) לָמָּה
    (C) מִשּׁוּם מָה
    (D) בְּאֵיזֶה עִנְיָן
    (E) מִתּוֹךְ כַּוָּנָה

20. הוּא יְבַקֵּר בָּאָרֶץ מִדֵּי שָׁנָה.

    (A) כָּל
    (B) פְּעָמִים
    (C) שָׁנָה
    (D) תּוֹךְ
    (E) אַחֲרֵי

יָבוֹא יוֹם וְכֻלָּנוּ נִשְׂמַח.

    (A) נִשְׁמַע
    (B) נִבְרַח
    (C) נִלְמַד
    (D) נִרְכַּב
    (E) נִכְנַס

21. הוּא אוֹהֵב אֶת הַמְּלָאכָה אֲשֶׁר הוּא עוֹשֶׂה.

    (A) מַצְלִיחַ
    (B) מְכַבֵּד
    (C) שׂוֹנֵא
    (D) מַעֲרִיךְ
    (E) מְבַזֶּה

22. הַיֶּלֶד הִרְגִּישׁ צַעַר גָּדוֹל.

    (A) יָגוֹן
    (B) כְּאֵב
    (C) שָׂמֵחַ
    (D) פַּחַד
    (E) עֶצֶב

23. הַיֶּלֶד קָרָא אֶת הַסֵּפֶר שֶׁהָיָה בְּיָדוֹ.

    (A) קָרַע
    (B) עָטַף
    (C) לִכְלֵךְ
    (D) הִשְׁלִיךְ
    (E) הִבִּיט

GO ON TO THE NEXT PAGE ➤

24. קָשֶׁה לִי לְהָבִין, מַדּוּעַ אֲנָשִׁים שׂוֹנְאִים אִישׁ אֶת אָחִיו.

   (A) מַרְגִּיזִים
   (B) הוֹרְגִים
   (C) רוֹצְחִים
   (D) כּוֹתְבִים
   (E) מַתְקִיפִים

25. הַתַּלְמִיד עָמַד בַּבְּחִינוֹת.

   (A) הִצְלִיחַ
   (B) הִצְטַיֵּן
   (C) נִגַּשׁ
   (D) נִכְשַׁל
   (E) הִתְבַּלְבֵּל

26. הוּא הִפְצִיר בִּי שֶׁאֶסַּע אִתּוֹ וְלֹא הִרְפָּה מִמֶּנִּי עַד שֶׁהִסְכַּמְתִּי.

   (A) סָר
   (B) נִפְרַד
   (C) זָז
   (D) הִנִּיחַ
   (E) הָלַךְ

27. הוּא עָסוּק בְּחֶשְׁבּוֹנוֹתָיו.

   (A) תִּקֵּן
   (B) שָׁגָה
   (C) הִתְבַּלְבֵּל
   (D) טָעָה
   (E) צָדַק

28. הוּא סִיֵּם אֶת הַסֵּפֶר.

   (A) סָגַר
   (B) עִיֵּן
   (C) הִפִּיל
   (D) פָּתַח
   (E) קָרַע

29. הוּא כּוֹעֵס עָלַי וְרוֹצֶה לְהִנָּקֵם בִּי.

   (A) לְהִלָּחֵם
   (B) לִגְעֹר
   (C) לִפְגֹּעַ
   (D) לַעֲנֹשׁ
   (E) לִמְרֹד

30. לִכְבוֹד חַג הַפֶּסַח צְרִיכִים לֶאֱפוֹת מַצּוֹת.

   (A) לִקְנוֹת
   (B) לְהָכִין
   (C) לְהַשִּׂיג
   (D) לְהַזְמִין
   (E) לְבָרֵךְ

31. קָנִיתִי בַּחֲנוּת שְׁמוֹנָה סְפָרִים.

   (A) עִתּוֹנִים
   (B) לוּחוֹת
   (C) עֶפְרוֹנוֹת
   (D) בֵּיצִים
   (E) יַלְקוּטִים

GO ON TO THE NEXT PAGE ➤

.32 עָלַי לְשַׁלֵּם לְךָ אֶת הַחוֹב.

(A) לִתְבֹּעַ

(B) לִשְׁלֹחַ

(C) לְהַחֲזִיר

(D) לָתֵת

(E) לִפְרֹעַ

.33 הַסֵּפֶר הַזֶּה מְצֻיָּן.

(A) כָּתוּב בְּטַעַם

(B) מְתֻרְגָּם

(C) מְעַנְיֵן

(D) נִפְלָא

(E) מְרַתֵּק

.34 הַאִם יָדוּעַ לְךָ הַדָּבָר?

(A) גֻּלָּה

(B) הֻגְלָה

(C) יִגָּלֶה

(D) נִגְלָה

(E) נִתְגַּלָּה

.35 אוּרִי הִסְתַּכֵּל בַּתְּמוּנָה שֶׁלְּפָנָיו.

(A) הִתְבּוֹנֵן

(B) לֹא גָּרַע עַיִן

(C) הֵצִיץ

(D) הִשְׂבִּיעַ עֵינָיו

(E) הִתְאַהֵב

.36 הוּא רָשַׁם בַּפִּנְקָס שֵׁמוֹת רַבִּים.

(A) רְשָׁמִים

(B) חֶשְׁבּוֹנוֹת

(C) רְשִׁימוֹת

(D) מִקְצוֹעוֹת

(E) הִרְהוּרִים

.37 הַוַּעַד הֶחְלִיט לִשְׁמֹעַ אֶת בַּקָּשָׁתוֹ.

(A) לְהַרְכִּיב

(B) לְאַשֵּׁר

(C) לְקַבֵּל

(D) לִדְחוֹת

(E) לְבַטֵּל

GO ON TO THE NEXT PAGE

Part C

<u>Directions:</u> Read the following passages carefully for comprehension. Each passage is followed by a number of incomplete statements or questions. Select the completion or answer that is best according to the passage and blacken the corresponding space on the answer sheet.

Be sure to note that the questions are numbered on the RIGHT side of each column and begin on the RIGHT side of the page.

בְּמוֹשָׁבָה קְטַנָּה שֶׁבִּיהוּדָה יָשְׁבוּ מֵרֵאשִׁית הִוָּסְדָהּ שְׁנֵי זוּגוֹת, וְקִשְׁרֵי יְדִידוּת נִקְשְׁרוּ בֵּינֵיהֶם. הַזּוּג הָאֶחָד — שְׁמוֹ שֶׁל הַגֶּבֶר חַיִּים, וְשֵׁם הָאִשָּׁה צִפּוֹרָה. הַזּוּג הַשֵּׁנִי — שְׁמוֹתָם זַנְוִיל וּדְבוֹרָה. חַיִּים וְזַנְוִיל שְׁנֵיהֶם עֶגְלוֹנִים הָיוּ. חַיִּים בַּעַל עֲגָלָה הָיָה, סוּס וַעֲגָלָה לוֹ מִשֶּׁלּוֹ וְהוּא מַסִּיעַ יוֹם יוֹם "נוֹסְעִים" וּמַשָּׂאוֹת מִמּוֹשַׁבְתּוֹ לְיָפוֹ וּמִיָּפוֹ לַמּוֹשָׁבָה. עִם צֵאת הַשַּׁחַר הָיָה יוֹצֵא לְדַרְכּוֹ וְהַנּוֹסְעִים מַמְתִּינִים לוֹ בְּמוֹצָאֵי הַמּוֹשָׁבָה, וְעִם צֵאת הַכּוֹכָבִים הָיָה חוֹזֵר מִדַּרְכּוֹ. אֵין הַדֶּרֶךְ רְחוֹקָה כָּל כָּךְ, אֶלָּא שֶׁהִיא עֲשׂוּיָה חוֹל וְגַלְגַּלֵּי הָעֲגָלָה שׁוֹקְעִים בּוֹ, וְרַק בִּקְשֵׁי תֵּחָלֵץ. שְׁלֹשֶׁת רִבְעֵי הַזְּמַן מְהַלְּכִים "הַנּוֹסְעִים" בְּצִדֵּי הָעֲגָלָה וּמֵאֲחוֹרֶיהָ. זַנְוִיל לֹא הָיָה כִּי אִם עֶגְלוֹן, נָהַג בִּשְׁנֵי סוּסָיו שֶׁל אַחַד הָאִכָּרִים הָאַמִּידִים בַּמּוֹשָׁבָה. לְיָפוֹ הָיָה נוֹסֵעַ רַק לְעִתִּים רְחוֹקוֹת עִם בְּעָלָיו וּבְנֵי בֵּיתוֹ. אֶת הַדֶּרֶךְ לְיָפוֹ הָיָה עוֹשֶׂה בְּמֶשֶׁךְ שָׁעֳתַיִם, וְהוּא הַדָּבָר גַּם בַּחֲזָרָה, שֶׁכֵּן סוּסֵי בְּעָלָיו זְרִיזִים הָיוּ וּמְהִירִים. בִּימוֹת הַחֹרֶף הָיָה זַנְוִיל וְעוֹזְרוֹ הָעַרְבִי חוֹרְשִׁים בַּשָּׂדֶה, וּבִימוֹת הַקַּיִץ הָיָה מוֹבִיל זֶבֶל, חַמְרָה וַאֲבָנִים.

38. הַהֶבְדֵּל בֵּין חַיִּים וְזַנְוִיל הָיָה בָּזֶה

(A) שֶׁחַיִּים בַּעַל רְכוּשׁ רַב הָיָה וְזַנְוִיל — עָנִי

(B) שֶׁרְכוּשׁוֹ שֶׁל חַיִּים הָיָה בְּקַרְקַע וְשֶׁל זַנְוִיל בִּסְחוֹרָה

(C) שֶׁחַיִּים הָיָה סוֹחֵר זָרִיז וְזַנְוִיל — אִכָּר פָּשׁוּט

(D) שֶׁחַיִּים הָיָה בַּעַל עֲגָלָה וְסוּס, וְזַנְוִיל הָיָה עֶגְלוֹן שֶׁל יְהוּדִי אַחֵר

(E) שֶׁחַיִּים הָיָה יוֹצֵא לְמַסָּעוֹת רְחוֹקִים וְזַנְוִיל הָיָה יוֹשֵׁב בֵּית מִטְבְּעוֹ

39. חַיִּים הָיָה נוֹסֵעַ לְיָפוֹ כְּדֵי

(A) לְהָבִיא חוֹל

(B) לְהַעֲבִיר אֲנָשִׁים וּמַשָּׂאוֹת

(C) לְהִתְרָאוֹת עִם בְּנֵי בֵּיתוֹ

(D) לַעֲשׂוֹת עֲסָקִים

(E) לַעֲשׂוֹת אֶת רְצוֹן בְּעָלָיו

40. מֶה עָשָׂה זַנְוִיל בִּימוֹת הַחֹרֶף?

(A) הָיָה מְזָרֵז אֶת סוּסֵי בְּעָלָיו.

(B) הָיָה מוֹבִיל חָמְרֵי בִּנְיָן.

(C) יָשַׁב בָּטֵל מִמְּלָאכָה.

(D) הָיָה נוֹסֵעַ לְעִתִּים רְחוֹקוֹת עִם בְּעָלָיו.

(E) הָיָה עוֹבֵד אֶת הָאֲדָמָה.

GO ON TO THE NEXT PAGE →

מרדכי עמנואל נוח נולד בשנת 1785 בעיר פִילָדֶלְפְיָה. בהיותו בן עשרים ושש נתמנה לציר ארצות־הברית בְּטוּנִיס. את שליחותו וחובותיו מילא באמונה, אולם אויביו הפוליטיים העלילו עליו עלילות שונות, שהשפיעו על שר החוץ לְפַטֵר אותו ממשרתו. בכתב הפיטורים שלו נאמר, שאמונתו היהודית היא בעוכריו, ולכן אינו יכול למלא את תפקידו. המקרה הזה ציער אותו מאוד, ועורר בו את הרעיון לְיַסֵד מדינה יהודית באמריקה הצפונית.

בשנת 1824 עשה את הצעד הראשון לייסוד המדינה היהודית. באותה שנה נמכר האי גְרֶנְד אשר באמצע הנהר נִיאָגְרָה. מרדכי עמנואל נוח החליט כי זהו המקום הראוי לייסוד המדינה היהודית. בעזרת עשירים הצליח לקנות חבל אדמה גדול במקום ההוא, כדי לבנות שם עיר בשם אֲרָרָט, שתשמש מקלט בטוח ליהודים הנידחים. הוא מיהר להניח את אבן היסוד לעיר זו לפני שהיו בידו האמצעים לבנות אותה. הוא קרא ליהודי העולם לתמוך במפעלו, אבל הם לא נענו לו. העיר לא נבנתה, אולם אבן הפנה נמצאת בבית אוסף העתיקות של העיר בּוּפָאלוֹ.

41. מרדכי עמנואל נוח רצה להקים מדינה יהודית עצמאית כי

(A) הושפע מלימוד התנ״ך

(B) סבל מאנטישמיות

(C) שאף להיות נשיא המדינה

(D) היה מעוניין להחיות את השפה העברית

(E) המיסים בארצות־הברית היו גבוהים מאוד

42. מרדכי עמנואל נוח החליט ליסד את המדינה היהודית באי גְרֶנְד מפני

(A) שהיתה אוכלוסיה יהודית גדולה במקום ההוא

(B) שמזג האויר שם היה נעים מאוד

(C) שאפשר היה לקנות אדמה במקום ההוא

(D) שהאי קרוב לעיר מולדתו

(E) שהקהילה היהודית רצתה בכך

43. מרדכי עמנואל נוח לא הגשים את רעיונו כי

(A) לא הקדיש לו את כל כוחותיו

(B) ממשלת ארצות הברית התנגדה לו

(C) מת זמן קצר אחרי שנתעורר בו הרעיון

(D) היהודים לא באו לעזרתו

(E) הוא לא היה איש מעשה

44. זכר למפעלו של מרדכי עמנואל נוח נמצא

(A) בבית כנסת עתיק

(B) בתל־אביב

(C) בספר שכתב מרדכי עמנואל נוח

(D) במוזיאון היהודי אשר בְּנְיוּ יוֹרְק

(E) בעיר בּוּפָאלוֹ

GO ON TO THE NEXT PAGE ➡

הֶרְשְׁל יָדוּעַ בְּכָל הַסְּבִיבָה כְּצַיָּר נִפְלָא. הַנְּסִיכִים בַּעֲלֵי הָאֲחֻזּוֹת הַגְּדוֹלוֹת מַזְמִינִים אוֹתוֹ לְצַיֵּר אֶת הֵיכְלֵיהֶם וּמְשַׁלְּמִים לוֹ שָׂכָר הָגוּן. הֶרְשְׁל יוֹדֵעַ אֶת הַמְּלָאכָה וְיוֹדֵעַ גַּם לָקַחַת שְׂכָרָהּ. בְּעַד אוּלָם אֶחָד הוּא לוֹקֵחַ לִפְעָמִים אֶלֶף רֶבֶל.

וְהֶרְשְׁל מַכְנִיס וְאֵינוּ מוֹצִיא: אִשָּׁה וּבָנִים אֵין לוֹ, דִּירָתוֹ צָרָה וּמְלֻכְלֶכֶת, לְבוּשׁוֹ סְמַרְטוּטִים, כְּאִלּוּ הַקַּבְּצָנוּת אֻמָּנוּתוֹ, וּמַאֲכָלוֹ — לֶחֶם וּקְצָת מֵי גְרִיסִין. רַק בַּשַּׁבָּתוֹת הוּא סָמוּךְ עַל שֻׁלְחַן נֹחַ־לֵיב הַמְּלַמֵּד וּמְשַׁלֵּם לוֹ מְחִיר שָׁלשׁ סְעֻדּוֹת שְׁלשִׁים פְּרוּטוֹת. מוּבָן מֵאֵלָיו, שֶׁהוּא הוֹלֵךְ וּמְאַסֵּף מָמוֹן כְּקֹרַח.

אַךְ הֵיכָן הוּא שָׂם אֶת כָּל הַכֶּסֶף הַזֶּה?

הַרְבֵּה עָמְלוּ יוֹשְׁבֵי הָעִיר לִמְצֹא פִּתְרוֹן לְחִידָה זוֹ וְהֶעֱלוּ חֶרֶס בְּיָדָם. לִצְדָקָה, לְמָשָׁל, אֵינוּ נוֹתֵן פְּרוּטָה וְגַם בְּרִבִּית אֵינוּ מַלְוֶה.

סָבְבוּ אוֹתוֹ הַסַּרְסוּרִים בִּלְהָטֵיהֶם, שֶׁיִּתֵּן אֶת כַּסְפּוֹ בְּנֶשֶׁךְ, וְלֹא יָכְלוּ. הוֹכִיחַ אוֹתוֹ הָרַב שֶׁיִּתֵּן לִצְדָקָה וְלֹא הוֹעִיל. תְּשׁוּבָה אַחַת בְּפִיו: אֵין לִי.

כַּמּוּבָן, הַכֹּל יָדְעוּ כִּי שֶׁקֶר בְּפִיו.

לֹא פַעַם בָּדְקוּ גַּנָּבִים בְּאַרְגָּזוֹ וּמָצְאוּ שָׁם — תַּכְרִיכִים, וַיֵּשׁוּבוּ בְּבוּשָׁה. בְּתַכְרִיכִים גַּם גַּנָּב לֹא יִגַּע.

מִי הָיָה הָאִישׁ? מֵאַיִן מוֹצָאוֹ? — אִישׁ לֹא יָדַע בְּבֵרוּר. שִׂיחָה נָפְלָה בְּפִי הַבְּרִיּוֹת כִּי הִכְרִיחוּהוּ בְּיַלְדוּתוֹ לְהָמִיר אֶת דָּתוֹ וְלֹא עָמַד בַּנִּסָּיוֹן. אֲבָל אַחַר כָּךְ חָזַר בִּתְשׁוּבָה וַיְהִי לִיהוּדִי.

וְאָמְנָם יְרֵא שָׁמַיִם הוּא הֶרְשְׁל. אָמְנָם בּוּר הוּא, עַם הָאָרֶץ, אֲבָל אֶת הָאֱלֹהִים הוּא יָרֵא, וּמַה שֶּׁהוּא יוֹדֵעַ הוּא מְקַיֵּם בִּזְהִירוּת רַבָּה. גַּם יוֹם אֶחָד לֹא יַעֲבֹר עָלָיו שֶׁלֹּא יֹאמַר אֶת מִזְמוֹרֵי הַתְּהִלִּים מֵרֹאשָׁם עַד סוֹפָם; וּבְשַׁבָּת, מִלְּבַד שֶׁהוּא שׁוֹמֵעַ אֶת הַסִּדְרָה עִם פֵּרוּשׁ רַשִׁ"י מִפִּי נֹחַ־לֵיב, הוּא קוֹרֵא תָּמִיד תְּהִלִּים. פַּעַם הִזְמִין אוֹתוֹ שַׂר הָעִיר בְּשַׁבָּת וְלֹא רָצָה לָלֶכֶת. אִיְּמוּ עָלָיו שֶׁיִּסְחָבוּהוּ בְּחָזְקָה, וְהוּא לֹא מָשׁ מִמְּקוֹמוֹ. מְבִינֵי הַתּוֹרָה בִּקְּשׁוּ לְהַתִּיר לוֹ אֶת הַדָּבָר, וְלֹא קִבֵּל.

וְיַחַד עִם זֶה קַמְצָן הוּא מֵאֵין כָּמוֹהוּ.

45. יוֹשְׁבֵי הָעִיר עָמְלוּ הַרְבֵּה לִמְצֹא אֶת פִּתְרוֹן הַחִידָה וְהִיא:

(A) מַדּוּעַ דִּירָתוֹ שֶׁל הֶרְשְׁל צָרָה וּמְלֻכְלָכָה?

(B) אֵיפֹה הוּא שׁוֹמֵר אֶת כַּסְפּוֹ?

(C) הַאִם בֶּאֱמֶת הֶרְשְׁל צוֹבֵר הוֹן רַב?

(D) מַדּוּעַ אוֹכֵל הוּא שָׁלשׁ סְעֻדּוֹת רַק בַּשַּׁבָּתוֹת?

(E) כַּמָּה מְשַׁלְּמִים לוֹ בְּעַד מְלַאכְתּוֹ?

46. הַסַּרְסוּרִים הִשְׁתַּדְּלוּ לְשַׁכְנֵעַ אֶת הֶרְשְׁל שֶׁיִּתֵּן אֶת כַּסְפּוֹ

(A) בְּרִבִּית

(B) לִקְרוֹבָיו

(C) בְּתַכְרִיכִים

(D) לַעֲנִיִּים

(E) לָאֻמָּנוּת

47. יוֹשְׁבֵי הָעִיר יָדְעוּ שֶׁהֶרְשְׁל הוּא עָשִׁיר מִפְּנֵי

(A) שֶׁשִּׁלֵּם לַמְּלַמֵּד שְׁלשִׁים פְּרוּטוֹת מְחִיר שָׁלשׁ סְעֻדּוֹת

(B) שֶׁמַּאֲכָלוֹ הָיָה לֶחֶם וּמְעַט מֵי גְרִיסִין

(C) שֶׁלֹּא הָיוּ לוֹ לֹא אִשָּׁה וְלֹא יוֹרְשִׁים אֲחֵרִים

(D) שֶׁקִּבֵּל שָׂכָר הָגוּן בְּעַד צִיּוּרָיו וְלֹא הוֹצִיא כְּלוּם

(E) שֶׁנָּתַן אֶת רֹב כַּסְפּוֹ לִצְדָקָה לַעֲנִיִּים

48. לְפִי קֶטַע זֶה, הֶרְשְׁל הָיָה יְרֵא שָׁמַיִם מִפְּנֵי

(A) שֶׁאִיְּמוּ עָלָיו שֶׁיִּסְחָבוּהוּ בְּשַׁבָּת אִם לֹא יָבוֹא לְבֵית הַנָּסִיךְ

(B) שֶׁלֹּא נָתַן כַּסְפּוֹ בְּנֶשֶׁךְ

(C) שֶׁלֹּא נַעֲנָה לְהַזְמָנַת שַׂר הָעִיר בְּשַׁבָּת לַמְרוֹת הָאִיּוּמִים

(D) שֶׁבִּקְּשׁוּ הָרַבָּנִים לְהַתִּיר לוֹ לְחַלֵּל שַׁבָּת בְּפַרְהֶסְיָה

(E) שֶׁקָּרָא אֶת פָּרָשַׁת הַשָּׁבוּעַ עִם פֵּרוּשׁ רַשִׁ"י בְּכָל יוֹם

GO ON TO THE NEXT PAGE ➡

בְּאַחַד הַקְּרָבוֹת נִפְצַע דָּנִי בְּרַגְלוֹ. לֹא הַבַּיְתָה הוּבָא אֶלָּא לְבֵית-הַחוֹלִים בָּעֵמֶק הֶבִיאוּהוּ, יַחַד עִם פְּצוּעִים אֲחֵרִים. זָקוּק הָיָה לְנִתּוּחַ וְהוֹדִיעוּ לְהוֹרָיו. הֵם נָסְעוּ אֵלָיו וּמְצָאוּהוּ שׁוֹכֵב בַּמִּטָּה. בְּחֶדֶר גָּדוֹל מָלֵא מִטּוֹת וְחוֹלִים שָׁכַב, וְהָיָה מְחַיֵּךְ לִקְרָאתָם וּמְנַעְנֵעַ לָהֶם בְּיָדוֹ. עַל שְׁאֵלַת הָאֵם, אִם הוּא מַרְגִּישׁ עַצְמוֹ כָּאן בְּטוֹב, הֵשִׁיב: "מָה אָחוּז!" וְהִצְטַעֵר שֶׁהִטְרִיחוּ אוֹתָם לִנְסֹעַ נְסִיעָה רְחוֹקָה בִּתְנָאֵי תַּחְבּוּרָה רָעִים כָּל-כָּךְ.

וְהַהוֹרִים חָזְרוּ מוּדְאָגִים. פֶּצַע מְסוּכָּן בָּרֶגֶל. כַּדּוּר פָּגַע בְּעֶצֶם הָרֶגֶל, וְסָפֵק אִם אֶפְשָׁר יִהְיֶה לְהַצִּילָהּ. וּמִי יוֹדֵעַ? חֻמּוֹ אֵינוֹ פוֹסֵק, וּמִפִּי הָרוֹפְאִים אֵין לְהַצִּיל דָּבָר בָּרוּר. וְהוּא, הַמִּסְכֵּן, שׁוֹכֵב בְּחֹם וּמִתְבַּדֵּחַ וְטוֹעֵן שֶׁאֵין לוֹ מַכְאוֹבִים, אַף כִּי מִתּוֹךְ פָּנָיו צוֹעֵק הַכְּאֵב. הָרוֹפְאִים אֵינָם אוֹמְרִים מָתַי יֵעָשֶׂה הַנִּתּוּחַ. כַּנִּרְאֶה, לֹא מַהֵר. וְעַל-כֵּן לֹא יָכְלוּ לְהִשָּׁאֵר וְחָזְרוּ.

49. אֶת דָּנִי הֵבִיאוּ לְבֵית-הַחוֹלִים

(A) כְּדֵי שֶׁיִּשְׁכַּב בַּמִּטָּה

(B) כְּדֵי שֶׁיִּהְיֶה יַחַד עִם פְּצוּעִים אֲחֵרִים

(C) כִּי נִפְצַע קָשֶׁה בַּקְּרָב

(D) כִּי בֵּית-הַחוֹלִים הָיָה קָרוֹב לִמְקוֹם הַקְּרָבוֹת

(E) כִּי לֹא הָיָה מָקוֹם בַּבַּיִת

50. הוֹרֵי דָּנִי חָזְרוּ הַבַּיְתָה מוּדְאָגִים, כִּי

(A) חֻמּוֹ אֵינוֹ פוֹסֵק

(B) תְּנָאֵי הַנְּסִיעָה הָיוּ קָשִׁים מְאֹד

(C) דָּנִי אָמַר, שֶׁהוּא מַרְגִּישׁ עַצְמוֹ בְּטוֹב

(D) דָּנִי שָׁכַב בְּחֹם וְצָחַק

(E) דָּנִי הָיָה פָּצוּעַ קָשֶׁה

51. הָרוֹפְאִים לֹא גִּלּוּ אֶת כָּל הָאֱמֶת, כִּי

(A) דָּנִי הִרְגִּישׁ עַצְמוֹ בְּטוֹב

(B) הַחֹם שֶׁל דָּנִי הָיָה גָּבֹהַּ מְאֹד

(C) דָּנִי לֹא הִצְלִיחַ לְרַמּוֹת אוֹתָם עַל-יְדֵי צְחוֹק

(D) הָיוּ פְּצוּעִים רַבִּים בְּבֵית-הַחוֹלִים

(E) לֹא יָדְעוּ אִם יוּכְלוּ לְהַצִּיל אֶת חַיֵּי דָּנִי

52. דָּנִי הִצְטַעֵר מִפְּנֵי

(A) שֶׁנִּפְצַע בְּרַגְלוֹ

(B) שֶׁהָרוֹפְאִים לֹא אָמְרוּ מָתַי יֵעָשֶׂה הַנִּתּוּחַ

(C) שֶׁהוֹרָיו נָסְעוּ נְסִיעָה אֲרֻכָּה וּמְעַיֶּפֶת

(D) שֶׁהוֹרָיו לֹא יָכְלוּ לְהִשָּׁאֵר אֶצְלוֹ

(E) שֶׁפָּנָיו הִבִּיעוּ כְּאֵב נוֹרָא

53. הַסִּפּוּר מַרְאֶה בְּעִקָּר אֶת

(A) חֲרִיצוּת הָרוֹפְאִים וּשְׁתִיקָתָם

(B) אֹמֶץ לִבּוֹ שֶׁל דָּנִי

(C) מַרְאֵה בֵּית הַחוֹלִים

(D) מַהֲלַךְ הַקְּרָבוֹת

(E) סַכָּנוֹת הַנְּסִיעָה

GO ON TO THE NEXT PAGE →

בָּעֵת הַהִיא שָׁלַח מְרֹאדַךְ בַּלְאֲדָן בֶּן־בַּלְאֲדָן מֶלֶךְ־בָּבֶל סְפָרִים וּמִנְחָה אֶל־חִזְקִיָּהוּ וַיִּשְׁמַע כִּי חָלָה וַיֶּחֱזָק: וַיִּשְׂמַח עֲלֵיהֶם חִזְקִיָּהוּ וַיַּרְאֵם אֶת־בֵּית נְכֹתֹה אֶת־הַכֶּסֶף וְאֶת־הַזָּהָב וְאֶת־הַבְּשָׂמִים וְאֵת הַשֶּׁמֶן הַטּוֹב וְאֵת כָּל־בֵּית כֵּלָיו וְאֵת כָּל־אֲשֶׁר נִמְצָא בְּאוֹצְרֹתָיו לֹא־הָיָה דָבָר אֲשֶׁר לֹא־הֶרְאָם חִזְקִיָּהוּ בְּבֵיתוֹ וּבְכָל־מֶמְשַׁלְתּוֹ: וַיָּבֹא יְשַׁעְיָהוּ הַנָּבִיא אֶל־הַמֶּלֶךְ חִזְקִיָּהוּ וַיֹּאמֶר אֵלָיו מָה־אָמְרוּ הָאֲנָשִׁים הָאֵלֶּה וּמֵאַיִן יָבֹאוּ אֵלֶיךָ ?

וַיֹּאמֶר חִזְקִיָּהוּ מֵאֶרֶץ רְחוֹקָה בָּאוּ אֵלַי מִבָּבֶל: וַיֹּאמֶר מָה רָאוּ בְּבֵיתֶךָ וַיֹּאמֶר חִזְקִיָּהוּ אֵת כָּל־אֲשֶׁר בְּבֵיתִי רָאוּ לֹא־הָיָה דָבָר אֲשֶׁר לֹא־הִרְאִיתִים בְּאוֹצְרֹתָי: וַיֹּאמֶר יְשַׁעְיָהוּ אֶל־חִזְקִיָּהוּ שְׁמַע דְּבַר־יְהֹוָה צְבָאוֹת: הִנֵּה יָמִים בָּאִים וְנִשָּׂא כָּל־אֲשֶׁר בְּבֵיתֶךָ וַאֲשֶׁר אָצְרוּ אֲבֹתֶיךָ עַד־הַיּוֹם הַזֶּה בָּבֶלָה לֹא־יִוָּתֵר דָּבָר אָמַר יְהֹוָה: וּמִבָּנֶיךָ אֲשֶׁר יֵצְאוּ מִמְּךָ אֲשֶׁר תּוֹלִיד יִקָּחוּ וְהָיוּ סָרִיסִים בְּהֵיכַל מֶלֶךְ בָּבֶל: וַיֹּאמֶר חִזְקִיָּהוּ אֶל־יְשַׁעְיָהוּ טוֹב דְּבַר־יְהֹוָה אֲשֶׁר דִּבַּרְתָּ וַיֹּאמֶר כִּי יִהְיֶה שָׁלוֹם וֶאֱמֶת בְּיָמָי:

56. חִזְקִיָּהוּ הַמֶּלֶךְ הֶרְאָה לִשְׁלִיחֵי הַמֶּלֶךְ בָּבֶל אֶת כָּל אֲשֶׁר בְּאוֹצְרוֹתָיו

(A) מִפְּנֵי שֶׁקִּבֵּל מַתָּנוֹת מִמֶּלֶךְ בָּבֶל

(B) מִפְּנֵי שֶׁשָּׂמַח עַל בּוֹאָם לְבַקֵּר אוֹתוֹ

(C) לְפִי עֲצָתוֹ שֶׁל יְשַׁעְיָהוּ הַנָּבִיא

(D) מִפְּנֵי שֶׁרָצָה לְקַבֵּל יוֹתֵר מַתָּנוֹת וּסְפָרִים

(E) מִפְּנֵי שֶׁהֵם בָּאוּ מֵאֶרֶץ רְחוֹקָה

57. לְפִי דִּבְרֵי יְשַׁעְיָהוּ הַנָּבִיא

(A) חִזְקִיָּהוּ יוֹלִיד בָּנִים וּבָנוֹת

(B) בְּנֵי חִזְקִיָּהוּ יִהְיוּ שָׂרִים בְּבָבֶל

(C) מֶלֶךְ בָּבֶל יִקַּח אֶת אַרְמְנוֹת חִזְקִיָּהוּ

(D) מֶלֶךְ בָּבֶל יִקַּח אֶת בְּנֵי חִזְקִיָּהוּ לְסָרִיסִים בְּהֵיכָלוֹ

(E) מֶלֶךְ בָּבֶל וְסָרִיסָיו יִקְּחוּ אֶת חִזְקִיָּהוּ לְאֶרֶץ בָּבֶל

54. לְפִי הַפָּסוּק הָרִאשׁוֹן בַּפֶּרֶק הַזֶּה, מֶלֶךְ בָּבֶל

(A) הִתְחַזֵּק כַּאֲשֶׁר שָׁמַע עַל מַחֲלָתוֹ שֶׁל חִזְקִיָּהוּ

(B) שָׁלַח סְפָרִים לְחִזְקִיָּהוּ הַחוֹלֶה לְחַזֵּק אוֹתוֹ

(C) שָׁמַע כִּי חִזְקִיָּהוּ חָלָה וּכְבָר הִבְרִיא

(D) שָׂמַח לִשְׁמֹעַ עַל מַחֲלָתוֹ שֶׁל חִזְקִיָּהוּ וְנִהְיָה חָזָק

(E) שָׁלַח סְפָרִים וּמַתָּנוֹת לִמְרֹאדַךְ בַּלְאֲדָן

58. חִזְקִיָּהוּ הָיָה מְרֻצֶּה מִדִּבְרֵי יְשַׁעְיָהוּ

(A) כִּי הַנָּבִיא דִּבֵּר אֱמֶת

(B) לֹא הָיָה לוֹ כֹּחַ לְהִתְנַגֵּד

(C) כָּל עוֹד לֹא תִּפְרֹץ מִלְחָמָה בְּיָמָיו

(D) כִּי זֶה הָיָה דְּבַר ה'

(E) וּבִלְבַד שֶׁלֹּא יָרִיקוּ אֶת אוֹצְרוֹתָיו

55. כַּאֲשֶׁר שָׁמַע מֶלֶךְ בָּבֶל כִּי חָלָה חִזְקִיָּהוּ

(A) שָׁלַח לוֹ סְפָרִים וּמַתָּנוֹת

(B) שָׂמַח מְאֹד וַיִּתְחַזַּק

(C) שָׁלַח לוֹ כֶּסֶף וְזָהָב וּבְשָׂמִים

(D) הָלַךְ לְבַקֵּר אוֹתוֹ בִּשְׁעַת מִנְחָה

(E) שָׁלַח לוֹ סִפְרֵי תּוֹרָה לִקְרִיאָה

GO ON TO THE NEXT PAGE ➜

לא יכולתי להבין כיצד הצליחו האנשים לשאת את
הסבל הנורא, במחנות המוות הללו, בְּאוֹשְׁוִיץ וכו', את
הציפיה התמידית לקץ המר, כיצד לא נשברו ברוחם
עוד בטרם . . . מה הצילם מהדיכאון הנפשי האיום?
עד שהבינותי: הרעב!
הם היו רעבים תמיד, תמיד, וכל מחשבותיהם
נתרכזו בנקודה זו בלבד, ברעב. הם התהלכו והביטו
תמיד למטה, אל הקרקע, בחפשם משהו לאכול,
לבלוע, כתרנגולת זו שמחפשת גרעין.
הרעב הצילם.

59. השאלה שמעסיקה את הסופר היא:

(A) מדוע לא מתו אסירי המחנות מרעב?

(B) מדוע לא ציפו לרעב שיגאלם מהמוות?

(C) איך החזיקו מעמד ורוחם לא נשברה?

(D) כיצד לא התעודדו ברוחם?

(E) מה העיק על לבם?

60. כוונת התשובה, שהרעב הצילם, כי:

(A) השקיעו את כל כוחם בחיפוש מזון

(B) אכילה יתירה מזיקה יותר מאכילה דלה

(C) במידה שהגוף נחלש מתחזק הרוח

(D) האדם מתחזק על ידי הרעב

(E) היו כמו תרנגולות ואכלו מכל הבא לידם

GO ON TO THE NEXT PAGE

בתוך אולם מלא אנשים, לאחר ששני הרבנים נשאו
את דבריהם הלבביים מעל הבימה קם הַגֵר הַיַּפַאנִי
שישב על ידם עצמו, ודיבר בעברית טובה על הסיבות
שהביאוהו לחסות תחת כנפי אלוהי ישראל. קודם
כל — התנ״ך. והתחיל לדקלם בהתלהבות רבה: ״בראשית
ברא אלהים את השמים ואת הארץ. והארץ היתה תהו
ובהו וחשך על פני תהום ורוח אלהים מרחפת על פני
המים. ויאמר אלהים: יהי אור, ויהי אור״ . . .
אכן אוצר כזה, פסוקים ראשונים כאלה, יש לנו
ואנחנו לא ידענו !

61. בקטע זו מעלה לפנינו הסופר

(A) אסיפת אבל ביפאן

(B) כינוס רבנים יפאניים דוברי עברית

(C) את המבוכה ששררה ביפאן אחרי המלחמה

(D) את אהבתו לבעלי הכנפיים

(E) את דברי הגר על הגורמים שהביאוהו ליהדות

62. הסיבה לצעדו זה של היפאני היתה

(A) הלשון העברית

(B) השפעת הרבנים

(C) אהבתו לדיקלומים

(D) השפעת המקרא

(E) תנועת הנוער בישראל

63. המחבר רוצה להדגיש

(A) שאין אנו יודעים את התנ״ך

(B) שהחלק היפה בתנ״ך הוא סיפור הבריאה

(C) שיש להפיץ את היהדות בעולם

(D) שאנו אוהבים לשמוע את שבחנו מפי זרים

(E) שזר מעמיק לראות מבן בית

GO ON TO THE NEXT PAGE →

תנועת ה"השכלה" היתה תנועה אירופית. אירופית לא רק מבחינת מקורה, אלא בעיקר מבחינת עתידה ומטרותיה. האמונה שאירופה היא המולדת, דירת קבע ולא ארעית, ארץ מושב ולא גלות — מתגלה לנו בצורה ברורה ברוב יצירות התקופה. כל האידיאולוגיה שלה, הדורשת ללמוד את לשון המדינה, להתלבש כאזרחיה, לעסוק בפרנסות המועילות לכלל, לרכוש את תרבותה של הסביבה ולסגל את מנהגיה ודרך מחשבתה, כל אלה מבטאים את השאיפה היסודית להשתלב בחברה ולהיות לאזרחים בה. מבחינה זו ההשכלה היא גם אנטי־גלותית וגם אנטי־ציונית.

64. לפי דעת המחבר, מטרתה של ההשכלה היתה שכל היהודים

(A) ימצאו את לחמם בדרך כבוד

(B) יעבדו שכם אחד לטובת כל האנושיות כולה

(C) יקנו דעת ביהדות ובחילוניות גם יחד

(D) ירכשו להם תרבות חילונית

(E) יהיו חלק בלתי־נפרד מסביבותם

65. המחבר חושב שההשכלה היתה גם אנטי־גלותית וגם אנטי־ציונית בגלל

(A) חיפושיה אחר דירת קבע

(B) החברה שבה השתלבה

(C) מטרת ההתבוללות שקבעה לעצמה

(D) המקום שבו צמחה

(E) הסתגלותה לאורחות חיים חדשים

66. כדי לקיים את שאיפותיה, ההשכלה

(A) קראה ליהודים להתנכר לתרבותה של הסביבה

(B) קראה ליחידים לא לפרוש מן הציבור

(C) המריצה את היהודים לחקות את החברה הכללית

(D) נמשכה אחרי היצירות המובחרות של התקופה

(E) שקדה על הבנת טענותיהם של שוללי הגלות

GO ON TO THE NEXT PAGE

Part D

<u>Directions</u>: Each of the sentences below contains a blank space indicating that a word or a phrase has been omitted. Following each sentence are five words or phrases. Select the word or phrase that best completes the sentence <u>logically</u> and <u>structurally</u>, and then blacken the corresponding space on the answer sheet.

Be sure to note that the questions are numbered on the RIGHT side of each column and begin on the RIGHT side of the page.

67. עָלָה עַל . . . לִלְמֹד אֶת הַתַּנַ"ךְ בְּעַל פֶּה.

    (A) רֹאשׁוֹ

    (B) דַּעְתּוֹ

    (C) רַעְיוֹנוֹ

    (D) מֹחוֹ

    (E) שִׂכְלוֹ

68. בְּסוֹפוֹ שֶׁל דָּבָר צָרִיךְ כָּל אֶחָד לָתֵת דִּין . . . עַל מַעֲשָׂיו.

    (A) וְחֶשְׁבּוֹן

    (B) תּוֹרָה

    (C) צֶדֶק

    (D) וּדְבָרִים

    (E) וָאֱמֶת

69. אֵין . . . כִּי תַּצְלִיחַ בְּדַרְכְּךָ.

    (A) שִׁנּוּי

    (B) סָפֵק

    (C) בְּרֵרָה

    (D) גּוֹרֵם

    (E) סִפּוּק

70. שְׁמוּאֵל עָמַד מִן הַצַּד, . . . מִן הַצִּבּוּר וְלֹא הִתְעָרֵב בְּשִׂיחָה.

    (A) לְבַד

    (B) פָּרוּשׁ

    (C) גָּדוּר

    (D) בָּדָד

    (E) חָפְשִׁי

71. הַשּׁוֹפֵט נָהַג בַּנֶּאֱשָׁם לְפָנִים . . . הַדִּין.

    (A) מִתּוֹרַת

    (B) מִפְּנֵי

    (C) מִצֹּרֶךְ

    (D) מֵחֹק

    (E) מִשּׁוּרַת

72. הַתַּלְמִיד . . . שֶׁמָּא לֹא יַצְלִיחַ.

    (A) שָׂמֵחַ

    (B) סוֹמֵךְ

    (C) חוֹשֵׁשׁ

    (D) נִכְשָׁל

    (E) חָכָם

73. בְּנֵי עַקְשָׁן מְאֹד . . . לַעֲשׂוֹת מַה שֶּׁדּוֹרְשִׁים מִמֶּנּוּ.

    (A) וּמַסְכִּים

    (B) וּמְמַהֵר

    (C) וּמְסָרֵב

    (D) וּמַכְחִישׁ

    (E) וּמִשְׁתַּדֵּל

74. צָרִיךְ לְעַיֵּן בַּדָּבָר בְּדֵעָה . . .

    (A) נְבוּכָה

    (B) מִסְעֶרֶת

    (C) נִרְגֶּשֶׁת

    (D) צְלוּלָה

    (E) מְפַקְפֶּקֶת

GO ON TO THE NEXT PAGE →

75. . . . טִפְּסוּ עַל תֹּרֶן הַסְּפִינָה.

   (A) הַסַּפָּנִים

   (B) הַחַבְּלָנִים

   (C) הַנּוֹסְעִים

   (D) הַמְּלָכִים

   (E) הַמַּלְאָכִים

76. עִם בּוֹא הַסְּתָו . . . הֶעָלִים.

   (A) נוֹשְׁרִים

   (B) מַחְוִירִים

   (C) מוֹרִיקִים

   (D) מְרַשְׁרְשִׁים

   (E) נֶעֱלָמִים

77. הַגֶּשֶׁם יָרַד בְּזַעַף, וּבַכְּבִישִׁים נִפְסְקָה . . .

   (A) הַסְּעָרָה

   (B) הַתְּנוּעָה

   (C) הַחֶבְרָה

   (D) הַיְצִיאָה

   (E) הַתְּנוּדָה

78. כְּשֶׁנֶּפְצָה הַשֶּׁמְשָׁה הִזְמַנְתִּי . . .

   (A) מְכוֹנַאי

   (B) שַׁמָּשׁ

   (C) זַגָּג

   (D) נַגָּר

   (E) סַיָּד

79. בָּאוֹטוֹבּוּס עָלֶיךָ לְהִזָּהֵר . . . , בְּיִחוּד כַּאֲשֶׁר מִסְפַּר הַנּוֹסְעִים גָּדוֹל.

   (A) מְשׁוֹדְדִים

   (B) מַתִּירִים

   (C) מְנַהֲגִים

   (D) מְטַרְדָּנִים

   (E) מְכַיְּסִים

80. הוּא . . . פָּנִים כְּאִלּוּ אֵינוּ מַכִּירֵנִי.

   (A) הֶחֱלִיף

   (B) הִבִּיעַ

   (C) הוֹסִיף

   (D) הֶעֱמִיד

   (E) הִתְחַפֵּשׂ

81. הַנֶּאֱשָׁם . . . בְּחֶטְאוֹ.

   (A) הִזְכִּיר

   (B) הוֹדִיעַ

   (C) הִכְרִיז

   (D) כָּחַשׁ

   (E) הוֹדָה

82. הַנָּהָר מָלֵא עַל . . .

   (A) עֲבָרָיו

   (B) חֲלָקָיו

   (C) צְדָדָיו

   (D) שְׂפָתָיו

   (E) גְּדוֹתָיו

GO ON TO THE NEXT PAGE ➤

HEBREW TEST—Continued

87. ‏. . . לוֹ מְאֹד, כִּי הֶעֱלִיבוּ אוֹתוֹ בִּפְנֵי קָהָל רַב.

(A) ‏הִצְטַעֵר
(B) ‏כָּעַס
(C) ‏הִתְנַגֵּד
(D) ‏הִתְבַּיֵּשׁ
(E) ‏חָרָה

83. ‏אֲנִי מַכִּיר לְךָ . . . עַל עֶזְרָתְךָ.

(A) ‏טוֹבָה
(B) ‏בְּרָכָה
(C) ‏חֶסֶד
(D) ‏אֱמֶת
(E) ‏צֹרֶךְ

88. ‏הָעֲרָפֶל הַכָּבֵד עִכֵּב אֶתְמוֹל אֶת . . . שֶׁל הַמְּטוֹסִים.

(A) ‏הֲכָנָתָם
(B) ‏מִפְעָלָם
(C) ‏צֵאתָם
(D) ‏תִּקּוּנָם
(E) ‏מִבְצָעָם

84. ‏הוּא חִכָּה לָהּ שָׁנִים רַבּוֹת וְשָׁמַר לָהּ . . .

(A) ‏תִּקְוָה
(B) ‏אֱמוּנִים
(C) ‏רַחֲמִים
(D) ‏מַתָּנָה
(E) ‏הַבְטָחָה

89. ‏הִיא הִתְבַּיְּשָׁה . . . פָּנֶיהָ בַּקַּרְקַע.

(A) ‏וְכִסְּתָה
(B) ‏וְהוֹרִידָה
(C) ‏וְשָׂמָה
(D) ‏וְהִשְׁפִּילָה
(E) ‏וְכָבְשָׁה

85. ‏הַצּוֹרֵף . . . אֶבֶן יְקָרָה בַּטַּבַּעַת.

(A) ‏שִׁבֵּץ
(B) ‏הִשְׁחִיז
(C) ‏נָעַץ
(D) ‏שִׁפֵּץ
(E) ‏חִבֵּר

90. ‏מִשְׁמַר הַכָּבוֹד שֶׁל צַהַ"ל הָיָה מֻרְכָּב מִפִּרְחֵי . . .

(A) ‏קְצוּנָה
(B) ‏שׁוֹשַׁנִּים
(C) ‏כְּהֻנָּה
(D) ‏הֲדָרִים
(E) ‏בָּר

86. ‏הוּא . . . אוֹתִי עַל טָעוּתִי.

(A) ‏הֶרְאָה
(B) ‏הוֹדִיעַ
(C) ‏הִדְרִיךְ
(D) ‏תִּקֵּן
(E) ‏הֶעֱמִיד

S T O P

IF YOU FINISH BEFORE TIME IS CALLED, YOU MAY CHECK YOUR WORK ON THIS TEST ONLY.
DO NOT WORK ON ANY OTHER TEST IN THIS BOOK.

How to Score the Hebrew Achievement Test

When you take the Hebrew Achievement Test, your answer sheet will be "read" by a scanning machine that will record your responses to each question. Then a computer will compare your answers with the correct answers and produce your raw score. You get one point for each correct answer. For each wrong answer, you lose one-fourth of a point. Questions you omit (and any for which you mark more than one answer) are not counted. This raw score is converted to a College Board scaled score that is reported to you and to the colleges you specify. After you have taken this test, you can get an idea of what your score might be by following the instructions in the next two sections.

Determining Your Raw Score

Step 1: Table A on the next page lists the correct answers for all the questions on the test.* Compare your answer with the correct answer and
- Put a check in the column marked "Right" if your answer is correct.
- Put a check in the column marked "Wrong" if your answer is incorrect.
- Leave both columns blank if you omitted the question.

Step 2: Count the number of right answers and enter the number here . . . . _____

Step 3: Count the number of wrong answers and enter the number here . . . . 4) ‾‾‾‾‾‾‾

Enter the result of dividing by 4 here . . . . _____

Step 4: Subtract the number you obtained in Step 3 from the number in Step 2; round the result to the nearest whole number (.5 is rounded up) and enter here . . _____

The number you obtained in Step 4 is your raw score. (The correction for guessing — subtraction of a quarter of a point for each incorrect answer — adjusts for the fact that random guessing on a large number of questions will result in some questions being answered correctly by chance.) Instructions for converting your raw score to a scaled score follow.

*The last column in Table A gives the percentage of a selected sample of students who took the test in December 1982 that answered the question correctly. (See page 144 for further explanation.)

TABLE A

Answers to Hebrew Achievement Test, Form 3EAC, and Percentage of Students Answering Each Question Correctly

Question Number	Correct Answer	Right	Wrong	Percentage of Students Answering the Question Correctly	Question Number	Correct Answer	Right	Wrong	Percentage of Students Answering the Question Correctly
1	B			94%	46	A			32%
2	C			94	47	D			76
3	A			97	48	C			48
4	B			86	49	C			77
5	C			93	50	E			62
6	D			85	51	E			54
7	D			88	52	C			73
8	A			80	53	B			72
9	A			78	54	C			25
10	B			85	55	A			60
11	B			65	56	B			48
12	C			72	57	D			64
13	D			57	58	C			29
14	A			35	59	C			73
15	B			54	60	A			60
16	A			64	61	E			60
17	A			26	62	D			49
18	D			79	63	E			19
19	E			85	64	E			34
20	B			66	65	C			32
21	A			78	66	C			18
22	C			72	67	B			76
23	E			76	68	A			74
24	D			82	69	B			78
25	C			73	70	B			67
26	D			66	71	E			59
27	A			64	72	C			72
28	B			72	73	C			55
29	D			55	74	D			23
30	E			56	75	A			24
31	D			35	76	A			30
32	A			48	77	B			42
33	C			22	78	C			11
34	B			32	79	E			31
35	B			29	80	D			31
36	C			23	81	E			36
37	A			42	82	E			27
38	D			70	83	A			32
39	B			72	84	B			18
40	E			93	85	A			18
41	B			67	86	E			15
42	C			75	87	E			17
43	D			78	88	C			49
44	E			79	89	E			17
45	B			74	90	A			07

Note: The percentages are based on the analysis of the answer sheets for a random sample of students who took the test in December 1982 and whose mean score was 607.

Finding Your College Board Scaled Score ■■■

When you take Achievement Tests, the scores sent to the colleges you specify will be reported on the College Board scale, ranging from 200 to 800. The raw score that you obtained above (Step 4) can be converted to a scaled score by using Table B.

To find your scaled score on this test, locate your raw score in the left column of Table B; the corresponding score in the right column will be your College Board scaled score. For example, a raw score of 32 on this particular edition of the Hebrew Achievement Test corresponds to a College Board scaled score of 550. Raw scores are converted to scaled scores to ensure that a score earned on any one edition of the Hebrew Achievement Test is comparable to the same scaled score earned on any other edition of the test.

Because some editions of the Hebrew Achievement Test may be slightly easier or more difficult than others, statistical adjustments are made in the scores so that each College Board scaled score indicates the same level of performance, regardless of the edition of the test you take and the ability of the group you take it with. A given raw score will correspond to different College Board scores, depending on the edi-

TABLE B — SCORE CONVERSION TABLE					
Hebrew Achievement Test, Form 3EAC					
Raw Score	College Board Scaled Score	Raw Score	College Board Scaled Score	Raw Score	College Board Scaled Score
90	800	50	650	10	430
89	800	49	640	9	430
88	800	48	630	8	420
87	800	47	630	7	420
86	800	46	620	6	410
85	800	45	620	5	410
84	800	44	610	4	400
83	800	43	610	3	400
82	800	42	600	2	390
81	800	41	600	1	390
80	800	40	590	0	380
79	800	39	590	−1	380
78	790	38	580	−2	370
77	790	37	580	−3	370
76	780	36	570	−4	360
75	780	35	570	−5	350
74	770	34	560	−6	350
73	770	33	560	−7	340
72	760	32	550	−8	340
71	760	31	540	−9	330
70	750	30	540	−10	330
69	750	29	530	−11	320
68	740	28	530	−12	320
67	730	27	520	−13	310
66	730	26	520	−14	310
65	720	25	510	−15	300
64	720	24	510	−16	300
63	710	23	500	−17	290
62	710	22	500	−18	290
61	700	21	490	−19	280
60	700	20	490	−20	280
59	690	19	480	−21	270
58	690	18	480	−22	260
57	680	17	470		
56	680	16	470		
55	670	15	460		
54	670	14	450		
53	660	13	450		
52	660	12	440		
51	650	11	440		

tion of the test taken. A raw score of 40, for example, may convert to a College Board score of 590 on one edition of the test, but that raw score might convert to a College Board score of 610 on a slightly more difficult edition. When you take the Hebrew Achievement Test on the actual test day, your score is likely to differ somewhat from the score you obtained on this test. People perform at different levels at different times, for reasons unrelated to the test itself. The precision of any test is also limited because it represents only a sample of all the possible questions that could be asked. (See page 12, "How Precise Are Your Scores?" for further information.)

Reviewing Your Test Performance

After you have scored your test, you should take some time to consider the following points in relation to your performance on the test.

- *Did you run out of time before you reached the end of the test?*

  If you did, you may want to consider tactics that will help you pace yourself better. For example, you may have spent too much time working on one or two difficult questions. A better approach might have been to continue the test and return to those questions after you had attempted to answer the remaining questions on the test.

- *Did you take a long time reading the directions for the test?*

  The directions in this test are the same as those in the Hebrew Achievement Tests now being administered. You will save time when you read the directions on the test day if you become thoroughly familiar with them in advance.

- *How did you handle questions you were unsure of?*

  If you were able to eliminate one or more of the answer choices and you guessed from the remaining choices, then your approach probably worked to your advantage. On the other hand, omitting questions about which you have some knowledge or guessing answers haphazardly would probably be a mistake.

- *How difficult were the questions for you compared with other students who took the test?*

  By referring to Table A on page 142 you can find out how difficult each question was for a selected sample of the students who took the test in December 1982. The right-hand column in the table tells you what percentage of that group of students answered the question correctly. It is important to remember that these percentages are based on only one group of students; had this edition of the test been given to all students in the class of 1983 who took a Hebrew Achievement Test, the percentages would probably have been different. A question that was answered correctly by almost everyone in the group, obviously, is an easy question. Question 3, for example, was answered correctly by 97 percent of the students in the sample. On the other hand, question 90 was answered correctly by only 7 percent of the students. If you find that you missed several questions that would be considered easy, you may want to review those questions carefully. They may cover some aspect of the subject that you need to review. Perhaps you misunderstood the directions for one part of the test or you thought the questions were so easy that you did not spend as much time on them as you might have.

About the Latin Achievement Test

The Latin Achievement Test is written to reflect general trends in high school curriculums and is independent of particular textbooks or methods of instruction. Most students taking the Latin Achievement Test have studied two to four years of Latin in high school (the equivalent of two to four semesters in college). The best preparation for the test is the gradual development of competence in sight-reading Latin over a period of years, but you may also prepare for the Latin Achievement Test as you would for any comprehensive examination that requires knowledge of facts and concepts and the ability to apply them. Reading the explanations and descriptions in this book should give you an indication of what to expect.

Since the Latin Achievement Test is intended to measure the Latin reading and grammatical skills of secondary school students between the second and fourth year of language study, the difficulty level of the questions varies. Some questions are directed toward students who have had only two years of Latin study and some to students who have had three or four years. The questions range from very easy ones that can be answered correctly by almost all of the students to difficult ones that only 15 percent to 20 percent can answer.

Colleges that require their applicants to take the Latin Achievement Test may use the scores for course placement. Because scores are not adjusted on the basis of years of study, colleges should consider the preparation of students when evaluating their scores.

Content of the Test

The Latin Achievement Test measures knowledge and ability in the following areas of reading skill: grammar and syntax, derivatives, and translation and reading comprehension. These skills are tested in certain percentages (see below) by six different types of questions.

Skills Measured	Approxmate Percentage of Test
Grammar and Syntax	30
Derivatives	5
Translation and Reading Comprehension	65

70-75 Questions; Time — 60 minutes

Questions Used in the Test

Forms

This type of question asks you to select a specific grammatical form of a Latin word. Any form of a noun, pronoun, adjective, adverb, or verb can be asked for.

Directions: In the statement below, you are asked to give a specific form of the underlined word. Select the correct form from the choices given. Then blacken the corresponding space on the answer sheet.

1. The present subjunctive passive of capitis is

   (A) capiāminī

   (B) capiēminī

   (C) caperēminī

   (D) capiminī

In this question, you are given the present indicative active of the verb *capere* in the second person plural. The correct answer is (A). (B) is the future indicative passive; (C) the imperfect subjunctive passive; and (D) the present indicative passive.

Derivatives

In this type of question, you are given an English sentence with one word underlined. You must choose the Latin word from which the underlined English word is derived.

Directions: The English sentence below contains a word that is underlined. Select from among the choices the Latin word to which the underlined word is related. Then blacken the corresponding space on the answer sheet.

2. The event ruptured the relationship.

   (A) reperiō

   (B) rapiō

   (C) reficiō

   (D) rumpō

The English word *ruptured* is derived from Latin *ruptus*, the past participle of *rumpō*. So, (D) is the correct answer. Note that you will need to know the various forms of different Latin words to answer questions.

Translation

You must choose the correct translation of the underlined Latin word or words. This type of question is more complex than the previous types, as it is based on the syntax of a complete Latin sentence.

Directions: In this part, part or all of the sentence is underlined. Select from among the choices the best translation for the underlined words. Then blacken the corresponding space on the answer sheet.

3. <u>Amīcitia est cārior mihi quam pecūnia.</u>

   (A) Friendship and money are as dear as possible to me.

   (B) Friendship is dearer to me than money.

   (C) Friendship which is dearer than money is mine.

   (D) Friendship which brings money is dearer to me.

In order to answer this question correctly, you must note that the word *cārior* is followed by *quam*. The word *cārior* is the comparative form of *cārus* and the comparative followed by *quam* is translated "more than." Thus, choices (A) and (D) are incorrect. (C) is incorrect because (among other reasons) *quam* cannot be the nominative relative pronoun and *pecūnia* is not the ablative case. The correct answer is (B).

Sentence Completion

This type of question contains a Latin sentence in which a word or phrase has been omitted. You must select the Latin word or phrase that best fits grammatically into the sentence.

Directions: The sentence below contains a blank space indicating that a word or phrase has been omitted. Following the sentence are four words or phrases. Select the word or phrase that best completes the sentence and blacken the corresponding space on the answer sheet.

4. Servus . . . vulnerātur.

   (A) ā saxō

   (B) saxum

   (C) cum saxō

   (D) saxō

In order to answer this question correctly, you must be able to translate the two words *servus vulnerātur* ("the slave is wounded") and then select

the only choice that can be added to these two words to make a complete, grammatical Latin sentence. Here the correct answer is (D) *saxō*, which expresses the means or instrument by which the slave is wounded.

Substitution

This type of question contains a complete Latin sentence, part of which is underlined. You are asked to select the substitution that is closest in meaning to the underlined words.

Directions: In the sentence below, part of the sentence is underlined. Select from the choices the expression that, when substituted for the underlined portion of the sentence changes the meaning of the sentence LEAST. Then blacken the corresponding space on the answer sheet.

5. <u>Quod parentēs occīsī sunt,</u> omnēs cīvēs miserē flēbant.

   (A) <u>Parentēs occīdentēs</u>

   (B) <u>Dum parentēs occīduntur</u>

   (C) <u>Parentibus occīsīs</u>

   (D) <u>Parentium occīdendōrum causā</u>

In this example, the underlined clause is translated: "Because the parents were killed." You must select the answer choice whose translation is closest in meaning to this underlined clause. The correct answer is (C), the ablative absolute. None of the other choices is an appropriate substitution.

Reading Comprehension

This type of question presents you with a series of short passages of prose or poetry followed by several questions. These questions test either grammatical points (8, 9, and 10 below), translation of a phrase or clause (6) or of a word (11), grammatical reference (7), or summary/comprehension (12). In addition, poetry passages always have one question on the scansion of the first four feet of a line of dactylic hexameter verse. Note that uncommon words that appear in the passages are defined and that the passages are adapted from Latin authors. There are approximately four or five passages with a total of 32 to 37 questions on the test. At least one (and no more than two) poetry passage appears on the test.

Directions: Read the following selection carefully for comprehension. The selection is followed by a number of related questions and incomplete statements. Select the best answer or completion. Then blacken the corresponding space on the answer sheet.

Urbe captā, dux Rōmānus cīvibus victīs
spem pācis amīcitiamque suam dābat.
Dīxit sē urbem eōrum restitūtūrum
esse.[1] Quod vīdit cīvēs lībertātem
(5) magis quam pācem cupere, aedificiīs
urbis incēnsīs, exercitum ex urbe redūxit.
Cīvēs īrātissimī eum secūtī sunt
ut proelium committerent.

[1]restituō, restituere, restituī, restitūtus: to rebuild

6. The words Urbe captā (line 1) are translated

(A) When the city had been taken
(B) In order to take the city
(C) While the city was being taken
(D) So that the city would be taken

The words Urbe captā make up an ablative absolute. Since captā is the perfect participle and the main verb dābat is in a past (imperfect) tense, the ablative absolute should be translated by the pluperfect (past perfect) tense: "When the city had been taken." The correct answer is (A).

7. sē (line 3) refers to

(A) Urbe (line 1)
(B) dux (line 1)
(C) cīvibus (line 1)
(D) amīcitiam (line 2)

The reflexive pronoun sē (used here in an indirect statement) refers to the subject of the main verb Dīxit (line 3). The understood subject of Dīxit is dux. The correct answer is (B).

8. restitūtūrum (line 3) agrees in case and number with

(A) spem (line 2)
(B) sē (line 3)
(C) urbem (line 3)
(D) eōrum (line 3)

The word restitūtūrum modifies the subject of the indirect statement, namely, sē. The correct answer is (B). Note that none of the other options is nominative, singular, and masculine.

9. lībertātem (line 4) is the direct object of

(A) vīdit (line 4)
(B) cupere (line 5)
(C) incēnsīs (line 6)
(D) redūxit (line 6)

The word lībertātem appears in the indirect statement following the verb vīdit (line 4): "Because he saw that the citizens desired liberty more than peace . . ." Therefore, lībertātem is the direct object of cupere. The correct answer is (B).

10. secūtī sunt (line 7) is a form of the verb

(A) secō
(B) sēcēdō
(C) sequor
(D) sector

The verb secūtī sunt is the perfect tense of the deponent verb sequor, sequī: to follow. The correct answer is (C).

11. ut proelium committerent (line 7) is translated

(A) to begin battle
(B) to finish the battle
(C) to win the battle
(D) to prolong the battle

The words ut proelium committerent make up a purpose clause. The verb committere when used with words for battle (proelium, certāmen, bellum, etc.) means to engage in battle. The correct answer, therefore, is (A).

12. Which of the following is true about the Roman leader described in the passage above?

(A) He established peace.
(B) He followed the enemy.
(C) He burned buildings.
(D) He restored the city.

In lines 5-6, the words aedificiīs urbis incēnsīs show that the Roman leader had burned the buildings before he led his army out of the city. The correct answer is (C).

Latin Achievement Test

The test that follows is an edition of the Latin Achievement Test administered in December 1982. So that you will have an idea of what the actual test administration will be like, try to take this test under conditions as close as possible to those of the actual test. It will probably help if you

- Set aside an hour for the test when you will not be interrupted, so that you can complete all of it in one sitting.

- Sit at a desk with no other papers or books. You can't take a calculator, a dictionary, other books, or notes into the test room.

- Have a kitchen timer or clock in front of you for timing yourself.

- Tear out an answer sheet from the back of this book and fill it in just as you would on the day of the test. You can use one answer sheet for as many as three Achievement Tests.

- Read the instructions that precede the test. When you take the test, you will be asked to read them before you begin answering questions.

- After you finish the test, read the sections on "How to Score the Latin Achievement Test," and "Reviewing Your Test Performance," which follow the test.

LATIN TEST

The top portion of the section of the answer sheet which you will use in taking the Latin test must be filled in exactly as shown in the illustration below. Note carefully that you have to do all of the following on your answer sheet:

1. Print LATIN on the line to the right of the words "Achievement Test."

2. Blacken spaces 4 and 7 in the row of spaces immediately under the words "Test Code."

3. Blacken space 2 in the group of five spaces labeled X.

4. Blacken space 3 in the group of five spaces labeled Y.

In the group of nine spaces labeled Q, you are to blacken ONE and ONLY ONE space, as described below, to indicate how you obtained your knowledge of Latin. The information that you provide is for statistical purposes only and will not influence your score on the test.

If your knowledge of Latin does not come primarily from courses taken in grades 9 through 12, blacken space 9 and leave the remaining spaces blank, regardless of how long you studied the subject in school. For example, you are to blacken space 9 if your knowledge of Latin comes primarily from any of the following sources: study prior to the ninth grade, courses taken at a college, or special study.

If your knowledge of Latin does come primarily from courses taken in grades 9 through 12, blacken the space that indicates the level of the Latin course in which you are currently enrolled. If you are not now enrolled in a Latin course, blacken the space that indicates the level of the most advanced course in Latin that you have completed.

Level I:	first or second half	–	blacken space 1
Level II:	first half	–	blacken space 2
	second half	–	blacken space 3
Level III:	first half	–	blacken space 4
	second half	–	blacken space 5
Level IV:	first half	–	blacken space 6
	second half	–	blacken space 7

Advanced Placement or course that represents a level of study higher than Level IV: second half – blacken space 8

If you are in doubt about whether to mark space 9 rather than one of the spaces 1-8, mark space 9.

When the supervisor gives the signal, turn the page and begin the Latin test. There are 100 numbered spaces on the answer sheet and 73 questions in the Latin test. Therefore, use only spaces 1 to 73 for recording your answers.

LATIN TEST

PLEASE NOTE THAT YOUR ANSWER SHEET HAS FIVE ANSWER POSITIONS MARKED A, B, C, D, E, WHILE THE QUESTIONS THROUGHOUT THIS TEST CONTAIN ONLY FOUR CHOICES. BE SURE <u>NOT</u> TO MAKE ANY MARKS IN COLUMN E.

<u>Note:</u> In some questions in this test variations of Latin terms will appear in parentheses.

Part A

<u>Directions:</u> In each statement below, you are asked to give a specific form of the underlined word. Select the correct form from the choices given. Then blacken the corresponding space on the answer sheet.

1. The dative singular of <u>diēs</u> is
   (A) <u>diem</u>
   (B) <u>diēs</u>
   (C) <u>diēbus</u>
   (D) <u>diēī</u>

2. The perfect indicative active of <u>iubet</u> (<u>jubet</u>) is
   (A) <u>iusserat</u> (<u>jusserat</u>)
   (B) <u>iussit</u> (<u>jussit</u>)
   (C) <u>iussus est</u> (<u>jussus est</u>)
   (D) <u>iusserit</u> (<u>jusserit</u>)

3. The nominative plural neuter of <u>brevis</u> is
   (A) <u>brevēs</u>
   (B) <u>brevia</u>
   (C) <u>brevī</u>
   (D) <u>brevium</u>

4. The imperfect indicative of <u>sum</u> is
   (A) <u>eram</u>
   (B) <u>fuī</u>
   (C) <u>fueram</u>
   (D) <u>erō</u>

5. The perfect passive infinitive of <u>audiō</u> is
   (A) <u>audīre</u>
   (B) <u>audīrī</u>
   (C) <u>audīvisse</u>
   (D) <u>audītum esse</u>

6. The ablative singular of <u>id</u> is
   (A) <u>eī</u>
   (B) <u>eae</u>
   (C) <u>eō</u>
   (D) <u>eīs</u>

7. The future indicative passive of <u>video</u> is
   (A) <u>vidēbor</u>
   (B) <u>vidēbar</u>
   (C) <u>videor</u>
   (D) <u>videar</u>

8. The genitive singular of <u>alter</u> is
   (A) <u>alterī</u>
   (B) <u>alterae</u>
   (C) <u>alterīus</u>
   (D) <u>alterīs</u>

GO ON TO THE NEXT PAGE →

Part B

Directions: Each of the following English sentences contains a word that is underlined. Select from among the choices the Latin word to which the underlined word is related. Then blacken the corresponding space on the answer sheet.

9. He served as president for several <u>consecutive</u> terms.

    (A) <u>sequor</u>

    (B) <u>secō</u>

    (C) <u>sēcernō</u>

    (D) <u>sēcēdō</u>

10. <u>Access</u> to the highway is limited.

    (A) <u>cēdō</u>

    (B) <u>cadō</u>

    (C) <u>cēnō</u>

    (D) <u>cēnseō</u>

11. She does not know how to <u>react</u> to that.

    (A) <u>ācer</u>

    (B) <u>recēns</u>

    (C) <u>agō</u>

    (D) <u>regō</u>

12. I do not expect much <u>opposition</u>.

    (A) <u>pōnō</u>

    (B) <u>possum</u>

    (C) <u>post</u>

    (D) <u>possideō</u>

GO ON TO THE NEXT PAGE

LATIN TEST—*Continued*

Part C

Directions: In each of the sentences below, part or all of the sentence is underlined. Select from among the choices the best translation for the underlined word or words. Then blacken the corresponding space on the answer sheet.

13. Sī librōs mittās, eōs legāmus.

    (A) If you had sent the books
    (B) If you will send the books
    (C) If you would have sent the books
    (D) If you should send the books

14. Flūmen quod videō est lātum.

    (A) because
    (B) who
    (C) which
    (D) the fact that

15. Cōnēmur Rōmānōs coniungere (conjungere).

    (A) Let us try to unite the Romans.
    (B) We shall try to unite the Romans.
    (C) The Romans will attempt to unite.
    (D) The Romans tried to unite.

16. Difficile est scrībere multōs librōs.

    (A) He is writing many difficult books.
    (B) It is said that he is writing many difficult books.
    (C) Many books are written with difficulty.
    (D) Writing many books is difficult.

17. Vir amīcōs hortātus est nē audīrent.

    (A) urged that they listen to his friends
    (B) urged his friends not to listen
    (C) was urged by his friends not to listen
    (D) was urged to listen to his friends

18. Multa nōbīs facienda sunt.

    (A) We are doing many things.
    (B) Many things were done by us.
    (C) Many things must be done by us.
    (D) They did many things for us.

19. Tanta fēcit ut urbem servāret.

    (A) She did such great things as saving the city.
    (B) She did it so that the city could save great things.
    (C) She did great things as she saved the city.
    (D) She did such great things that she saved the city.

20. Celeriter Rōmam properāvit.

    (A) from Rome
    (B) near Rome
    (C) to Rome
    (D) at Rome

21. Dīxit Rōmam captam esse.

    (A) is being captured
    (B) would be captured
    (C) will be captured
    (D) had been captured

22. Ignāvus contemnit labōrantem.

    (A) The lazy person despises working.
    (B) The lazy person despises the working person.
    (C) The lazy worker despises himself.
    (D) The lazy person despises the person who has worked.

23. Vōbīs salūtī erō.

    (A) I shall be a source of safety for you.
    (B) I shall seek safety for you.
    (C) I shall be saved by you.
    (D) I shall not be safe for you.

24. Mihi aegra esse vīsa est.

    (A) she is seen
    (B) she was visible
    (C) she is caught sight of
    (D) she seemed

25. Ponte faciendō exercitum flūmen altissimum trādūcet.

    (A) The bridge having been built
    (B) After the bridge had been built
    (C) By building a bridge
    (D) The bridge being built

26. Timēbant nē quem vidērent.

    (A) that they would not see it
    (B) that they would not see him
    (C) that they would not see anybody
    (D) that they would see somebody

GO ON TO THE NEXT PAGE

Part D

Directions: Each of the sentences below contains a blank space indicating that a word or phrase has been omitted. Following each sentence are four words or phrases. Select the word or phrase that best completes the sentence. Then blacken the corresponding space on the answer sheet.

27. Lēgātōs cum equitātū in Menapiīs . . . Caesar.

    (A) ā duce

    (B) nōbīs

    (C) relīquit

    (D) dum

28. Equōs . . . puerōs in campō vidēbant.

    (A) māgnōs

    (B) et

    (C) patris

    (D) vir

29. Eōs ōrāvī . . . mē līberārent.

    (A) quīn
    (B) quō
    (C) utrum
    (D) ut

30. . . . vir occīsus est?

    (A) Quī annus

    (B) Cui annō

    (C) Quō annō

    (D) Quem annum

31. Puer . . . pater in Galliam mittētur meus amīcus est.

    (A) cuius (cujus)

    (B) et

    (C) quem

    (D) parvum

32. Multōs hominēs fortūnam . . . dīcitur.

    (A) timendōs esse

    (B) timērī

    (C) timēre

    (D) timentem

33. Cūr haec . . . nōn intellegēbam.

    (A) faciet

    (B) faciēbat

    (C) fēcisset

    (D) fēcerat

34. Cīvēs ducem . . . urbs dēfēnsa erat laudāvērunt.

    (A) quī

    (B) ā quō

    (C) ad quem

    (D) quem

GO ON TO THE NEXT PAGE

LATIN TEST—*Continued*

Part E

Directions: In each of the sentences below, part or all of the sentence is underlined. Select from the choices the expression that, when substituted for the underlined portion of the sentence, changes the meaning of the sentence LEAST. Then blacken the corresponding space on the answer sheet.

35. Timet virōs quī multa dīcunt.

    (A) multīs dictīs

    (B) multa dīcentēs

    (C) multīs dīcentibus

    (D) multa dīcentia

36. Caesare duce, Rōmānī nihil timuērunt.

    (A) Ut Caesar dux esset

    (B) Quod Caesar dux erat

    (C) Sī Caesar dux sit

    (D) Caesar dux

37. Quī ōrātōrēs meliōrēs erant Rōmānīs veteribus?

    (A) quam Rōmānīs veteribus

    (B) Rōmānī veterēs

    (C) Rōmānōs veterēs

    (D) quam Rōmānī veterēs

38. Sī fīlia tibi est, eam vocā.

    (A) Sī fīliam habēs

    (B) Sī mea fīlia est

    (C) Sī fīlia tē habet

    (D) Sī fīlia tēcum est

GO ON TO THE NEXT PAGE

LATIN TEST—*Continued*

Part F

Directions: Read each of the following selections carefully for comprehension. Each selection is followed by a number of related questions and incomplete statements. Select the best answer or completion. Then blacken the corresponding space on the answer sheet.

Cato was versatile and learned.

In omnibus rēbus Catō fuit vir māximae industriae. Nam et agricola bonus fuit et māgnus imperātor. Studiō litterārum[1] sē dedit cum senex esset. Tantum sciēbat ut nihil invenīrī posset
(5) quod eī novum esset. Ab adulēscentiā fēcit ōrātiōnēs et posteā historiās[2] scrībere coepit quārum sunt librī septem.

[1] litterae, litterārum, f.: literature
[2] historia, historiae, f.: history, book on history

39. industriae (line 2) is

   (A) dative singular
   (B) genitive singular
   (C) accusative plural
   (D) nominative plural

40. The case of Studiō (line 3) is

   (A) dative
   (B) nominative
   (C) genitive
   (D) ablative

41. What does dedit (line 3) mean?

   (A) he relaxed
   (B) he granted
   (C) he devoted
   (D) he conceded

42. How is esset (line 4) translated?

   (A) he was
   (B) he had been
   (C) he would be
   (D) he has been

43. The sentence Studiō . . . esset (lines 3-4) tells us that Cato

   (A) was too old to study literature
   (B) urged an old man to study literature
   (C) studied literature that was old
   (D) studied literature when he was old

44. ut (line 4) means

   (A) as
   (B) that
   (C) to
   (D) in order that

45. The sentence Tantum . . . esset (lines 4-5) tells us that

   (A) Cato did not try to learn everything
   (B) Cato was able to find out what he did not know
   (C) it was impossible for Cato to learn everything
   (D) there was nothing that Cato did not know

46. The words Ab adulēscentiā fēcit ōrātiōnēs (lines 5-6) tell us that Cato

   (A) was addressed by a young man
   (B) learned about public speaking from his youthful contemporaries
   (C) gave young men advice on public speaking
   (D) began public speaking while still a young man

GO ON TO THE NEXT PAGE ➤

The state, war, and peace

Dīcendum est hōc locō, quid sit cīvitās.
Cīvitās autem est hominum multitūdō ad rēctē
vīvendum collēcta. Cum erit cīvitās cōnstitūta,
necesse est ut prīmō bella patiātur, posteā
(5) pācem agat. Pāx enim esse nōn potest, nisi
causa praecēdat, id est bellum. Hoc et multī
dīxērunt, cum dē rēbus Rōmānīs loquerentur:
prius bella gesta esse, posteā pācem esse fundātam.

47. Dīcendum est (line 1) is translated

   (A) it is a discussion
   (B) it ought to be discussed
   (C) it has been discussed
   (D) it is discussed

48. hōc locō (line 1) is translated

   (A) because of this place
   (B) from this place
   (C) at this point
   (D) to this point

49. collēcta (line 3) modifies

   (A) hominum (line 2)

   (B) multitūdō (line 2)

   (C) rēctē (line 2)

   (D) pāx (understood)

50. The first two sentences tell us that a state is
    founded to enable its citizens to

   (A) live properly
   (B) establish peace
   (C) wage wars
   (D) protect themselves

51. The words ut . . . bella patiātur (line 4) are
    translated

   (A) so that wars may be endured
   (B) that he endure wars
   (C) so that they may endure wars
   (D) that it endure wars

52. nisi (line 5) is translated

   (A) unless
   (B) if
   (C) and not
   (D) nonetheless

53. Hoc (line 6) is

   (A) nominative singular
   (B) accusative singular
   (C) ablative singular
   (D) accusative plural

54. posteā (line 8) is translated

   (A) after
   (B) afterward
   (C) behind
   (D) since

55. The passage tells us, among other things, that

   (A) war must occur before peace is possible
   (B) many people disagree with the author
   (C) a state exists for the sake of war
   (D) peace is better than war

GO ON TO THE NEXT PAGE

Two Roman generals, Sempronius and Fulvius,
are compared.

Cum servōrum exercitus Semprōniō datus esset,
hic exercitus praesidium sociīs et hostibus terror
fīēbat. Fulvius exercituī cīvium Rōmānōrum
servīlia[1] vitia[2] imposuit. Effēcit ut ferōcēs inter
5) sociōs, ignāvī inter hostēs essent. Nec impetum
hostium nec clāmōrem sustinēre potuērunt.

[1]servīlis, -e: of a slave, slavish

[2]vitium, -ī, n.: weakness, fault

56. The case of Sempronio (line 1) is

(A) nominative
(B) genitive
(C) dative
(D) ablative

57. The tense and voice of datus esset (line 1) is

(A) imperfect active
(B) perfect active
(C) present passive
(D) pluperfect (past perfect) passive

58. What does the first sentence tell us about
Sempronius?

(A) He was successful both with the allies and
against the enemy.
(B) He was effective because of the enemy's
terror.
(C) He controlled his troops with the help of
comrades.
(D) He provided training to allies out of fear of
the enemy.

59. What is the case and number of exercituī (line 3) ?

(A) Genitive singular
(B) Dative singular
(C) Ablative singular
(D) Nominative plural

60. What is the case and number of ferōcēs (line 4) ?

(A) Nominative singular
(B) Genitive singular
(C) Nominative plural
(D) Vocative plural

61. The understood subject of potuērunt (line 6) is

(A) Sempronius and Fulvius
(B) the Roman citizens
(C) the allies
(D) the enemy

62. What does the passage tell us about Sempronius
and Fulvius as generals?

(A) Sempronius was a better general.
(B) Fulvius was a better general.
(C) They were both equally good.
(D) They were both equally bad.

GO ON TO THE NEXT PAGE

LATIN TEST—*Continued*

Ajax criticizes Ulysses.

Ājāx inquit dux "Mēcum cōnfertur[1] Ulixēs.
Tūtius est[2] illī fictīs contendere verbīs
quam pugnāre manū. Nōn est mihi dīcere prōmptum,[3]
nec facere est istī; quantumque ego Marte ferōcī
(5) inque aciē valeō, tantum valet iste loquendō.
Nec memoranda tamen vōbīs mea facta, Pelasgī,[4]
esse reor; vīdistis enim. Sua narret Ulixēs,
quae sine teste gerit, quōrum nox cōnscia sōla est!"

[1]cōnferō, cōnferre, contulī, collātus: to compare

[2]Tūtius est: it is safer

[3]prōmptus, -a, -um: easy

[4]Pelasgī: Greeks

63. Which of the following is closest in meaning to inquit (line 1) ?

(A) āit
(B) clāmat
(C) putat
(D) imperat

64. The case and number of illī (line 2) is

(A) genitive singular
(B) dative singular
(C) ablative singular
(D) nominative plural

65. The words fictīs . . . verbīs (line 2) are translated

(A) because of lies
(B) for lies
(C) from lies
(D) by means of lies

66. quam (line 3) means

(A) whom
(B) than
(C) as
(D) what

67. How many elisions occur in line 4 ?

(A) 1
(B) 2
(C) 3
(D) 4

68. iste (line 5) refers to

(A) Marte (line 4)
(B) aciē (line 5)
(C) Ulixēs (understood)
(D) manus (understood)

69. loquendō (line 5) is translated

(A) in speaking
(B) speaking
(C) having spoken
(D) I speak

70. The words memoranda . . . esse (lines 6-7) are translated

(A) to be recounted
(B) to have been recounted
(C) have been recounted
(D) have to be recounted

71. narret Ulixēs (line 7) is translated

(A) Ulysses will recount
(B) let Ulysses recount
(C) Ulysses is recounting
(D) Ulysses recounted

72. The passage tells us that, in Ajax's view, Ulysses is most skilled at

(A) fighting
(B) doing great deeds
(C) speaking
(D) remembering the past

73. In this passage Ajax takes pride in his

(A) accomplishments in war
(B) ability to speak
(C) fellow Greeks
(D) father Mars

160

S T O P
IF YOU FINISH BEFORE TIME IS CALLED, YOU MAY CHECK YOUR WORK ON THIS TEST ONLY.
DO NOT WORK ON ANY OTHER TEST IN THIS BOOK.

How to Score the Latin Achievement Test

When you take the Latin Achievement Test, your answer sheet will be "read" by a scanning machine that will record your responses to each question. Then a computer will compare your answers with the correct answers and produce your raw score. You get one point for each correct answer. For each wrong answer, you lose one-third of a point. Questions you omit (and any for which you mark more than one answer) are not counted. This raw score is converted to a College Board scaled score that is reported to you and to the colleges you specify. After you have taken this test, you can get an idea of what your score might be by following the instructions in the next two sections.

Determining Your Raw Score

Step 1: Table A on the next page lists the correct answers for all the questions on the test.* Compare your answer with the correct answer and
- Put a check in the column marked "Right" if your answer is correct.
- Put a check in the column marked "Wrong" if your answer is incorrect.
- Leave both columns blank if you omitted the question.

Step 2: Count the number of right answers and enter the number here . . . . _____

Step 3: Count the number of wrong answers and enter the number here . . . . 3)‾‾‾‾‾‾‾‾‾‾

Enter the result of dividing by 3 here . . . . _____

Step 4: Subtract the number you obtained in Step 3 from the number in Step 2; round the result to the nearest whole number and enter here . . . . _____

The number you obtained in Step 4 is your raw score. (The correction for guessing — subtraction of a third of a point for each incorrect answer — adjusts for the fact that random guessing on a large number of questions will result in some questions being answered correctly by chance.) Instructions for converting your raw score to a scaled score follow.

*The last column in Table A gives the percentage of a selected sample of the students who took the test in December 1982 that answered the question correctly. (See page 164 for further explanation.)

TABLE A

Answers to Latin Achievement Test, Form K-3DAC1, and Percentage of Students Answering Each Question Correctly

Question Number	Correct Answer	Right	Wrong	Percentage of Students Answering the Question Correctly	Question Number	Correct Answer	Right	Wrong	Percentage of Students Answering the Question Correctly
1	D			89%	41	C			68%
2	B			82	42	A			68
3	B			72	43	D			79
4	A			84	44	B			73
5	D			57	45	D			63
6	C			83	46	D			68
7	A			65	47	B			47
8	C			25	48	C			63
9	A			70	49	B			26
10	A			70	50	A			50
11	C			62	51	D			50
12	A			51	52	A			68
13	D			41	53	B			33
14	C			82	54	B			79
15	A			53	55	A			76
16	D			83	56	C			64
17	B			67	57	D			80
18	C			54	58	A			46
19	D			71	59	B			59
20	C			78	60	C			74
21	D			56	61	B			16
22	B			28	62	A			43
23	A			37	63	A			35
24	D			58	64	B			44
25	C			37	65	D			70
26	D			28	66	B			79
27	C			81	67	B			43
28	B			91	68	C			42
29	D			67	69	A			50
30	C			58	70	D			25
31	A			56	71	B			52
32	C			52	72	C			44
33	C			28	73	A			38
34	B			33					
35	B			38					
36	B			64					
37	D			38					
38	A			44					
39	B			80					
40	A			50					

Note: The percentages are based on the analysis of the answer sheets for a sample of students who took this test in December 1982 and whose mean score was 537. The analysis sample was selected to represent students for whom the test is intended. Students whose knowledge of the language does not come almost entirely from high school courses were excluded and only those students who had at least three semesters of language study were included.

Finding Your College Board Scaled Score ■

When you take Achievement Tests, the scores sent to the colleges you specify will be reported on the College Board scale, ranging from 200 to 800. The raw score that you obtained above (Step 4) can be converted to a scaled score by using Table B.

To find your scaled score on this test, locate your raw score in the left column of Table B; the corresponding score in the right column will be your College Board scaled score. For example, a raw score of 40 on this particular edition of the Latin Achievement Test corresponds to a College Board scaled score of 570. Raw scores are converted to scaled scores to ensure that a score earned on any one edition of the Latin Achievement Test is comparable to the same scaled score earned on any other edition of the test.

Because some editions of the Latin Achievement Test may be slightly easier or more difficult than others, statistical adjustments are made in the scores so that each College Board scaled score indicates the same level of performance, regardless of the edition of the test you take and the ability of the group you take it with. A given raw score will correspond to different College Board scores, depending on the edition of the test taken. A raw score of 40, for example, may convert to a College Board score of 570 on one edition of the test, but that raw score might convert to a College Board score of 590 on a slightly more difficult edition. When you take the Latin Achievement Test on the actual test day, your score is likely to differ somewhat from the score you obtained on this test. People perform at different levels at different

TABLE B — SCORE CONVERSION TABLE
Latin Achievement Test, Form K-3DAC1

Raw Score	College Board Scaled Score	Raw Score	College Board Scaled Score	Raw Score	College Board Scaled Score
73	800	38	560	3	380
72	800	37	550	2	380
71	800	36	540	1	370
70	790	35	540	0	370
69	780	34	530	−1	370
68	770	33	530	−2	360
67	760	32	520	−3	360
66	750	31	510	−4	350
65	740	30	510	−5	350
64	730	29	500	−6	350
63	720	28	500	−7	340
62	720	27	490	−8	340
61	710	26	490	−9	330
60	710	25	480	−10	330
59	700	24	480	−11	320
58	690	23	470	−12	320
57	690	22	470	−13	320
56	680	21	460	−14	310
55	670	20	460	−15	310
54	670	19	450	−16	300
53	660	18	450	−17	300
52	650	17	440	−18	300
51	640	16	440	−19	290
50	640	15	430	−20	290
49	630	14	430	−21	280
48	620	13	420	−22	280
47	620	12	420	−23	280
46	610	11	410	−24	270
45	600	10	410		
44	600	9	410		
43	590	8	400		
42	580	7	400		
41	580	6	390		
40	570	5	390		
39	560	4	390		

times, for reasons unrelated to the test itself. The precision of any test is also limited because it represents only a sample of all the possible questions that could be asked. (See page 12, "How Precise Are Your Scores?" for further information.)

Reviewing Your Test Performance

After you have scored your test, you should take some time to consider the following points in relation to your performance on the test.

- *Did you run out of time before you reached the end of the test?*

  If you did, you may want to consider tactics that will help you pace yourself better. For example, you may have spent too much time working on one or two difficult questions. A better approach might have been to continue the test and return to those questions after you had attempted to answer the remaining questions on the test.

- *Did you take a long time reading the directions for the test?*

  The directions in this test are the same as those in the Latin Achievement Tests now being administered. You will save time when you read the directions on the test day if you become thoroughly familiar with them in advance.

- *How did you handle questions you were unsure of?*

  If you were able to eliminate one or more of the answer choices and you guessed from the remaining choices, then your approach probably worked to your advantage. On the other hand, omitting questions about which you have some knowledge or guessing answers haphazardly would probably be a mistake.

- *How difficult were the questions for you compared with other students who took the test?*

  By referring to Table A on page 162 you can find out how difficult each question was for a selected sample of the students who took the test in December 1982. The right-hand column in the table tells you what percentage of that group of students answered the question correctly. It is important to remember that these percentages are based on only one group of students; had this edition of the test been given to all students in the class of 1983 who took a Latin Achievement Test, the percentages would probably have been different. A question that was answered correctly by almost everyone in the group, obviously, is an easy question. Question 28, for example, was answered correctly by 91 percent of the students in the sample. On the other hand, question 61 was answered correctly by only 16 percent of the students. If you find that you missed several questions that would be considered easy, you may want to review those questions carefully. They may cover some aspect of the subject that you need to review. Perhaps you misunderstood the directions for one part of the test or you thought the questions were so easy that you did not spend as much time on them as you might have.

About the Spanish Achievement Test

The Spanish Achievement Test is written to reflect general trends in secondary school curriculums and is independent of particular textbooks or methods of instruction. Students who take the Spanish Achievement Test have studied Spanish two to four years in junior high and/or high school (the equivalent of two to four semesters in college). The best preparation for the test is the gradual development of competence in Spanish over a period of years. You may also prepare for the Spanish Achievement Test as you would for any comprehensive examination that requires knowledge of facts and concepts and the ability to apply them. Reading the explanations and descriptions in this book should give you an indication of what to expect.

Since the Spanish Achievement Test is intended to measure the Spanish reading skills of secondary school students between the second and fourth year of language study, the difficulty level of the questions varies. Some questions are directed toward students who have had only two years of study and some to students who have three or four years of Spanish. The questions range from very easy ones that can be answered correctly by almost all of the students to difficult ones that only 15 to 20 percent can answer.

Colleges that require their applicants to take the Spanish Achievement Test may use the scores for course placement. Because scores are not adjusted on the basis of years of study, colleges should consider the preparation of students when evaluating their scores.

Content of the Test

The Spanish Achievement Test measures knowledge and ability in the following areas of reading skill: (1) vocabulary mastery, tested in the vocabulary-in-context section; (2) grammatical control, tested in the structure section; and (3) reading comprehension. A certain percentage of each test is devoted to questions testing skill in these three areas (see below).

Skills Measured	Approximate Percentage of Test
Vocabulary in Context	30
Structure	40
Reading Comprehension	30

85-90 Questions; Time — 60 minutes

Although knowledge of vocabulary is tested implicitly throughout the test, some questions specifically test word meaning in the context of a sentence that resembles spoken or written language. Various parts of speech and idiomatic expressions are tested (nouns, verbs, adjectives, adverbs). Since the extensive vocabulary reflected in the test is acquired only through much study and practice, a last-minute review of word lists will probably not affect your performance on the test.

Grammatical control, the ability to use correct language patterns, is essential to the command of a language. A number of questions test your ability to identify usage that is structurally correct and appropriate in context. Structure is tested through a variety of language patterns, such as prepositions, gender and number agreement, and conjunctions that require the use of the subjunctive.

The reading comprehension section consists of a series of passages, each followed by questions designed to test your understanding of the passages selected. The questions are diversified and test points such as main and supporting ideas and themes, spatial and temporal setting, and the motivation of characters and their relationship to one another. Prose fiction, historical works, and newspaper and magazine articles are used in order to include varied selections.

Questions Used in the Test

The Spanish Achievement Test measures reading skills through questions that cover vocabulary, structure, and reading comprehension.

In all multiple-choice questions, the wrong choices are selected with as much care as the correct answer. If you are sure of the correct answer, you will not be attracted by any of the wrong choices. If you are in some doubt, however, you may find yourself debating among two or three of the choices. In this case, you will have to call upon your knowledge and analytical skills to select the correct answer and reject the others.

Vocabulary in Context

Directions: This part consists of a number of incomplete statements, each having four suggested completions. Select the best completion and blacken the corresponding space on the answer sheet.

1. Si a Enrique no le gustan las tareas caseras, debe buscar una . . .

    (A) escoba
    (B) limpieza
    (C) criada
    (D) castaña

The correct choice is (C). In order to answer the question correctly, you have to understand both the right answer, *criada*, and the phrase *tareas caseras* in the sentence. All the other choices are unacceptable because they make no sense in the context of the sentence. They are, however, related to the sentence and to the right answer in terms of meaning (semantically) or in terms of sound (phonologically). Choices (A) and (B), *escoba* and *limpieza*, are words related to housekeeping; choice (D), *castaña*, sounds like *caseras*.

2. El niño no quiere comer porque no le gusta . . .

    (A) el jabón
    (B) el hambre
    (C) la comedia
    (D) el pollo

The correct choice is (D), *el pollo*. None of the other choices is a possible answer in the context of this sentence. Choice (A) is sometimes mistaken for *jamón*, which would be a possible answer. Choice (B), *el hambre*, is a related idea, and (C), *la comedia*, sounds like the word *comer* in the sentence.

Situation Questions

Some Spanish Achievement Tests also test knowledge of vocabulary by means of situation questions. This type of question will not be used in the Spanish Achievement Test after 1984.

Directions: In each of the following questions a certain situation is suggested. From the four choices given, select the remark which is most likely to be made in the situation suggested and blacken the corresponding space on the answer sheet.

3. Alvarez cree que Vega es un antipático. Así es que cuando éste entra, Alvarez le dice a un amigo:

    (A) Poca gracia me hace este tipo.
    (B) Le tengo mucha simpatía.
    (C) Pobre hombre; se ve que se siente mal.
    (D) A Vega le estimo mucho.

The correct choice is (A) because it expresses Alvarez' negative emotion. None of the other choices is an appropriate response to the situation: (B), (C), and (D) are all positive responses.

Structure

All Spanish Achievement Tests measure your ability to recognize correct structure. You should remember that you must select the choice that is *structurally* correct in the context of the sentence. All of the choices contain appropriate vocabulary and are forms that exist in Spanish, but only one will be grammatically correct in the context given.

Directions: Each of the following sentences contains a blank. From the four choices given, select the one that can be inserted in the blank to form a grammatically correct sentence and blacken the corresponding space on the answer sheet.

4. ¿La maleta? Jorge ————— dio.

    (A) me lo
    (B) le
    (C) te la
    (D) lo

The correct choice is (C), *te la*. In order to choose the correct answer, you need to know that the direct object pronoun has to be feminine to agree with *la maleta*, the noun it replaces. (C) is the only choice that includes the feminine direct object pronoun *la*. The context also demands that the sentence *Jorge ----- dio* be completed with both a direct object pronoun and an indirect object pronoun. Thus choices (B) and (D), which consist of one pronoun only, cannot complete the sentence adequately.

5. Quiero que tú y Lázaro ————— conmigo.

   (A) fueron

   (B) vayan

   (C) van

   (D) irán

The correct choice is (B), *vayan*. In order to answer correctly, you must know that the construction *Quiero que* is always followed by a verb in the subjunctive mood. All of the choices make sense in terms of meaning (they are all forms of the verb "to go"), but only choice (B) forms a grammatically correct sentence.

Some Spanish Achievement Tests measure your knowledge of structure by asking you to select the one choice that does *not* fit grammatically into the sentence. As in the structure questions described above, you should focus on structure rather than on meaning in choosing your answers. This type of question will not appear in the Spanish Achievement Test after 1984.

Directions: Each of the following sentences contains a blank. Three of the four choices that follow can be inserted in the blank to form sentences that are grammatically correct though they may differ in meaning from each other. You are to select the one choice that does NOT fit grammatically into the incomplete sentence.

6. Miguel quiere hablar con —————.

   (A) ti

   (B) ella

   (C) usted

   (D) todos

The choice that does *not* fit grammatically into the sentence is (A), *ti*. In order to respond correctly, you must know that the pronoun *ti* is used after most prepositions, but that with the preposition *con*, the expression would be *contigo*.

Reading Comprehension

All Spanish Achievement Tests contain several prose passages followed by questions that test understanding of the literal meaning of the passage. The passage and questions that follow are typical of the material that appears on the test.

Directions: Read the following passages carefully for comprehension. Each passage is followed by a number of questions and incomplete statements. Select the answer or completion that is best according to the passage and blacken the corresponding space on the answer sheet.

Alcanzó la carretera central y pisó el acelerador. Se cruzó con varios camiones del ejército y con una ambulancia de la Cruz Roja. Sara hablaba incoherentemente a su lado.
(5)   — Pararemos en algún lugar. Un café nos hará bien.
En Santa Fe cayeron las primeras gotas. Alvaro las vio caer en los cristales como frutas maduras y, a los pocos segundos, el espacio se
(10) convirtió en una cortina de agua. Era la lluvia del trópico violenta, acompañada de un viento colérico y del fuego brutal de los relámpagos. Los limpiacristales oscilaban inútilmente en abanico con un ruido sordo.

7. ¿Dónde se desarrolla esta narración?

   (A) En una casa

   (B) En un automóvil

   (C) En un café

   (D) En un cuartel

8. ¿Qué tiempo hace?

   (A) Hace frío.

   (B) Hace sol.

   (C) Está lloviendo.

   (D) Está nevando.

9. ¿Quién acompaña a Alvaro?

   (A) Un soldado

   (B) Un chofer

   (C) Nadie

   (D) Una mujer

10. ¿Qué desea Alvaro?

   (A) Abrir la cortina

   (B) Comer una fruta

   (C) Tomar un café

   (D) Encender la luz

11. Alvaro se enfrenta con

   (A) una tormenta

   (B) el ejército

   (C) una ambulancia

   (D) la cólera de una mujer

Questions 7 and 8 test how well you understand the setting in which the events of the passage take place. Question 7 deals with the physical location of the characters, and question 8 with the weather.

The correct answer to question 7 is (B), *En un automóvil*. Evidence that the couple is in a car is found throughout the passage, although it will be obvious to you by the end of the first paragraph (lines 1-4). The passage does not use the words *automóvil, carro,* or *coche;* you must infer that the passage takes place in a car by such words as *carretera* and *acelerador* (lines 1-2) and *camiones del ejército* and *ambulancia* (lines 2-3).

The correct answer to question 8 is (C), *Está lloviendo*. The last paragraph of the passage describes the rain in some detail. You can answer the question correctly by looking for paraphrases of *está lloviendo* in the passage: *cayeron las primeras gotas* (line 7), *cortina de agua* (line 10), and *lluvia del trópico* (lines 10-11).

Questions 9 and 10 deal with facts about the passage. As in the previous questions, you can choose the correct answers if you read the passage carefully. In question 9, the correct answer is (D), *Una mujer.* You can find the information in the first paragraph, *Sara hablaba incoherentemente a su lado.*

The correct answer to question 10 is (C), *Tomar un café.* You can answer correctly by drawing the inference from Alvaro's words in lines 5-6, *"Pararemos en algún lugar. Un café nos hará bien."*

Question 11 deals with the main idea of the passage. Questions that treat the passage as a whole are usually placed at the beginning or at the end of the series of questions. The correct answer is (A), *una tormenta.* The problem that Alvaro faces in the passage is a storm, whose increasing intensity is described in considerable detail in the last paragraph, lines 7-14.

Spanish Achievement Test

The test that follows is an edition of the Spanish Achievement Test administered in May 1983. So that you will have an idea of what the actual test administration will be like, try to take this test under conditions as close as possible to those of the actual test. It will probably help if you

- Set aside an hour for the test when you will not be interrupted, so that you can complete all of it in one sitting.

- Sit at a desk with no other papers or books. You can't take a calculator, a dictionary, other books, or notes into the test room.

- Have a kitchen timer or clock in front of you for timing yourself.

- Tear out an answer sheet from the back of this book and fill it in just as you would on the day of the test. You can use one answer sheet for as many as three Achievement Tests.

- Read the instructions that precede the test. When you take the test, you will be asked to read them before you begin answering questions.

- After you finish the test, read the sections on "How to Score the Spanish Achievement Test" and "Reviewing Your Test Performance," which follow the test.

SPANISH TEST

The top portion of the section of the answer sheet which you will use in taking the Spanish test must be filled in exactly as shown in the illustration below. Note carefully that you have to do all of the following on your answer sheet:

1. Print SPANISH on the line to the right of the words "Achievement Test."
2. Blacken spaces 4 and 6 in the row of spaces immediately under the words "Test Code."
3. Blacken space 3 in the group of five spaces labeled X.
4. Blacken space 2 in the group of five spaces labeled Y.

TEST CODE

```
        1  2  3  ●  5     ●  7  8  9  0      ACHIEVEMENT
 X      1  2  ●  4  5   Y  1  ●  3  4  5      TEST:        SPANISH
 Q      1  2  3  4  5  6  7  8  9                          (Print)
```

In the group of nine spaces labeled Q, you are to blacken ONE and ONLY ONE space, as described below, to indicate how you obtained your knowledge of Spanish. The information that you provide is for statistical purposes only and will not influence your score on the test.

If your knowledge of Spanish does not come primarily from courses taken in grades 9 through 12, blacken space 9 and leave the remaining spaces blank, regardless of how long you studied the subject in school. For example, you are to blacken space 9 if your knowledge of Spanish comes primarily from any of the following sources: study prior to the ninth grade, courses taken at a college, special study, residence abroad, or living in a home in which Spanish is spoken.

If your knowledge of Spanish does come primarily from courses taken in grades 9 through 12, blacken the space that indicates the level of the Spanish course in which you are currently enrolled. If you are not now enrolled in a Spanish course, blacken the space that indicates the level of the most advanced course in Spanish that you have completed.

Level I:	first or second half	— blacken space 1
Level II:	first half	— blacken space 2
	second half	— blacken space 3
Level III:	first half	— blacken space 4
	second half	— blacken space 5
Level IV:	first half	— blacken space 6
	second half	— blacken space 7
Advanced Placement or course that represents a level of study higher than Level IV: second half		— blacken space 8

If you are in doubt about whether to mark space 9 rather than one of the spaces 1-8, mark space 9.

When the supervisor gives the signal, turn the page and begin the Spanish test. There are 100 numbered spaces on the answer sheet and 88 questions in the Spanish test. Therefore, use only spaces 1 to 88 for recording your answers.

SPANISH TEST

PLEASE NOTE THAT YOUR ANSWER SHEET HAS FIVE ANSWER POSITIONS MARKED A, B, C, D, E, WHILE THE QUESTIONS THROUGHOUT THIS TEST CONTAIN ONLY FOUR CHOICES. BE SURE <u>NOT</u> TO MAKE ANY MARKS IN COLUMN E.

Part A

<u>Directions:</u> This part consists of a number of incomplete statements, each having four suggested completions. Select the most appropriate completion and blacken the corresponding space on the answer sheet.

1. Si quieres comer con nosotros, vuelve . . .

   (A) a tiempo
   (B) a fondo
   (C) con profundidad
   (D) por regla general

2. Al llegar a viejos los señores González desean una vida tranquila y reposada. Por eso han decidido . . .

   (A) comprar una casa en el campo
   (B) dar la vuelta al mundo en quince días
   (C) participar en las carreras de automóviles
   (D) buscar trabajo en el circo

3. Te digo que no tengo apetito, por eso . . .

   (A) tengo mucha hambre
   (B) necesito ver al cartero
   (C) tengo frío en las manos
   (D) no quiero comer nada más

4. Juan Pablo tuvo que esperar unos minutos antes de tomar la sopa porque estaba demasiado . . .

   (A) caliente
   (B) calurosa
   (C) mojada
   (D) perfumada

5. Tiene más años que yo; es decir, es . . .

   (A) mayor
   (B) menor
   (C) mejor
   (D) peor

6. En los periódicos se leen . . .

   (A) carteras
   (B) recitales
   (C) noticias
   (D) películas

7. No tengo ningún inconveniente; lo haré . . .

   (A) de buena gana
   (B) en marcha
   (C) con disgusto
   (D) a contrapelo

8. Cada vez que el dentista me saca una muela siento . . .

   (A) mucho dolor
   (B) muchos espejos
   (C) muchas gomas
   (D) mucha simpatía

9. Vaya por este . . . para ir a la ciudad.

   (A) camino
   (B) piso
   (C) viaje
   (D) caso

10. La hija de mi tío es mi . . .

    (A) sobrina
    (B) tía
    (C) prima
    (D) nieta

11. El dependiente le ofrece camisetas, corbatas, calcetines y pañuelos. Ramón está en . . .

    (A) un desfile
    (B) una zapatería
    (C) un almacén
    (D) una farmacia

GO ON TO THE NEXT PAGE

12. Pepe le dijo a María: —Al salir de clase te . . .
    el libro que me prestaste.

    (A) escribiré
    (B) devolveré
    (C) olvidaré
    (D) ahorraré

13. Aquí no se plantan árboles porque . . .
    muy poco.

    (A) llama
    (B) limpia
    (C) llueve
    (D) lava

14. Amelia, estudia y no dejes para mañana lo que
    puedas hacer . . .

    (A) ayer
    (B) hoy
    (C) el día próximo
    (D) el día de mañana

15. ¡Qué música tan estupenda! Esta orquesta
    . . . muy bien.

    (A) juega
    (B) sabe
    (C) maneja
    (D) toca

16. Marta fue a ver al médico porque estaba . . .

    (A) enferma
    (B) dormida
    (C) sentada
    (D) oscura

17. Por dondequiera que vaya, nunca lo rechazan;
    nadie lo . . .

    (A) acepta
    (B) advierte
    (C) sufre
    (D) odia

GO ON TO THE NEXT PAGE

SPANISH TEST—*Continued*

Part B

Directions: In each of the following questions a certain situation is suggested. From the four choices given, select the remark that is most likely to be made in the situation suggested and blacken the corresponding space on the answer sheet.

18. Cuando Anita entró en la librería, le preguntó al empleado:

    (A) ¿Me lleva a la calle Paz, número 44, por favor?
    (B) ¿Tienen libros de arte medieval?
    (C) ¿Sirven el desayuno aquí?
    (D) ¿Tienen muebles de estilo contemporáneo?

19. La madre, al ver que el hijo tenía las manos sucias, le dijo:

    (A) Ponte a comer en seguida.
    (B) Lávatelas con jabón.
    (C) Pon las manos en el suelo.
    (D) No salgas sin abrigo.

20. Como no sabía la fecha, mi hermano me preguntó:

    (A) ¿Qué hora es?
    (B) ¿Cómo te sientes?
    (C) ¿Quién eres?
    (D) ¿A cómo estamos?

21. El camarero, al servir la comida muy caliente al señor, le dice:

    (A) ¡Cuidado, no se queme!
    (B) ¡No se preocupe!
    (C) ¡Qué gracia tiene Ud.!
    (D) Tenga Ud. la cuenta, señor.

22. Como el torero resultó mediocre, el crítico escribió:

    (A) Salió sin pena ni gloria.
    (B) Empezó fuera de la plaza.
    (C) No iba vestido de torero.
    (D) Obtuvo una gran ovación.

23. Cuando regañaron a Carlitos por romper el plato, él se defendió diciendo:

    (A) ¡Dile que no estoy!
    (B) ¡No tuve la culpa!
    (C) ¡Ya hice la tarea!
    (D) ¡Lo comí sin querer!

24. Carmen acababa de ganar el premio gordo. Al verla, su amigo Carlos le dijo:

    (A) ¡Cómo que no!
    (B) ¡Ya lo creo!
    (C) ¡De ninguna forma!
    (D) ¡Felicitaciones!

25. Mi amiga estaba preocupada porque tenía mucho que hacer. Por eso yo le dije:

    (A) Pasé unas vacaciones estupendas.
    (B) ¿Tienes algo que hacer?
    (C) Quiero comprarme un barco de vela.
    (D) No te apures, muchacha.

26. Un mendigo me pidió limosna. Yo no tenía dinero, pero queriendo ser cortés le dije:

    (A) ¿Con qué derecho se dirige a mí?
    (B) ¡A otro tonto con ese cuento!
    (C) ¡Que Dios le ampare!
    (D) ¡Vaya Ud. a trabajar!

27. Le compré a mi madre un regalo de cumpleaños y la empleada me preguntó:

    (A) ¿Se lo rompo?
    (B) ¿Cuántos años cumplió su hija?
    (C) ¿Por qué no ahorra el dinero?
    (D) ¿Se lo envuelvo?

28. Después de ver el programa de televisión que terminó a las once de la noche, el niño oyó a su madre que le decía:

    (A) Ya es hora de acostarte.
    (B) Tienes que ir a la escuela ahora mismo.
    (C) ¡Despiértate, que ya es tarde!
    (D) Tu programa acaba de empezar.

29. El médico cree que el señor está demasiado gordo y por eso le dice:

    (A) ¿Por qué no engorda Ud. más?
    (B) Hay que comer más.
    (C) Hay que ponerse más delgado.
    (D) ¿Por qué le falta el apetito?

GO ON TO THE NEXT PAGE

30. Cuando Federico quemó el arroz, su mamá comentó con la familia:

    (A) El arroz está frío.
    (B) Es demasiado distraído.
    (C) Tendrá que servir el arroz en una taza.
    (D) No le gusta el pollo.

31. Martín le pregunta a Federico cuándo llegó. Federico le contesta:

    (A) Lo hice bien.
    (B) Hace un rato.
    (C) El martes próximo.
    (D) Habrá tiempo.

32. Después de terminar toda su tarea, Antonio se levantó y dijo:

    (A) Sólo me falta estudiar el libro de biología.
    (B) ¡Qué cantidad de trabajo me queda todavía!
    (C) Media hora más y le pongo fin a esto.
    (D) Ahora puedo salir con mis amigos.

33. Juana volvió a la taquilla del teatro y se quejó al empleado:

    (A) Me ha dado unas butacas muy incómodas.
    (B) La escenografía es magnífica.
    (C) La taquillera es monísima.
    (D) Me impresiona la buena calidad de los artistas.

GO ON TO THE NEXT PAGE

Part C

<u>Directions</u>: Each of the following sentences contains a blank. Three of the four choices that follow can be inserted in the blank to form sentences that are grammatically correct though they may differ in meaning from each other. You are to select the one choice that does NOT fit grammatically into the incomplete sentence.

34. ------- sufrieron heridas graves.

    (A) Todos
    (B) Las víctimas
    (C) Cada uno
    (D) Los de enfrente

35. ¿------- vino a verte ayer?

    (A) Quién
    (B) Quiénes
    (C) Qué persona
    (D) Quién es la que

36. La profesora me -------, pero no pude creerlo.

    (A) lo mostró
    (B) mostró aquello
    (C) mostró eso
    (D) mostró lo

37. Ponga ese vaso más cerca de -------.

    (A) él
    (B) usted
    (C) me
    (D) nosotros

38. Teresa y Gloria quieren ir al partido -------.

    (A) conmigo
    (B) para ellas
    (C) solas
    (D) sin él

39. En cuanto acabe, ------- contigo.

    (A) voy
    (B) hablo
    (C) salgo
    (D) hago

40. Pedro ------- regaló unas revistas.

    (A) te
    (B) les
    (C) mí
    (D) os

41. Se lo dije cuando ------- la noticia.

    (A) supe
    (B) vi
    (C) pude
    (D) obtuve

42. Durante el viaje compramos ------- tela de lujo.

    (A) suficiente
    (B) mucha
    (C) ninguna
    (D) poca

43. María es tan ------- como mi hermano Jorge.

    (A) alta
    (B) delgada
    (C) feliz
    (D) bien

44. La calle ------- llena de gente.

    (A) estuviese
    (B) estaba
    (C) está
    (D) estuvo

45. Tuvo que sacar ------- dólares del banco.

    (A) diez
    (B) millón
    (C) mil
    (D) cien

46. Este hombre no es ------- ese otro.

    (A) como
    (B) lo mismo que
    (C) como el que
    (D) igual a

47. El chico se ríe de ------- chistes.

    (A) sus
    (B) suyos
    (C) los
    (D) tus

48. Rafael es un artista -------.

    (A) famoso
    (B) aplaudida
    (C) popular
    (D) inteligente

GO ON TO THE NEXT PAGE

49. Carolina se ------- siempre a las ocho de la mañana.

    (A) lo toma
    (B) levanta
    (C) le llama
    (D) le queja

50. Aquellos señores son -------.

    (A) de la capital
    (B) de origen humilde
    (C) en la ciudad
    (D) amigos míos

51. Todavía no lo ha -------.

    (A) devuelto
    (B) trecho
    (C) abierto
    (D) vendido

52. José no ------- en la clase de español.

    (A) presta atención
    (B) duerme
    (C) sienta
    (D) levanta la mano

53. Quiero que nos ------- traiga inmediatamente.

    (A) lo
    (B) las
    (C) la
    (D) les

54. Queríamos -------.

    (A) que Paco leyera aquella novela
    (B) que ellos tengan buena suerte
    (C) que el examen fuese fácil
    (D) levantarnos de madrugada

55. A pesar de todo -------, Cecilia no dijo nada.

    (A) esto
    (B) lo referido
    (C) lo demás
    (D) este

56. Salgamos antes de que ------- a llover.

    (A) comience
    (B) vaya
    (C) vuelva
    (D) parezca

57. ------- necesitamos dinero.

    (A) Todo
    (B) Sólo
    (C) Nunca
    (D) Todavía

58. Hablas muy -------.

    (A) alto
    (B) bajo
    (C) bueno
    (D) despacio

59. Han encontrado a ------- alemanes.

    (A) varios
    (B) tres mujeres
    (C) varios representantes
    (D) unos

60. A Pepe le gustará -------.

    (A) acompañarnos al teatro
    (B) esa película
    (C) los regalos que escogimos
    (D) lo que hicimos

61. Mi abuela ------- su cartera encima de la mesa.

    (A) vio
    (B) dejó
    (C) puso
    (D) quedó

62. Mi amigo me prestó ------- libro.

    (A) eso
    (B) aquel
    (C) su
    (D) cierto

63. ------- en mimar a la criatura.

    (A) Insistieron
    (B) Se empeñaron
    (C) Estuvieron de acuerdo
    (D) Se negaron

64. El profesor pedía que los estudiantes ------- durante la conferencia.

    (A) dejaron de fumar
    (B) se sentasen
    (C) prestaran atención
    (D) no hablaran

65. Le mandaremos el lavaplatos en cuanto -------.

    (A) nos lo indique
    (B) usted nos diga
    (C) recibamos su cheque
    (D) llega del almacén

GO ON TO THE NEXT PAGE

Part D

Directions: Read the following passages carefully for comprehension. Each passage is followed by a number of questions and incomplete statements. Select the answer or completion that is best according to the passage and blacken the corresponding space on the answer sheet.

Según algunos educadores, existe en la actualidad tal predominio de la "imagen" que a los niños les gusta cada vez menos leer. En la televisión, los avisos publicitarios, el cine y las revistas, las imágenes acaparan la atención. La razón es muy sencilla: la imagen exige menos esfuerzo y es más directa.

Pero los padres no hacen mucho para fomentar la lectura. De nada sirve que la escuela obligue a leer tal o cual libro. Siempre será una obligación, un deber. Pero una cosa es innegable: el gusto por la lectura tiene que nacer en la casa. El niño de hoy sufre de más ansiedad ya que comparte demasiado los problemas de los adultos. Por eso la lectura es imprescindible: para entretenerlo, relajarlo, transportarlo al mundo de la fantasía y para darle conocimientos.

66. ¿De qué trata este artículo?

   (A) La necesidad de leer
   (B) La importancia de la televisión
   (C) Cómo aprender a leer
   (D) Cómo usar la "imagen"

67. El autor atribuye el problema educativo que comenta a la

   (A) influencia de la escuela
   (B) falta de enseñanza
   (C) falta de buenos materiales
   (D) influencia de las representaciones visuales

68. Según el artículo, el placer por la lectura debe surgir en

   (A) la escuela únicamente
   (B) el hogar
   (C) el niño mismo
   (D) la sociedad

GO ON TO THE NEXT PAGE

Johnny Logan, el alto y guapo irlandés que este año ganó el concurso de canto de Eurovisión con la canción "Otro año", lleva una vida muy atareada desde su triunfo en La Haya.

Hasta entonces este ex-electricista de veinticuatro años apenas había conseguido ganar más de cien dólares a la semana cantando en clubs nocturnos, pero ahora está excelentemente encarrilado hacia un futuro brillante.

En los escenarios, Johnny Logan se mueve con seguridad y aplomo admirables, pero fuera de ellos da la impresión de no tener mucha confianza en sí mismo.

"Sinceramente, no esperaba ganar el concurso de Eurovisión. Sabía, esto sí, que contaba con una buena canción, pero todos me decían que no era la más apta para el Festival. Yo pensaba que ellos tenían razón, ya que debían saber de eso más que yo. Después de haberla cantado aquella noche, tuve la certeza de haberlo hecho bien . . . y, como esto era lo que más me preocupaba, me sentí satisfecho."

69. La vida de Johnny Logan cambió cuando éste

   (A) viajó a Irlanda
   (B) empezó a cantar por las noches
   (C) tuvo éxito como cantante
   (D) decidió hacerse electricista

70. ¿Qué tipo de trabajo hacía Johnny Logan antes?

   (A) Vendía cerveza.
   (B) Hacía instalaciones eléctricas.
   (C) Era mozo en un club.
   (D) Trabajaba en los ferrocarriles.

71. Algunos opinaban que la canción que Johnny Logan había escogido para el concurso

   (A) era muy alegre
   (B) no estaba de moda
   (C) era la mejor del concurso
   (D) no era apropiada

72. ¿Cómo se sintió Johnny Logan inmediatamente después de cantar en el concurso?

   (A) Contento de su actuación
   (B) Satisfecho porque iba a ganar el concurso
   (C) Fatigado por su gran esfuerzo
   (D) Preocupado porque necesitaba el dinero del premio

73. ¿Qué le pasó a Johnny Logan cuando le anunciaron el resultado del concurso?

   (A) Se sorprendió.
   (B) Perdió la confianza.
   (C) Se desmayó.
   (D) Se enojó.

GO ON TO THE NEXT PAGE

La señora del Administrador ha permanecido dormida, mientras los campesinos, desesperados, han tratado de quemar el edificio de la Dirección para vengarse de que les hayan inundado sus cosechas, después de expulsarlos de su pueblo y de sus tierras. Ella, la señora del Administrador, sigue en la cama, tapándose el escote con las manos y oyendo las explicaciones que le dan.

74. Los campesinos han intentado

    (A) una huelga
    (B) un robo
    (C) una venganza
    (D) un asalto a la señora del Administrador

75. La señora del Administrador ha estado

    (A) furiosa
    (B) dormida
    (C) contentísima
    (D) desesperada

76. Los campesinos están furiosos porque

    (A) no les suben el sueldo
    (B) los han echado del pueblo
    (C) les obligan a trabajar más
    (D) se ha dormido la señora del Administrador

En la Residencia del Seguro de Enfermedad de Oviedo acaba de ser practicada una operación quirúrgica rara: la extracción de 132 pesetas en monedas del estómago de Manuel Soages, fogonero de un barco de pesca. El enfermo, de cincuenta y cinco años, venía quejándose de dolores de estómago y le fue falsamente diagnosticada una úlcera. Lo que no ha sido aclarado aún es si las comía como postre riquísimo o si se trataba de una manía ahorrativa.

77. La enfermedad de Manuel Soages se debió a

    (A) una úlcera
    (B) un exceso de postres
    (C) unas monedas
    (D) pescado podrido

78. La operación consistió en

    (A) congelar la úlcera
    (B) sacar las monedas
    (C) quitar el estómago
    (D) sustituir el estómago

79. La noticia da a entender que el paciente estaba motivado por

    (A) exhibicionismo
    (B) una dieta insuficiente
    (C) una manía de ahorrar
    (D) causas desconocidas

GO ON TO THE NEXT PAGE

Voy a ver la puesta del sol: un incendio volcánico entre montañas de ceniza. Y luego me envuelve la melancolía otoñal de una ciudad desconocida. Pensando en cosas melancólicas voy a comer, que es una brutalidad fisiológica independiente del alma.

Por fortuna, los últimos días de noviembre son muy cortos y pude acostarme a las siete con una novela de Camilo a la cabecera de la cama. No sin antes dar un paseo por la ciudad y pararme ante la imagen de la Virgen en el rincón del arco para pensar: ¡de qué tragedias calladas habrás sido muda confidente!

80. El melancólico paseante de este fragmento opina que la comida

(A) es una barbaridad nada espiritual
(B) es una necesidad del alma
(C) es una consecuencia de la melancolía
(D) produce mal humor

81. Para el autor de este fragmento, los días de otoño tienen la ventaja de que

(A) provocan pensamientos románticos
(B) son muy tristes y deprimentes
(C) permiten ir pronto a la cama
(D) son muy fríos y tranquilos

82. El autor dice que, antes de acostarse

(A) lee el periódico
(B) prepara un discurso
(C) reza sus oraciones
(D) da un paseo por el pueblo

83. La imagen a la que el autor se refiere es

(A) una imagen poética
(B) una fantasía
(C) un símbolo del hambre
(D) una figura religiosa

84. Ante la imagen, el autor piensa:

(A) ¡Qué aficionada eres al drama!
(B) ¡Cuántos te habrán contado sus penas!
(C) ¡Qué lugar tan desconocido!
(D) ¡Qué lejos estoy de mi mundo!

La señora García le entregó a Adolfo un segundo trozo de pastel y le propuso que pasara a felicitar a los novios. Adolfo trató de excusarse, pero debió seguir a la señora, abriéndose paso entre la gente, hasta el rincón del comedor donde los novios recibían las felicitaciones de los invitados. La novia era una muchacha pálida, acaso rubia, con un sombrerito redondo, un vestido muy corto y zapatos de tacón alto. El novio era un hombre corpulento y canoso; su traje negro y su notorio aseo sugerían un paisano de visita en Buenos Aires; contradictoriamente, las manos eran suaves, pequeñas y delicadas. Después de saludarlos, Adolfo se encaminó, a fuerza de empujones y codazos, hacia el patio; pensó que tenía que ventilar los pulmones, porque en la casa no corría el aire y francamente ya no se podía respirar.

85. Según la selección, ¿qué es lo primero que Adolfo hace en la fiesta?

(A) Saluda a los padres de los novios.
(B) Toma dos pedazos de pastel.
(C) Charla con mucha gente.
(D) Camina mucho por el patio.

86. ¿Qué hizo Adolfo después de seguir a la señora?

(A) Les presentó sus excusas a los novios.
(B) Se escondió en un rincón.
(C) Le dio varios empujones a la novia.
(D) Saludó a los recién casados.

87. Puede notarse que en el comedor

(A) los novios estaban recibiendo a sus invitados
(B) los pasteles estaban en un rincón
(C) había poca gente
(D) había unas paisanas pequeñas y delicadas

88. Según la selección, en la casa tenían

(A) todas las ventanas abiertas
(B) dos comedores pequeños
(C) demasiados invitados y poca ventilación
(D) un corpulento panadero ofreciendo pasteles

S T O P

IF YOU FINISH BEFORE TIME IS CALLED, YOU MAY CHECK YOUR WORK ON THIS TEST ONLY.
DO NOT WORK ON ANY OTHER TEST IN THIS BOOK.

How to Score the
Spanish Achievement Test

When you take the Spanish Achievement Test, your answer sheet will be "read" by a scanning machine that will record your responses to each question. Then a computer will compare your answers with the correct answers and produce your raw score. You get one point for each correct answer. For each wrong answer, you lose one-third of a point. This raw score is converted to a College Board scaled score that is reported to you and to the colleges you specify. Questions you omit (and any for which you mark more than one answer) are not counted. After you have taken this test, you can get an idea of what your score might be by following the instructions in the next two sections.

Determining Your Raw Score

Step 1:	Table A on the next page lists the correct answers for all the questions on the test.* Compare your answer with the correct answer and • Put a check in the column marked "Right" if your answer is correct. • Put a check in the column marked "Wrong" if your answer is incorrect. • Leave both columns blank if you omitted the question.
Step 2:	Count the number of right answers and enter the number here . . . . _____
Step 3:	Count the number of wrong answers and enter the number here . . . . 3)‾‾‾‾‾‾‾‾‾‾ Enter the result of dividing by 3 here . . . . _____
Step 4:	Subtract the number you obtained in Step 3 from the number in Step 2; round the result to the nearest whole number and enter here. . . . . _____

The number you obtained in Step 4 is your raw score. (The correction for guessing — subtraction of a third of a point for each incorrect answer — adjusts for the fact that random guessing on a large number of questions will result in some questions being answered correctly by chance.) Instructions for converting your raw score to a scaled score follow.

*The last column in Table A gives the percentage of a selected sample of the students who took the test in May 1983 that answered the question correctly. (See page 185 for further explanation.)

TABLE A
Answers to Spanish Achievement Test, Form 3FAC, and Percentage of Students Answering Each Question Correctly

Question Number	Correct Answer	Right	Wrong	Percentage of Students Answering the Question Correctly	Question Number	Correct Answer	Right	Wrong	Percentage of Students Answering the Question Correctly
1	A			89%	46	C			61%
2	A			89	47	B			71
3	D			93	48	B			64
4	A			76	49	C			20
5	A			85	50	C			52
6	C			91	51	B			60
7	A			53	52	C			53
8	A			73	53	D			66
9	A			72	54	B			27
10	C			80	55	D			37
11	C			57	56	D			24
12	B			71	57	A			40
13	C			88	58	C			46
14	B			71	59	B			36
15	D			86	60	C			29
16	A			98	61	D			40
17	D			16	62	A			23
18	B			90	63	D			18
19	B			82	64	A			52
20	D			49	65	D			32
21	A			70	66	A			61
22	A			72	67	D			72
23	B			67	68	B			34
24	D			57	69	C			34
25	D			59	70	B			73
26	C			29	71	D			44
27	D			60	72	A			38
28	A			46	73	A			50
29	C			60	74	C			46
30	B			42	75	B			68
31	B			34	76	B			44
32	D			84	77	C			46
33	A			33	78	B			60
34	C			80	79	D			23
35	B			78	80	A			34
36	D			64	81	C			36
37	C			64	82	D			51
38	B			70	83	D			53
39	D			60	84	B			29
40	C			64	85	B			42
41	C			55	86	D			22
42	C			50	87	A			46
43	D			69	88	C			50
44	A			66					
45	B			70					

Note: The percentages are based on the analysis of the answer sheets of students who took this test in May 1983 and whose mean score was 518. The analysis sample was selected to represent the students for whom the test is intended. Students whose knowledge of the language does not come almost entirely from high school courses were excluded, and only those students who had at least four semesters of language study were included.

Finding Your College Board Scaled Score ▰

When you take Achievement Tests, the scores sent to the colleges you specify will be reported on the College Board scale, ranging from 200 to 800. The raw score that you obtained above (Step 4) can be converted to a scaled score on the College Board scale of 200 to 800 by using Table B.

To find your scaled score on the practice test, locate your raw score in the left column of Table B; the corresponding score in the right column will be your College Board scaled score. For example, a raw score of 50 on this particular edition of the Spanish Achievement Test corresponds to a College Board scaled score of 570. Raw scores are converted to scaled scores to ensure that a score earned on any one edition of the Spanish Achievement Test is comparable to the same scaled score earned on any other edition of the test.

Because some editions of the Spanish Achievement Test may be slightly easier or more difficult than others, statistical adjustments are made in the scores so that each College Board scaled score indicates the same level of performance, regardless of the edition of the test you take and the ability of the group you

TABLE B — SCORE CONVERSION TABLE					
Spanish Achievement Test, Form 3FAC					
Raw Score	College Board Scaled Score	Raw Score	College Board Scaled Score	Raw Score	College Board Scaled Score
88	780	48	560	8	390
87	770	47	550	7	380
86	760	46	550	6	380
85	750	45	540	5	370
84	740	44	540	4	370
83	730	43	530	3	360
82	730	42	530	2	360
81	720	41	530	1	350
80	720	40	520	0	340
79	710	39	520	−1	340
78	710	38	510	−2	330
77	700	37	500	−3	330
76	700	36	500	−4	320
75	690	35	490	−5	320
74	690	34	480	−6	310
73	680	33	480	−7	310
72	680	32	480	−8	300
71	670	31	470	−9	300
70	670	30	470	−10	300
69	660	29	470	−11	290
68	660	28	460	−12	290
67	650	27	460	−13	280
66	650	26	450	−14	280
65	640	25	450	−15	270
64	640	24	450	−16	270
63	630	23	440	−17	260
62	630	22	440	−18	260
61	620	21	430	−19	250
60	620	20	430	−20	250
59	610	19	430	−21	240
58	610	18	420	−22	240
57	600	17	420	−23	240
56	600	16	420	−24	230
55	590	15	410	−25	230
54	590	14	410	−26	220
53	590	13	410	−27	220
52	580	12	400	−28	210
51	570	11	400	−29	210
50	570	10	400		
49	560	9	390		

take it with. A given raw score will correspond to different College Board scores, depending on the edition of the test taken. A raw score of 40, for example, may convert to a College Board score of 520 on one edition of the test, but that raw score might convert to a College Board score of 540 on a slightly more difficult edition. When you take the Spanish Achievement Test on the actual test day, your score is likely to differ somewhat from the score you obtained on this test. People perform at different levels at different times, for reasons unrelated to the test itself. The precision of any test is also limited because it represents only a sample of all the possible questions that could be asked. (See page 12, "How Precise Are Your Scores?" for further information.)

Reviewing Your Test Performance

After you have scored your test, you should take some time to consider the following points in relation to your performance on the test.

- *Did you run out of time before you reached the end of the test?*

  If you did, you may want to consider tactics that will help you pace yourself better. For example, you may have spent too much time working on one or two difficult questions. A better approach might have been to continue the test and return to those questions after you had attempted to answer the remaining questions on the test.

- *Did you take a long time reading the directions for the test?*

  The directions in this test are the same as those in the Spanish Achievement Tests now being administered. You will save time when you read the directions on the test day if you become thoroughly familiar with them in advance.

- *How did you handle questions you were unsure of?*

  If you were able to eliminate one or more of the answer choices and you guessed from the remaining choices, then your approach probably worked to your advantage. On the other hand, omitting questions about which you have some knowledge or guessing answers haphazardly would probably be a mistake.

- *How difficult were the questions for you compared with other students who took the test?*

  By referring to Table A on page 183 you can find out how difficult each question was for a selected sample of the students who took the test in May 1982. The right-hand column in the table tells you what percentage of that group of students answered the question correctly. It is important to remember that these percentages are based on only one group of students; had this edition of the test been given to all students in the class of 1983 who took a Spanish Achievement Test, the percentages would probably have been different. A question that was answered correctly by almost everyone in the group, obviously, is an easy question. Question 16, for example, was answered correctly by 98 percent of the students in the sample. On the other hand, question 63 was answered correctly by only 18 percent of the students. If you find that you missed several questions that would be considered easy, you may want to review those questions carefully. They may cover some aspect of the subject that you need to review. Perhaps you misunderstood the directions for one part of the test or you thought the questions were so easy that you didn't spend as much time on them as you might have.

About the American History and Social Studies Achievement Test

The American History and Social Studies Achievement Test is a one-hour test consisting of 95 to 100 multiple-choice questions. The principal focus of the test is American history from pre-Columbian times to the present, with a lesser emphasis on measurement of basic social science concepts, methods, and generalizations as they are encountered in the study of history and in the areas of political science and law, international relations, economics, sociology, anthropology, social psychology, and geography. Among the history questions, the great majority fall in the post-1763 period and cover the following historical fields: political, economic, social, diplomatic, intellectual, and cultural. The test content and approximate percentages of questions covering each historical field are given below.

Content of the Test

Material Covered	Approximate Percentage of Test
Political History (including Political Science and Law)	31-35
Economic History (including Geography)	15-19
Social History (including Sociology, Anthropology, and Social Psychology)	18-22
Foreign Policy (including International Relations)	18-22
Intellectual and Cultural History	8-12
Periods covered:	
Pre-Columbian History to 1763	8
1763 to 1900	35
1900 to the Present	40
Cross-Period	12
Nonchronological	5

Most of the questions in the test are based on material that is commonly taught in American history courses in secondary schools, although the material in some questions may also be covered in such courses as American government, economics, and problems of democracy. Thus, knowledge of the latter areas, gained from course work or from outside reading, could prove helpful. The only necessary preparation, however, is a sound course in American history at the college preparatory level. No one textbook or method of instruction is considered better than another. You can use a variety of approaches to content and chronology, including in-depth studies of limited topics, provided you do not ignore large historical periods and fundamental subject-matter areas.

Questions Used in the Test

The types of questions used in the test and the abilities they measure are described below. These abilities should not be thought of as mutually exclusive, since many questions test several abilities at the same time. Questions may be presented as separate items or in sets based on quotations, maps, pictures, graphs, or tables.

Directions: Each of the questions or incomplete statements below is followed by five suggested answers or completions. Select the one that is best in each case and then blacken the corresponding space on the answer sheet.

Some questions require you to know facts, terms, concepts, and generalizations. They test your recall of basic information about significant aspects of American history and the social studies. Question 1 is a sample of this type.

1. **During his term as President, Andrew Jackson did all of the following EXCEPT**

   (A) veto the recharter of the Second Bank of the United States

   (B) support the rights of the Cherokee Indians against the state of Georgia

   (C) veto a congressional appropriation for road building in the West

   (D) threaten to use federal troops to stop South Carolina's nullification of federal laws

   (E) support the spoils system in the distribution of federal offices

This question asks you to identify the exception in a series of otherwise true statements. Familiarity with the policies of the Jackson administration and knowledge of the President's support of Georgia in its defiance of the Supreme Court's decision on the land claims of the Cherokee Indians should lead you to (B), a statement that is not true, as the answer.

Questions posed in the negative, such as the one discussed above, occur quite frequently in the test, but never account for more than 25 percent of the test questions. Variations of this question format employ the capitalized words NOT or LEAST, as in the following examples: "Which of the following is NOT true?" "Which of the following is LEAST likely to occur?"

Some questions require you to analyze and interpret materials. Question 2, based on a quotation, is in this category. A few questions test both your ability to interpret introductory material and your ability to recall information related to the material, or to make inferences and interpolations based on the material. Questions 3 and 4 are illustrations of questions that test a combination of interpretation and recall.

2. "What is man born for but to be a reformer, a remaker of what man has made; a renouncer of lies; a restorer of truth and good, imitating that great Nature which embosoms us all, and which sleeps no moment on an old past, but every hour repairs herself, yielding every morning a new day, and with every pulsation a new life?"

These sentiments are most characteristic of

(A) fundamentalism

(B) Social Darwinism

(C) pragmatism

(D) neoorthodoxy

(E) transcendentalism

Several elements in the quotation suggest that choice (E) is the correct answer, without requiring you to know the source of the quotation. The emphasis that the quotation places on reform, on nature as a source of moral truth, and on the infinite possibilities open to man mark it as an example of the thought of the Transcendentalist movement. This combination of elements is not pertinent to any of the other choices.

Questions 3-4 refer to the following map.

3. The controversy with Great Britain over the northern boundary of the shaded section was settled during the presidency of

(A) John Quincy Adams

(B) James K. Polk

(C) Franklin Pierce

(D) James Buchanan

(E) Andrew Johnson

4. To the north of the area shown on the map is a continental territory purchased by Secretary of State William H. Seward from

(A) Great Britain

(B) Canada

(C) Russia

(D) France

(E) Spain

To answer question 3, you must interpret the map and recognize the shaded section as part of the Oregon territory. Since the Oregon dispute with Great Britain was settled during the presidency of James K. Polk, choice (B) is the correct answer.

To answer question 4, you must go beyond the content of the map in order to determine that the territory referred to in the question is Alaska. If you recall that Secretary of State Seward purchased the territory from Russia in 1867, you can choose the correct answer, (C).

Some questions require you to select or relate hypotheses, concepts, principles, or generalizations to given data. The questions may begin with concrete particulars and ask for the appropriate concept, or they may begin with a concept and apply it to particular problems or situations. Thus, you may need to use inductive and deductive reasoning. Questions 5 and 6 are examples of questions in this category.

5. From 1870 to 1930, the trend in industry was for hours to be generally reduced, while both money wages and real wages rose. What factor was primarily responsible for this trend?

(A) A reduction in profit margins

(B) Minimum wage laws

(C) Restriction of the labor supply

(D) Increased output per hour of work

(E) Right-to-work legislation

The best answer to this question is choice (D). To arrive at this answer, you must be aware that the trend referred to in the question came about primarily because of technological advances that resulted in increased productivity. None of the other answer choices satisfactorily accounts for all the conditions described in the question.

6. Which of the following wars of the United States would fit the description of a war neither lost nor won?

I. The War of 1812

II. The Mexican War

III. The Spanish-American War

IV. The Second World War

(A) I only

(B) II only

(C) I and III only

(D) II and IV only

(E) III and IV only

In answering question 6, you must recognize that a war not won, though not necessarily lost, is one in which a country either fails to achieve clear victory on the battlefield or fails to sign a peace treaty that is definitive and fulfills its goals. Only Roman numeral I, the War of 1812, is an illustration of the kind of war defined by the question. Thus, (A) is the best answer.

Some questions require you to judge the value of data for a given purpose, either assessing by internal evidence, such as proof and logical consistency, or by external criteria, such as comparison with other works, established standards, and theories. Question 7 is an illustration of this kind of question.

7. Some historians have described the United States in the 1790's as a "developing" or "emerging" nation with conditions similar to those in Third World nations that gained their independence after the Second World War. Which of the following elements in United States history in the 1790's does NOT support this concept?

(A) America's division into separate regions with often conflicting interests

(B) America's efforts to remain neutral during the wars in Europe

(C) Americans' attempts to establish a "national" culture in which they could take pride

(D) The nation's shortage of capital for investments

(E) America's possession of a literacy rate higher than that of Europe

In answering this question, you must be able to eliminate from consideration choices that fail to differentiate between the experience of the young American republic and the experiences of the Third World nations that emerged following the Second World War. With the exception of (E), the correct answer, all the choices fall into this category: (A), (C), and (D) describe conditions in the America of the 1790's that were later paralleled in the new Third World nations, and (B) describes an early American policy of neutrality similar to the policy adopted by newly independent Third World countries in their earliest years. In contrast, (E) describes a condition in the newly independent United States not typically found in newly independent Third World nations.

American History and Social Studies Achievement Test

The test that follows is an edition of the American History and Social Studies Achievement Test administered in November 1982. So that you will have an idea of what the actual test administration will be like, try to take this test under conditions as close as possible to those of the actual test. It will probably help if you

- Set aside an hour for the test when you will not be interrupted, so that you can complete all of it in one sitting.

- Sit at a desk with no other papers or books. You can't take a calculator, a dictionary, other books, or notes into the test room.

- Have a kitchen timer or clock in front of you for timing yourself.

- Tear out an answer sheet from the back of this book and fill it in just as you would on the day of the test. You can use one answer sheet for as many as three Achievement Tests.

- Read the instructions that precede the test. When you take the test, you will be asked to read them before you begin answering questions.

- After you finish the test, read the sections on "How to Score the American History and Social Studies Achievement Test," and "Reviewing Your Test Performance," which follow the test.

AMERICAN HISTORY AND SOCIAL STUDIES TEST

The top portion of the section of the answer sheet which you will use in taking the American History and Social Studies test must be filled in exactly as shown in the illustration below. Note carefully that you have to do all of the following on your answer sheet:

1. Print AMERICAN HISTORY AND SOCIAL STUDIES on the line to the right of the words "Achievement Test."

2. Blacken spaces 2 and 0 in the row of spaces immediately under the words "Test Code."

3. Blacken space 5 in the group of five spaces labeled X.

4. Blacken space 3 in the group of five spaces labeled Y.

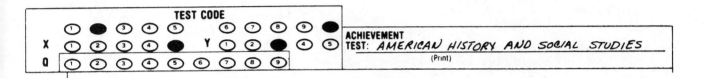

You are to leave blank the nine spaces which are labeled Q.

When the supervisor gives the signal, turn the page and begin the American History and Social Studies test. There are 100 numbered spaces on the answer sheet and 95 questions in the American History and Social Studies test. Therefore, use only spaces 1 to 95 for recording your answers.

AMERICAN HISTORY AND SOCIAL STUDIES TEST

<u>Directions</u>: Each of the questions or incomplete statements below is followed by five suggested answers or completions. Select the one that is best in each case and then blacken the corresponding space on the answer sheet.

1. The Stamp Act of 1765 was designed to
   (A) increase colonial postal rates
   (B) establish a colonial mint to stamp out silver coins
   (C) facilitate British postal censorship of colonial mails
   (D) establish a colonial postal service
   (E) increase British tax revenues from the colonies

2. The French government supported the American Revolution primarily because
   (A) there was general support for the political ideals of the Enlightenment in France
   (B) an American victory would enable France to recapture Canada
   (C) Benjamin Franklin and his scientific achievements inspired the admiration of the French
   (D) France wished to reduce the British empire and gain influence in North America
   (E) France's ally Spain was eager to recapture Gibraltar from Britain

3. At the 1787 Constitutional Convention, the members rejected a proposal that the President should have the power to declare war and instead voted to give that power to Congress. In actuality, the result of this decision has been to
   (A) make Congress more influential than the President in the conduct of American foreign policy
   (B) allow Congress to override a presidential veto of a declaration of war
   (C) make it impossible for the President to commit the nation to war when he has wanted to do so
   (D) create a deadlock between the President and Congress that has had to be broken by Supreme Court decisions
   (E) enable Congress to declare war, but only after the President has taken the initiative to ask Congress to do so

4. The direct economic and social consequences of the American Revolution included all of the following EXCEPT
   (A) expanded opportunities for settlement in the West
   (B) reforms in laws of inheritance
   (C) increased property holding rights for women
   (D) new opportunities for trade and manufacturing
   (E) confiscation of Loyalist property

5. The factory system of manufacturing was first applied in early nineteenth-century New England to the production of
   (A) textiles   (B) plows   (C) steel
   (D) clocks   (E) shoes

6. The Erie Canal linked New York to which of the following areas?
   (A) Delaware River
   (B) Great Lakes
   (C) Rio Grande-Sabine River
   (D) Missouri River
   (E) Potomac River-James River

7. Which of the following religious groups moved west during the first half of the nineteenth century to secure religious freedom?
   (A) Mormons
   (B) Unitarians
   (C) Presbyterians
   (D) Christian Scientists
   (E) Quakers

8. Social Darwinists believed that
   (A) there should be public ownership of the means of production
   (B) all men are created equal
   (C) society evolves in a cyclical fashion
   (D) man could, with proper effort, recover from any adversity in life
   (E) the theory of survival of the fittest explains individual success or failure in society

GO ON TO THE NEXT PAGE

9. Which of the following would most probably provide the widest range of information for a historian wishing to analyze the social composition of an American city in the 1880's?

(A) The minutes of the city council
(B) A debutante's diary
(C) A manuscript census tabulating the residence, ethnicity, occupation, and wealth of each city resident
(D) Precinct-level voting returns in a closely contested mayoral election held in a presidential election year
(E) A survey of slum housing conditions carried out by a Social Gospel minister in the year following several epidemics

10. Which of the following was NOT a characteristic of American industrialization between 1840 and 1920?

(A) Production increasingly by machines rather than by hand
(B) Production increasingly located in large, systematically organized factories
(C) Heavy dependence on foreign raw materials
(D) Accelerated technological innovation with emphasis on new inventions and applied science
(E) Enlarged markets stretching beyond local and regional limits

11.   AMERICAN FOREIGN TRADE, 1900-1920
            (in millions of dollars)

	Export	Import
1900	$1,499	$ 930
1905	1,660	1,199
1910	1,919	1,646
1915	2,966	1,875
1920	8,664	5,784

The table above shows which of the following for the period between 1900 and 1920?

(A) The United States was losing its industrial predominance in the world economy.
(B) The United States had a favorable trade balance.
(C) There was an excess of foreign investments in the United States.
(D) Farmers opposed the expansion of markets abroad.
(E) American merchants were becoming complacent in their competition with foreign merchants.

12. Major American writers of the 1930's generally concentrated on themes relating to which of the following?

(A) Collegiate life during the Jazz Age
(B) American expatriates in Europe
(C) The quest for religious truth
(D) Social problems and inequities
(E) An appreciation of nature

13. The Great Depression of the 1930's contributed LEAST to which of the following?

(A) Emergence of the Democratic party as the majority party
(B) Establishment of federal aid and support programs for agriculture
(C) Desegregation of federal facilities
(D) Unionization of mass production industries
(E) Establishment of a social security system

14. Which of the following Presidents reversed a long-standing foreign policy of the United States toward the People's Republic of China?

(A) Richard M. Nixon
(B) John F. Kennedy
(C) Lyndon B. Johnson
(D) Dwight D. Eisenhower
(E) Harry S. Truman

GO ON TO THE NEXT PAGE

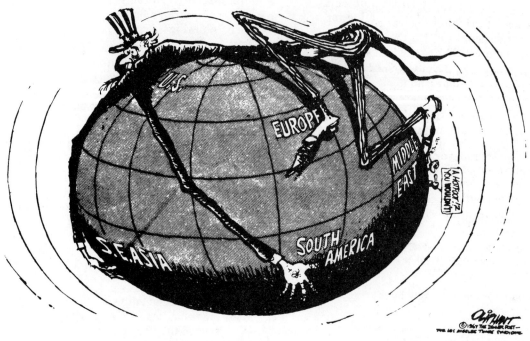

Reprinted by permission of Oliphant/1981.

15. Which of the following best summarizes the idea
expressed in the 1967 cartoon above?

(A) In order to win the world's respect, the
United States should behave in a more
dignified manner.

(B) The world regards the United States far-
flung aid programs as futile and
pointless.

(C) The United States should use military
power rather than economic and diplomatic methods to resolve international
problems.

(D) The United States should reduce its excessive consumption of the world's
resources.

(E) The United States should avoid involve-
ment in too many world problems at
once.

GO ON TO THE NEXT PAGE ➤

16. According to a current widely accepted hypothesis, which of the following was common to all of the native peoples of North and South America before 1492 ?

    (A) Accurate astronomical calendars
    (B) Domestication of wild horses
    (C) Rotation of agricultural crops
    (D) Descent from Asian peoples
    (E) Mining of gold and silver

17. In the creation of which of the following colonies was commercial profit the first and foremost motive?

    (A) Connecticut
    (B) Maryland
    (C) Virginia
    (D) Pennsylvania
    (E) Rhode Island

18. Great Britain's conquest of French North America was facilitated by which of the following?

    (A) The large number of English-speaking settlers in Canada
    (B) The discovery of the Northwest Passage
    (C) The thin settlement of France's North American colonies
    (D) The munitions industry in England's Atlantic Seaboard colonies
    (E) The Battle of Austerlitz

19. Which of the following statements represents a major theme in George Washington's 1796 farewell address?

    (A) The United States must free all slaves without delay.
    (B) The true interest of the United States is to steer clear of permanent alliances with foreign powers.
    (C) The practice of democracy must be strengthened by granting women suffrage with all deliberate speed.
    (D) It is imperative that the United States repair its differences with England immediately and forge an Anglo-American alliance.
    (E) The newly formed United States must ally itself closely with France, its only friend among the powers of Europe.

20. Benjamin Franklin's advice to eighteenth-century American colonists that hard work and thrift would lead them to wealth was an appropriate formula for the time because

    (A) taxes on income were needed by the government to raise revenues
    (B) land scarcity and a rapidly growing population seriously curtailed economic opportunities
    (C) most people of the period were unusually gullible and thus easily motivated by slogans and proverbs
    (D) formal education and specialized skills were less necessary to economic success than they would later become
    (E) legal restraints on the inheritance of wealth were increasing

21. The purpose of the Monroe Doctrine was to

    (A) stop revolutions in Latin America
    (B) win the presidential election of 1824
    (C) discredit the Federalist party, which supported Latin American revolutionaries
    (D) warn Russia, France, and Spain against further colonization or intervention in the New World
    (E) form close political ties with Simón Bolívar and other Latin American revolutionaries

22. Which of the following is true about the failure to recharter the Second Bank of the United States?

    (A) It was a political defeat for Andrew Jackson.
    (B) It was caused by British intervention.
    (C) It led to a growth in state-chartered banks.
    (D) It was followed immediately by falling prices in the United States.
    (E) It meant that the United States went off the gold standard.

GO ON TO THE NEXT PAGE →

23.

POPULAR VOTE FOR PRESIDENTIAL ELECTORS, GEORGIA, 1848 AND 1852

	Democratic Electors	Whig Electors	Webster Electors
1848	44,809	47,538	-----
1852	40,516	16,660	5,324

Using the table above, one might conclude that the most plausible explanation for the Georgia Democrats' victory in 1852 following their defeat in 1848 was that

(A) many new voters increased the turnout in 1852, to the advantage of the Democrats
(B) many voters abstained from voting in 1852, to the disadvantage of the Whigs
(C) Webster, who had not run in 1848, drew sufficient votes from the Whigs to cost them the election of 1852
(D) the Democrats, who had run a highly unpopular candidate in 1848, ran a highly popular candidate in 1852
(E) the Democrats cast fraudulent ballots to increase their share of the votes in 1852

---

24. "Manifest Destiny" was a slogan that referred to the

(A) ultimate triumph of the "fittest" in the progress of industrial capitalism
(B) eventual overthrow of slavery under God's design
(C) right of United States vessels to trade without interference anywhere in the world
(D) territorial expansion of the United States in North America
(E) eventual domination of slavery over the territories acquired from Mexico

25. The United States policy toward China at the turn of the century was expressed in the

(A) Open Door policy
(B) Gentlemen's Agreement
(C) Good Neighbor policy
(D) Lend-Lease Act
(E) Marshall Plan

26. Which of the following was an important factor in the American decision to enter the First World War?

(A) The Bolshevik Revolution in Russia
(B) German submarine operations in the Atlantic Ocean
(C) Formation of a German-Japanese alliance directed against the United States
(D) The outbreak of revolution in Mexico
(E) The German conquest of France

27. John T. Scopes was

(A) an anarchist accused of inciting the 1886 Haymarket bombing in Chicago
(B) the assassin of President James A. Garfield
(C) a teacher tried for discussing evolution in a Tennessee public school
(D) a character in a novel by William Faulkner
(E) an immigrant anarchist tried and executed on a murder and robbery charge in Massachusetts in the 1920's

GO ON TO THE NEXT PAGE →

28. The only amendment to the United States Constitution that has been repealed dealt with

    (A) the manufacture and sale of alcoholic beverages
    (B) prayer in public schools
    (C) the voting rights of Blacks
    (D) draft exemption for conscientious objectors
    (E) the federal income tax

29. The Works Progress Administration (WPA), established during the administration of Franklin D. Roosevelt, was the federal agency empowered to

    (A) protect employees from unfair labor practices
    (B) provide financial aid to western farmers suffering from low grain prices
    (C) provide aid to dependent children
    (D) investigate charges of discrimination against women in job hiring practices
    (E) provide jobs for the unemployed

30. Through the direct primary, voters have the right to

    (A) vote for potential party nominees
    (B) select delegates to the electoral college
    (C) initiate new legislation
    (D) approve or disapprove laws passed by legislative bodies
    (E) remove office holders

31. Since 1950, criticism of the method of electing American Presidents has focused on which of the following?

    (A) The electorate's lack of firm commitments to candidates
    (B) Overemphasis on the importance of minor candidates
    (C) The resolution of electoral deadlocks in the Senate
    (D) The winner-take-all aspect of the electoral college system
    (E) The relative lack of influence of the large states in deciding electoral outcomes

32. A person in the United States charged with murder should be convicted only if

    (A) he fails to prove his innocence
    (B) the prosecution proves his guilt beyond a reasonable doubt
    (C) the judge decides that he is guilty
    (D) he is arrested at the scene of the crime
    (E) at least one eyewitness to the crime identifies him as the guilty party

33. A central objective of the early New England Puritan leadership was to

    (A) establish religious liberty for all
    (B) eliminate the use of alcohol and tobacco
    (C) eliminate any distinction between church and state
    (D) reproduce the ecclesiastical structure of the Church of England
    (E) establish the moral authority of the community over individual self-interest

GO ON TO THE NEXT PAGE

THE GEOGRAPHY OF WITCHCRAFT : SALEM VILLAGE, 1692

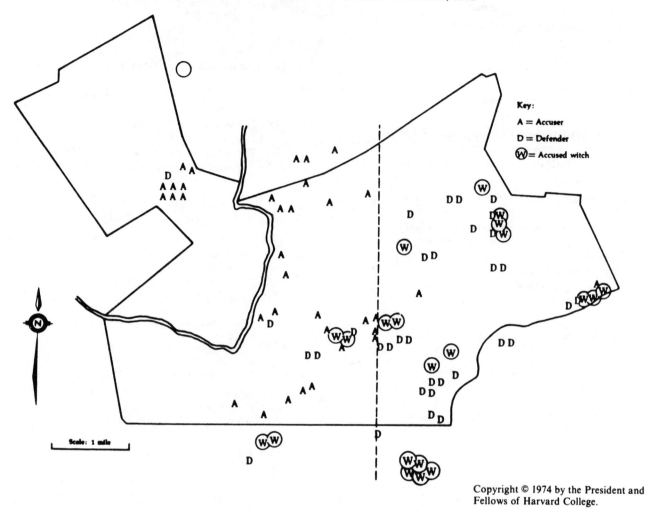

34. The map above is consistent with all of the following conclusions EXCEPT:

(A) The Salem witchcraft trials contributed to the enmity between persons of the east side of the village and persons on the west side of the village.

(B) Those persons who lived farthest from the village's geographic center were the ones who were most frequently accused of being witches.

(C) Accusers were more likely than defenders to be the close neighbors of accused witches.

(D) The majority of the persons from Salem Village who were accused of witchcraft lived on the east side of the village and the majority of accusers from the village lived on the west side.

(E) Some people were accused of witchcraft in spite of the efforts of their closest neighbors to defend them.

GO ON TO THE NEXT PAGE

35. An important factor in the creation of sectional differences among the English colonies in North America was the

    (A) wide variation in climate and geography among the colonies
    (B) strong opposition to slavery in the northern colonies
    (C) existence of large Catholic populations in some colonies
    (D) adherence of some colonies to the mercantile system
    (E) close political ties of the middle colonies to England

36. "But what do We mean by the American Revolution? Do we mean the American War? The Revolution was effected before the War commenced. The Revolution was in the Minds and Hearts of the People. A Change in their Religious Sentiments of their Duties and Obligations. While the King, and all in Authority under him, were believed to govern, in Justice and Mercy according to the Laws and Constitutions derived to them from the God of Nature, and transmitted to them by their Ancestors: they thought themselves bound to pray for the King and Queen and all the Royal Family, and all the Authority under them, as Ministers ordained of God for their good. But when they saw those Powers renouncing all the Principles of Authority, and bent upon the destruction of all the Securities of their Lives, Liberties and Properties, they thought it their Duty to pray for the Continental Congress and all the thirteen State Congresses, &c."

    In this extract from an 1818 letter reflecting on the American Revolution, John Adams' central point is that

    (A) the Revolution involved an intellectual and emotional component that preceded the military one
    (B) the Revolutionary War had a deep influence on the religious life of Americans
    (C) the American revolutionary leadership tried to focus popular hostility against the British Crown, rather than against Parliament
    (D) in the years before the Revolution, the British authorities flagrantly violated the rights and security of the American colonists
    (E) Americans always pray for the welfare of their political leaders, whoever they may be

37. Which of the following statements is most likely to have been made by an eighteenth-century Deist?

    (A) God cares about us and listens to our prayers.
    (B) We can discover the laws of God by studying the laws of Nature.
    (C) God has already decided who will be saved and who will be damned.
    (D) God is a figment of the imagination.
    (E) We can become holy by atoning for our sins.

38. American fur traders in the Trans-Mississippi West can be characterized as all of the following EXCEPT

    (A) adventurers who lived a rugged life of freedom amid the wilderness
    (B) people who, frequently with the help of Native American (Indian) guides, explored the trails, mountain passes, and rivers of the Trans-Mississippi West
    (C) frontiersmen who eased the way for the pioneers by establishing relations with Native American (Indian) tribes
    (D) advance scouts who extended American influence into regions contested by Spain and England
    (E) investors whose capital was crucial to the establishment of the ranching and mining industries

GO ON TO THE NEXT PAGE

BORN TO COMMAND

OF VETO MEMORY

HAD I BEEN CONSULTED.

KING ANDREW THE FIRST.

Courtesy of The New-York Historical Society.

39. The point of view expressed by this cartoon probably would have met with the approval of

(A) Daniel Webster
(B) James K. Polk
(C) Martin Van Buren
(D) Roger B. Taney
(E) Stephen A. Douglas

40. The works of America's major novelists and poets in the 1830's and 1840's reflected all of the following EXCEPT

(A) a concern with nature
(B) a desire to create a distinctly American culture
(C) transcendental philosophy
(D) an acute sense of human limitation
(E) a preoccupation with moral and spiritual questions

41. The chief factor delaying the annexation of Texas for nearly ten years was the

(A) danger of upsetting the negotiations for Oregon
(B) opposition of the antislavery forces
(C) insufficient population for Texas to qualify for statehood
(D) set of terms insisted on by the Texans
(E) problem posed by Mexican-owned California, which the United States also coveted

42. All of the following were economic and social consequences of the building of a national railway network EXCEPT the

(A) settlement of the Western plains
(B) encouragement of industrial growth in the Great Lakes region
(C) creation of the cotton textile industry in New England
(D) decline of canals and canal traffic
(E) rise of discontent among Western and Southern farmers toward business monopolies

43. "We demand a graduated income tax."

". . . the government should own and operate the railroads in the interest of the people."

"We demand a national currency, safe, sound and flexible, issued by the [federal] government."

These statements best reflect the views of the

(A) People's (Populist) party
(B) States' Rights party
(C) Know-Nothing party
(D) Progressive (Bull Moose) party
(E) Whig party

44. Which of the following novels had the greatest significance in arousing public interest in the need for a major social reform?

(A) *Huckleberry Finn*
(B) *Gone with the Wind*
(C) *The Scarlet Letter*
(D) *The Jungle*
(E) *All the King's Men*

GO ON TO THE NEXT PAGE

AMERICAN HISTORY AND SOCIAL STUDIES TEST—*Continued*

45. One reason why Woodrow Wilson won the United States presidential election in 1912 was that

    (A) the Socialist party supported the Democrats
    (B) an economic depression made Republicans unpopular
    (C) the Republican party divided its vote between two candidates
    (D) he promised to keep the nation out of any foreign wars
    (E) he received the political support of Theodore Roosevelt

46. The work of the "lost generation" of American writers in the 1920's was marked by

    (A) a rejection of prevailing middle-class values
    (B) extreme prudishness and morality
    (C) a glorification of God and country
    (D) an obvious desire to keep things as they were
    (E) an attempt to re-create the values of the pre-World War era

47. In 1936 a group of unions left the American Federation of Labor (AFL) and formed a new labor organization, the Congress of Industrial Organizations (CIO). Which of the following was the major issue that divided union leaders and brought about this split in the ranks of organized labor?

    (A) The CIO leaders favored the organization of all workers in a particular industry into a single union, whereas the AFL leaders favored organization of workers according to their skills or trades.
    (B) The AFL leaders felt that because of the depression labor should make no wage demands, whereas the CIO leaders favored militant activity to raise wages.
    (C) The AFL leaders favored giving active support to the Republican Party whereas the CIO leaders supported the Democrats.
    (D) The CIO leaders were far more radical than the AFL leaders, favoring government ownership of public utilities, the railroads, and the armament industries, and strict government regulation and control of big business.
    (E) The CIO leaders favored the creation of a new labor party in politics, whereas the AFL leaders wanted to eliminate labor involvement in politics altogether.

48. Which of the following statements best describes the attitude of most Americans toward the outbreak of the Second World War in Europe?

    (A) Americans were unconcerned about world politics and indifferent to which side won the war.
    (B) Americans were determined to avoid military involvement in the war.
    (C) Americans were outraged by the Axis powers and willing to use any excuse to go to war against them.
    (D) Americans wanted to sell all possible supplies and equipment on easy terms to both sides to end the Great Depression.
    (E) Americans wanted to remain out of the war until both sides exhausted each other and then enter the war to dictate peace terms.

49. During the quarter century after the Second World War, the populations of many large cities, such as Boston, Pittsburgh, Cleveland, Detroit, and St. Louis, decreased because

    (A) the death rates rose in the cities
    (B) new, independent towns were formed within the city limits
    (C) large numbers of people moved from the cities to the suburbs
    (D) census takers made errors on earlier counts
    (E) disastrous floods forced many people to leave the cities

50. All of the following usually take place at national political party conventions EXCEPT

    (A) nomination of a party presidential candidate
    (B) formal seating of delegates
    (C) approval of the party platform
    (D) election of state party chairmen
    (E) selection of a vice-presidential candidate

51. If a nation's foreign policy is based on balance-of-power politics, which of the following would be a necessary element of that foreign policy?

    (A) Economic self-sufficiency
    (B) The involvement of citizens' groups
    (C) Political isolationism
    (D) Religious idealism
    (E) Military force

GO ON TO THE NEXT PAGE

52. The initiative, referendum, and recall were intended primarily to

    (A) make politics at the state and local level more immediately responsive to popular opinion
    (B) speed the flow of legislation through Congress
    (C) strengthen the independence of office-holders
    (D) eliminate partisan influence over the federal courts
    (E) enable minority groups to have a more effective voice in national politics

53. The United States Constitution provides for all of the following EXCEPT

    (A) separation of powers
    (B) federalism
    (C) limited government
    (D) representative government
    (E) political parties

54. For which of the following reasons was the War of 1812 viewed as a "second war of independence" by many Americans?

    (A) Britain accepted the Monroe Doctrine.
    (B) Francis Scott Key wrote "The Star-spangled Banner."
    (C) European monarchs recognized the independence of new Latin American republics.
    (D) Although British forces had many military successes, the United States proved able to defend itself against a world power.
    (E) The war contributed to Napoleon's defeat at Waterloo.

55. The Missouri Compromise, the Wilmot Proviso, the Compromise of 1850, and the Kansas-Nebraska Act all involved which of the following issues?

    (A) The return of fugitive slaves
    (B) The underground railroad
    (C) The transcontinental railroad
    (D) The expansion of slavery in the West
    (E) The distribution of western lands

56. Which of the following factors was most responsible for the spread of slavery across the south central region of the United States during the period 1800-1860 ?

    (A) Competition between Northerners and Southerners for control of the Congress
    (B) Improved methods of overland and water-borne transportation
    (C) International demand for tobacco
    (D) Low prices of slaves due to increasing imports of slaves from Africa
    (E) International demand for cotton

57. The concept of the "noble savage" was reflected in the novels of

    (A) Washington Irving
    (B) James Fenimore Cooper
    (C) Nathaniel Hawthorne
    (D) Mark Twain
    (E) Frank Norris

58. Many Southern slave owners and proslavery leaders advocated training slaves to be artisans for all of the following reasons EXCEPT:

    (A) The value of slaves at sale would be increased.
    (B) The earnings of slaves put out to hire would be increased.
    (C) Slaves could be kept at productive work between harvest and planting time.
    (D) Slaves hired out to townspeople would be more closely supervised than those on the plantations.
    (E) Plantations could be made more economically self-sufficient.

59. Which of the following was true of the Socialist party of America during the period 1900-1918 ?

    (A) It advocated reforms which in many instances were subsequently espoused by the two major parties.
    (B) It gave women and Blacks positions of primary responsibility in the national party leadership.
    (C) It induced the American Federation of Labor to pursue a policy of industrial unionism.
    (D) It supported unanimously the entry of the United States into the First World War.
    (E) It led the fight for the adoption of the prohibition amendment in such cities as Milwaukee and St. Louis.

GO ON TO THE NEXT PAGE

60. Most of the immigrants who came to the United States between 1880 and 1920 were from

 (A) Northern and Western Europe
 (B) China and Japan
 (C) Ireland
 (D) Latin America
 (E) Southern and Eastern Europe

61. Which of the following was NOT a factor in the declining public significance of the organized feminist movement in the 1920's ?

 (A) The successful conclusion of the campaign for women's suffrage
 (B) The consequences of changing manners and morality
 (C) Dissension among women's groups concerning goals
 (D) Declining prominence of the Progressive reform movement
 (E) Passage of legislation requiring that women receive equal pay for equal work

62. Which of the following was a significant development in the United States during the 1920's?

 (A) The reduction of tariff barriers
 (B) The rapid growth of unions
 (C) The widespread purchase of common stock
 (D) Abandonment of the gold standard
 (E) Federal legislation governing wages and hours

63. In terms of relative voter support the most successful third-party movement in twentieth-century America was the

 (A) Progressive party of 1912
 (B) Socialist party of 1920
 (C) Union party of 1936
 (D) Progressive party of 1948
 (E) American party of 1968

64. Which of the following has traditionally been most effective in limiting presidential power?

 (A) The military forces
 (B) Senate filibusters
 (C) The national committees of the major political parties
 (D) Key congressional committees
 (E) Members of the cabinet

65. The victories of Dwight D. Eisenhower in the presidential elections of 1952 and 1956 are best explained as the

 (A) result of a new and lasting shift in party allegiances
 (B) personal triumphs of an attractive candidate
 (C) result of a large-scale return of Blacks to the Republican party
 (D) result of reforms that modernized the Republican party
 (E) political by-product of McCarthyism

66. During the 1950's and 1960's, the term "containment" was used in reference to the United States government's policy of

 (A) preventing the further spread of communism abroad
 (B) controlling inflation by using price controls
 (C) restraining the international arms race
 (D) checking the flow of drugs into the United States
 (E) curbing the flow of United States dollars to other countries

67. In the United States the power to regulate business and trade is

 (A) reserved to the national government
 (B) reserved to the state governments
 (C) denied to both the state and national governments
 (D) shared by the state and national governments
 (E) reserved to private business

GO ON TO THE NEXT PAGE

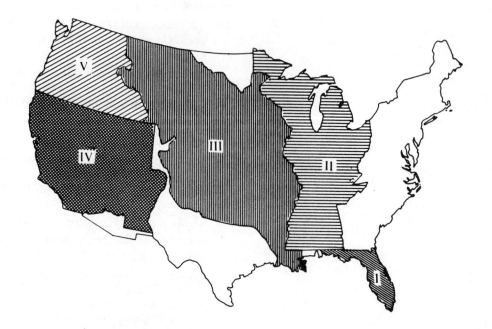

I.   Florida
II. Area bounded by the Appalachians and the Mississippi
III. Louisiana Purchase
IV. Mexican Cession
V.   Oregon Territory

68. Which of the following is true about United States acquisition of the territories shown in the map above?

   (A) V was purchased from Russia by Secretary of State William Seward.
   (B) I and II were won from Great Britain in the American Revolution.
   (C) I and III were purchased from Spain.
   (D) I and IV were ceded by Mexico.
   (E) II and IV were won by force of arms.

---

69. Which of the following was LEAST characteristic of the attitudes of Westerners during the years from 1830 to 1860 ?

   (A) Opposition to credit control by a central bank
   (B) Strong support for a liberal public land policy
   (C) Support for national policies of territorial expansion
   (D) Opposition to internal improvements at federal expense
   (E) Strong support for Native American (Indian) removal measures

70. An important consideration in Lincoln's decision to issue the Emancipation Proclamation was his

   (A) opposition on constitutional grounds to the continuation of slavery in the Southern states
   (B) hope that emancipation would rally anti-slavery opinion both at home and abroad to the Union cause
   (C) hope that the slave states of the Deep South would not secede
   (D) wish to quiet the Copperheads in the North who were demanding the end of the Union's war against the Confederacy
   (E) hope that it would bolster the position of the moderates within the Confederate government

GO ON TO THE NEXT PAGE

71. The book *A Century of Dishonor*, written by Helen Hunt Jackson and published in 1881, won wide fame by denouncing

    (A) continued exploitation of the South by Northern businessmen
    (B) the failure of state and federal governments to grant women the right to vote
    (C) federal policy toward Native Americans (Indians)
    (D) American foreign policy in Latin America
    (E) monopolistic tactics of railroads

72. Which of the following factors was NOT involved in the rise of political machines in nineteenth-century American cities?

    (A) The gap between the need for social services and the willingness of city governments to provide them
    (B) The increasing proportion of immigrant residents in American cities
    (C) Construction of public works on an unprecedented scale
    (D) The limitation of suffrage to property owners
    (E) The desire of numerous urban residents to circumvent legal restrictions on gambling and the sale of alcohol

73. Which of the following reforms was LEAST frequently advocated during the Progressive Era?

    (A) Direct election of United States senators
    (B) Factory inspection laws
    (C) The use of the initiative and the referendum
    (D) Prosecution of trusts
    (E) Laws prohibiting racial discrimination

74. Prior to ratification of the Nineteenth Amendment to the United States Constitution, women could vote in

    (A) states that had granted them the right to do so
    (B) no state
    (C) all states
    (D) national elections only
    (E) state and local elections only

75. The federal statute that declared illegal "every contract, combination in the form of trust, or otherwise, or conspiracy in restraint of trade among the several states" was the

    (A) Sherman Act
    (B) Taft-Hartley Act
    (C) Wagner Act
    (D) Norris-La Guardia Act
    (E) Landrum-Griffin Act

76. The "clear and present danger" doctrine, adopted unanimously by the United States Supreme Court in 1919, declared that

    (A) the formation of the American Communist party was illegal because it constituted a "clear and present danger" to the security of the United States
    (B) the federal government may restrict the expression of ideas that tend to place the nation's security in imminent danger
    (C) the war danger having passed, governmental restrictions on freedom of speech and press were unconstitutional
    (D) governmental restrictions on freedom of speech and press comprised a "clear and present danger" to the liberties guaranteed by the First Amendment
    (E) constitutional guarantees of due process of law could legally be suspended in wartime

77. Garveyism was identified with all of the following EXCEPT

    (A) Pan-Africanism
    (B) Black nationalism
    (C) racial integration
    (D) Black economic development
    (E) Black pride

78. Which of the following accounts for the fact that in the United States in the 1920's real income per person increased despite the growth in population and the decline in hours worked?

    (A) Lowering of tariff barriers
    (B) The development of the corporate holding company
    (C) The growth of viable trade unions
    (D) The development of a sound banking system
    (E) Rapid technological advances

GO ON TO THE NEXT PAGE

79. As a leader of the civil rights movement, Martin Luther King, Jr., based his doctrine of non-violence on the teachings of

    (A) Billy Graham
    (B) Bertrand Russell
    (C) Albert Schweitzer
    (D) Mohandas Gandhi
    (E) Norman Thomas

80. The isolationist tradition in United States foreign policy can best be characterized as

    (A) total avoidance of involvement with other nations
    (B) avoidance of economic and political but not cultural involvement
    (C) avoidance of cultural and economic but not political involvement
    (D) rhetorical avoidance of involvement with other nations but covert political, economic, and cultural dealings
    (E) avoidance of political but not cultural or economic involvement

81. At the close of 1941, which of the following had NOT been occupied or invaded by the Japanese army?

    (A) French Indochina
    (B) Manchuria
    (C) Hong Kong
    (D) The Philippines
    (E) Pearl Harbor

82. A central figure in the investigations of alleged domestic communist influence during the 1950's was

    (A) Senator Eugene McCarthy
    (B) Senator Joseph McCarthy
    (C) General Douglas MacArthur
    (D) Senator Robert A. Taft
    (E) General George C. Marshall

83. Which of the following cases was NOT among the decisions of the Supreme Court during the term of Chief Justice Earl Warren?

    (A) *Plessy* v. *Ferguson*
    (B) *Miranda* v. *Arizona*
    (C) *Baker* v. *Carr*
    (D) *Gideon* v. *Wainwright*
    (E) *Brown* v. *Board of Education of Topeka*

84. All of the following policies were advocated by Alexander Hamilton EXCEPT

    (A) funding of the foreign and domestic debt at par
    (B) assumption by the federal government of debts incurred by states during the Revolution
    (C) encouragement of manufactures
    (D) sale of the public domain on terms that would encourage the settlement of the West
    (E) establishment of a Bank of the United States

85. "If Reason is a universal faculty, the universal decision of the masses is the nearest criterion of truth. The common mind winnows opinions; it is the sieve which separates error from certainty. . . .

    The passage above best reflects the political philosophy of which of the following?

    (A) Jacksonian Democrats
    (B) Federalists
    (C) Liberty party
    (D) Whigs
    (E) Mugwumps

86. Pre-Civil War reformers were active in all of the following causes EXCEPT

    (A) public education (B) temperance
     (C) minimum wage laws (D) women's rights
      (E) prison reform

87. The term "Radical Reconstruction" refers to

    (A) Abraham Lincoln's plan to restore the Confederate States to the Union
    (B) the program for the former Confederate States associated with Republicans led by Charles Sumner and Thaddeus Stevens
    (C) the federal policies put into effect by Andrew Johnson immediately after the Civil War
    (D) the implementation of the Thirteenth Amendment after the Civil War
    (E) the restoration of white conservative rule in the South after 1877

GO ON TO THE NEXT PAGE

88. Which of the following has NOT been suggested by historians as an explanation for the development of American imperialism in the 1890's ?

    (A) The search for markets and raw materials by business
    (B) Pressure for military action by a growing officer corps in the army
    (C) The example of European colonial powers in Asia and Africa
    (D) Support for the idea of the "White Man's Burden"
    (E) Competition for newspaper readership by the "yellow press"

89. Historian Frederick Jackson Turner asserted that the frontier was important in American history for which of the following reasons?

    I. It helped shape a distinctive American character.
    II. It enabled Eastern factory workers to escape bad economic conditions.
    III. It helped stimulate nationalism and individualism.

    (A) I only (B) II only (C) I and II only
    (D) II and III only (E) I, II, and III

90. The emergence of Black writers and artists in the Harlem Renaissance took place during the

    (A) 1860's
    (B) 1870's
    (C) 1890's
    (D) 1920's
    (E) 1930's

91. In the 1920's, the number of Mexicans and Puerto Ricans migrating to the continental United States increased. One reason for this was that

    (A) their transportation from home was subsidized by the United States government
    (B) they were accepted into unions whose members worked in sectors of the economy experiencing labor shortages
    (C) White Protestant Americans dropped their prejudices against people from Hispanic cultures
    (D) they wished to escape recurrent epidemics that were decimating their home populations
    (E) neither group was affected by the restrictive immigration acts of 1921 and 1924

92. The Employment Act of 1946 made the achievement of maximum employment a national economic goal. This goal was to be achieved primarily through

    (A) appropriate spending and taxing policies
    (B) subsidization of American exports
    (C) action against costly wage rates
    (D) a tariff-protected national economic development program
    (E) restrictions on the use of laborsaving machinery

93. The United States agreement to the North Atlantic Treaty of 1949 did which of the following?

    (A) Reaffirmed the Good Neighbor policy.
    (B) Marked a sharp departure from traditional American foreign policy.
    (C) Weakened the Truman Doctrine.
    (D) Weakened the Marshall Plan.
    (E) Appealed to American isolationists.

94. During the twentieth century the United States has intervened with its armed forces in all of the following EXCEPT

    (A) the Dominican Republic
    (B) Mexico
    (C) Cuba
    (D) China
    (E) South Africa

95. In 1965 President Lyndon B. Johnson introduced new civil rights legislation designed to

    (A) grant equal rights to women
    (B) guarantee equal access to housing by persons of all races
    (C) protect the voting rights of Southern Blacks
    (D) force universities to establish affirmative action programs
    (E) institute busing to achieve desegregation in public schools

S T O P

IF YOU FINISH BEFORE TIME IS CALLED, YOU MAY CHECK YOUR WORK ON THIS TEST ONLY.
DO NOT WORK ON ANY OTHER TEST IN THIS BOOK.

How to Score the American History and Social Studies Achievement Test

When you take the American History and Social Studies Achievement Test, your answer sheet will be "read" by a scanning machine that will record your responses to each question. Then a computer will compare your answers with the correct answers and produce your raw score. You get one point for each correct answer. For each wrong answer, you lose one-fourth of a point. Questions you omit (and any for which you mark more than one answer) are not counted. This raw score is converted to a College Board scaled score that is reported to you and to the colleges you specify. After you have taken this test, you can get an idea of what your score might be by following the instructions in the next two sections.

Determining Your Raw Score

Step 1: Table A on the next page lists the correct answers for all the questions on the test.* Compare your answer with the correct answer and
- Put a check in the column marked "Right" if your answer is correct.
- Put a check in the column marked "Wrong" if your answer is incorrect.
- Leave both columns blank if you omitted the question.

Step 2: Count the number of right answers and enter the number here . . . . _____

Step 3: Count the number of wrong answers and enter

the number here . . . . 4)‾‾‾‾‾‾‾‾‾‾‾

Enter the result of dividing by 4 here . . . . _____

Step 4: Subtract the number you obtained in Step 3 from the number in Step 2; round the result to the nearest whole number (.5 is rounded up) and enter here. . _____

The number you obtained in Step 4 is your raw score. (The correction for guessing — subtraction of a quarter of a point for each incorrect answer — adjusts for the fact that random guessing on a large number of questions will result in some questions being answered correctly by chance.) Instructions for converting your raw score to a scaled score follow.

*The last column in Table A gives the percentage of students who took the test in November 1982 that answered the question correctly. (See page 213 for further explanation.)

TABLE A

Answers to American History and Social Studies Achievement Test, Form 3EAC2, and Percentage of Students Answering Each Question Correctly

Question Number	Correct Answer	Right	Wrong	Percentage of Students Answering the Question Correctly	Question Number	Correct Answer	Right	Wrong	Percentage of Students Answering the Question Correctly
1	E			89%	51	E			47%
2	D			80	52	A			59
3	E			61	53	E			67
4	C			78	54	D			78
5	A			77	55	D			60
6	B			75	56	E			62
7	A			83	57	B			39
8	E			78	58	D			53
9	C			83	59	A			42
10	C			81	60	E			36
11	B			79	61	E			40
12	D			79	62	C			37
13	C			64	63	A			45
14	A			84	64	D			51
15	E			91	65	B			41
16	D			54	66	A			72
17	C			52	67	D			52
18	C			50	68	E			31
19	B			71	69	D			33
20	D			65	70	B			37
21	D			80	71	C			35
22	C			47	72	D			27
23	B			56	73	E			43
24	D			80	74	A			33
25	A			72	75	A			54
26	B			71	76	B			29
27	C			58	77	C			25
28	A			84	78	E			27
29	E			79	79	D			58
30	A			74	80	E			34
31	D			59	81	E			28
32	B			80	82	B			61
33	E			53	83	A			22
34	C			47	84	D			22
35	A			37	85	A			23
36	A			56	86	C			26
37	B			20	87	B			26
38	E			77	88	B			33
39	A			27	89	E			37
40	D			35	90	D			28
41	B			48	91	E			35
42	C			54	92	A			16
43	A			52	93	B			36
44	D			64	94	E			43
45	C			45	95	C			20
46	A			32					
47	A			54					
48	B			58					
49	C			85					
50	D			37					

Note: The percentages are based on the analysis of the answer sheets for a random sample of students who took this test in November 1982 and whose mean score was 508.

Finding Your College Board Scaled Score ▬

When you take Achievement Tests, the scores sent to the colleges you specify will be reported on the College Board scale, ranging from 200 to 800. The raw score that you obtained above (Step 4) can be converted to a scaled score by using Table B.

To find your scaled score on this test, locate your raw score in the left column of Table B; the corresponding score in the right column will be your College Board scaled score. For example, a raw score of 49 on this particular edition of the American History and Social Studies Achievement Test corresponds to a College Board scaled score of 550. Raw scores are converted to scaled scores to ensure that a score earned on any one edition of the American History

and Social Studies Achievement Test is comparable to the same scaled score earned on any other edition of the test.

Because some editions of the American History and Social Studies Achievement Test may be slightly easier or more difficult than others, statistical adjustments are made in the scores so that each College Board scaled score indicates the same level of performance, regardless of the edition of the test you take and the ability of the group you take it with. A given raw score will correspond to different College Board scores, depending on the edition of the test taken. A raw score of 40, for example, may convert to a College Board score of 500 on one edition of the test, but that raw score might convert to a College Board score

| TABLE B — SCORE CONVERSION TABLE ||||||
| American History and Social Studies Achievement Test, Form 3EAC2 ||||||
Raw Score	College Board Scaled Score	Raw Score	College Board Scaled Score	Raw Score	College Board Scaled Score
95	800	60	610	25	410
94	800	59	610	24	400
93	800	58	600	23	400
92	800	57	600	22	390
91	800	56	590	21	390
90	790	55	590	20	380
89	780	54	580	19	370
88	780	53	570	18	370
87	770	52	570	17	360
86	770	51	560	16	360
85	760	50	560	15	350
84	760	49	550	14	350
83	750	48	540	13	340
82	740	47	540	12	330
81	740	46	530	11	330
80	730	45	530	10	320
79	730	44	520	9	320
78	720	43	520	8	310
77	710	42	510	7	300
76	710	41	500	6	300
75	700	40	500	5	290
74	700	39	490	4	290
73	690	38	490	3	280
72	690	37	480	2	280
71	680	36	470	1	270
70	670	35	470	0	260
69	670	34	460	−1	260
68	660	33	460	−2	250
67	660	32	450	−3	250
66	650	31	440	−4	240
65	640	30	440	−5	230
64	640	29	430	−6	230
63	630	28	430	−7	220
62	630	27	420	−8	220
61	620	26	420	−9	210
				−10 through −24	200

of 520 on a slightly more difficult edition. When you take the American History and Social Studies Achievement Test on the actual test day, your score is likely to differ somewhat from the score you obtained on this test. People perform at different levels at different times, for reasons unrelated to the test itself. The precision of any test is also limited because it represents only a sample of all the possible questions that could be asked. (See page 12, "How Precise Are Your Scores?" for further information.)

Reviewing Your Test Performance

After you have scored your test, you should take some time to consider the following points in relation to your performance on the test.

- *Did you run out of time before you reached the end of the test?*

  If you did, you may want to consider tactics that will help you pace yourself better. For example, you may have spent too much time working on one or two difficult questions. A better approach might have been to continue the test and return to those questions after you had attempted to answer the remaining questions on the test.

- *Did you take a long time reading the directions for the test?*

  The directions in this test are the same as those in the American History and Social Studies Achievement Tests now being administered. You will save time when you read the directions on the test day if you become thoroughly familiar with them in advance.

- *How did you handle questions you were unsure of?*

  If you were able to eliminate one or more of the answer choices and you guessed from the remaining choices, then your approach probably worked to your advantage. On the other hand, omitting questions about which you have some knowledge or guessing answers haphazardly would probably be a mistake.

- *How difficult were the questions for you compared with other students who took the test?*

  By referring to Table A on page 211 you can find out how difficult each question was for the group of students who took the test in November 1982. The right-hand column in the table tells you what percentage of that group of students answered the question correctly. It is important to remember that these percentages are based on only one group of students; had this edition of the test been given to all students in the class of 1983 who took an American History and Social Studies Achievement Test, the percentages would probably have been different. A question that was answered correctly by almost everyone in the group, obviously, is an easy question. Question 1, for example, was answered correctly by 89 percent of the students in the sample. On the other hand, question 92 was answered correctly by only 16 percent of the students. If you find that you missed several questions that would be considered easy, you may want to review those questions carefully. They may cover some aspect of the subject that you need to review. Perhaps you misunderstood the directions for one part of the test or you thought the questions were so easy that you did not spend as much time on them as you might have.

About the European History and World Cultures Achievement Test

The European History and World Cultures Achievement Test is a one-hour test consisting of 95 to 100 multiple-choice questions. The test measures your understanding of the development of Western and non-Western cultures, your comprehension of fundamental social science concepts as employed by the historian, and your ability to use basic historical techniques. These include the weighing and use of evidence and the ability to interpret and to generalize.

At least half the test questions deal with Western Europe, with the remainder covering other world areas: Eastern Europe, the Middle East, Africa, Southern Asia, Latin America, and China and Japan. Although history, and in particular historical development since the middle of the fifteenth century, furnishes the general frame of reference for questions, you should be familiar with the basic concepts of other social science disciplines to help you interpret historical evidence. All historical fields — political and diplomatic history, intellectual and cultural history, and social and economic history — are encompassed by the test questions.

Content of the Test

I. Chronological Material Covered	Approximate Percentage of Test
A. Ancient	5-10
B. Medieval	10-15
C. Early Modern	15-20
D. Modern	40-45
E. Cross-Chronological	10-15

II. Geographical Material Covered	Approximate Percentage of Test
A. Western Europe	40-50
B. Eastern Europe	10-12
C. Middle East	5-10
D. Africa	5-10
E. Southern Asia	5-10
F. China and Japan	5-10
G. Latin America	5-10
H. Cross-Geographical	15-20

III. Topical Material Covered	Approximate Percentage of Test
A. Major Political Developments	25-35
B. Values and Attitudes	10-15
C. Nature of the Economy	8-10
D. Literature	7-10
E. International Cultural Contacts and Conflicts	5-10
F. Social and Class Structure	4-5
G. Influence of Geography	4-5
H. Science and Technology	1-3
I. Major Historical Figures	1-3
J. Cross-Topical	18-22

Because secondary school programs differ, no one textbook or particular course of study is emphasized in the test. Test content lends itself to a variety of academic approaches. These include a course in European history against a global background, a course in world history as such, or a course in world history concentrating on either world cultures or area studies.

Questions Used in the Test

The sample multiple-choice questions that follow illustrate the types of questions used in the test and the abilities they measure. These abilities should not be thought of as mutually exclusive, since many questions test several abilities at the same time. Questions may be presented as separate items or in sets based on quotations, maps, pictures, graphs, or tables. The directions that begin every edition of the test are printed below.

Directions: Each of the questions or incomplete statements below is followed by five suggested answers or completions. Select the one that is best in each case and blacken the corresponding space on the answer sheet.

Some questions require you to know terms, factual cause-and-effect relationships, geography, and other data necessary for understanding major historical developments. Questions 1-3 fall into this category.

1. **Which of the following was immediately responsible for precipitating the French Revolution?**

   (A) **The threat of national bankruptcy**

   (B) **An attack upon the privileges of the middle class**

   (C) **The desire of the nobility for a written constitution**

   (D) **The sufferings of the peasantry**

   (E) **The king's attempt to restore feudalism**

To answer this question, you must recall the circumstances that led in May 1789 to the first meeting of the Estates-General in over a century and a half, an event that arrayed the Third Estate against the nobility and Louis XVI in the first stage of a political struggle that was to evolve into the French Revolution. With his debt-ridden government brought to a halt, the king, by mid-1788, was left with no other recourse than a promise to convene the Estates-General in the months ahead. The correct answer is (A).

Questions 2-3 refer to the map below. Arabic numerals refer to cities; Roman numerals to arrows.

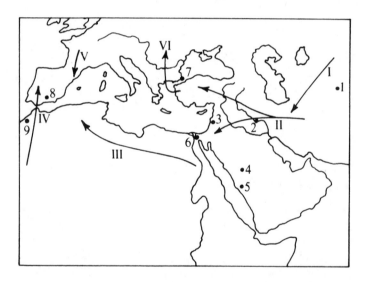

2. **In the eighth century which cities were near the east-west limits of the Islamic world?**

   (A) 1 and 7 (B) 1 and 9 (C) 2 and 6

   (D) 2 and 8 (E) 5 and 8

3. **Which arrow indicates a major threat to Europe in the seventeenth century?**

   (A) II (B) III (C) IV (D) V (E) VI

Both questions 2 and 3 test your knowledge of geography and familiarity with the movements of non-European peoples in different time periods. In question 2, you must recall that by the early years of the eighth century, the Islamic world had expanded westward to the Atlantic coast of North Africa and eastward to the edge of the Central Asian steppes and the boundaries of India, an area whose limits are approximately marked by cities 1 and 9, choice (B). To answer question 3, you must be aware that after the Ottoman Turks captured Constantinople in 1453, they gradually moved into Hungary along a route approximating the direction of arrow VI, choice (E), so that by 1648 the Turkish power had reached to about 50 miles from Vienna.

Some questions test your understanding of concepts essential to history and social science, your capacity to interpret artistic materials, and your ability to assess quotations from speeches, documents, and other published materials. Questions 4 and 5 fall into this category.

4. **Totalitarian regimes of the Fascist, Nazi, and communist variety have all**

   (A) **encouraged class struggle**

   (B) **ruthlessly suppressed capitalism**

   (C) **favored the state over the individual**

   (D) **urged extermination of the Jews**

   (E) **promoted revolutions of the colonial peoples of Africa south of the Sahara**

To answer this question, you must know about the preeminence of the totalitarian state over the individual, stated in choice (C), and recognize that the remaining four choices are not all applicable to all forms of totalitarianism. For example, although choices (A), (B), and (E) reflect communist ideology, they do not represent the policies of either Fascist Italy and Spain or Nazi Germany; and though choice (D) was part of the policy of Nazi Germany, it has not been promulgated by communist regimes. Thus, choice (C) is the correct answer.

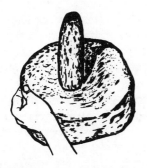

5. Which of the following hypotheses derived from the stone artifact above is LEAST likely to be valid?

(A) It was made by hunters.

(B) It was made by people skilled in stone craft.

(C) It was probably used in food preparation.

(D) The people who used it ate grain.

(E) It was probably used in the same way as a present-day mortar and pestle.

The question above asks you to identify the statement that has the *least* likelihood of being true among the answer choices offered. To answer question 5, you need to recognize that the object shown in the drawing is similar to the mortar and pestle of today, to deduce that stone craft skills were required for its manufacture, and to know that such an object was typically used by early agricultural peoples to grind grain they used for food. You also need to know that hunters were generally nomadic and therefore unlikely to cultivate cereals or use the tools that process them. Hence choice (A) is the answer choice least likely to be true, and, in the format of this question, therefore, the correct answer.

Questions posed in the negative, such as the one discussed above, occur quite frequently in the test, but never account for more than 25 percent of the test questions. Variations of this question format employ the capitalized words EXCEPT or NOT, as in the following examples: "All of the following are shown EXCEPT:" "Which of the following is NOT true?"

Questions based on graphs, charts, or cartoons require you to use historical knowledge in interpreting data. Questions 6 and 7 fall into this category.

ANNUAL PRODUCTION OF STEEL (in thousands of metric tons)				
Year				
1865	225	13	97	41
1870	286	68	169	83
1875	723	396	370	258
1880	1,320	1,267	660	388
1885	2,020	1,739	1,202	533
1890	3,637	4,346	2,161	566
1895	3,444	6,212	3,941	899
1900	5,130	10,382	6,645	1,565
1905	5,983	20,354	10,066	2,110
1910	6,374	26,512	13,698	3,506

6. Read from left to right, the column headings for the table above should be

(A) Great Britain, United States, Germany, and France

(B) Italy, Great Britain, Russia, and Germany

(C) Germany, Great Britain, Russia, and France

(D) Great Britain, United States, France, and Germany

(E) Germany, Russia, Great Britain, and United States

The correct answer is choice (A). To answer this question, you need to know where and when the first large-scale production of steel occurred, and when changes took place in the relative size of national production levels in the nineteenth and early twentieth centuries.

PERILOUS PASSAGE

Reprinted by permission of the Chicago *Tribune*,
the copyright owner

7. **Which of the following statements correctly interprets the cartoon above?**

   (A) Latin America has a history of strong constitutional government.

   (B) Dictatorship and constitutional government are really quite closely related.

   (C) Political turmoil is a direct result of the use of dictatorship in government.

   (D) Latin America is precariously maintaining a course of constitutional government between the threats of political turmoil and dictatorship.

   (E) It is perilous to visit Latin America because most constitutional governments are moving politically toward dictatorship.

In the question above, you are asked to interpret a political cartoon showing what the cartoonist believes are the dangers that menace constitutional government in Latin America. The best answer is choice (D) because it correctly states what the cartoonist depicts.

Some questions will ask you to analyze historical judgments and hypotheses. Questions 8 and 9 fall into this category.

8. **Which of the following statements would be most difficult for the historian to prove true or false?**

   (A) There was little organized education in Europe during the Middle Ages.

   (B) Greece contributed more to Western civilization than Rome did.

   (C) The invention of the steam engine influenced the way people lived.

   (D) The Soviet Union is the largest country in the world.

   (E) The tourist industry in Europe increased markedly after the Second World War.

For questions such as the one above, you must make the distinction between statements that need only the citation of facts for confirmation or denial and statements that also need a value judgment. The latter type is more difficult than the former to prove true or false, since value judgments, while they may be based on facts, are ultimately expressions of assumptions, preferences, or beliefs. In this question, choice (B) is the correct answer since the assertion that Greece contributed more to Western civilization than did Rome is based not simply on a citation of the accomplishments of each but on placement of a higher value on Greek than on Roman contributions.

9. **"It was a period marked by a great deal of chaos and turbulence, including internal disunity and invasion from without by alien peoples of a lower cultural level."**

   The quotation above can be applied to which of the following?

   I. China during the thirteenth and fourteenth centuries

   II. Western Europe during the fourth to the eleventh centuries

   III. Western Europe during the fourteenth and fifteenth centuries

   IV. The Middle East during the eleventh to the thirteenth centuries

   (A) III and IV only

   (B) I, II, and III only

   (C) I, II, and IV only

   (D) II, III, and IV only

   (E) I, II, III, and IV

To answer this question, you must recognize that of the four eras in different world regions, numbered I to IV, only three, I, II, and IV, were marked by invasions of the region from the outside: the period in China when internal anarchy was compounded by the Mongol infiltration of Peking, Kansu, and Szechwan; the period in Western Europe when the disintegration of Roman institutions and the influx of peoples ignorant of Roman tradition combined to throw the region into chaos; and the period in the Middle East when the region was invaded by such groups as the Seljuk Turks, the Mongols, and the European crusaders. Thus the best answer is choice (C).

European History and World Cultures Achievement Test

The test that follows is an edition of the European History and World Cultures Achievement Test administered in May 1983. So that you will have an idea of what the actual test administration will be like, try to take this test under conditions as close as possible to those of the actual test. It will probably help if you

- Set aside an hour for the test when you will not be interrupted, so that you can complete all of it in one sitting.

- Sit at a desk with no other papers or books. You can't take a calculator, a dictionary, other books, or notes into the test room.

- Have a kitchen timer or clock in front of you for timing yourself.

- Tear out an answer sheet from the back of this book and fill it in just as you would on the day of the test. You can use one answer sheet for as many as three Achievement Tests.

- Read the instructions that precede the test. When you take the test, you will be asked to read them before you begin answering questions.

- After you finish the test, read the sections on "How to Score the European History and World Cultures Achievement Test" and "Reviewing Your Test Performance," which follow the test.

EUROPEAN HISTORY AND WORLD CULTURES TEST

The top portion of the section of the answer sheet which you will use in taking the European History and World Cultures test must be filled in exactly as shown in the illustration below. Note carefully that you have to do all of the following on your answer sheet:

1. Print EUROPEAN HISTORY AND WORLD CULTURES on the line to the right of the words "Achievement Test."

2. Blacken spaces 4 and 0 in the row of spaces immediately under the words "Test Code."

3. Blacken space 3 in the group of five spaces labeled X.

4. Blacken space 4 in the group of five spaces labeled Y.

You are to leave blank the nine spaces which are labeled Q.

When the supervisor gives the signal, turn the page and begin the European History and World Cultures test. There are 100 numbered spaces on the answer sheet and 100 questions in the European History and World Cultures test.

EUROPEAN HISTORY AND WORLD CULTURES TEST

<u>Directions:</u> Each of the questions or incomplete statements below is followed by five suggested answers or completions. Select the one that is best in each case and then blacken the corresponding space on the answer sheet.

1. "Having disregarded the conciliatory and peaceable reply of the Serbian government and having declined [our] well-intentioned mediation, Austria hastened to launch an attack. We commanded that the army be put on a war footing but, at the same time, we made every effort to obtain a peaceable issue of the negotiation that had been started. In the midst of friendly communications, Austria's ally, Germany, contrary to our trust suddenly declared war."

   This quotation expresses one view of the beginning of the

   (A) Thirty Years' War
   (B) Crimean War
   (C) Franco-Prussian War
   (D) First World War
   (E) Second World War

2. In 1453 the Ottoman Turks conquered Constantinople and by so doing

   (A) gained territory in Europe for the first time
   (B) destroyed Christendom's most powerful state
   (C) completed for Islam the conquest of the Balkans
   (D) destroyed what was left of the Byzantine Empire
   (E) surrendered the city to Pope Pius II

CHINA—NET GRAIN IMPORTS 1961-1963
(million metric tons)

	Rice	Wheat	Barley	Flour	Total (commodity weight)
From Burma	0.35	—	—	—	0.35
From Canada	—	5.89	1.28	0.03	7.20
From Australia	—	2.08	0.30	0.04	2.42
From Europe	—	0.03	—	—	0.03
Total	0.35	8.00	1.58	0.07	10.00

3. On the basis of the table above, one may conclude that in the early 1960's China

   (A) could supply all of its industrial needs
   (B) was a developing country
   (C) had only limited access to international trade
   (D) could not pay for its imports
   (E) did not raise enough food to feed all of its people

GO ON TO THE NEXT PAGE ▶

Questions 4-5 refer to the following passage.

The work of the priest is to pray to God, that of the knight is to do justice, and of the laborer to provide their bread. One provides food, one prays, the other defends. In the fields, in the city, and in the church these three help each other by providing their skills according to a well-planned arrangement.

4. Which of the following statements can be made on the basis of the passage above?

   (A) Peasants are to be treated like dirt.
   (B) The knight is a parasite offering nothing to society.
   (C) Society is composed of interdependent parts.
   (D) Man needs government to help him reach God.
   (E) Each man's role on earth is ordained before his birth.

5. The social analysis above best fits

   (A) ancient Rome
   (B) France in the Middle Ages
   (C) Florence in the Renaissance
   (D) nineteenth-century France
   (E) nineteenth-century England

6. Which of the following civilizations produced the temple above?

   (A) Aztec (B) Egyptian (C) Roman
   (D) Harappa (E) Greek

7. Dutch power and prosperity in the seventeenth century were based on all of the following EXCEPT

   (A) control of the spice trade in the East Indies
   (B) development of a large shipbuilding industry
   (C) active participation in international banking
   (D) the development of a large standing army
   (E) a large and active burgher class

8. Rivers have been LEAST important in the historical development of which of the following?

   (A) Japan (B) Russia (C) Egypt
   (D) India (E) Babylonia

9. Medieval Scholasticism was heavily influenced by the writings of

   (A) Aristotle (B) Lucretius (C) Seneca
   (D) Ovid (E) Erasmus

Reprinted with the permission of the copyright owner.

10. The cartoon above refers to the

   (A) Lateran Act (1929)
   (B) Anschluss (1938)
   (C) Munich Agreement (1938)
   (D) German-Russian Pact (1939)
   (E) invasion of Finland (1939)

GO ON TO THE NEXT PAGE

11. In the sixteenth century, Christian explorers and traders came into contact with Islam and the important Muslim states in all of the following EXCEPT

    (A) South Asia
    (B) North Africa
    (C) the Near East
    (D) South America
    (E) East Asia

12. "His whole nature appears utterly at variance with the surroundings into which he was born. He has no prejudices, and his Russian subjects brim over with them. They are fanatics in their own religion; he is almost a freethinker. They look askance at novelty; he is never weary of innovations."

    The statement above describes

    (A) Ivan the Terrible
    (B) Peter the Great
    (C) Alexander I
    (D) Nicholas I
    (E) Nicholas II

13. The chart above depicts

    (A) size of population
    (B) per capita wealth
    (C) approximate land area
    (D) size of armed forces
    (E) daily food calorie consumption

GO ON TO THE NEXT PAGE

14. All of the following directed invasions of what is now territory of the Soviet Union EXCEPT

    (A) Attila   (B) Julius Caesar   (C) Charles XII
    (D) Napoleon I   (E) Hitler

15. The Russian Revolution of 1905 was precipitated by Russia's defeats in war against

    (A) Turkey   (B) China   (C) Germany
    (D) Sweden   (E) Japan

16. World population increased from approximately 8 million 10,000 years ago to approximately 300 million 2,000 years ago. This dramatic increase in the world population was triggered by

    (A) a substantial increase in the size of herds of wild game
    (B) the domestication of animals and plants
    (C) the use and control of fire
    (D) the invention of better weapons for hunting wild game
    (E) the invention of the wheel

17. The French Revolution resulted in all of the following EXCEPT the

    (A) mass conscription for national armies
    (B) alteration of the relationship between church and state
    (C) removal of feudal economic restrictions and trade barriers
    (D) granting of equal political rights to women
    (E) introduction of basic changes in law and education

18. All of the following are characteristics of Chinese civilization as it had developed by the time of the Shang dynasty (approximately 1766 B.C. to 1122 B.C.) EXCEPT

    (A) a written language using ideographs
    (B) the veneration of ancestors
    (C) artistic decoration of bronzeware
    (D) the importance of the family as a social unit
    (E) the worship of a single god

Questions 19-20 refer to the following passage.

The state of monarchy is the supremest thing upon earth, for kings are not only God's lieutenants upon earth and sit upon God's throne, but even by God himself are called gods. In the scriptures kings are called gods, and their power is compared to the divine power. Kings are also compared to fathers of families, for a king is truly *parens patriae,* the politic father of his people. And lastly, kings are compared to the head of this microcosm of the body of man.

19. The passage above embodies the seventeenth-century concept of

    (A) mercantilism
    (B) dynasticism
    (C) feudalism
    (D) divine right monarchy
    (E) state of nature

20. Which of the following might have written the passage above?

    (A) Joseph II of Austria
    (B) James I of England
    (C) Oliver Cromwell
    (D) John Locke
    (E) Martin Luther

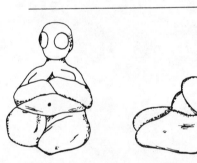

21. An archaeologist examining the figure illustrated above would find it most difficult to substantiate which of the following statements?

    (A) It is made of clay.
    (B) It is characteristic of figures found in ancient Near Eastern sites.
    (C) It is a religious symbol.
    (D) It was hand-fashioned.
    (E) It is 3 inches high.

GO ON TO THE NEXT PAGE

22. "Nor would I have him speak always of grave matters, but of amusing things, of games, jests, and waggery, according to the occasion; but sensibly of everything, and with readiness and lucid fullness; and in no place let him show vanity or childish folly. I would have him more than passably accomplished in letters, at least in those studies that are called the humanities, and conversant not only with the Latin language but with the Greek, for the sake of the many different things that have been admirably written therein."

The description above was most likely written as advice for

(A) a Renaissance courtier
(B) a sixteenth-century merchant
(C) a seventeenth-century nonconformist
(D) a medieval noble
(E) an eighteenth-century deist

23. Two Asian countries whose relations have been embittered by religious differences are

(A) India and Pakistan
(B) India and China
(C) Indonesia and Malaysia
(D) Pakistan and Japan
(E) China and Japan

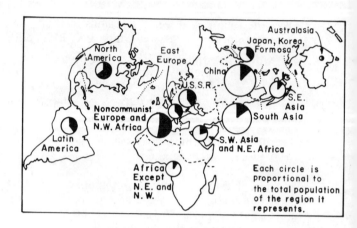

24. On the map above, the shaded portions of the circles represent the proportion of the population in the middle of the twentieth century that is

(A) native-born
(B) over the age of 25
(C) urban
(D) Muslim
(E) Roman Catholic

GO ON TO THE NEXT PAGE

25. "The battle grows more hard and harder yet,
Franks and pagans, with marvelous onset,
Each other strike and each himself defends.
So many Franks lose their young lustihead.
Who'll see no more their mothers nor their
  friends,
Nor hosts of France that in the pass attend."

The quotation above comes from

(A) *El Cid*
(B) *Song of Roland*
(C) *The Nibelungenlied*
(D) *Tristan and Iseult*
(E) *Le Morte D'Arthur*

26. The Muscovy Company (1553), the East India
Company (1600), the Virginia Company (1606),
and the Hudson's Bay Company (1670) were
alike in that they all

(A) founded permanent settlements
(B) traded with the Far East
(C) were joint-stock ventures, precursors of
   the modern corporation
(D) restricted their membership to the
   aristocracy
(E) engaged in manufacturing activities, fore-
   shadowing the factory system

27. The use of mosaics in religious art is most
closely associated with which of the following
societies?

(A) Ancient Egypt
(B) Ancient Athens
(C) Ancient Vikings
(D) The Byzantine Empire
(E) Twelfth-century France

28. Which of the following statements about the
Southeast Asian countries is LEAST accurate?

(A) They are ethnically homogeneous.
(B) They have long histories of invasion and
   occupation by foreign powers.
(C) There are very few centers of heavy
   industry in the region.
(D) They have gained their independence since
   the Second World War.
(E) Their cultural development was influenced
   by India or China.

29. Most eighteenth-century *philosophes* espoused
all of the following as goals for society
EXCEPT

(A) freedom of expression
(B) religious toleration
(C) a reformed legal system
(D) careers open to talent
(E) equal distribution of property

30. "We may likewise diminish our importations if
we would soberly refrain from mass
consumption of foreign wares. The value of
our exportations likewise may be much
advanced when we perform it in our own ships.
Also we ought to esteem and cherish those
trades which we have in remote countries."

Which of the following groups of economic
theorists is associated with the ideas expressed
in this passage?

(A) Keynesian economists
(B) Utopian socialists
(C) Economic liberals
(D) Mercantilists
(E) Physiocrats

31. The Russian Empire of the nineteenth century
differed from that of the colonial empires of
Western Europe in that it was

(A) acquired from nomadic tribes
(B) confined to a land mass contiguous with
   its home country
(C) acquired primarily to convert peoples to
   Christianity
(D) made up of many tiny Pacific islands
(E) a loose confederation of autonomous
   republics

32. The Tokugawa shogunate, which provided
Japan with over two centuries of peace and
stability, pursued a policy of

(A) expanding maritime trade
(B) submission to China
(C) alliance with England
(D) complete religious toleration
(E) almost complete isolation

GO ON TO THE NEXT PAGE

33. "Men are born, and always continue, free and equal in respect of their rights. Civil distinctions, therefore, can be founded only on public utility."

Which of the following would probably be the reaction of a typical, educated member of the Third Estate in 1789 to this statement?

(A) I agree. This should be the first article of the Declaration of the Rights of Man and the Citizen. It reaffirms what the philosophes said.
(B) I agree. These principles will destroy the foundations of organized religion.
(C) I disagree. The revolution should bring about a total elimination of civil distinctions.
(D) I disagree. Such pernicious doctrines will only encourage unrest among the lower orders of society.
(E) I disagree. The statement is a misrepresentation of the teachings of such men as Rousseau.

34. In the seventeenth century, knowledge of scientific discoveries was disseminated by all of the following EXCEPT

(A) university lectures
(B) daily newspapers
(C) learned societies
(D) private correspondence
(E) published treatises

Questions 35-38 are based on the following map of the ancient world. For the description in each question, select the appropriate location on the map.

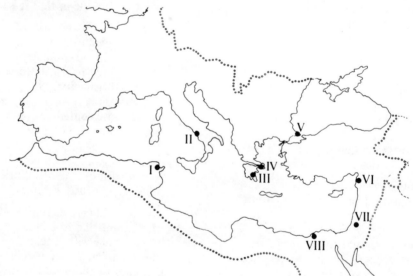

35. Site of an ancient city buried under volcanic lava and rediscovered in the eighteenth century

(A) I (B) II (C) III (D) V (E) VI

36. Site of the development of the first Western comedies and tragedies as dramatic forms

(A) II (B) III (C) IV (D) V (E) VIII

37. Center of a major sea power that was crushed by Rome in the second century B.C.

(A) I (B) IV (C) V (D) VII (E) VIII

38. Capital of the Eastern portion of the later Roman Empire

(A) IV (B) V (C) VI (D) VII (E) VIII

GO ON TO THE NEXT PAGE

39. On January 28, 1690, the Commons declared: "that King James II, having endeavored to subvert the constitution of the kingdom by breaking the original contract between king and people...has abdicated the government, and that the throne is vacant."

The concept of government expressed above finds its closest expression in the writings of

(A) Thomas More
(B) Bossuet
(C) Adam Smith
(D) Machiavelli
(E) Locke

40. The ancient civilization of the Indus River valley was characterized by all of the following EXCEPT

(A) cities built according to plan
(B) a system of writing
(C) an economy based mainly on foreign trade
(D) inhabitants skilled in techniques of water control
(E) contacts with Mesopotamia

41. "We must therefore accept as our basic principle the fact that a hierarchy of races and civilizations exists, and that we belong to the highest race, the highest civilization. But we must realize, too, that our superiority imposes important duties on us, as well as giving us certain rights. For we are superior not only in the economic and military, but especially in the moral, sense. That fact constitutes our main justification for the conquest of native peoples. To it we owe our position, our right to lead the rest of mankind."

Which of the following would most likely have made the statement above?

(A) A minister of Louis XIV
(B) A British diplomat of the late nineteenth century
(C) A twelfth-century Crusader
(D) An eighteenth-century philosopher
(E) A foreign minister of the Soviet Union

42.
I. The European woman is part of an inferior "second sex." From childhood onward she is taught passivity. The goal is to please men; unmarried women seem somehow to have failed. We need a fundamental revolution in values if woman's true potential is to be realized.

II. The position of European women has changed since the early nineteenth century. Reforms in legislation obviously broadened women's political and economic rights. Still more important were growing opportunities to work and earn outside the home and the steady reduction of the high birth rate. Indeed, feminist protest derived from previous changes in women's life.

Which of the following best expresses the relationship between these two passages?

(A) Commentator I is writing from a feminine perspective; Commentator II from a masculine perspective.
(B) Commentator I and Commentator II must be talking about different countries, although they claim to be generalizing about the whole continent.
(C) Both Commentator I and Commentator II have a Marxist perspective, despite their disagreement about feminism.
(D) Commentator I measures the position of women without reference to the past; Commentator II is interested in a historical assessment.
(E) Commentator I and Commentator II are writing at different times because Commentator II is clearly unaware of the feminist movement since the Second World War.

43. From about the first century B.C. until the early twentieth century, China was normally ruled by

(A) emperors, governing through the feudal nobility
(B) emperors, governing through scholar-bureaucrats
(C) regents, who were the powers behind the thrones of figurehead emperors
(D) military chieftains, governing through regional military commanders
(E) mandarins who presided over councils of elders

GO ON TO THE NEXT PAGE

Questions 44-45 refer to the following.

    (A) Prussia
    (B) Holland
    (C) France
    (D) Spain
    (E) England

44. During the period 1648-1815, which country, on a number of occasions, threatened to establish political and military domination over all Europe?

45. During the period 1618-1776, the institutions of which country underwent the most revolutionary changes?

---

46. Belief in which of the following was NOT part of the ethic of Western European middle classes in the nineteenth century?

    (A) The importance of education
    (B) A rigorous sexual morality
    (C) The possibility and desirability of personal and social improvement
    (D) Equality in economic and political rights for all adults
    (E) Personal and public hygiene

47. In the late fifteenth century, the rise of strong monarchs such as the early Tudors was facilitated by

    (A) the ability of the monarch to maintain internal order
    (B) the separation of church and state
    (C) an extension of democratic institutions to the new and growing middle class
    (D) the organization of state churches
    (E) the example of national unification in Renaissance Italy

Questions 48-49 refer to the following passage.

Between 1870 and 1920 Europe was described as having two zones, an inner zone of steam and an outer, or agricultural, zone. The inner zone was bounded by an imaginary circle drawn through Glasgow, Stockholm, Danzig, Trieste, Florence, and Barcelona.

48. Which of the following lay entirely within the inner zone?

    (A) England, Germany, and Spain
    (B) Germany, Italy, and France
    (C) The Netherlands, Russia, and Switzerland
    (D) England, Belgium, and France
    (E) Italy, Denmark, and Austria-Hungary

49. Which of the following traveled primarily from the inner zone to the outer zone?

    I. Engineers and technicians
    II. Immigrants
    III. Political ideas
    IV. Manufactured goods

    (A) I only
    (B) II and III only
    (C) II and IV only
    (D) I, III, and IV only
    (E) I, II, III, and IV

GO ON TO THE NEXT PAGE

Questions 50-51 refer to the following passage.

A crisis is made by people, who enter into the crisis with their own prejudices, propensities, and predispositions. A crisis is the sum of intuition and blind spots, a blend of facts noted and facts ignored.

Yet underlying the uniqueness of each crisis is a disturbing sameness. A characteristic of crises is their predictability, in retrospect. They seem to have a certain inevitability, they seem predestined. This is not true of all crises, but it is true of sufficiently many to make the most hardened historian cynical and misanthropic.

50. Which of the following statements is correct concerning the view of the past expressed in this passage?

(A) It indicates that the author has a Marxist view of history.
(B) It asserts that since history is inevitable, historians can predict crises.
(C) It maintains that historians are biased and malicious.
(D) It maintains that people have no role in shaping events.
(E) It indicates that though crises are unique, they are comparable.

51. Which of the following pairs of events would be LEAST effective as an illustration of the ''disturbing sameness'' referred to in the passage?

(A) The treatment of the defeated powers by the Congress of Vienna, 1814-1815, and the treatment of the defeated powers by the Versailles conference after the First World War
(B) The French Revolution and the Russian Revolution
(C) The trial of Servetus by Calvinists in Geneva and the trial of Galileo by the Church of Rome
(D) The French defeat in Vietnam and the American defeat in Vietnam
(E) Napoleon's invasion of Russia and Hitler's invasion of Russia

52. By the early seventeenth century the center of international trade in Europe had shifted from the

(A) Low Countries to the Mediterranean
(B) Mediterranean to the Baltic
(C) Mediterranean to the Low Countries
(D) Atlantic to the Mediterranean
(E) eastern to the western Mediterranean

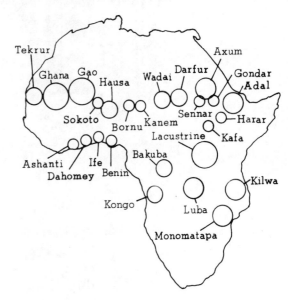

53. The best title for the map above would be

(A) Twenty-five early African Kingdoms
(B) Major Life-Styles in Africa
(C) Africa's Twenty-five Languages
(D) Africa's Twenty-five Tribes
(E) Major Population Centers in Africa Today

GO ON TO THE NEXT PAGE

Hirmer Fotoarchiv München

54. The statue pictured above was probably created in

(A) Egypt during the fourteenth dynasty
(B) Mesopotamia under Hammurabi
(C) Persia under Cyrus
(D) Greece in the Age of Pericles
(E) Rome under Augustus

GO ON TO THE NEXT PAGE

55. The greatest number of nation-states in Africa south of the Sahara became independent

    (A) before 1800
    (B) between 1800 and 1885
    (C) between 1885 and 1915
    (D) between 1915 and 1950
    (E) after 1950

56. A conservative at the Congress of Vienna would probably have supported all of the following EXCEPT

    (A) the return of the legitimate rulers to their thrones
    (B) suppression of liberal thought through censorship and police surveillance
    (C) reestablishment of a European balance of power
    (D) a formal constitution for each European country
    (E) control of government by the upper class

57. The fundamental causes of the Latin-American wars of independence included all of the following EXCEPT

    (A) resentment against the mercantilist system
    (B) the effects of the Enlightenment
    (C) the expulsion of the Jesuits
    (D) Creole bitterness toward the special privileges of those of pure Spanish ancestry
    (E) the displacement of the Bourbon dynasty in Spain by Napoleon Bonaparte

58. The early Mesopotamians used all of the following EXCEPT

    (A) the wheel
    (B) irrigation techniques
    (C) the phonetic alphabet
    (D) the sail
    (E) bronze weapons

Questions 59-60 are based on the following passage.

The system of communal land ownership and the social organization of the local government unit have remained a strong heritage for the past four hundred years. Corn, beans, and squash remain the staple crops.

Many colonial elements that still exist in the village culture were introduced early in the sixteenth century. The most important of these traits are the physical layout of the village with its residential areas, streets, and central plaza, Catholicism and the churches, the language, the money economy, domestic animals, and the plow and other agricultural tools.

Side by side are many items of modern civilization. These include corn mills and sewing machines, a modern highway and buses, clocks, poolrooms, patent medicines, powdered milk, battery radios, and a few automobiles.

59. The passage is describing rural life in

    (A) Africa
    (B) the Middle East
    (C) Latin America
    (D) Southern Asia
    (E) China

60. Which of the following concepts is evidenced in the passage?

    (A) Economic determinism
    (B) Racism
    (C) Social stratification
    (D) Urbanism
    (E) Cultural diffusion

61. Which of the following does NOT accurately describe the political characteristics of Gaullism in France after the Second World War?

    (A) Belief in strong executive leadership
    (B) Belief in national glory
    (C) Commitment to economic planning
    (D) Anticommunism
    (E) Anticlericalism

GO ON TO THE NEXT PAGE

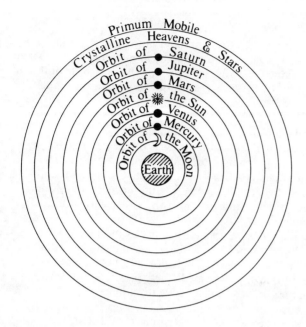

66. Most of the land in Africa south of the Sahara is covered by

    (A) deserts (B) jungles (C) swamps
    (D) grasslands (E) mountains

67. A demographer would be interested in all of the following historical developments EXCEPT the

    (A) rise of cities during the Middle Ages
    (B) effects of the Black Death
    (C) medical discoveries of the nineteenth century
    (D) fall of the Bastille
    (E) increase in wheat production per acre

62. The idea of the solar system portrayed above was most basically challenged by the work of

    (A) Aristotle (B) Copernicus (C) Vesalius
    (D) Leonardo da Vinci (E) Francis Bacon

63. Of all the religions that came into East Asia, the one that has influenced the greatest number of people has proved to be

    (A) Christianity (B) Buddhism (C) Islam
    (D) Jainism (E) Zoroastrianism

64. Most early Protestant movements differed from the Roman Catholic church with respect to all of the following EXCEPT

    (A) the doctrine of the Trinity
    (B) the nature of the mass
    (C) papal supremacy
    (D) the necessity of a celibate priesthood
    (E) monasticism

65. Beginning with the earliest, what is the correct chronological order of events in the history of Russia?

    I. Decembrist revolt
    II. Emancipation of serfs
    III. Treaty of Brest-Litovsk
    IV. New Economic Policy
    V. October Revolution

    (A) I, II, V, III, IV
    (B) I, V, II, IV, III
    (C) II, I, IV, V, III
    (D) III, IV, V, I, II
    (E) V, IV, I, II, III

68. The style of architecture pictured above is

    (A) Byzantine (B) Romanesque (C) Gothic
    (D) Renaissance (E) Classical

GO ON TO THE NEXT PAGE

69. Which of the following seemed to represent an improvement in French-German relations after the First World War?

    (A) The French military occupation of the Ruhr
    (B) The Locarno Pact
    (C) The Treaty of Rapallo
    (D) The formation of the League of Nations
    (E) Hitler's occupation of the Rhineland

70. All of the following were results of the Hundred Years' War EXCEPT:

    (A) Foot soldiers armed with longbows gained military importance at the expense of knights on horseback.
    (B) The English Parliament increased its control over the king's expenditures.
    (C) The English lost all of their French possessions except Calais.
    (D) The leadership of Joan of Arc helped revive the French monarchy.
    (E) French nobles were allowed to choose whether their territories should be Catholic, Lutheran, or Calvinist.

71. A term associated with Western European feudalism is correctly matched with its equivalent in Japanese feudalism in which of the following pairs?

    I. Knights..Samurai
    II. Lord..Daimyo
    III. Castle..Shogun

    (A) I only
    (B) I and II only
    (C) I and III only
    (D) II and III only
    (E) I, II, and III

72. "According to this theory, which prevailed until the early twentieth century, Heaven conferred a mandate upon whoever was appointed to exercise political authority, but the mandate might be withdrawn at any time in the same mysterious way in which it had been initially conferred."

    The country in which the theory described above prevailed was

    (A) Russia (B) China (C) Spain
      (D) the Ottoman Empire (E) Greece

73. Interpreted as "the first instance of Indian nationalism," or simply as religious unrest, the most startling incident in British India in the nineteenth century was the

    (A) First Afghan War
    (B) Great (Sepoy) Mutiny
    (C) formation of the Indian National Congress
    (D) Amritsar Massacre
    (E) proclamation of Victoria as Empress of India

74. Which of the following is part of the policy of apartheid as advocated by the government of the Republic of South Africa?

    (A) The establishment of separate homelands for African tribes within the boundaries of South Africa
    (B) The annihilation or deportation of the nonwhite peoples from South Africa
    (C) The partition of South Africa among colonial powers
    (D) The withdrawal of South Africa from the British Commonwealth
    (E) The isolation of South Africa from the other nations of the continent

75. Of the following, which was fundamental to Bismarck's foreign policy?

    (A) Enlarging Germany's navy
    (B) Isolating Great Britain
    (C) Establishing a colonial empire
    (D) Supporting Turkey
    (E) Keeping France and Russia separated

76. Charles Fourier, Louis Blanc, and Robert Owen all believed in

    (A) economic laissez faire
    (B) cooperation rather than competition
    (C) the class struggle
    (D) economic determinism
    (E) the necessity for violent revolution

77. "Our tsar has grandiose plans in his head: to capture Manchuria and to annex Korea. He is dreaming also of bringing Tibet under his dominion. He desires to take Persia and to seize not only the Bosporus but also the Dardanelles."

    This statement was most probably written in

    (A) 1775 (B) 1815 (C) 1835
      (D) 1903 (E) 1913

GO ON TO THE NEXT PAGE

78. Before the coming of the Europeans in the fifteenth century, the people who lived in East Africa carried on a measurable overseas trade with all of the following EXCEPT the

    (A) Chinese   (B) Malays   (C) Indians
    (D) Arabs   (E) Japanese

Questions 79-80 are based on the following information.

The Revolutions of 1848 failed to effect most of the political reforms the revolutionaries intended. Italy and Germany were not unified, for example, and parliaments were abolished in most of the countries involved in the revolutions.

Within two and a half decades many of the goals sought in the Revolutions of 1848 had been achieved, though sometimes in modified form, for conservatives came to realize that they had to make some concessions to the new forces of liberalism and nationalism. The national unifications were joined with advances in the power of parliaments and constitutional rights in Central and Western Europe.

79. Which of the following is the most appropriate conclusion from the information above?

    (A) The Revolutions of 1848 resulted in the unifications of Italy and Germany.
    (B) The Revolutions of 1848 had little political impact.
    (C) The results of 1848 confirmed that Germany was a less liberal country than France.
    (D) Although the Revolutions of 1848 prompted an initial conservative reaction, they encouraged important new political forces.
    (E) National unifications contented potential revolutionaries, who dropped their demands for internal political reforms.

80. Which of the following was NOT a durable result of the Revolutions of 1848 in at least one of the following: Austrian Empire; France; Prussia; Piedmont?

    (A) Universal manhood suffrage
    (B) Abolition of serfdom
    (C) Nationalization of major industries
    (D) Decline of liberal revolutionary agitation
    (E) An interest in territorial expansion

81. About which of the following are historians or social scientists most likely to DISAGREE?

    (A) The major participants at the signing of the Treaty of Versailles
    (B) The number of members in the British House of Commons in 1850
    (C) The date for the end of the War of 1812
    (D) The most important reason for the decline of the Roman Empire
    (E) Germany's population in 1936

82. During the Middle Ages, there was LEAST controversy between the Church and lay rulers over which of the following?

    (A) The right of the state to tax the clergy
    (B) The right of the state to make appointments to ecclesiastical offices
    (C) The right of the Church to try laymen for heresy
    (D) The right of the Church to administer justice in cases involving the clergy
    (E) The right of the Church to criticize the activities of secular monarchs

GO ON TO THE NEXT PAGE

83. Which of the following help(s) to account for the development of a Russian culture distinct from that of Western Europe?

    I. Geographical remoteness
    II. Two centuries of Mongol rule
    III. The dominance of the Russian Orthodox church

    (A) II only   (B) III only   (C) I and II only
    (D) II and III only   (E) I, II, and III

84. Economic and social development in twelfth- and thirteenth-century Europe was characterized by all of the following EXCEPT

    (A) rapid growth of population
    (B) an increase in the number and size of towns
    (C) rapid growth in manufacturing activity in Northern Italy and the Low Countries
    (D) rapid growth of trade between Italy and the western Mediterranean
    (E) opening of an all-water trade route to Asia

85. "The humanists were by no means the major architects of the modern world, nor the makers of the modern mind. Insofar as the sixteenth and seventeenth centuries went to make us what we are, others were more important than the humanists."

    The author of the passage above might have cited all of the following as examples of "major architects" EXCEPT

    (A) Protestants
    (B) natural scientists
    (C) secular political philosophers
    (D) Scholastics
    (E) mathematicians

86. The principles of social stratification are embodied or reflected in which of the following?

    I. The caste system
    II. The code of the samurai
    III. The Greek polis
    IV. Chivalry

    (A) I only   (B) IV only   (C) II and III only
    (D) I, II, and III only   (E) I, II, III, and IV

GO ON TO THE NEXT PAGE

Questions 87-92 refer to the following round-table discussion.

Speaker I: In this grave crisis the great majority cf my people and of the citizens of Europe wanted peace. I tried to prevent the catastrophe of war and to ensure peace in our time. No one wanted to fight, and in fact neither my country nor its chief ally was militarily prepared to enter a struggle against a large continental army, recently rearmed and revitalized. Thus, we made the best agreement possible, even though certain rights of a smaller power had to be infringed.

Speaker II: Of course, I appreciate that your intentions were honorable. But think of the cost: the agreement vitiated the morale of my people and their trust in the West. Our allies to the east were similarly affected. The agreement permitted the enemy to split Europe, to pick us off one by one, and it was widely interpreted as a "sell-out" of our interests by the very nations that only recently had helped us to gain our independence.

Speaker III: But that is ridiculous. The agreement simply recognized the position in Europe to which the resources of a great power entitled my country, and it provided for the reunification with its own *Volk* of a minority which was being oppressed by the Slavs. Moreover, if it had not been for the threats and aggressions which followed, my nation would have been perfectly satisfied with the gains recognized under this agreement.

Speaker IV: My country was quite prepared to take a stand and fight; in fact we would have come to the aid of our small ally to the west if the French had done so. But it is clear that the intention of the "democratic" leaders was to save themselves by turning the aggressor against us in the hope that we would destroy each other and leave the field clear for their imperialist domination of Europe and the world.

87. The grave crisis referred to is the

(A) Berlin Airlift
(B) Soviet suppression of the Hungarian revolt
(C) Spanish Civil War
(D) Danzig question
(E) Sudeten crisis that led to the Munich Conference

88. Speaker I most clearly reflects the view of

(A) Winston Churchill
(B) Lloyd George
(C) Neville Chamberlain
(D) Franklin D. Roosevelt
(E) Benito Mussolini

89. Speaker II is most likely

(A) Czech   (B) German   (C) Spanish
   (D) Hungarian   (E) Russian

90. Speaker IV would most likely be supported by which of the following parties?

(A) Nazi   (B) Communist   (C) Fascist
   (D) Fabian Socialist   (E) Christian Socialist

91. Speaker III most clearly reflects the views of

(A) de Gaulle   (B) Daladier   (C) Franco
   (D) Stalin   (E) Hitler

92. The policy described by Speaker I has been traditionally called

(A) isolationism   (B) adventurism
   (C) neutralism   (D) appeasement
      (E) fortress Europe

93. The majority of the people of Northern Ireland (Ulster) differ from the majority of the people of the Irish Republic in which of the following respects?

   I. They are the descendants of English and Scottish settlers.
   II. They are Protestants.
   III. They live in the most heavily industrialized section of Ireland.
   IV. They are Roman Catholic.

(A) I and II only
(B) II and III only
(C) III and IV only
(D) I, II, and III only
(E) I, III, and IV only

94. All of the following statements about Islam are correct EXCEPT:

    (A) It esteems Abraham, Moses, and Jesus.
    (B) It is monotheistic.
    (C) It permits polygamy.
    (D) It permits the use of religious statues.
    (E) Its holy book is the Koran.

95. Which of the following was NOT an accomplishment of the Frankish kingdom under Charlemagne?

    (A) Decisive defeat of Norse invaders
    (B) Defeat and occupation of the lands of the Lombard Kingdom
    (C) Creation of a court culture centered around his person
    (D) Establishment of a defensive border in Northern Spain against the Muslims
    (E) Creation of an alliance with the papacy which resulted in Charlemagne's coronation as emperor in 800

96. The North Atlantic Treaty was signed for the purpose of

    (A) implementing the Helsinki Agreement
    (B) bringing about world union
    (C) bringing about greater economic cooperation among countries of the Western Hemisphere
    (D) coordinating the defense preparations of Western Europe
    (E) putting into effect the declarations made in the Atlantic Charter

97. In the early period of their historical relationship, the Aryans were to the Dravidians what the Japanese were to the

    (A) Chinese (B) Mongols (C) Ainu
      (D) Dayaks (E) Moros

98. Which of the following was a Leninist addition to Marxist theory?

    (A) Under capitalism, the state is the tool of the bourgeoisie.
    (B) Imperialism makes communist revolutions possible in nonindustrialized countries.
    (C) Because of the power of industrial capitalism, a dictatorship must follow the proletarian revolution to complete the revolution.
    (D) Communism should be an international movement.
    (E) Pragmatic trade unionism is a danger to the cause of proletarian revolution.

99. Which of the following best describes the role of Cavour in the movement for Italian unification?

    (A) He preached a doctrine of radical nationalism which appealed to the youth of many nations other than Italy.
    (B) He was an inspiring military leader who led his peasant army to many victories.
    (C) He was an agent of Austria who used severe repressive measures against the nationalist revolutionaries.
    (D) He favored Italian national unity only until it endangered the independence of the Papal States.
    (E) He sponsored economic and political reform in Piedmont and used diplomacy to make it the nucleus of a new Italian nation.

100. The age of industrialism was ushered into Britain in the late eighteenth century by basic new inventions in which of the following industries?

    (A) Lumber
    (B) Petroleum
    (C) Shipbuilding
    (D) Cotton textiles
    (E) Electric power

S T O P

IF YOU FINISH BEFORE TIME IS CALLED, YOU MAY CHECK YOUR WORK ON THIS TEST ONLY.
DO NOT WORK ON ANY OTHER TEST IN THIS BOOK.

How to Score the European History and World Cultures Achievement Test

When you take an actual European History and World Cultures Achievement Test, your answer sheet will be "read" by a scanning machine that will record your responses to each question. Then a computer will compare your answers with the correct answers and produce your raw score. You get one point for each correct answer. For each wrong answer, you lose one-fourth of a point. Questions you omit (and any for which you mark more than one answer) are not counted. This raw score is converted to a College Board scaled score that is reported to you and to the colleges you specify. After you have taken this test, you can get an idea of what your score might be by following the instructions in the next two sections.

Determining Your Raw Score

Step 1: Table A on the next page lists the correct answers for all the questions on the test.* Compare your answer with the correct answer and
- Put a check in the column marked "Right" if your answer is correct.
- Put a check in the column marked "Wrong" if your answer is incorrect.
- Leave both columns blank if you omitted the question.

Step 2: Count the number of right answers and enter the number here . . . . _____

Step 3: Count the number of wrong answers and enter

the number here . . . . 4)‾‾‾‾‾‾‾‾‾‾‾‾

Enter the result of dividing by 4 here . . . . _____

Step 4: Subtract the number you obtained in Step 3 from the number in Step 2; round the result to the nearest whole number (.5 is rounded up) and enter here. . _____

The number you obtained in Step 4 is your raw score. (The correction for guessing — subtraction of a quarter of a point for each incorrect answer — adjusts for the fact that random guessing on a large number of questions will result in some questions being answered correctly by chance.) Instructions for converting your raw score to a scaled score follow.

*The last column in Table A gives the percentage of students who took the test in May 1983 that answered the question correctly. (See page 243 for further explanation.)

TABLE A

Answers to European History and World Cultures Test, Form 3FAC, and Percentage of Students Answering Each Question Correctly

Question Number	Correct Answer	Right	Wrong	Percentage of Students Answering the Question Correctly	Question Number	Correct Answer	Right	Wrong	Percentage of Students Answering the Question Correctly
1	D			87%	51	A			30%
2	D			59	52	C			38
3	E			80	53	A			49
4	C			92	54	D			82
5	B			83	55	E			45
6	A			88	56	D			52
7	D			66	57	C			27
8	A			71	58	C			29
9	A			51	59	C			71
10	D			71	60	E			38
11	D			86	61	E			53
12	B			68	62	B			74
13	C			79	63	B			60
14	B			53	64	A			40
15	E			64	65	A			39
16	B			65	66	D			45
17	D			87	67	D			58
18	E			71	68	B			28
19	D			97	69	B			35
20	B			75	70	E			46
21	C			73	71	B			50
22	A			70	72	B			33
23	A			69	73	B			44
24	C			61	74	A			40
25	B			36	75	E			45
26	C			58	76	B			25
27	D			56	77	D			34
28	A			41	78	E			48
29	E			51	79	D			57
30	D			63	80	C			21
31	B			67	81	D			80
32	E			76	82	C			27
33	A			53	83	E			50
34	B			58	84	E			39
35	B			62	85	D			14
36	C			50	86	E			22
37	A			61	87	E			39
38	B			62	88	C			38
39	E			52	89	A			35
40	C			50	90	B			35
41	B			44	91	E			36
42	D			43	92	D			40
43	B			18	93	D			24
44	C			67	94	D			30
45	E			62	95	A			25
46	D			37	96	D			44
47	A			47	97	C			10
48	D			48	98	B			13
49	D			44	99	E			28
50	E			53	100	D			55

Note: The percentages are based on the analysis of the answer sheets for a random sample of students who took this test in May 1983 and whose mean score was 545.

Finding Your College Board Scaled Score ■

When you take Achievement Tests, the scores sent to the colleges you specify will be reported on the College Board scale, ranging from 200 to 800. The raw score that you obtained above (Step 4) can be converted to a scaled score by using Table B.

To find your scaled score on this test, locate your raw score in the left column of Table B; the corresponding score in the right column will be your College Board scaled score. For example, a raw score of 47 on this particular edition of the European History and World Cultures Achievement Test corresponds to a College Board scaled score of 570. Raw scores are converted to scaled scores to ensure that a score earned on any one edition of the European History and World Cultures Achievement Test is comparable to the same scaled score earned on any other edition of the test.

Because some editions of the European History and World Cultures Achievement Test may be slightly easier or more difficult than others, statistical adjustments are made in the scores so that each College Board scaled score indicates the same level of performance, regardless of the edition of the test you take

TABLE B — SCORE CONVERSION TABLE					
European History and World Cultures Achievement Test, Form 3FAC					
Raw Score	College Board Scaled Score	Raw Score	College Board Scaled Score	Raw Score	College Board Scaled Score
100	800	60	650	20	400
99	800	59	640	19	390
98	800	58	640	18	390
97	800	57	630	17	380
96	800	56	630	16	380
95	800	55	620	15	370
94	800	54	610	14	360
93	800	53	610	13	360
92	800	52	600	12	350
91	800	51	590	11	340
90	800	50	590	10	340
89	800	49	580	9	330
88	800	48	580	8	330
87	800	47	570	7	320
86	800	46	560	6	310
85	800	45	560	5	310
84	800	44	550	4	300
83	790	43	540	3	290
82	790	42	540	2	290
81	780	41	530	1	280
80	780	40	530	0	280
79	770	39	520	−1	270
78	760	38	510	−2	260
77	760	37	510	−3	260
76	750	36	500	−4	250
75	740	35	490	−5	250
74	740	34	490	−6	240
73	730	33	480	−7	230
72	730	32	480	−8	230
71	720	31	470	−9	220
70	710	30	460	−10	210
69	710	29	460	−11	210
68	700	28	450	−12	200
67	690	27	440	through −25	
66	690	26	440		
65	680	25	430		
64	680	24	430		
63	670	23	420		
62	660	22	410		
61	660	21	410		

and the ability of the group you take it with. A given raw score will correspond to different College Board scores, depending on the edition of the test taken. A raw score of 40, for example, may convert to a College Board score of 530 on one edition of the test, but that raw score might convert to a College Board score of 550 on a slightly more difficult edition. When you take the European History and World Cultures Achievement Test on the actual test day, your score is likely to differ somewhat from the score you obtained on this test. People perform at different levels at different times, for reasons unrelated to the test itself. The precision of any test is also limited because it represents only a sample of all the possible questions that could be asked. (See page 12, "How Precise Are Your Scores?" for further information.)

Reviewing Your Test Performance

After you have scored your test, you should take some time to consider the following points in relation to your performance on the test.

- *Did you run out of time before you reached the end of the test?*

  If you did, you may want to consider tactics that will help you pace yourself better. For example, you may have spent too much time working on one or two difficult questions. A better approach might have been to continue the test and return to those questions after you had attempted to answer the remaining questions on the test.

- *Did you take a long time reading the directions for the test?*

  The directions in this test are the same as those in the European History and World Cultures Achievement Tests now being administered. You will save time when you take the test if you become thoroughly familiar with them in advance.

- *How did you handle questions you were unsure of?*

  If you were able to eliminate one or more of the answer choices and you guessed from the remaining choices, then your approach probably worked to your advantage. On the other hand, omitting questions about which you have some knowledge or guessing answers haphazardly would probably be a mistake.

- *How difficult were the questions for you compared with other students who took the test?*

  By referring to Table A on page 241 you can find out how difficult each question was for the group of students who took the test in May 1983. The right-hand column in the table tells you what percentage of that group of students answered the question correctly. It is important to remember that these percentages are based on only one group of students; had this edition of the test been given to all students in the class of 1983 who took a European History and World Cultures Achievement Test, the percentages would probably have been different. A question that was answered correctly by almost everyone in the group, obviously, is an easy question. Question 19, for example, was answered correctly by 97 percent of the students in the sample. On the other hand, question 98 was answered correctly by only 13 percent of the students. If you find that you missed several questions that would be considered easy, you may want to review those questions carefully. They may cover some aspect of the subject that you need to review. Perhaps you misunderstood the directions for one part of the test or you thought the questions were so easy that you did not spend as much time on them as you might have.

About the Mathematics Achievement Tests

The two Achievement Tests in mathematics are Mathematics Level I and Mathematics Level II. Level I is the College Board's principal Mathematics Achievement Test for use in college admissions.

All editions of the test are linked statistically to previous editions. In general, however, because the content measured by the two tests differs considerably, your score on one of the Mathematics Achievement Tests should not be used to predict your score on the other test.

Content of the Tests

Mathematics Level I, one hour in length, is a broad survey test, composed of 50 multiple-choice questions, covering content typical of three years of college-preparatory mathematics. It contains questions in algebra, geometry, trigonometry, elementary functions, mathematical reasoning, logic, and elementary number theory.

The Mathematics Level II test, also a one-hour, 50-question, multiple-choice test, is intended for students who have taken college-preparatory mathematics for three and one-half years or more, but it is also suitable for able students who have had three years of a strong mathematics curriculum. The Level II test contains questions in algebra, geometry, trigonometry, elementary functions, sequences and limits, logic and proof, probability and statistics, and elementary number theory.

The chart below shows approximately how the questions in each test are distributed among the major curriculum areas. Comparison of the percentages for both levels should help you decide which test you are better prepared to take.

Topic	Approximate Percentage of Test	
	Level I	Level II
Algebra	30	18
Plane Geometry	20	—
Solid Geometry	6	8
Coordinate Geometry	12	12
Trigonometry	8	20
Elementary Functions	12	24
Other	12	18

There is some overlap in content between the Level I and Level II tests, especially in questions on elementary algebra, coordinate geometry, and basic trigonometry. Consequently, some questions may be appropriate for either test. However, as you can see from the chart, the emphasis in the Level II test is on more advanced material, with a greater percentage of questions devoted to trigonometry, elementary functions, and advanced precalculus topics. Further, a significant percentage of questions in Level I is devoted to plane Euclidean geometry, a topic not tested directly in Level II; the geometry questions in Level II cover topics from coordinate geometry in two or three dimensions, transformations, solid Euclidean geometry, and vectors. The trigonometry questions in Level I are primarily limited to right triangle trigonometry and the fundamental relationships among the trigonometric ratios, whereas Level II places more emphasis on the properties and graphs of the trigonometric functions, the inverse trigonometric functions, and identities.

Students who have had preparation in trigonometry and elementary functions should select the Level II test, particularly if they have attained grades of B or better in their mathematics courses. Those who are sufficiently prepared to take the Level II test, but who elect to take the Level I test in the hope of receiving high scores, sometimes do not do as well as they expect because of weak performance in areas they have not studied recently. However, no student taking either Level I or Level II is expected to have studied every topic on the test.

Questions Used in the Tests

As much as possible, test questions are constructed so that they can be understood by all students regardless of the mathematics curriculums and textbooks they have studied. Symbolism has been kept simple; for example, the symbol *PQ* may be used to denote a line, a ray, a segment, or the measure (length) of a segment; the particular interpretation of the symbol is indicated by its context in the problem.

The five-choice completion question is widely used in objective tests and is probably the type of question with which you are most familiar. It is written either as an incomplete statement or as a question. In its simplest application, this type of question poses a problem that has a unique solution. It is also appropriate when: (1) the problem presented is clearly delineated by the wording of the question so that you choose not a universal solution but the best of the solutions offered; (2) the problem is such that you are required to evaluate the relevance of five plausible choices and to select the one most pertinent; (3) the problem has several pertinent solutions and you are required to select the one inappropriate solution that is presented. In the last case the best answer to the question is the choice that is least or not applicable to the situation described by the question.

A special type of five-choice completion question is used in some tests to allow for the possibility of several correct answers. Unlike many quantitative problems that must by their nature have a unique solution, situations do arise in which there may be more than one correct response to a question. In such situations, you should evaluate each response independently of the others in order to select the most appropriate combination. (See example 20.) In questions of this type there are usually three statements each labeled with a Roman numeral. None or one or more of these statements may correctly answer the question. The statements are followed by five lettered choices, each choice consisting of some combination of the Roman numerals that label the statements. You are to select from among the five lettered choices the one that gives the combination of statements that best answers the question. Questions of this type are intermixed among the standard five-choice completion questions.

The five-choice completion question is also used to test your problem-solving skills. This type of question may present a word problem and require you to convert the information into graphical form or to select and use the mathematical relationship necessary to solve the problem. Alternatively, you may be required to interpret data, graphical material, or mathematical expressions. Thus, the five-choice completion question can be adapted to test several kinds of abilities.

The sample questions that follow illustrate the kinds of mathematical knowledge and techniques required for the tests; they do not describe the specific content of any test. The best test-taking approach is to solve each problem and then look for the choice that best fits the answer you obtained. Trying to work each problem by testing each of the choices is time-consuming and, in many instances, will not work. However, you should look at all the answer choices while studying each question, since the form of the answer choices may help to point out the best approach to solve the problem.

Sample Questions — Mathematics Level I

Directions: For each of the following problems, decide which is the best of the choices given.

Notes: (1) Figures that accompany problems in this test are intended to provide information useful in solving the problems. They are drawn as accurately as possible EXCEPT when it is stated in a specific problem that its figure is not drawn to scale. All figures lie in a plane unless otherwise indicated.

(2) Unless otherwise specified, the domain of a function f is assumed to be the set of all real numbers x for which $f(x)$ is a real number.

Algebra

1. Each of c cases contains b boxes, and each box contains k items. What is the total number of items in the c cases?

   (A) $b + c + k$ (B) $\dfrac{bc}{k}$ (C) $\dfrac{ck}{b}$
   (D) $\dfrac{bk}{c}$ (E) bck

The total number of items in the c cases is found by multiplying the number c of cases by the number b of boxes in each case by the number k of items in each box. The answer is (E).

2. The solution set of $2x^2 - 4x = 30$ is $\{-3,5\}$. What is the solution set of $2(x - 4)^2 - 4(x - 4) = 30$?

   (A) $\{-12,20\}$ (B) $\{-7,1\}$ (C) $\{-\dfrac{3}{4},\dfrac{5}{4}\}$
   (D) $\{1,9\}$ (E) $\{12,-20\}$

There are several ways to approach this problem. You could expand the terms in the equation $2(x - 4)^2 - 4(x - 4) = 30$, collect like terms, and solve the resulting equation. Or you could notice the similarity between the equation $2x^2 - 4x = 30$ that has solution set $\{-3,5\}$ and the equation $2(x - 4)^2 - 4(x - 4) = 30$ that is to be solved. By letting $z = x - 4$, the equation to be solved becomes $2z^2 - 4z = 30$, which has solutions $z = -3$ and $z = 5$. Thus the solution set to be determined consists of the numbers $x = z + 4$, that is, the numbers $x = 1$ and $x = 9$, and the answer is (D).

3. If $i = \sqrt{-1}$, which of the following is an expression for $\sqrt{-49} - \sqrt{-25}$ in the form $a + bi$, where a and b are real numbers?

   (A) $0 + (\sqrt{24})i$ (B) $0 + (\sqrt{74})i$ (C) $0 + 24i$
   (D) $0 + 2i$ (E) $2 + 0i$

For k positive, $\sqrt{-k}$ means $\sqrt{k}\sqrt{-1}$, which equals $\sqrt{k}\,i$. Thus, $\sqrt{-49} - \sqrt{-25} = \sqrt{49}i - \sqrt{25}i = 7i - 5i = 2i$, which is equivalent to $0 + 2i$, and the answer is (D).

Plane Geometry

4. What is the area of a triangle whose sides are 13, 13, and 10?

   (A) $2\sqrt{65}$ (B) $36\sqrt{2}$ (C) 60   (D) 72   (E) 120

In this, as in many geometry questions, a figure may help.

This triangle is isosceles; so the altitude shown bisects the base. You can find the altitude by using the Pythagorean Theorem. $13^2 = h^2 + 5^2$, so $h^2 = 144$, and $h = 12$. Hence the area, $\frac{1}{2} \times$ base $\times$ altitude, is $\frac{1}{2}(10)(12) = 60$ and the answer is (C).

5. If the measure of one angle of a rhombus is 60°, then the ratio of the length of its longer diagonal to the length of its shorter diagonal is

   (A) 2   (B) $\sqrt{3}$ (C) $\sqrt{2}$ (D) $\dfrac{\sqrt{3}}{2}$ (E) $\dfrac{\sqrt{2}}{2}$

Again, drawing a figure helps to clarify the problem.

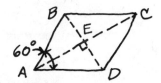

According to the figure, you must find the ratio $\dfrac{AC}{BD}$. Since $ABCD$ is a rhombus, $\triangle ABC$ and $\triangle ADC$ are congruent isosceles triangles. Therefore $\angle BAE = \angle DAE$. Also, since the diagonals of a rhombus are perpendicular, $\angle AED$ is a right angle. If $\angle BAD = 60°$, then $\angle BDA = 60°$ and $\angle EAD = 30°$. Since $\triangle ADE$ is a 30°-60°-90° triangle, $ED = \frac{1}{2}(AD)$ and $AE = \frac{1}{2}\sqrt{3}(AD)$. The diagonals of a rhombus bisect each other; therefore $AC = 2(AE) = \sqrt{3}(AD)$ and $BD = 2(ED) = 1(AD)$. Thus $\dfrac{AC}{BD} = \dfrac{\sqrt{3}}{1} = \sqrt{3}$ and the answer is (B).

Coordinate Geometry

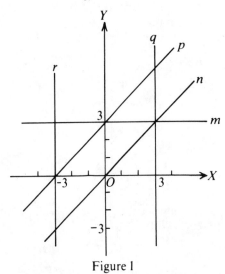

Figure 1

6. Which of the lines in Figure 1 is the graph of $x = 3$?

   (A) m (B) n (C) p (D) q (E) r

The graph of $x = 3$ is a vertical line with x-intercept 3. The answer is (D).

7. Which quadrants of the plane contain points of the graph of $2x - y > 4$?

   (A) First, second, and third only
   (B) First, second, and fourth only
   (C) First, third, and fourth only
   (D) Second, third, and fourth only
   (E) First, second, third, and fourth

This problem can be solved by first sketching the graph of the inequality.

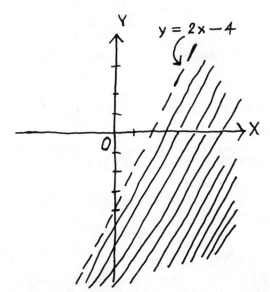

$2x - y > 4$ is equivalent to $y < 2x - 4$. The equation for the boundary of the half-plane represented

247

by this inequality is $y = 2x - 4$, and the points that satisfy the inequality are in the half-plane below this boundary as shown. The answer is (C).

Solid Geometry

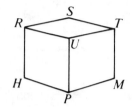

Figure 2

8. **Figure 2 represents a cube. The intersection of plane *RSM* and plane *TSH* is line**

(A) *RM*   (B) *SP*   (C) *TH*   (D) *TP*   (E) *SH*

Since $RS \parallel PM$, the lines RS and PM determine a plane. This plane must be the plane determined by points R, S, and M. Therefore P lies in plane RSM. Similarly, P lies in plane TSH. Since P and S lie in both planes RSM and TSH, line SP is contained in RSM and TSH and therefore in their intersection. The answer is (B).

Trigonometry

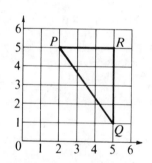

Figure 3

9. **In right triangle *PRQ* in Figure 3, cos ∠ *QPR* =**

(A) $\frac{3}{5}$ (B) $\frac{3}{4}$ (C) $\frac{4}{5}$ (D) $\frac{4}{3}$ (E) $\frac{5}{3}$

In right triangle PRQ, $\cos \angle QPR = \dfrac{PR}{PQ}$. By counting the spaces on the grid, you can determine that $PR = 3$ and $RQ = 4$. The length of PQ can be found by using the Pythagorean Theorem: $(PQ)^2 = (PR)^2 + (RQ)^2$. $PR = 3$ and $RQ = 4$, therefore $PQ = \sqrt{3^2 + 4^2} = \sqrt{9 + 16} = \sqrt{25} = 5$; thus $\cos \angle QPR = \frac{3}{5}$ and the answer is (A).

Elementary Functions

10. **If $f(x) = 3x + 6$ and $g(x) = 5x - 4$, what is the real number r such that $f(r) = g(r)$?**

(A) -2 (B) 0 (C) $\frac{1}{4}$ (D) $\frac{4}{5}$ (E) 5

Since $f(x) = 3x + 6$ and $g(x) = 5x - 4$, we have $f(r) = 3r + 6$ and $g(r) = 5r - 4$. To find the real number r such that $f(r) = g(r)$, the equation $3r + 6 = 5r - 4$ must be solved. The solution is $r = 5$; the answer is (E).

Figure 4

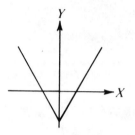

11. **Figure 4 is the graph of $y = f(x)$. Which of the following is the graph of $y = |f(x)|$?**

(A)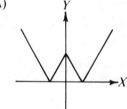

(B)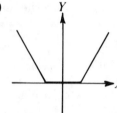

(C)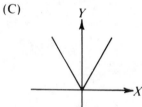

(D)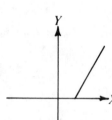

(E)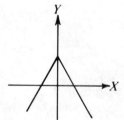

This problem can be solved by using the fact that the absolute value of any number is greater than or equal to 0; thus the absolute value of a negative number x is equal to $-x$, for example $|-2| = -(-2) = 2$. Thus the portion of the graph below the X-axis in Figure 4 (that is, where $y = f(x) < 0$) would be reflected in that axis to become positive. The answer is (A).

Miscellaneous

12. Let P be the set of multiples of 2, Q be the set of multiples of 3, and R be the set of multiples of 7. Which of the following contains 63?

(A) $P \cap Q \cap R$ (B) $Q \cap R$ (C) $P \cap Q$ (D) $P \cap R$ (E) P

If 63 is factored into its prime factors, that is, $63 = 3^2 \times 7$, it is apparent that 63 is a multiple of 3 and a multiple of 7, but not a multiple of 2. Hence 63 is in the intersection of Q and R and the answer is (B).

Sample Questions — Mathematics Level II ∎

Directions: For each of the following problems, decide which is the best of the choices given.

Notes: (1) Figures that accompany problems in this test are intended to provide information useful in solving the problems. They are drawn as accurately as possible EXCEPT when it is stated in a specific problem that its figure is not drawn to scale. All figures lie in a plane unless otherwise indicated.

(2) Unless otherwise specified, the domain of a function f is assumed to be the set of all real numbers x for which $f(x)$ is a real number.

Algebra

13. For what real numbers x is $y = 2^{-x}$ a negative number?

(A) All real numbers x (B) $x > 0$ only (C) $x \geq 0$ only
(D) $x < 0$ only   (E) No real number x

Since $2^{-x} = \frac{1}{2^x}$ and 2^x is always positive, 2^{-x} is positive for all x and the answer is (E).

14. If $Z = p + qi$ and $\overline{Z} = p - qi$ are two complex numbers and p and q are real numbers, which of the following statements is true?

(A) $Z = -\overline{Z}$

(B) $(\overline{Z})^2$ is a real number.

(C) $Z \cdot \overline{Z}$ is a real number.

(D) $(\overline{Z})^2 = Z^2$

(E) $Z^2 = -(\overline{Z})^2$

To solve this problem, you should check the options.

(A): $-\overline{Z} = -(p - qi) = -p + qi \neq p + qi = Z$.

(B): $(\overline{Z})^2 = (p - qi)^2 = p^2 + q^2 - 2pqi$, which is not necessarily a real number.

(C): $Z \cdot \overline{Z} = (p + qi)(p - qi) = p^2 + q^2$, which is a real number. Thus (C) is the answer.

Although you can verify that (D) and (E) are not true, you do not have to check the remaining choices once you find the correct one. In fact, if you had realized that Z and $\overline{Z}$ are conjugate complex numbers and

that the product of conjugates is always a real number, you could have found the correct answer more quickly.

15. A teacher gives a test to 20 students. Grades on the test range from 0 to 10 inclusive. The average grade for the first 12 papers is 6.5. If x is the average grade for the class, then which of the following is true?

(A) $0.33 \leq x \leq 6.50$ (B) $3.25 \leq x \leq 6.50$

(C) $3.90 \leq x \leq 6.50$ (D) $3.90 \leq x \leq 7.90$

(E) $4.00 \leq x \leq 7.90$

Since the average grade of the first 12 papers is 6.5, the sum of these grades is 12(6.5) or 78. The least possible sum of the grades for the other 8 papers is 0 and the maximum possible sum is 80. Therefore the average grade for the class is between $\frac{78 + 0}{20} = 3.90$ and $\frac{78 + 80}{20} = 7.90$ inclusive. The answer is (D).

Solid Geometry

Figure 5

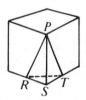

16. In Figure 5, R and T are the midpoints of two adjacent edges of the cube. If the length of each edge of the cube is h, what is the volume of the pyramid $PRST$?

(A) $\frac{h^3}{24}$ (B) $\frac{h^3}{12}$ (C) $\frac{h^3}{8}$ (D) $\frac{h^3}{6}$ (E) $\frac{h^3}{4}$

The volume of a pyramid is $\frac{1}{3}bh$, where b is the area of the base of the pyramid and h is the length of its altitude. It may be helpful to mark the figure to indicate those parts whose lengths are given or that can be deduced.

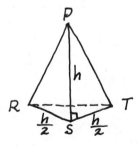

Since PS is perpendicular to $\triangle RST$, its length h is the length of the altitude of the pyramid $PRST$. The base of the pyramid is $\triangle RST$. R and T are the midpoints of two adjacent edges of the cube, therefore the lengths of RS and ST are both $\frac{h}{2}$. Since $\triangle RST$ is a right triangle, its area is $(\frac{1}{2})\,(\frac{h}{2})\,(\frac{h}{2}) = \frac{h^2}{8}$. Thus the volume of $PRST$ is $(\frac{1}{3})\,(\frac{h^2}{8})\,(h) = \frac{h^3}{24}$ and the answer is (A).

Coordinate Geometry

17. Which of the following figures represents the rectangular-coordinate graph of

$$\begin{cases} x = 2\cos\theta \\ y = 4\sin\theta \end{cases} ?$$

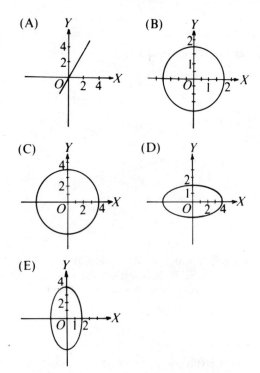

The two equations given in this problem are parametric equations that relate polar coordinates to rectangular coordinates. Since $x = 2\cos\theta$ and $y = 4\sin\theta$, $\cos\theta = \frac{x}{2}$ and $\sin\theta = \frac{y}{4}$. From the fact that $\cos^2\theta + \sin^2\theta = 1$, the equation $\frac{x^2}{4} + \frac{y^2}{16} = 1$ results. This is the equation of an ellipse that has center $(0,0)$ and passes through $(2,0)$ and $(0,4)$. The answer is (E).

Figure 6

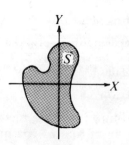

18. In Figure 6, shaded region S has area 10. What is the area of region T, which consists of all points $(x - 1, y + 4)$ where the point (x, y) is in S?

(A) 40   (B) 30   (C) 20   (D) $10\sqrt{2}$ (E) 10

For each point (x, y) in S, there is a point in T one unit to the left of and four units above (x, y); similarly, for each point $(x - 1, y + 4)$ in T, there is a point in S one unit to the right of and four units below $(x - 1, y + 4)$. Thus T is a region that has points to the left of and above points in S and that is congruent to S. Hence the area of T is the same as the area of S, and the answer is (E).

You can solve this problem by using transformational geometry. The mapping $S \rightarrow T$ or $(x, y) \rightarrow (x - 1, y + 4)$ is a translation. A translation is an isometry, and an isometry maps congruent figures onto congruent figures. Since regions S and T are congruent, their areas are equal.

Trigonometry

19. If $\sin(\sin x) = 0$ and $0 \le x \le \frac{\pi}{2}$, then $x =$

(A) 0   (B) $\frac{\pi}{6}$ (C) $\frac{\pi}{4}$ (D) $\frac{\pi}{3}$ (E) $\frac{\pi}{2}$

Let $y = \sin x$. Then $\sin(\sin x) = \sin y = 0$ and y must be $k\pi$, where k is an integer. Since $k\pi = \sin x$ and $0 \le x \le \frac{\pi}{2}$, the only possible integer value of k is 0 and x must be 0. The answer is (A).

20. If $0 < y < x < \frac{\pi}{2}$, which of the following must be true?

   I. $\sin y < \sin x$
   II. $\cos y < \cos x$
   III. $\tan y < \tan x$

(A) None   (B) I and II only
   (C) I and III only   (D) II and III only
      (E) I, II, and III

In this problem it is helpful to sketch or make a mental image of the graphs of the three functions.

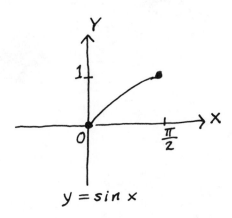

$y = \sin x$

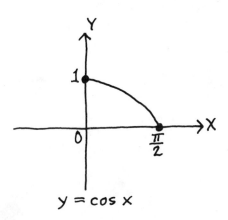

$y = \cos x$

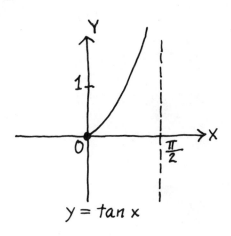

$y = \tan x$

From the graphs, it can be observed that sin x and tan x are increasing over the interval $0 < x < \frac{\pi}{2}$, but cos x is decreasing over that interval. The answer is (C).

Elementary Functions

21. If $f(x) = 2x$ and $f(g(x)) = -x$, then $g(x) =$

(A) $-3x$ (B) $-\frac{x}{2}$ (C) $\frac{x}{2}$ (D) $2 - \frac{x}{2}$ (E) x

The solution to this problem depends on your understanding of function notation. Since $f(x) = 2x$, $f(g(x)) = 2(g(x)) = -x$. Solving the latter equation for $g(x)$ gives $\frac{-x}{2}$. The answer is (B).

22. If $f(x) = 10^x$, where x is real, and if the inverse function of f is denoted by f^{-1}, then what is $\frac{f^{-1}(a)}{f^{-1}(b)}$ where $a > 1$ and $b > 1$?

(A) $\log_{10}a - \log_{10}b$ (B) $\log_{10}(a - b)$

(C) $\frac{\log_{10}a}{\log_{10}b}$ (D) $\frac{10^b}{10^a}$

(E) **None of the above**

Since the inverse of the exponential function $f(x) = 10^x$ is the logarithmic function $f^{-1}(x) = \log_{10}x$, $\frac{f^{-1}(a)}{f^{-1}(b)} = \frac{\log_{10}a}{\log_{10}b}$ and the answer is (C).

Miscellaneous

23. For all positive real numbers, $a * b$ is defined by the equation $a * b = \frac{ab}{a+b}$. If $2 * x = 3 * 4$, then $x =$

(A) 12   (B) 8   (C) 6   (D) 4   (E) 3

You can solve this problem by substituting in the given equation and solving for x.

$2 * x = \frac{2x}{2 + x}$ and $3 * 4 = \frac{3(4)}{3 + 4}$

$\frac{2x}{2 + x} = \frac{12}{7}$

$14x = 24 + 12x$

$x = 12$

The answer is (A).

24. The probability that R hits a certain target is $\frac{3}{5}$ and the probability that T hits it is $\frac{5}{7}$. What is the probability that R hits the target and T misses it?

(A) $\frac{4}{35}$ (B) $\frac{6}{35}$ (C) $\frac{3}{7}$ (D) $\frac{21}{25}$ (E) $\frac{31}{35}$

Since you can assume that the two events are independent, the probability that R hits the target and T misses it is the product of the two probabilities. The former probability is given. The latter is the complement of the probability that T hits the target, that is, $1 - \frac{5}{7}$ or $\frac{2}{7}$. Therefore $P = \left(\frac{3}{5}\right)\left(\frac{2}{7}\right) = \frac{6}{35}$. The answer is (B).

Mathematics Achievement Test, Level I

The test that follows is an edition of the Mathematics Achievement Test, Level I, administered in May 1983. So that you will have an idea of what the actual test administration will be like, try to take this test under conditions as close as possible to those of the actual test. It will probably help if you

- Set aside an hour for the test when you will not be interrupted, so that you can complete all of it in one sitting.

- Sit at a desk with no other papers or books. You can't take a calculator, a dictionary, other books, or notes into the test room.

- Have a kitchen timer or clock in front of you for timing yourself.

- Tear out an answer sheet from the back of this book and fill it in just as you would on the day of the test. You can use one answer sheet for as many as three Achievement Tests.

- Read the instructions that precede the test. When you take the test, you will be asked to read them before you begin answering questions.

- After you finish the test, read the sections on "How to Score the Mathematics Achievement Test, Level I," and "Reviewing Your Test Performance," which follow the test.

MATHEMATICS LEVEL I

The top portion of the section of the answer sheet which you will use in taking the Mathematics Level I test must be filled in exactly as shown in the illustration below. Note carefully that you have to do all of the following on your answer sheet:

1. Print MATHEMATICS LEVEL I on the line to the right of the words "Achievement Test."
2. Blacken spaces 1 and 6 in the row of spaces immediately under the words "Test Code."
3. Blacken space 5 in the group of five spaces labeled X.
4. Blacken space 1 in the group of five spaces labeled Y.

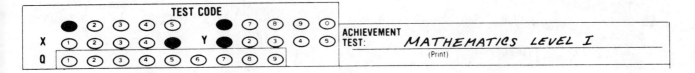

You are to leave blank the nine spaces which are labeled Q.

When the supervisor gives the signal, turn the page and begin the Mathematics Level I test. There are 100 numbered spaces on the answer sheet and 50 questions in the Mathematics Level I test. Therefore, use only spaces 1 to 50 for recording your answers.

MATHEMATICS LEVEL I

For each of the following problems, decide which is the best of the choices given. Then blacken the corresponding space on the answer sheet.

Notes: (1) Figures that accompany problems in this test are intended to provide information useful in solving the problems. They are drawn as accurately as possible EXCEPT when it is stated in a specific problem that its figure is not drawn to scale. All figures lie in a plane unless otherwise indicated.

(2) Unless otherwise specified, the domain of a function f is assumed to be the set of all real numbers x for which $f(x)$ is a real number.

USE THIS SPACE FOR SCRATCHWORK.

1. If $\dfrac{5}{b+8} = \dfrac{3}{b+4}$, then $b =$

   (A) $\dfrac{15}{32}$ (B) $\dfrac{1}{2}$ (C) $\dfrac{11}{8}$ (D) 2   (E) 4

2. If $x = (a+2)^2$ and $a = -1$, then $x =$

   (A) 9   (B) 4   (C) 3   (D) 2   (E) 1

3. If the cost of a dozen pencils is \$1.56, and if the cost of a pen and one of these pencils together is \$2.98, what is the cost of the pen alone?

   (A) \$1.42   (B) \$2.85   (C) \$3.11
   (D) \$3.15   (E) \$4.54

4. If $3^{2x} = 9$, then $x =$

   (A) 1   (B) $\dfrac{3}{2}$ (C) 3   (D) $\dfrac{9}{2}$ (E) 6

5. In Figure 1, if Q is the midpoint of segment PT, then the length of segment RT is

   (A) $\dfrac{13}{8}$ (B) $\dfrac{23}{12}$ (C) $\dfrac{55}{24}$ (D) $\dfrac{55}{12}$ (E) $\dfrac{13}{2}$

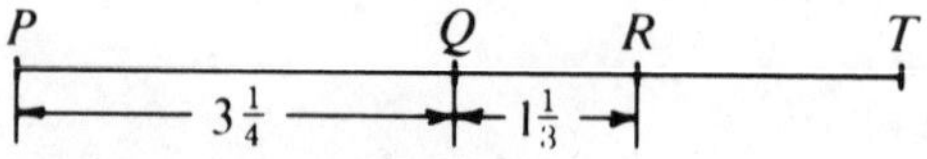

Figure 1

6. The distance between the points $(-5, 0)$ and $(-12, 0)$ is

   (A) $\sqrt{17}$ (B) 7   (C) 13   (D) 17   (E) $\sqrt{119}$

GO ON TO THE NEXT PAGE

256

MATHEMATICS LEVEL I—*Continued*

7. If $\frac{3}{4}x = 0$, then $\frac{3}{4} + x =$

   (A) $\frac{25}{12}$ (B) $\frac{7}{4}$ (C) 1   (D) $\frac{3}{4}$ (E) 0

8. If $4 < x < 9$ and $6 < y < 12$, then

   (A) $48 < xy < 54$ (B) $36 < xy < 72$ (C) $24 < xy < 108$
   (D) $10 < xy < 21$ (E) $4 < xy < 12$

9. In Figure 2, two chords of the circle intersect, making the angles shown. What is the value of $x + y$?

   (A) 40   (B) 50   (C) 80   (D) 160   (E) 320

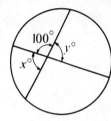

Figure 2

10. If $\frac{r}{s} = 3$, then $r^2 - 9s^2 =$

    (A) -9 (B) -8 (C) 0   (D) 8   (E) 9

11. If $xy - x = 15$ and $y - 1 = 5$, then $x =$

    (A) 20   (B) 15   (C) 5   (D) 4   (E) 3

12. If $\frac{1}{\frac{x}{2}} = \frac{1}{5}$, then $x =$

    (A) $\frac{1}{5}$ (B) $\frac{2}{5}$ (C) $\frac{11}{5}$ (D) $\frac{5}{2}$ (E) 10

GO ON TO THE NEXT PAGE →

USE THIS SPACE FOR SCRATCHWORK.

13. $\sqrt{27} + 2\sqrt{12} - 7\sqrt{3} =$

(A) $3 - 3\sqrt{3}$ (B) 0   (C) $6\sqrt{2} - 4\sqrt{3}$
(D) $4\sqrt{3}$ (E) $10\sqrt{3}$

14. In Figure 3, if $BE = BD = DC$, then $x =$

(A) 35   (B) 75   (C) 105   (D) 115   (E) 120

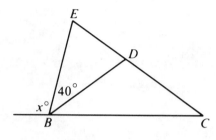

Figure 3

15. The solution to the pair of equations $\begin{cases} kx + my = 11 \\ mx + ky = 10 \end{cases}$

is $x = 2$, $y = 1$. What are the values of k and m?

(A) $k = 4$ (B) $k = 5$ (C) $k = 6$
     $m = 3$ $m = 1$ $m = -1$

(D) $k = 3$ (E) $k = 1$
     $m = 4$ $m = 5$

16. If an operation ϕ is defined for all real numbers x and y by the equation $x \phi y = x - y + xy$, then $2 \phi (-2) =$

(A) -8 (B) -4 (C) 0   (D) 4   (E) 8

17. A theorem states that if perpendiculars are drawn to each of the three sides of an equilateral triangle T from any point P inside T, as in Figure 4, then the sum of the lengths of the perpendiculars is constant. This sum is equal to

(A) half the perimeter of T
(B) the altitude of T
(C) the square root of the area of T
(D) $\sqrt{2}$ times the length of a side of T
(E) $\sqrt{3}$ times the length of a side of T

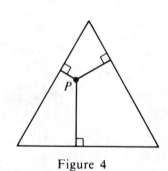

Figure 4

GO ON TO THE NEXT PAGE

USE THIS SPACE FOR SCRATCHWORK.

18. What is the least positive integer k for which $9 - k$ and $16 - k$ will be nonzero and have opposite signs?

   (A) 8   (B) 10   (C) 12   (D) 15   (E) 17

19. If $f(x) = 3x - 2$ and $0 < x < 3$, then $f(x)$ is between

   (A) -6 and -3
   (B) -3 and 0
   (C) -2 and 7
   (D) -1 and 8
   (E) 0 and 9

20. In Figure 5, $\triangle DAB$ is a right isosceles triangle. If $CA = 6$ and $AB = 4$, what is the area of $\triangle CDB$?

   (A) 2   (B) 4   (C) $4\sqrt{2}$ (D) 8   (E) 12

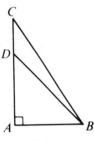

Figure 5

21. If $f(x) = \dfrac{x-1}{x}$ and $g(x) = \dfrac{1}{x}$, then $f(g(3)) =$

   (A) $\dfrac{3}{2}$ (B) $\dfrac{2}{3}$ (C) $-\dfrac{2}{9}$ (D) $-\dfrac{2}{3}$ (E) -2

22. If $xyz \neq 0$, then $\dfrac{9x^2yz^6}{27xy^2z^3} =$

   (A) $3xyz^3$ (B) $\dfrac{3xz^2}{y}$ (C) $\dfrac{xz^2}{3y}$ (D) $\dfrac{xz^3}{3y}$ (E) $\dfrac{x^2z^3}{3y^2}$

23. Of all rectangles with a given perimeter, the square has maximum area. What is the maximum area of a rectangle with perimeter 28 ?

   (A) 784   (B) 196   (C) 49   (D) 28   (E) $2\sqrt{7}$

GO ON TO THE NEXT PAGE

24. If there exist positive integers u and v such that
$$6u + 10v = q,$$
then q must be divisible by which of the following?

(A) 2   (B) 3   (C) 5   (D) 10   (E) 60

25. How many integers are in the solution set of $|2x - 6| > 1$?

(A) None   (B) One   (C) Two

(D) Three   (E) Infinitely many

26. In right triangle ABC in Figure 6, if $\sin A = \frac{1}{2}$, then the length of BC is

(A) 1   (B) $2\frac{1}{2}$ (C) 5   (D) $2\sqrt{5}$ (E) $5\sqrt{3}$

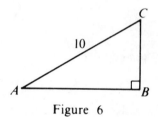

Figure 6

27. Which of the following is NOT the graph of a function of x?

(A) 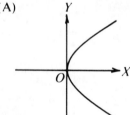   (B)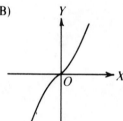

(C) 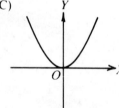   (D)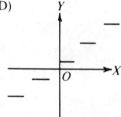

(E)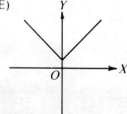

GO ON TO THE NEXT PAGE

28. The following instructions to a computer are carried out in the order specified.

   1. LET $S = 0$.
   2. LET $N = 1$.
   3. IF $N^2 > 16$ GO TO INSTRUCTION 6 OTHERWISE GO TO INSTRUCTION 4.
   4. INCREASE S BY 10 AND INCREASE N BY 1.
   5. GO BACK TO INSTRUCTION 3.
   6. WRITE THE FINAL VALUE OF S.

   What is the final value of S ?

   (A) 10   (B) 20   (C) 30   (D) 40   (E) 50

29. An equation for the circle that has its center at the origin and passes through the point (3, 4) is

   (A) $x^2 + y^2 = 4$ (B) $x^2 + y^2 = 5$ (C) $x^2 + y^2 = 16$
   (D) $x^2 + y^2 = 25$ (E) $x^2 + y^2 = 49$

30. If x and y are even integers, which of the following must be an odd integer?

   I. $\dfrac{x + y}{2}$

   II. $xy - 1$

   III. $\dfrac{xy - 1}{2}$

   (A) I only   (B) II only   (C) I and II only
   (D) II and III only   (E) I, II, and III

31. If $f(x) = 8x - 2$ for all x, then the slope of the line given by $y = f(x + 1)$ is

   (A) -3 (B) 1   (C) 7   (D) 8   (E) 9

GO ON TO THE NEXT PAGE

32. If $0° \leqq \theta \leqq 90°$, the value of $1 + \cos^2\theta + \sin^2\theta$ is

   (A) -2 (B) -1 (C) 0 (D) 1 (E) 2

33. If $f(x) = 2x - 3$ and $g(f(x)) = x$, then $g(x) =$

   (A) $\dfrac{x+3}{2}$ (B) $\dfrac{x}{2} + 3$ (C) $2x$

   (D) $2x + 3$ (E) $4x - 9$

34. In Figure 7, if $AC \parallel DF$ and if $AC = x$ and $BC = y$, then $\dfrac{DE}{EF} =$

   (A) $\dfrac{x}{y}$ (B) $\dfrac{x}{y} + 1$ (C) $\dfrac{x}{y} - 1$

   (D) $\dfrac{y}{x}$ (E) $\dfrac{y}{x} - 1$

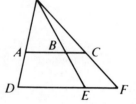

Figure 7

35. If $i^2 = -1$ and if $x = 3 + 2i$, then $x^2 =$

   (A) $5 + 12i$ (B) $7 + 12i$ (C) $9 + 8i$

   (D) $9 + 16i$ (E) $13 + 12i$

36. In Figure 8, if square $ABCD$ has a side of length r, then the ratio 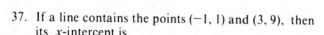 $=$

   (A) $\dfrac{2\sqrt{2}}{1}$ (B) $\dfrac{2}{1}$ (C) $\dfrac{\sqrt{2}}{1}$ (D) $\dfrac{1}{\sqrt{2}}$ (E) $\dfrac{1}{2}$

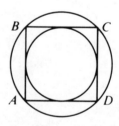

Figure 8

37. If a line contains the points $(-1, 1)$ and $(3, 9)$, then its x-intercept is

   (A) $-\dfrac{3}{2}$ (B) $-\dfrac{2}{3}$ (C) $\dfrac{2}{5}$ (D) 2 (E) 3

GO ON TO THE NEXT PAGE

USE THIS SPACE FOR SCRATCHWORK.

38. If $\frac{1}{x} = \frac{1}{\frac{1}{y}}$, then $1 < x < 10$ if and only if

   (A) $\frac{1}{10} < y < 1$ (B) $\frac{1}{10} < y < 10$ (C) $1 < y < 10$

   (D) $1 < y < 100$ (E) $10 < y < 100$

39. A solid cube that measures 1 meter on an edge has a mass of 150 kilograms. What is the mass, in kilograms, of a solid cube of the same kind of material that measures 2 meters on an edge?

   (A) 300   (B) 450   (C) 600   (D) 900   (E) 1,200

40. In the right triangle in Figure 9, $\sin \theta$ is equal to which of the following?

   I. $\cos \omega$

   II. $\frac{r}{t}$

   III. $\frac{s}{t}$

   (A) I only   (B) II only   (C) III only

   (D) I and II   (E) I and III

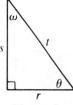

Figure 9

41. If the points $P(5, 0)$, $Q(0, -1)$, $R(2, 0)$, and $S(0, 3)$ are connected in that order to form a quadrilateral with sides PQ, QR, RS, and SP, the area of the quadrilateral will be

   (A) 6   (B) 9   (C) 10   (D) 12   (E) 15

42. Two planes are necessarily perpendicular to each other if they are respectively

   (A) parallel to two perpendicular lines
   (B) perpendicular to two parallel lines
   (C) parallel to two perpendicular planes
   (D) perpendicular to two parallel planes
   (E) perpendicular to two perpendicular planes

GO ON TO THE NEXT PAGE

USE THIS SPACE FOR SCRATCHWORK.

43. If θ is an acute angle and $\sin \theta = \dfrac{t}{s}$, where $t > 0$, $s > 0$, and $t \neq s$, then $\cos \theta =$

(A) $\dfrac{\sqrt{t^2 - s^2}}{s}$ (B) $\dfrac{\sqrt{s^2 - t^2}}{s}$ (C) $\dfrac{\sqrt{t^2 - s^2}}{t}$

(D) $\dfrac{\sqrt{s^2 - t^2}}{t}$ (E) $\dfrac{s}{t}$

44. Which of the following represents the graph of the equation $y = |x - 5|$?

(A)
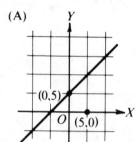

(B)
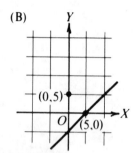

(C)
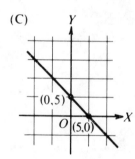

(D)
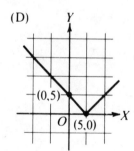

(E)
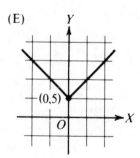

45. If $a \neq 0$, then $(9^{3a})(3^{9a}) =$

(A) 27^{12a} (B) 9^{9a} (C) 9^{6a} (D) 3^{18a} (E) 3^{15a}

GO ON TO THE NEXT PAGE

USE THIS SPACE FOR SCRATCHWORK.

46. In Figure 10, $\triangle ABC \sim \triangle A'B'C'$ and $a = ka'$. If the area of $\triangle ABC$ is $\frac{1}{2}ah$, what is the area of $\triangle A'B'C'$ in terms of k, a, and h?

(A) $\frac{kah}{2}$ (B) $\frac{k^2ah}{2}$ (C) $\frac{ah}{2k}$ (D) $\frac{k^2ah}{4}$ (E) $\frac{ah}{2k^2}$

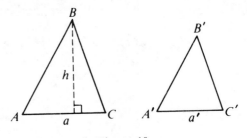

Figure 10

47. "If p, then q" is logically equivalent to which of the following?

(A) If not p, then q.
(B) If not p, then not q.
(C) If q, then p.
(D) If not q, then not p.
(E) If not q, then p.

48. If one vertex of a cube with volume 64 is the center of a sphere of radius 6, how many vertices of the cube are <u>outside</u> the sphere?

(A) None (B) One (C) Three (D) Four (E) Seven

49. The coordinates of the point of intersection of the lines having equations $\sqrt{2}x + 2y = 1$ and $x - \sqrt{2}y = \sqrt{2}$ are

(A) $\left(\frac{3}{2\sqrt{2}}, \frac{1}{4}\right)$ (B) $\left(\frac{3}{2\sqrt{2}}, -\frac{1}{4}\right)$ (C) $\left(\frac{1}{2\sqrt{2}}, \frac{1}{2}\right)$

(D) $\left(\frac{1}{2\sqrt{2}}, -\frac{1}{2}\right)$ (E) $\left(\sqrt{2}, \frac{1}{2\sqrt{2}}\right)$

50. In Figure 11, R and S are the centers of circles that intersect at P and at T. If arc PRT has length 2π, what is the area of the circle with center S?

(A) 4π (B) 6π (C) 9π (D) 36π (E) 64π

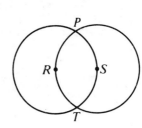

Figure 11

S T O P

IF YOU FINISH BEFORE TIME IS CALLED, YOU MAY CHECK YOUR WORK ON THIS TEST ONLY.
DO NOT WORK ON ANY OTHER TEST IN THIS BOOK.

How to Score the Mathematics Achievement Test, Level I

When you take the Mathematics Achievement Test, Level I, your answer sheet will be "read" by a scanning machine that will record your responses to each question. Then a computer will compare your answers with the correct answers and produce your raw score. You get one point for each correct answer. For each wrong answer, you lose one-fourth of a point. Questions you omit (and any for which you mark more than one answer) are not counted. This raw score is converted to a College Board scaled score that is reported to you and to the colleges you specify. After you have taken this test, you can get an idea of what your score might be by following the instructions in the next two sections.

Determining Your Raw Score

Step 1: Table A on the next page lists the correct answers for all the questions on the test.* Compare your answer with the correct answer and
- Put a check in the column marked "Right" if your answer is correct.
- Put a check in the column marked "Wrong" if your answer is incorrect.
- Leave both columns blank if you omitted the question.

Step 2: Count the number of right answers and enter the number here . . . . _____

Step 3: Count the number of wrong answers and enter

the number here . . . . 4) ‾‾‾‾‾‾‾‾‾‾‾

Enter the result of dividing by 4 here . . . . _____

Step 4: Subtract the number you obtained in Step 3 from the number in Step 2; round the result to the nearest whole number (.5 is rounded up) and enter here. . _____

The number you obtained in Step 4 is your raw score. (The correction for guessing — subtraction of a quarter of a point for each incorrect answer — adjusts for the fact that random guessing on a large number of questions will result in some questions being answered correctly by chance.) Instructions for converting your raw score to a scaled score follow.

*The last column in Table A gives the percentage of students who took the test in May 1983 that answered the question correctly. (See page 269 for further explanation.)

TABLE A

Answers to Mathematics Test, Level I, Form 3FAC, and Percentage of Students Answering Each Question Correctly

Question Number	Correct Answer	Right	Wrong	Percentage of Students Answering the Question Correctly
1	D			84%
2	E			92
3	B			92
4	A			93
5	B			85
6	B			82
7	D			92
8	C			82
9	D			85
10	C			82
11	E			85
12	E			90
13	B			82
14	C			67
15	A			82
16	C			65
17	B			44
18	B			65
19	C			43
20	B			33
21	E			57
22	D			74
23	C			59
24	A			82
25	E			77
26	C			62
27	A			45
28	D			53
29	D			59
30	B			31
31	D			43
32	E			47
33	A			29
34	C			23
35	A			54
36	C			22
37	A			37
38	A			43
39	E			27
40	E			42
41	A			18
42	C			28
43	B			33
44	D			36
45	E			19
46	E			07
47	D			12
48	B			10
49	B			18
50	C			14

Note: The percentages are based on the analysis of the answer sheets for a random sample of students who took this test in May 1983 and whose mean score was 547.

Finding Your College Board Scaled Score ▬

When you take Achievement Tests, the scores sent to the colleges you specify will be reported on the College Board scale, ranging from 200 to 800. The raw score that you obtained above (Step 4) can be converted to a scaled score by using Table B.

To find your scaled score on this test, locate your raw score in the left column of Table B; the corresponding score in the right column will be your College Board scaled score. For example, a raw score of 25 on this particular edition of the Mathematics Achievement Test, Level I, corresponds to a College Board scaled score of 570. Raw scores are converted to scaled scores to ensure that a score earned on any one edition of the Mathematics Achievement Test, Level I, is comparable to the same scaled score earned on any other edition of the test.

Because some editions of the Mathematics Achievement Test, Level I, may be slightly easier or more difficult than others, statistical adjustments are made in the scores so that each College Board scaled score indicates the same level of performance, regardless of the edition of the test you take and the ability of the group you take it with. A given raw score will correspond to different College Board scores, depending on the edition of the test taken. A raw score of 40, for example, may convert to a College Board score of 720 on one edition of the test, but that raw score might convert to a College Board score of 740 on a slightly more difficult edition. When you take the Mathematics Achievement Test, Level I, on the actual test day, your score is likely to differ somewhat from the score you obtained on this test. People perform at different levels at different times, for reasons unrelated to the test itself. The precision of any test is also limited because it represents only a sample of all the possible questions that could be asked. (See page 12, "How Precise Are Your Scores?" for further information.)

TABLE B — SCORE CONVERSION TABLE			
Mathematics Achievement Test, Level I, Form 3FAC			
Raw Score	College Board Scaled Score	Raw Score	College Board Scaled Score
50	800	15	470
49	800	14	460
48	800	13	450
47	790	12	440
46	780	11	430
45	770	10	420
44	760	9	410
43	750	8	390
42	740	7	380
41	730	6	370
40	720	5	360
39	710	4	350
38	700	3	340
37	690	2	330
36	680	1	320
35	670	0	310
34	660	−1	300
33	650	−2	290
32	640	−3	280
31	630	−4	270
30	620	−5	260
29	610	−6	250
28	600	−7	240
27	590	−8	230
26	580	−9	220
25	570	−10	210
24	560	−11	200
23	550	−12	200
22	540		
21	530		
20	520		
19	510		
18	500		
17	490		
16	480		

Reviewing Your Test Performance

After you have scored your test, you should take some time to consider the following points in relation to your performance on the test.

- *Did you run out of time before you reached the end of the test?*

  If you did, you may want to consider tactics that will help you pace yourself better. For example, you may have spent too much time working on one or two difficult questions. A better approach might have been to continue the test and return to those questions after you had attempted to answer the remaining questions on the test.

- *Did you take a long time reading the directions for the test?*

  The directions in this test are the same as those in the Mathematics Achievement Tests, Level I now being administered. You will save time when you read the directions on the test day if you become thoroughly familiar with them in advance.

- *How did you handle questions you were unsure of?*

  If you were able to eliminate one or more of the answer choices and you guessed from the remaining choices, then your approach probably worked to your advantage. On the other hand, omitting questions about which you have some knowledge or guessing answers haphazardly would probably be a mistake.

• *How difficult were the questions for you compared with other students who took the test?*

By referring to Table A on page 267 you can find out how difficult each question was for the group of students who took the test in May 1983. The right-hand column in the table tells you what percentage of that group of students answered the question correctly. It is important to remember that these percentages are based on only one group of students; had this edition of the test been given to all students in the class of 1983 who took a Mathematics Achievement Test, Level I, the percentages would probably have been different. A question that was answered correctly by almost everyone in the group, obviously, is an easy question. Question 4, for example, was answered correctly by 93 percent of the students in the sample. On the other hand, question 46 was answered correctly by only 7 percent of the students. If you find that you missed several questions that would be considered easy, you may want to review those questions carefully. They may cover some aspect of the subject that you need to review. Perhaps you misunderstood the directions for one part of the test or you thought the questions were so easy that you did not spend as much time on them as you might have.

Mathematics Achievement Test, Level II

The test that follows is an edition of the Mathematics Achievement Test, Level II, administered in November 1982. So that you will have an idea of what the actual test administration will be like, try to take this test under conditions as close as possible to those of the actual test. It will probably help if you

- Set aside an hour for the test when you will not be interrupted, so that you can complete all of it in one sitting.

- Sit at a desk with no other papers or books. You can't take a calculator, a dictionary, other books, or notes into the test room.

- Have a kitchen timer or clock in front of you for timing yourself.

- Tear out an answer sheet from the back of this book and fill it in just as you would on the day of the test. You can use one answer sheet for as many as three Achievement Tests.

- Read the instructions that precede the test. When you take the test, you will be asked to read them before you begin answering questions.

- After you finish the test, read the sections on "How to Score the Mathematics Achievement Test, Level II," and "Reviewing Your Test Performance," which follow the test.

MATHEMATICS LEVEL II

The top portion of the section of the answer sheet which you will use in taking the Mathematics Level II test must be filled in exactly as shown in the illustration below. Note carefully that you have to do all of the following on your answer sheet:

1. Print MATHEMATICS LEVEL II on the line to the right of the words "Achievement Test."
2. Blacken spaces 1 and 7 in the row of spaces immediately under the words "Test Code."
3. Blacken space 5 in the group of five spaces labeled X.
4. Blacken space 4 in the group of five spaces labeled Y.

You are to leave blank the nine spaces which are labeled Q.

When the supervisor gives the signal, turn the page and begin the Mathematics Level II test. There are 100 numbered spaces on the answer sheet and 50 questions in the Mathematics Level II test. Therefore, use only spaces 1 to 50 for recording your answers.

MATHEMATICS LEVEL II

For each of the following problems, decide which is the best of the choices given. Then blacken the corresponding space on the answer sheet.

<u>Notes:</u> (1) Figures that accompany problems in this test are intended to provide information useful in solving the problems. They are drawn as accurately as possible EXCEPT when it is stated in a specific problem that its figure is not drawn to scale. All figures lie in a plane unless otherwise indicated.

(2) Unless otherwise specified, the domain of a function f is assumed to be the set of all real numbers x for which $f(x)$ is a real number.

USE THIS SPACE FOR SCRATCHWORK.

1. The set of all ordered pairs (x, y) that satisfy the system $\begin{cases} y = x \\ xy = 1 \end{cases}$ is

   (A) $\{(-1, -1)\}$ (B) $\{(-1, 1)\}$ (C) $\{(1, 1)\}$
   (D) $\{(-1, -1), (1, 1)\}$ (E) $\{(-1, 1), (1, -1)\}$

2. If k is an integer less than zero, which of the following is less than zero?

   (A) $-k$ (B) $-(-k)$ (C) $(-k)^2$ (D) $(k)^2$ (E) $-(k)^3$

3. When a certain integer is divided by 5, the remainder is 3. What is the remainder when 4 times that integer is divided by 5 ?

   (A) 0   (B) 1   (C) 2   (D) 3   (E) 4

4. If $f(x) = -x^2 + 3x + k$ and if $f(-1) = 0$, then $k =$

   (A) 4   (B) 2   (C) 0   (D) -2 (E) -4

5. If functions f, g, and h are defined by $f(x) = 2x$, $g(x) = x + 1$, and $h(x) = x^2$, then $f(g(h(3))) =$

   (A) 14   (B) 16   (C) 18   (D) 20   (E) 22

GO ON TO THE NEXT PAGE

6. During the first 2 hours of a 300-mile trip, a car is driven at an average speed of k miles per hour. At what average speed, in miles per hour, must the car be driven for the rest of the distance if the trip takes 4 more hours?

(A) $\dfrac{k}{2} - 75$　(B) $75 - \dfrac{k}{2}$　(C) $\dfrac{1}{75} - \dfrac{2}{k}$

(D) $\dfrac{2}{k} - \dfrac{1}{75}$　(E) $75 - k$

7. If $f(x) = x^2 - x$, then $f(a - 1) =$

(A) $a^2 - a$　(B) $a^2 - a - 1$　(C) $a^2 - a + 1$
(D) $a^2 - a + 2$　(E) $a^2 - 3a + 2$

8. The midpoint of the line segment joining the points (4, 3) and (3, 4) is

(A) $(7, 7)$　(B) $\left(\dfrac{7}{2}, \dfrac{7}{2}\right)$　(C) $\left(\dfrac{5}{2}, \dfrac{5}{2}\right)$

(D) $\left(2, \dfrac{3}{2}\right)$　(E) $\left(\dfrac{1}{2}, -\dfrac{1}{2}\right)$

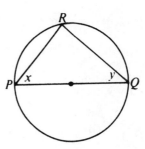

Figure 1

9. In Figure 1, if PQ is a diameter of the circle, R is a point on the circle, and $\cos x = \dfrac{2}{3}$, then $\cos y =$

(A) $\dfrac{2\sqrt{5}}{25}$　(B) $\dfrac{\sqrt{5}}{3}$　(C) $\dfrac{2\sqrt{5}}{5}$　(D) $\dfrac{3\sqrt{5}}{5}$　(E) $\dfrac{3\sqrt{5}}{2}$

10. The "spread" of a point (x, y) in the rectangular coordinate plane is defined as $|x| + |y|$. Which of the following points has the same spread as $\left(\dfrac{3}{2}, -\dfrac{1}{2}\right)$?

(A) $(-1, 0)$　(B) $\left(0, \dfrac{1}{2}\right)$　(C) $\left(\dfrac{1}{2}, \dfrac{1}{2}\right)$

(D) $(1, -1)$　(E) $(2, 1)$

GO ON TO THE NEXT PAGE

USE THIS SPACE FOR SCRATCHWORK.

11. If a square region is rotated 360° around one of its sides as an axis, the solid generated is a

    (A) cube
    (B) rectangular parallelepiped
    (C) cone
    (D) sphere
    (E) cylinder

12. If $f(x, y) = x^2 + xy + y^2$ for all real numbers x and y, which of the following are true?

    I. $f(x, y) = f(x, -y)$
    II. $f(x, y) = f(-x, y)$
    III. $f(x, y) = f(-x, -y)$

    (A) I only   (B) II only   (C) III only
    (D) I and II only   (E) I, II, and III

13. An angle measure of $\frac{\pi}{12}$ radians is equivalent to an angle measure of

    (A) 15°   (B) 18°   (C) 30°   (D) 36°   (E) 45°

14. If f is the function defined by $f(x) = 2x - 4$, and if $g(f(x)) = x$, then $g(x) =$

    (A) $\frac{1}{2x - 4}$ (B) $-2x + 4$ (C) $x - 2$

    (D) $-\frac{1}{2}x - 2$ (E) $\frac{1}{2}x + 2$

15. The solution set of $\frac{(x + 1)^2}{x} > 0$ is

    (A) the empty set   (B) $\{x \mid x > -1\}$ (C) $\{x \mid x > 0\}$
    (D) $\{x \mid x > 1\}$ (E) $\{x \mid x$ is any real number$\}$

GO ON TO THE NEXT PAGE

16. In Figure 2, the shaded region is bounded by an ellipse whose area A is given by the formula $A = \pi ab$. If the area of the ellipse is 6π and the area of the small circle with center at O is 4π, what is the area of the large circle with center at O?

   (A) 5π (B) 6π (C) 7π (D) 8π (E) 9π

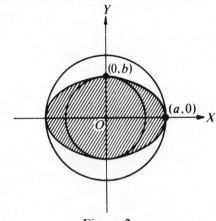

Figure 2

17. Where defined, $\dfrac{\sec x}{\csc x} =$

   (A) $\tan x$ (B) $\cot x$ (C) $\sin x \cos x$

   (D) $\dfrac{1}{\sin x \cos x}$ (E) 1

18. In Figure 3, the bases of the right prism are equilateral triangles, each with perimeter 30 centimeters. If the altitude of the prism is 10 centimeters, what is the total surface area of the solid in square centimeters?

   (A) 100 (B) $\dfrac{250}{\sqrt{3}}$ (C) $100\sqrt{3}$

   (D) 300 (E) $50\sqrt{3} + 300$

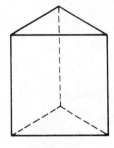

Figure 3

19. A club has 14 members, consisting of 6 men and 8 women. How many slates of 3 officers—president, vice-president, and secretary—can be formed if the president must be a woman and the vice-president must be a man?

   (A) 2,744   (B) 2,184   (C) 672   (D) 576   (E) 336

20. $\log_2 \sqrt{2} =$

   (A) -1 (B) $-\dfrac{1}{2}$ (C) $\dfrac{1}{2}$ (D) 1 (E) 2

21. If $f(x) = \dfrac{x + 4}{(x - 4)(x^2 + 4)}$, for what value of x is $f(x)$ undefined?

   (A) -4 (B) -2 (C) 0 (D) 2 (E) 4

GO ON TO THE NEXT PAGE

22. If $f(x) = \dfrac{1}{x}$, which of the following could be the graph
of $y = f(-x)$?

(A)
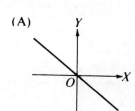

(B)
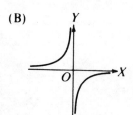

(C)
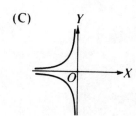

(D)
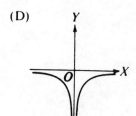

(E)
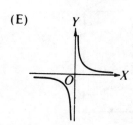

23. If $0 < x < \dfrac{3\pi}{2}$ and $\cos \dfrac{\pi}{2} = \sin\left(\dfrac{\pi}{2} + x\right)$, then $x =$

(A) $\dfrac{\pi}{4}$ (B) $\dfrac{\pi}{2}$ (C) $\dfrac{3\pi}{4}$ (D) π (E) $\dfrac{5\pi}{4}$

24. If the line $y = k$ is tangent to the circle
$(x - 2)^2 + y^2 = 9$, then $k =$

(A) -1 or 4   (B) -3 or 3   (C) -4 or 1
(D) -6 or 6   (E) -9 or 9

25. If, for all x, $3^x + 3^x + 3^x = k3^{x+1}$, then $k =$

(A) 9^{3x} (B) $3^{x^3 - x - 1}$ (C) 3^{2x-1} (D) 3   (E) 1

GO ON TO THE NEXT PAGE

USE THIS SPACE FOR SCRATCHWORK.

26. If $f(x) = (x + 3)^2 + 1$, what is the minimum value of the function f?

(A) -3 (B) 0 (C) 1 (D) 3 (E) 4

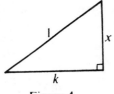

27. In Figure 4, if Arcsin x = Arccos x, then $k =$

(A) x (B) x^2 (C) 1 (D) $1 - x$ (E) $\frac{1}{x}$

Figure 4

Note: Figure not drawn to scale.

28. Which of the following could be the graph of the set of all pairs (x, y), where $x = \cos\theta$, $y = \sin\theta$, and $0 \leqq \theta < 2\pi$?

(A)

(B)

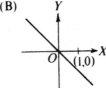

(C)

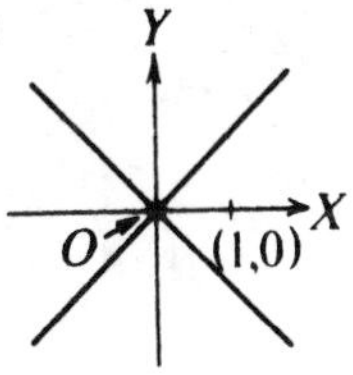

(D)

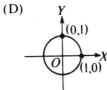

(E)

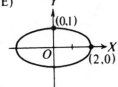

29. If $x + 2$ is a factor of $2x^3 + x^2 - 2kx + 4$, then k is

(A) -6 (B) -4 (C) 2 (D) 4 (E) 6

GO ON TO THE NEXT PAGE

30. If $f(x) = x^2 + x - 6$, then the set of all b for which $f(-b) = f(b)$ is

(A) all real numbers   (B) {−3, 2}   (C) {−2, 3}
(D) {0}   (E) {2}

31. If $\sin x = -\cos x$ and $0 \leqq x \leqq \pi$, then $x =$

(A) $\dfrac{\pi}{4}$ (B) $\dfrac{\pi}{3}$ (C) $\dfrac{\pi}{2}$ (D) $\dfrac{2\pi}{3}$ (E) $\dfrac{3\pi}{4}$

32. Which of the following could be an equation of the graph shown in Figure 5 ?

(A) $y = \sin x + 1$ (B) $y = \cos x - 1$ (C) $y = \csc x - 1$
(D) $y = \sec x - 1$ (E) $y = \csc x + 1$

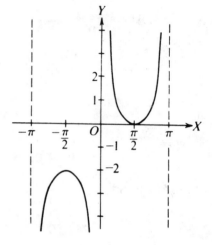

Figure 5

33. $(-i)^n$ is a negative real number if $n =$

(A) 21   (B) 22   (C) 23   (D) 24   (E) 25

34. If, for all x, $f(x) = a^x$ and $f(x + 3) = 8f(x)$, then $a =$

(A) 0   (B) 1   (C) 2   (D) 4   (E) 8

35. If $\sin x = \dfrac{1}{2}$ and $0 \leqq x \leqq \dfrac{\pi}{2}$, then $\sin 2x =$

(A) $-\dfrac{\sqrt{3}}{2}$ (B) $-\dfrac{1}{2}$ (C) 0   (D) $\dfrac{\sqrt{3}}{2}$ (E) 1

36. $\dfrac{(n-1)!}{n!} + \dfrac{(n+1)!}{n!} =$

(A) $\dfrac{n-1}{n}$ (B) $\dfrac{n^2+1}{n}$ (C) $\dfrac{n^2-1}{n}$

(D) $\dfrac{n+1}{n}$ (E) $\dfrac{n^2+n+1}{n}$

GO ON TO THE NEXT PAGE

37. What is the range of the function defined by

$$f(x) = \frac{1}{x} + 2 \,?$$

(A) All real numbers

(B) All real numbers except $-\frac{1}{2}$

(C) All real numbers except 0

(D) All real numbers except 2

(E) All real numbers between 2 and 3

38. If $a > b$ and $c > d$, which of the following must be true?

    I. $a + c > b + d$
   II. $ac > bd$
  III. $a > d$

(A) I only   (B) II only   (C) I and II only

(D) I and III only   (E) II and III only

39. If $\displaystyle\sum_{k=0}^{10} (3 + k) = X + \sum_{k=0}^{10} k$, then $X =$

(A) 3   (B) 10   (C) 11   (D) 30   (E) 33

40. How many different sets of two parallel edges are there in a cube?

(A) 6   (B) 8   (C) 12   (D) 18   (E) 24

41. Which of the following defines a function that will associate a positive integer y with each positive integer x so that x and y have the same tens' digit?

(A) $y = 10x$ (B) $y = 11x$ (C) $y = 100x$

(D) $y = 101x$ (E) $y = 111x$

42. If two fair dice are tossed, what is the probability that the sum of the number of dots on the top faces will be 10 ?

(A) $\frac{1}{36}$ (B) $\frac{1}{18}$ (C) $\frac{1}{12}$ (D) $\frac{1}{9}$ (E) $\frac{1}{6}$

GO ON TO THE NEXT PAGE

43. Three vertices of a cube, no two of which lie on the same edge, are joined to form a triangle. If an edge of the cube has length 1, what is the area of the triangle?

(A) $\dfrac{\sqrt{6}}{2}$ (B) $\dfrac{\sqrt{3}}{2}$ (C) $\dfrac{\sqrt{2}}{2}$ (D) $\dfrac{\sqrt{6}}{4}$ (E) $\dfrac{\sqrt{3}}{4}$

44. What is $\lim\limits_{x \to 2} \dfrac{x^3 + x^2 - 6x}{x - 2}$?

(A) 0   (B) 3   (C) 7   (D) 10

(E) The limit does not exist.

45. Which of the following graphs could represent the equation $y = ax^2 + bx + c$ where $b^2 - 4ac > 0$?

(A)
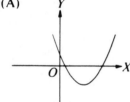

(B)
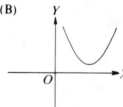

(C)
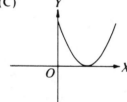

(D)
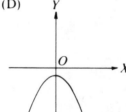

(E)
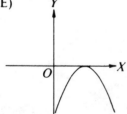

GO ON TO THE NEXT PAGE

USE THIS SPACE FOR SCRATCHWORK.

46. The least positive integer N for which each of
$\frac{N}{2}, \frac{N}{3}, \frac{N}{4}, \frac{N}{5}, \frac{N}{6}, \frac{N}{7}, \frac{N}{8}$, and $\frac{N}{9}$ is an integer is

   (A) $9 \cdot 8 \cdot 7 \cdot 6 \cdot 5 \cdot 4 \cdot 3 \cdot 2$
   (B) $9 \cdot 8 \cdot 6 \cdot 5 \cdot 4 \cdot 3 \cdot 2$
   (C) $9 \cdot 8 \cdot 7 \cdot 6 \cdot 5$
   (D) $9 \cdot 8 \cdot 7 \cdot 5$
   (E) $9 \cdot 8 \cdot 7$

47. The graph of $y = 3 + \cos 2x$ intersects the Y-axis at the point where $y =$

   (A) 0   (B) 1   (C) 3   (D) 4   (E) 5

48. The area of the parallelogram in Figure 6 is

   (A) ab (B) $ab \cos \theta$ (C) $ab \sin \theta$
   (D) $ab \tan \theta$ (E) $a^2 + b^2 - 2ab \cos \theta$

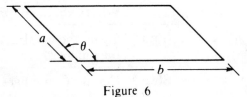

Figure 6

49. Which of the following equations describes the set of all points (x, y) that are equidistant from the X-axis and the point $(4, 6)$?

   (A) $(x - 4)^2 + (y - 6)^2 = 9$
   (B) $(x - 4)^2 = 12(y - 3)$
   (C) $(y - 3)^2 = 12(x - 4)$
   (D) $(x - 4)^2 = 6(y - 3)$
   (E) $(x - 4)^2 = 12(y - 6)$

50. "If A is true, then for some x, B is true." Which of the following is logically equivalent to the preceding statement?

   (A) If B is false for all x, then A is false.
   (B) If for some x, B is true, then A is true.
   (C) If A is false, then for all x, B is false.
   (D) If B is false for some x, then A is false.
   (E) There exists an x for which A is true and B is false.

S T O P

**IF YOU FINISH BEFORE TIME IS CALLED, YOU MAY CHECK YOUR WORK ON THIS TEST ONLY.
DO NOT WORK ON ANY OTHER TEST IN THIS BOOK.**

How to Score the Mathematics Achievement Test, Level II

When you take an actual Mathematics Achievement Test, Level II, your answer sheet will be "read" by a scanning machine that will record your responses to each question. Then a computer will compare your answers with the correct answers and produce your raw score. You get one point for each correct answer.

For each wrong answer, you lose one-fourth of a point. Questions you omit (and any for which you mark more than one answer) are not counted. This raw score is converted to a College Board scaled score that is reported to you and to the colleges you specify. After you have taken this test, you can get an idea of what your score might be by following the instructions in the next two sections.

Determining Your Raw Score

Step 1: Table A on the next page lists the correct answers for all the questions on the test.* Compare your answer with the correct answer and
- Put a check in the column marked "Right" if your answer is correct.
- Put a check in the column marked "Wrong" if your answer is incorrect.
- Leave both columns blank if you omitted the question.

Step 2: Count the number of right answers and enter the number here . . . . _____

Step 3: Count the number of wrong answers and enter

the number here . . . . 4)‾‾‾‾‾‾‾‾‾‾

Enter the result of dividing by 4 here . . . . _____

Step 4: Subtract the number you obtained in Step 3 from the number in Step 2; round the result to the nearest whole number (.5 is rounded up) and enter here. . _____

The number you obtained in Step 4 is your raw score. (The correction for guessing — subtraction of a quarter of a point for each incorrect answer — adjusts for the fact that random guessing on a large number of questions will result in some questions being answered correctly by chance.) Instructions for converting your raw score to a scaled score follow.

*The last column in Table A gives the percentage of students who took the test in November 1982 that answered the question correctly. (See pages 286 and 287 for further explanation.)

TABLE A

Answers to Mathematics Test, Level II, Form 3EAC2, and Percentage of Students Answering Each Question Correctly

Question Number	Correct Answer	Right	Wrong	Percentage of Students Answering the Question Correctly
1	D			92%
2	B			95
3	C			79
4	A			82
5	D			95
6	B			56
7	E			89
8	B			93
9	B			59
10	D			84
11	E			75
12	C			90
13	A			91
14	E			73
15	C			78
16	E			80
17	A			79
18	E			74
19	D			38
20	C			67
21	E			91
22	B			75
23	B			67
24	B			65
25	E			56
26	C			67
27	A			65
28	D			76
29	C			52
30	D			72
31	E			69
32	C			57
33	B			42
34	C			42
35	D			69
36	E			40
37	D			36
38	A			52
39	E			27
40	D			35
41	D			38
42	C			42
43	B			26
44	D			47
45	A			25
46	D			39
47	D			41
48	C			21
49	B			16
50	A			16

Note: The percentages are based on the analysis of the answer sheets for a random sample of students who took this test in November 1982 and whose mean score was 675.

Finding Your College Board Scaled Score

When you take Achievement Tests, the scores sent to the colleges you specify will be reported on the College Board scale, ranging from 200 to 800. The raw score that you obtained above (Step 4) can be converted to a scaled score by using Table B.

To find your scaled score on this test, locate your raw score in the left column of Table B; the corresponding score in the right column will be your College Board scaled score. For example, a raw score of 15 on this particular edition of the Mathematics Achievement Test, Level II, corresponds to a College Board scaled score of 570. Raw scores are converted to scaled scores to ensure that a score earned on any one edition of the Mathematics Achievement Test, Level II, is comparable to the same scaled score earned on any other edition of the test.

Because some editions of the Mathematics Achievement Test, Level II, may be slightly easier or more difficult than others, statistical adjustments are made in the scores so that each College Board scaled score indicates the same level of performance, regardless of the edition of the test you take and the ability of the group you take it with. A given raw score will correspond to different College Board scores, depending on the edition of the test taken. A raw score of 40, for example, may convert to a College Board score of 780 on one edition of the test, but that raw score might convert to a College Board score of 800 on a slightly more difficult edition. When you take the Mathematics Achievement Test, Level II, on the actual test day, your score is likely to differ somewhat from the score you obtained on this test. People perform at different levels at different times, for reasons unrelated to the test itself. The precision of any test is also limited because it represents only a sample of all the possible questions that could be asked.(See page 12, "How Precise Are Your Scores?" for further information.)

Reviewing Your Test Performance

After you have scored your test, you should take some time to consider the following points in relation to your performance on the test.

- *Did you run out of time before you reached the end of the test?*

  If you did, you may want to consider tactics that will help you pace yourself better. For example, you may have spent too much time working on one or two difficult questions. A better approach might have been to continue the test and return to those questions after you had attempted to answer the remaining questions on the test.

- *Did you take a long time reading the directions for the test?*

  The directions in this test are the same as those in the Mathematics Achievement Tests, Level II now being administered. You will save time when you read the directions on the test day if you become thoroughly familiar with them in advance.

- *How did you handle questions you were unsure of?*

  If you were able to eliminate one or more of the answer choices and you guessed from the remaining choices, then your approach probably worked to your advantage. On the other hand, omitting questions about which you have some knowledge or guessing answers haphazardly would probably be a mistake.

- *How difficult were the questions for you compared with other students who took the test?*

  By referring to Table A on page 285 you can find out how difficult each question was for the group

TABLE B — SCORE CONVERSION TABLE			
Mathematics Achievement Test, Level II, Form 3EAC2			
Raw Score	College Board Scaled Score	Raw Score	College Board Scaled Score
50	800	20	610
49	800	19	610
48	800	18	600
47	800	17	590
46	800	16	580
45	800	15	570
44	800	14	560
43	800	13	560
42	800	12	550
41	790	11	530
40	780	10	520
39	770	9	500
38	760	8	480
37	760	7	470
36	750	6	450
35	740	5	430
34	730	4	420
33	720	3	400
32	710	2	380
31	710	1	370
30	700	0	350
29	690	−1	330
28	680	−2	320
27	670	−3	300
26	660	−4	280
25	660	−5	270
24	650	−6	250
23	640	−7	230
22	630	−8	220
21	620	−9 through −12	200

of students who took the test in November 1982. The right-hand column in the table tells you what percentage of that group of students answered the question correctly. It is important to remember that these percentages are based on only one group of students; had this edition of the test been given to all students in the class of 1983 who took a Mathematics Achievement Test, Level II, the percentages would probably have been different. A question that was answered correctly by almost everyone in the group, obviously, is an easy question. Question 2, for example, was answered correctly by 95 percent of the students in the sample. On the other hand, question 48 was answered correctly by only 21 percent of the students. If you find that you missed several questions that would be considered easy, you may want to review those questions carefully. They may cover some aspect of the subject that you need to review. Perhaps you misunderstood the directions for one part of the test or you thought the questions were so easy that you did not spend as much time on them as you might have.

About the Biology Achievement Test

The Biology Achievement Test is a one-hour test that consists of 95 to 100 multiple-choice questions. The test assumes that you have had a one-year introductory course in biology and that the course content was at a level suitable for college preparation. The test covers the topics outlined in the description of test content given below. Different aspects of each topic are stressed from year to year. Because high school courses differ, both in the percentage of time devoted to each major topic and in the specific subtopics covered, you may encounter questions on topics with which you have little or no familiarity. However, in any typical high school biology course, more topics are usually covered — and in more detail — than there are questions in the Biology Achievement Test. So, even if high school biology curriculums weren't different, the questions in any particular test edition could be only a sample of all the questions that might be asked. The questions in all of the editions, however, test knowledge and abilities that might reasonably be expected of high school biology students intending to go to college.

Questions in the Biology Achievement Test have been tried out on entering college students who have had high school biology; the questions have also been approved by a committee of college and secondary school biology teachers appointed by the College Board. (See "How the Tests Are Developed" in the introduction to this book.)

No one instructional approach is better than another in helping you prepare for the test, provided that you are able to recall and understand the major concepts of biology and to apply the principles you have learned to solve specific scientific problems in biology. In addition, you should be able to organize and interpret results obtained by observation and experimentation and to draw conclusions or make inferences from experimental data. Laboratory experience is a significant factor in developing reasoning and problem-solving skills. Although testing laboratory skills in a standardized test is necessarily limited, reasonable experience in the laboratory is an asset to you in preparing for the Biology Achievement Test.

You will *not* be allowed to use electronic calculators or slide rules during the test. Numerical calculations are limited to simple arithmetic. In this test, the metric system of units is used.

Content of the Test

Topics Covered	Approximate Percentage of Test
I. Cellular and Molecular Biology	20
II. Organismal Reproduction, Development, Growth, and Nutrition	15
III. Ecology	15
IV. Heredity and Evolution	15
V. Organismal Biology (structure and function)	20
VI. Systematics	10
VII. Behavior	5

Cognitive Abilities	Approximate Percentage of Test
Level I: Essentially Recall: remembering specific facts; demonstrating straight-forward knowledge of information and familiarity with terminology	50
Level II: Essentially Application: understanding concepts and reformulating information into other equivalent terms; applying knowledge to unfamiliar and/or practical situations; solving mathematical problems	30
Level III: Essentially Interpretation: inferring and deducing from data available and integrating information to form conclusions; recognizing unstated assumptions	20

Questions Used in the Test

Classification Questions

Each set of classification questions has, in the heading, five lettered choices that are used in answering all of the questions in the set. The choices may be statements that refer to concepts, principles, organisms, substances, or observable phenomena; or they may be graphs, pictures, equations, formulas, or experimental settings or situations. The questions themselves may be presented in one of these formats or may be given in the question format directly. To answer each question you should select the choice that is most appropriate to it. You should consider all of the choices before you answer a question. The directions for this type of question specifically state that you should not eliminate a choice simply because it is the correct answer to a previous question.

Because the same five choices are applicable to several questions, classification questions usually require less reading than other types of multiple-choice questions. Therefore, this type of question is a quick means, in terms of testing time, of determining how well you have mastered the topics represented in the choices. The degree of mastery required to answer a question correctly depends to a large extent on the sophistication of the set of questions. One set may probe your familiarity with choices that test recall; another may ask you to apply your knowledge to a specific situation or to translate information from one form to another (descriptive, graphical, mathematical). Thus several types of abilities can be tested by this type of question.

Following are directions for and an example of a classification set.

Directions: Each set of lettered choices below refers to the numbered statements immediately following it. Select the one lettered choice that best fits each statement and then blacken the corresponding space on the answer sheet. A choice may be used once, more than once, or not at all in each set.

Questions 1-3

(A) Decomposers (e.g., bacteria)

(B) Producers (e.g., grasses)

(C) Primary consumers (e.g., mice)

(D) Secondary consumers (e.g., snakes)

(E) Tertiary consumers (e.g., hawks)

1. Organisms that comprise the greatest mass of living substance (biomass) in a terrestrial food chain

2. Organisms that convert nitrogen-containing organic molecules into nitrates

3. Organisms that would be the first to experience adverse effects if significant amounts of carbon dioxide were withdrawn from the biosphere

This group of questions deals with ecology and in particular with the identification of the proper trophic level for the organisms described in each question. To answer question 1 correctly, you need to know that terrestrial-based food chains begin with the capture of the sun's energy by autotrophic organisms, typically the green plants that carry on photosynthesis. These are the producers that provide the energy (in the form of chemical energy) for subsequent links in a food chain. Only a small fraction of the energy at any trophic level in a food chain can effectively be passed on to the next level, resulting in a steady draining of energy from the ecosystem. The producers, of which grasses are an example, are the first trophic level and, as a group of organisms, they have the greatest amount of energy. Hence, producers account for the greatest biomass of all organisms in a terrestrial food chain. The correct answer to question 1 is, therefore, (B).

For question 2, you need to know that matter is recycled in an ecosystem. Organic molecules from dead organisms are broken down into inorganic compounds by microorganisms specifically adapted for such decomposition, that is, the decomposers. The inorganic compounds, of which the nitrates are an example, are thereby made available to producers such as the green plants for synthesis of fresh organic matter. Thus, (A) is the correct answer to question 2.

For question 3, you need to recognize that carbon dioxide is a raw material for photosynthesis. If its supply were severely limited, the first organisms to be affected would be those at the beginning of the food chain, that is, the producers that carry on photosynthesis. Thus, (B) is the correct answer to question 3.

Five-Choice Completion Questions ■■■■

The five-choice completion question is widely used in objective tests and is probably the type with which you are most familiar. It is written either as an incomplete statement or as a question. In its simplest application, this type of question poses a problem that intrinsically has a unique solution. It is also appropriate when: (1) the problem presented is clearly delineated by the wording of the question so that you are asked to choose not a universal solution but the best of the solutions offered; (2) the problem is such that you are required to evaluate the relevance of five plausible, or even scientifically accurate, options and to select the one most pertinent; (3) the problem has several pertinent solutions and you are required to select the one inappropriate solution that is presented. In the latter case, the correct answer to the question is the choice that is *least* applicable to the situation described by the question. Such questions will normally contain a word in capital letters such as NOT, EXCEPT, or LEAST. (Question 6 is an example of this type of question.)

A special type of five-choice completion question is used in some tests, including the Biology Achievement Test, to allow for the possibility of multiple correct answers. Unlike many quantitative problems that must by their nature have a unique solution, some questions have more than one correct response. For these questions, you must evaluate each response independently of the others in order to select the most appropriate combination. In questions of this type, several (usually three to five) statements labeled by Roman numerals are given with the question. One or more of these statements may correctly answer the question. The statements are followed by five lettered choices, each consisting of some combination of the Roman numerals that label the statements. You must select from among the five lettered choices the one combination of statements that best answers the question. In the test, questions of this type are intermixed among the more standard five-choice completion questions. (Question 5 is an example of this type of question.)

The five-choice completion question is also used in conjunction with introductory material (such as a summary of an experiment, an outline of a problem, a graph, a chart) to assess your ability to use learned concepts and to apply them to unfamiliar laboratory or experimental situations. (Question 4 is an example of this type of question.) When the experimental data or other scientific problems to be analyzed are comparatively long, several five-choice completion questions may be organized into sets, that is, the material that precedes each set is common to all questions in the set. This type of question allows you to respond to several questions based on scientific information that may take considerable testing time to read and comprehend. However, it is not necessary for you to know the answer to one question in order to answer a subsequent question correctly. Each question in a set is independent of the others and refers directly to the common material given for the entire set.

Sets of questions describing laboratory or experimental situations test your understanding of a problem in greater depth than is generally possible with some other formats. In particular, they test your ability to: (1) identify a problem, (2) evaluate experimental situations, (3) suggest hypotheses, (4) interpret data, (5) make inferences and draw conclusions, (6) check the logical consistency of hypotheses based on relevant observations, and (7) select appropriate procedures for further investigation of the problem described. In the Biology Achievement Test, questions pertaining to laboratory or experimental situa-

tions are grouped together in the latter part of the test. (Questions 7-9 are examples of this type of question.)

Directions: Each of the questions or incomplete statements below is followed by five suggested answers or completions. Select the one that is best in each case and then blacken the corresponding space on the answer sheet.

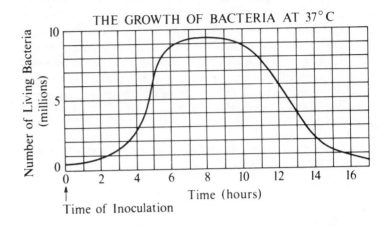

4. **In the graph above, the time when the number of living bacteria is increasing at the greatest rate occurs**

   (A) **during the first 2 hours**
   (B) **between the 2nd and the 4th hour**
   (C) **between the 4th and the 6th hour**
   (D) **between the 6th and the 10th hour**
   (E) **between the 11th and the 13th hour**

This is a straightforward question that tests your ability to interpret experimental data given in graphical form. The number of bacteria is increasing at the greatest rate for the part of the curve that has the steepest positive slope. This occurs between the 4th and 6th hour after the innoculation of bacteria to the medium. Thus the correct answer is (C).

5. **ATP is produced during which of the following processes?**

   I. **Photosynthesis**
   II. **Aerobic respiration**
   III. **Fermentation**

   (A) **I only**   (B) **II only**   (C) **I and III only**
   (D) **II and III only**   (E) **I, II, and III**

This is a question on cellular and molecular biology that asks you to consider whether or not ATP is produced by more than one metabolic pathway. Each of the processes designated by a Roman numeral must be evaluated independently. In photosynthesis, solar energy captured by chlorophyll-containing plants creates a flow of electrons that results in the synthesis of ATP. Thus I is correct. Aerobic respiration, the process by which glucose is broken down to CO_2 and H_2O in the presence of O_2, is the most efficient mechanism by which cells produce the ATP they need to carry on their other metabolic activities. Thus II is also correct. Fermentation also involves the breakdown of glucose but without O_2. Under these conditions, substances such as lactic acid or ethyl alcohol and CO_2 are produced, together with limited quantities of ATP. Although the carbon-containing end products of fermentation still have much of the energy contained in the original glucose, fermentation permits a cell to produce some ATP under anaerobic conditions. Thus III is also correct and the correct answer to the question is (E).

6. Darwin's theory of evolution by natural selection incorporated all of the following EXCEPT

    (A) hereditary variation

    (B) high reproductive potential

    (C) inheritance of acquired characteristics

    (D) struggle for existence

    (E) differential survival

For this question, you must know the premises upon which Darwin based his explanation of evolutionary change in terms of natural selection. Darwin observed that variation exists among individuals in a species. He also recognized hereditary variation was a major factor in evolutionary change. Thus choice (A) is true. Darwin also observed that all organisms have high reproductive capacity under optimal conditions; that is, organisms have a high capacity for population growth. Thus choice (B) is also true. Darwin further pointed out that the food supply for any population is necessarily limited and that this results in a continual competition among organisms of the same kind; that is, a struggle for existence occurs. Therefore, choice (D) is also true. Finally, Darwin pointed out that organisms possessing favorable variations for a given environment will be better able to survive than those with less favorable variations, that is, there is a difference among organisms of a species in their ability to leave more offspring in the next generation. Thus choice (E) is also true. Choice (C) refers to a theory of evolutionary change proposed by Lamarck that has since been disproved. Since this question asks for the one answer choice that is *not* attributable to Darwin, the correct answer is (C).

Directions: Each group of questions below concerns a laboratory or experimental situation. In each case, first study the description of the situation. Then choose the one best answer to each question following it and blacken the corresponding space on the answer sheet.

Questions 7-9

In a breeding experiment using gray and white mice of unknown genotypes, the following results were obtained.

Cross	Parents		Offspring	
	Female	Male	Gray	White
I	Gray × White		82	78
II	Gray × Gray		118	39
III	White × White		0	50
IV	Gray × White		74	0

7. Heterozygous gray female parents occur in

    (A) cross I only

    (B) cross II only

    (C) cross IV only

    (D) crosses I and II only

    (E) crosses II and IV only

8. If two gray progeny of cross IV mate with each other, what is the probability that any one of their offspring will be gray?

    (A) 100%   (B) 75%   (C) 50%   (D) 25%   (E) 0%

9. If the gray female from cross IV were mated with the gray male from cross II, then which of the following would most likely be true?

    (A) All of the offspring would be gray.

    (B) All of the offspring would be white.

    (C) Half of the offspring would be gray.

    (D) One-quarter of the offspring would be gray.

    (E) One-quarter of the offspring would be white.

Questions 7-9 are questions on heredity that refer directly to the experiment described in the introductory material. You are asked to draw conclusions from the results of the experiment and to predict the results of further experimentation on the basis of the information obtained.

Question 7 asks you to determine which gray female mice were heterozygous. First you must realize from the ratio of offspring obtained in all the crosses that gray coat color is dominant over white in these mice. Next, you should note that no white offspring were obtained in cross IV. Thus the gray female in this cross was homozygous gray. In cross I, approximately 50 percent of the offspring were gray. Therefore, the gray female, mated with a white male, must have been heterozygous. In cross II, a gray female was mated with a gray male, and a 3:1 ratio of gray to white offspring was obtained. Therefore both gray female and gray male parents were heterozygous. Thus heterozygous females occurred in crosses I and II only and (D) is the correct answer to the question.

Question 8 assumes that two gray progeny of cross IV were mated with each other. Since this progeny resulted from a cross between a gray female and a white male and no white offspring were produced, you can conclude that the female parent was homozygous gray and that all the offspring are heterozygous gray. Therefore, the mating of the gray progeny of cross IV will produce offspring in the ratio of 3 gray to 1 white. The probability, therefore, of such an offspring being gray is 75 percent. The correct answer to the question is (B).

Question 9 asks you to predict the results of a cross between the gray female from cross IV and the gray male from cross II. From the data given, you can determine that the gray female in cross IV is homozygous, and the male in cross II is heterozygous. Thus you could expect that all the offspring from such a mating would be gray, and the correct answer to the question is (A).

Diagram-Referenced Questions

Questions of this type are also organized in sets, each of which pertains to a diagram (with labeled parts) common to all the questions in the set. Each question in a diagram-referenced set has its own group of five lettered choices that may refer either directly to some of the labeled parts in the diagram or to a function associated with those structures. This type of question is particularly useful for testing your knowledge of the morphology of plants and animals and your understanding of the relationships of structure to function. Questions in a diagram-based set are generally not as complex as questions in the sets on laboratory or experimental situations.

Directions: Each of the following questions refers to the diagram with certain parts labeled with numbers. Each question is followed by five suggested labels or answers. For each question select the one best answer and then blacken the corresponding space on the answer sheet.

Questions 10-12

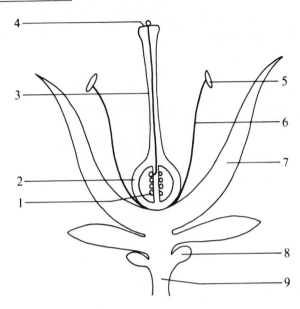

10. Commonly, the fruit is derived from

(A) 2   (B) 4   (C) 7   (D) 8   (E) 9

11. Pollination involves a transfer of pollen from

(A) 4 to 1

(B) 4 to 2

(C) 4 to 5

(D) 5 to 4

(E) 5 to 9

12. The structures most directly involved in the formation of haploid cells through meiosis are

(A) 1 and 5

(B) 1 and 7

(C) 3 and 4

(D) 1, 7, and 8

(E) 4, 7, and 9

The diagram to which these questions refer illustrates a flowering plant. To answer these questions correctly, you need to identify the structures labeled in the diagram and associate each of them with their correct functions.

To answer question 10 correctly, you need to know that the fruit is derived from the ovary of the plant and that the ovary is the structure labeled 2 in the diagram. The correct answer is (A).

Question 11 deals with the process of pollination in angiosperms, which involves the transfer of pollen from the anther, the tip of the stamen, to the stigma, the tip of the pistil. In the diagram, the anther is labeled 5 and the stigma is labeled 4, so the correct answer to the question is (D).

Question 12 asks you to identify the structures of a flowering plant in which meiosis occurs, producing the haploid cells necessary for reproduction. The egg cells are produced in the ovules (structure 1) located inside the ovary and the pollen grains are formed in the anther (structure 5). Thus the correct answer to this question is (A).

Biology Achievement Test

The test that follows is an edition of the Biology Achievement Test administered in November 1982. So that you will have an idea of what the actual test administration will be like, try to take this test under conditions as close as possible to those of the actual test. It will probably help if you

- Set aside an hour for the test when you will not be interrupted, so that you can complete all of it in one sitting.

- Sit at a desk with no other papers or books. You can't take a calculator, a dictionary, other books, or notes into the test room.

- Have a kitchen timer or clock in front of you for timing yourself.

- Tear out an answer sheet from the back of this book and fill it in just as you would on the day of the test. You can use one answer sheet for as many as three Achievement Tests.

- Read the instructions that precede the test. When you take the test, you will be asked to read them before you begin answering questions.

- After you finish this test, read the sections on "How to Score the Biology Achievement Test" and "Reviewing Your Test Performance," which follow the test.

BIOLOGY TEST

The top portion of the section of the answer sheet which you will use in taking the Biology test must be filled in exactly as shown in the illustration below. Note carefully that you have to do all of the following on your answer sheet:

1. Print BIOLOGY on the line to the right of the words "Achievement Test."
2. Blacken spaces 2 and 6 in the row of spaces immediately under the words "Test Code."
3. Blacken space 1 in the group of five spaces labeled X.
4. Blacken space 1 in the group of five spaces labeled Y.

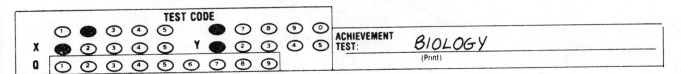

You are to leave blank the nine spaces which are labeled Q.

When the supervisor gives the signal, turn the page and begin the Biology test. There are 100 numbered spaces on the answer sheet and 100 questions in the Biology test.

BIOLOGY TEST

Part A

Directions: Each of the questions or incomplete statements below is followed by five suggested answers or completions. Select the one that is best in each case and then blacken the corresponding space on the answer sheet.

1. Which of the following neurons gathers information directly from the external environment?

   (A) Sensory
   (B) Effector
   (C) Association
   (D) Postsynaptic
   (E) Motor

2. Which of the following adaptive features would be found in wind-pollinated flowers?

   (A) Brightly colored petals
   (B) Freely exposed anthers or stigmas
   (C) Strong odors
   (D) Petals forming landing stages
   (E) Abundant nectar

3. Which of the following cellular organelles is most closely associated with the translation activity of messenger RNA ?

   (A) Mitochondrion
   (B) Ribosome
   (C) Lysosome
   (D) Chloroplast
   (E) Golgi apparatus

GO ON TO THE NEXT PAGE

AMOUNT OF FERTILIZER APPLIED AND AREA OF LAND
CULTIVATED IN THE UNITED STATES FROM 1940 TO 1963

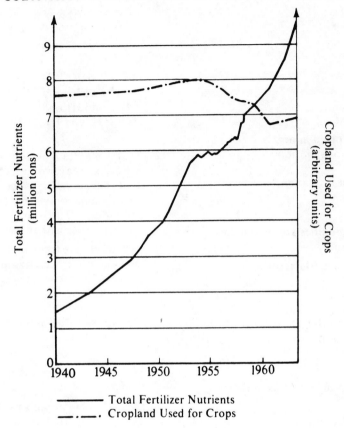

———— Total Fertilizer Nutrients
—·—· Cropland Used for Crops

4. From the graph above, which of the following is
   true about the change in the amount of cropland
   and of fertilizer used between 1955 and 1963 ?

	FERTILIZER	CROPLAND
(A)	Increased	Increased
(B)	Decreased	Increased
(C)	Increased	Decreased
(D)	Decreased	Decreased
(E)	No significant change	No significant change

GO ON TO THE NEXT PAGE

5. Movement of materials across animal cell membranes can be accomplished by all of the following EXCEPT

   (A) pinocytosis
   (B) phagocytosis
   (C) diffusion
   (D) active transport
   (E) denaturation

6. Root hairs of plants serve to

   (A) absorb water and dissolved minerals
   (B) release water during transpiration
   (C) protect the root cap
   (D) initiate secondary root formation
   (E) excrete organic wastes

7. Deep ocean (abyssal) communities are similar to cave communities in that both

   (A) have temperatures close to the freezing point of water
   (B) lack photosynthetic producers
   (C) have water supplies rich in calcium
   (D) include animals adapted to high pressures
   (E) are formed as a result of the activity of water

8. Mitochondria are similar to chloroplasts in that both

   (A) contain structures called grana
   (B) are sites for ATP synthesis
   (C) occur in animal cells
   (D) utilize the rays of the Sun
   (E) function only during daylight hours

9. According to our present system of classification, which of the following is LEAST closely related to the others?

   (A) Dog (B) Cat (C) Whale
   (D) Salmon (E) Man

10. In human pregnancy, the structure through which materials in solution are interchanged between the blood of the fetus and that of the mother is the

    (A) fallopian tube
    (B) ureter
    (C) navel
    (D) endometrium
    (E) placenta

11. Animals that possess a closed circulatory system include which of the following?

    I. Earthworm
    II. Frog
    III. Grasshopper

    (A) II only
    (B) III only
    (C) I and II only
    (D) I and III only
    (E) I, II, and III

12. Tracheophytes have four major characteristics: a protective layer of cells around the gametes, multicellular embryos, cuticles on parts above the soil, and conducting tissue such as xylem and phloem. The primary importance of these characteristics is that they all

    (A) accelerate transpiration in tracheophytes
    (B) aid in nitrogen fixation
    (C) enable tracheophytes to survive in land habitats
    (D) aid in the distribution of the pollen
    (E) are essential in the process of photosynthesis

13. Which of the following most accurately defines the term "species"?

    (A) All those organisms, within a certain group, that are the same color
    (B) Those members of a population capable of exchanging genetic material and producing fertile offspring
    (C) Members of a local population that share the same habitat
    (D) Organisms that look alike and share the same niche throughout the world
    (E) All organisms within the same genus

GO ON TO THE NEXT PAGE

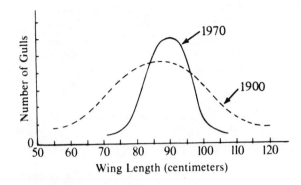

14. In 1900 and 1970, equal-sized samples of an adult gull population were studied and wing lengths were measured. The data collected are shown on the graph above. The best explanation for the change in the wing length is

   (A) migration
   (B) maturation
   (C) disease
   (D) natural selection
   (E) natural disaster

15. Which of the following is NOT found in DNA molecules?

   (A) Adenine
   (B) Deoxyribose
   (C) Phosphorus
   (D) Uracil
   (E) Thymine

16. In a prairie ecosystem, there is a delicate balance between populations of prairie grasses, coyotes, and jackrabbits. If the coyote population is reduced by hunting, which of the following is likely to occur?

   (A) The prairie grasses will be reduced over the next few years.
   (B) The number of jackrabbits will be reduced significantly.
   (C) The prairie grasses will be the predominant vegetation for a short time.
   (D) The jackrabbits will become predators of coyotes.
   (E) No change in interspecies relationships will occur.

17. All of the following organisms reproduce both sexually and asexually EXCEPT the

   (A) lobster (B) hydra (C) sponge
   (D) planarian (E) fluke

18. All of the following are characteristics of enzymes EXCEPT:

   (A) They are proteins.
   (B) They are inactivated by high temperature.
   (C) They are organic catalysts.
   (D) Each binds temporarily with its substrate.
   (E) Each is active within a wide range of pH.

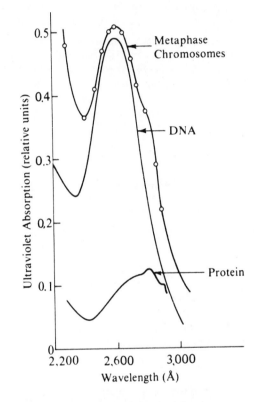

19. From the graph above showing the degree of ultraviolet absorption by metaphase chromosomes, pure DNA, and protein, which of the following can be inferred?

   (A) Ultraviolet light promotes the pairing of chromosomes during metaphase.
   (B) Chromosomes contain DNA.
   (C) Chromosomes contain neither protein nor DNA.
   (D) Chromosomes in metaphase do not absorb ultraviolet light.
   (E) Proteins absorb ultraviolet light to a higher degree than does DNA.

GO ON TO THE NEXT PAGE

20. The eighteenth-century biologist who devised the binomial system of nomenclature for the classification of plants and animals was

    (A) Anton van Leeuwenhoek
    (B) Charles Darwin
    (C) Edward Jenner
    (D) Robert Hooke
    (E) Carolus Linnaeus

21. Which of the following statements about bioluminescence and photosynthesis is correct?

    (A) In photosynthesis, chemical reactions produce light; in bioluminescence, light promotes chemical reactions.
    (B) In photosynthesis, light promotes chemical reactions; in bioluminescence, chemical reactions produce light.
    (C) Both photosynthesis and bioluminescence produce light from chemical reactions.
    (D) Light promotes chemical reactions in both photosynthesis and bioluminescence.
    (E) Both photosynthesis and bioluminescence are inhibited by light.

22. The fact that humans have a coccyx (the vestigial tail vertebrae) can best be explained by which of the following?

    (A) Tails are functional in some animals.
    (B) Tails are probably mutations.
    (C) Tail formation is a recessive characteristic.
    (D) Tails were a characteristic of ancestors of humans.
    (E) Tails are required for good balance.

23. All of the following statements related to evolution are correct EXCEPT:

    (A) Characteristics of living things change with time.
    (B) Changes in species are influenced by natural selection.
    (C) Individuals cannot evolve, but populations can.
    (D) The genetic makeup of an individual is set at the time of fertilization.
    (E) Change occurs within species, but new species do not evolve.

24. Each of the following represents one of the four protozoan groups: *Plasmodium* (malarial protozoan), *Trypanosoma*, *Amoeba*, and *Paramecium* . This classification is based on

    (A) cell pigmentation
    (B) the manner in which movement is accomplished
    (C) the method employed in the uptake of oxygen
    (D) the kind of habitat in which the organisms live
    (E) the characteristics of the contractile vacuole

25. Many vitamins function as

    (A) hormones
    (B) coenzymes
    (C) nucleic acids
    (D) antibodies
    (E) buffers

26. The small intestine absorbs digested food rapidly because it

    (A) has a large surface area
    (B) has a smooth lining
    (C) lacks an appendix
    (D) is short
    (E) has a large diameter

27. During embryonic development, the germ layer from which the inner lining of the digestive tract develops is the

    (A) ectoderm
    (B) epidermis
    (C) mesenchyme
    (D) endoderm
    (E) mesoderm

28. Which of the following invertebrates is considered to be most primitive?

    (A) Arthropods
    (B) Coelenterates (Cnidaria)
    (C) Mollusks
    (D) Annelids (segmented worms)
    (E) Echinoderms

GO ON TO THE NEXT PAGE

29. Of the following, which is the best procedure for sterilizing glass test tubes?

    (A) Washing the tubes thoroughly with hot water and soap
    (B) Exposing the tubes to direct sunlight for 30 minutes
    (C) Refrigerating the tubes for 12 hours
    (D) Placing the tubes in an oven for 5 hours at 37° C
    (E) Placing the tubes in an oven for 2 hours at 200° C

30. The crab, spider, ant, and lobster are classified in the same phylum. Which of the following sets of characteristics do they share?

    (A) Segmented body and six appendages
    (B) Jointed appendages and a digestive system with a single opening
    (C) Jointed appendages and a chitinous exoskeleton
    (D) A dorsal nerve cord and a chitinous exoskeleton
    (E) A dorsal nerve cord and jointed appendages

31. The chemical element that is always present in protein but absent from fats and carbohydrates is

    (A) carbon (B) hydrogen (C) oxygen
    (D) nitrogen (E) sodium

32. Which of the following provides the best evidence that water is a limiting factor in the growth of plants in the desert?

    (A) A cactus transplanted to a coastal area fails to survive.
    (B) Rainfall in the desert is more common in the winter than in the summer.
    (C) Flash floods destroy many desert plants.
    (D) The volume of plant life increases when desert areas are irrigated.
    (E) Deciduous trees transplanted to the desert fail to survive.

33. Which of the following contributes most to genetic variability?

    (A) Mitosis (B) Regeneration (C) Meiosis
    (D) Linkage (E) Vegetative propagation

34. Although termites eat wood, they cannot digest cellulose. If newly hatched termite nymphs are prevented from eating the adults' feces, the nymphs will die. This situation is best understood if one recognizes that termites

    (A) harbor mutualistic intestinal protozoa
    (B) are highly specialized social insects
    (C) belong to the same order as the cockroach
    (D) live in the dark and thus have poorly developed eyesight
    (E) are important decomposers in the forest

35. All of the following are endocrine glands EXCEPT the

    (A) salivary
    (B) adrenal
    (C) pituitary
    (D) testis
    (E) thyroid

36. Which of the following is true about the flow of energy through a food chain?

    (A) There is more energy available to consumers than to producers.
    (B) There is more energy available to secondary consumers than to primary consumers.
    (C) There is more energy available to primary consumers than to secondary consumers.
    (D) The energy available to producers is determined by their interactions with primary and secondary consumers.
    (E) There is more energy available to decomposers than to producers.

37. Which of the following is NOT a characteristic of primates?

    (A) Flat nails
    (B) Opposable thumb
    (C) Binocular vision
    (D) Body hair
    (E) Three-chambered heart

38. The most important function of nitrates in the nitrogen cycle is to

    (A) provide a source of nitrogen for protein synthesis by plants
    (B) facilitate excretion of waste products in mammals
    (C) establish a symbiotic relationship between plants and fungi
    (D) act as a toxic agent to kill harmful bacteria
    (E) restore nitrogen gas to the atmosphere

GO ON TO THE NEXT PAGE

39. The study of crossing-over between homologous chromosomes is most useful for determining which of the following?

    (A) Number of mutations on a chromosome
    (B) Length of a chromosome
    (C) Position of genes on a chromosome
    (D) Presence of dominant genes
    (E) Occurrence of polyploidy

40. In an organism that is heterozygous for three independently assorting traits (*AaBbCc*), what fraction of its gametes will contain all three recessive genes (*abc*)?

    (A) 0 (B) 1/8 (C) 1/4 (D) 1/2 (E) 3/4

41. All of the following kinds of organisms are capable of converting light energy to chemical energy EXCEPT

    (A) maple trees
    (B) cactus plants
    (C) red algae
    (D) mushrooms
    (E) mosses

42. The primary function of NAD in the Krebs cycle is to serve as

    (A) an oxygen acceptor
    (B) an oxygen donor
    (C) a source of phosphate ions
    (D) a hydrogen ion and electron acceptor
    (E) a photosynthetic pigment

43. All of the following statements about cartilage are correct EXCEPT:

    (A) It is a part of the skeletal system.
    (B) It is less rigid than bone.
    (C) It contains salts and proteins.
    (D) It appears earlier than does bone during embryonic development.
    (E) It is richly supplied with blood vessels.

44. The oxygen given off by plants is a product of

    (A) aerobic respiration
    (B) anaerobic respiration
    (C) the light phase of photosynthesis
    (D) the dark phase of photosynthesis
    (E) oxidation of carbohydrates

45. All of the following processes are involved in translocation in plants EXCEPT

    (A) root pressure
    (B) cohesion
    (C) transpiration
    (D) capillarity
    (E) phototropism

46. The brewing of beer is an application of which of the following cellular processes?

    (A) Photosynthesis
    (B) Oxidative phosphorylation
    (C) Aerobic respiration
    (D) Fermentation
    (E) Transformation

47. Which of the following is NOT a part of the pistil?

    (A) Stigma (B) Style (C) Anther
    (D) Ovule (E) Ovary

48. As one travels northward from the geographical center of the United States, the correct sequence of major biomes (life zones) encountered is

    (A) grassland, taiga, arctic tundra
    (B) deciduous forest, alpine tundra, arctic tundra
    (C) grassland, desert, alpine tundra
    (D) desert, deciduous forest, taiga
    (E) desert, grassland, taiga

49. For which of the following pairs does the molecule given as the first term NOT contribute to the synthesis of the molecule given as the second term?

    (A) Amino acid..protein
    (B) Glucose..starch
    (C) Urea..glycogen
    (D) Phosphoric acid..nucleotide
    (E) Fatty acid..lipid

GO ON TO THE NEXT PAGE

50. Which of the following is NOT characteristic of monocots?

    (A) The flower parts are usually in threes or multiples of three.
    (B) The leaves have parallel veins.
    (C) The stems contain cambium for production of secondary xylem.
    (D) The seeds contain a single cotyledon.
    (E) The seeds at maturity usually contain a large endosperm.

51. Which of the following occurs in meiosis but not in mitosis?

    (A) Production of diploid cells
    (B) Synapsis of homologous chromosomes
    (C) Duplication of DNA
    (D) Duplication of the centrioles
    (E) Appearance of spindle fibers

52. Scientists who study evolution look for homologous structures when determining similarities among species. These structures are said to have been inherited from common ancestors. All of the following are examples of homologous structures EXCEPT the

    (A) wings of a robin and the wings of an owl
    (B) wings of a blue jay and the wings of a butterfly
    (C) wings of an ostrich and the front legs of a dog
    (D) front legs of a horse and the arms of a human
    (E) legs of a chicken and the hind legs of a lizard

53. Factors that may contribute to divergent evolution include which of the following?

    I. Separation of populations by geographic barriers, such as mountains or rivers
    II. Breeding of populations at different times of the year
    III. Spreading of populations into different habitats

    (A) I only   (B) III only   (C) I and II only
    (D) II and III only   (E) I, II, and III

54. If a cell uses 100 amino acid molecules to produce a particular polypeptide chain in a protein, the number of water molecules formed during the process is

    (A) 1
    (B) 50
    (C) 99
    (D) 100
    (E) 101

55. The primitive atmosphere existing just before the time that life arose on Earth is believed to have contained all of the following gases EXCEPT

    (A) hydrogen
    (B) water vapor
    (C) ammonia
    (D) oxygen
    (E) methane

56. Which of the following represents the normal sequence of animal development?

    (A) Gastrula formation→blastula formation→mesoderm formation→cleavage→somite formation
    (B) Cleavage→blastula formation→somite formation→gastrula formation→mesoderm formation
    (C) Cleavage→blastula formation→mesoderm formation→gastrula formation→somite formation
    (D) Cleavage→blastula formation→gastrula formation→mesoderm formation→somite formation
    (E) Blastula formation→gastrula formation→mesoderm formation→cleavage→somite formation

57. Replacing inorganic nutrients in soil is accomplished primarily by the

    (A) first-order consumers
    (B) second-order consumers
    (C) herbivores
    (D) producers
    (E) decomposers

GO ON TO THE NEXT PAGE

ECOLOGICAL SUCCESSION

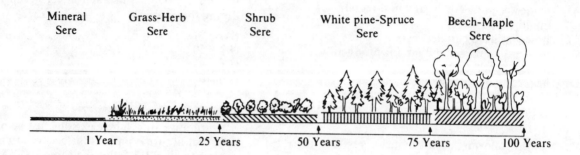

58. The climax community in the ecosystem above is
    (A) shrub
    (B) white pine-spruce
    (C) beech-maple
    (D) mineral
    (E) grass-herb

GO ON TO THE NEXT PAGE

BIOLOGY TEST—*Continued*

Part B

Directions: Each set of lettered choices below refers to the numbered statements immediately following it. Select the one lettered choice that best fits each statement and then blacken the corresponding space on the answer sheet. A choice may be used once, more than once, or not at all in each set.

Questions 59-62

    (A) Trial and error
    (B) Habituation
    (C) Imprinting
    (D) Reasoning
    (E) Conditioning

59. The most complex type of learning; an ability that can be demonstrated by primates

60. Learning demonstrated when an animal randomly displays several forms of behavior until the "right" one is found or rewarded

61. Demonstrated in newly hatched chicks or ducklings when they follow the first moving object they see as though it were their mother

62. Occurs when a dog salivates at the sound of a bell because the dog has learned to associate the bell with food

Questions 63-65

    (A) Amnion
    (B) Allantois
    (C) Yolk sac
    (D) Chorion
    (E) Eggshell

63. Provides for storage of the nitrogenous wastes of a developing chick embryo and functions in respiratory gas exchange

64. Forms a fluid-filled chamber in which a terrestrial animal may develop in an aquatic medium

65. Stores an adequate amount of nourishment for the egg stage of a chick's development

Questions 66-68

    (A) Grafting
    (B) Fission
    (C) Sexual reproduction
    (D) Parthenogenesis
    (E) Hermaphroditism

66. A unicellular organism divides to give rise to new individuals.

67. Both male and female reproductive organs are present in the same individual.

68. In the absence of fertilization, an egg develops into a new individual.

Questions 69-70

    (A) Birds
    (B) Bony fish
    (C) Amphibians
    (D) Cartilaginous fish
    (E) Reptiles

69. Have bones that are light, porous, and sometimes air-filled

70. Have toes that are soft and generally lack claws

GO ON TO THE NEXT PAGE

BIOLOGY TEST—*Continued*

Questions 71-74

(A) Xylem vessel
(B) Companion cell
(C) Guard cell
(D) Apical meristem
(E) Sieve-tube element

71. Regulates the opening and closing of stomates

72. Accounts for continual growth in length of plants

73. Is usually dead in a mature plant; is cut when a finished board of lumber is sawed

74. Transports manufactured food from leaves to roots in green plants

Questions 75-78

In cats, tiger stripe (S) is an autosomal trait that is dominant over plain coat (s). In order to study this trait, breeding experiments were conducted. The lettered headings below represent the percentages of tiger-striped cats in first-generation offspring produced by different crosses that were made during the breeding experiments.

(A) 0% striped
(B) 25% striped
(C) 50% striped
(D) 75% striped
(E) 100% striped

75. Result from crosses between a homozygous, striped male and a homozygous, plain female

76. Result from crosses between a homozygous, striped female and a homozygous, plain male

77. Result from crosses between a striped male, whose mother was plain, and a plain female

78. Result from crosses between two heterozygous, striped cats

GO ON TO THE NEXT PAGE

Part C

Directions: Each of the following questions refers to the diagram with certain parts labeled with numbers. Each question is followed by five suggested labels or answers. For each question select the one best answer and then blacken the corresponding space on the answer sheet.

Questions 79-83

MALE UROGENITAL SYSTEM

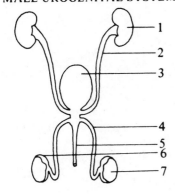

79. Sperm are produced in

    (A) 1
    (B) 3
    (C) 4
    (D) 5
    (E) 7

80. Urine is stored in

    (A) 1
    (B) 2
    (C) 3
    (D) 4
    (E) 5

81. In a vasectomy, the tube that is tied off or cut is

    (A) 2
    (B) 3
    (C) 4
    (D) 5
    (E) 6

82. Nitrogenous wastes are removed from the blood in

    (A) 1
    (B) 2
    (C) 3
    (D) 4
    (E) 5

83. Both sperm and urine are released through

    (A) 2
    (B) 3
    (C) 4
    (D) 5
    (E) 6

GO ON TO THE NEXT PAGE

BIOLOGY TEST—*Continued*

Part D

<u>Directions</u>: Each group of questions below concerns a laboratory or experimental situation. In each case, first study the description of the situation. Then choose the one best answer to each question following it and blacken the corresponding space on the answer sheet.

<u>Questions 84-86</u> refer to the two graphs given below. Graph I shows the growth curve of *Paramecium aurelia* and *Paramecium caudatum* cultured in separate dishes. Graph II shows the growth curve of these two species cultured in the same dish. Similar conditions of food and other requirements were provided in each case.

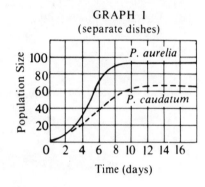

GRAPH I
(separate dishes)

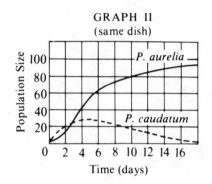

GRAPH II
(same dish)

84. The population *P. aurelia* when cultured by itself increases most rapidly

   (A) between days 0 and 2
   (B) between days 2 and 4
   (C) between days 4 and 6
   (D) between days 6 and 8
   (E) after 8 days

85. In graph I, the most likely explanation for the fact that the population curves of both *P. aurelia* and *P. caudatum* flatten out after an initial period of growth is that

   (A) organisms of both populations are no longer reproducing
   (B) population sizes have reached the maximum capacity that their environment can support
   (C) organisms of both populations have used up all the food
   (D) organisms of both populations are dying faster than they are reproducing
   (E) oxygen required by the organisms for survival has been all used up

86. The effects shown in graph II are most likely the result of

   (A) mutualism between two species
   (B) parasitism of one species by another
   (C) competition between members of the same species
   (D) competition between members of different species
   (E) toxic poisoning of one species after the first day

GO ON TO THE NEXT PAGE

Questions 87-90 pertain to the muscle twitch of the gastrocnemius muscle of a frog in response to a stimulus. The diagram below illustrates a muscle twitch recorded on a kymograph.

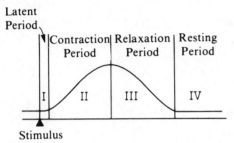

87. The energy for the movement during the contraction period (II) is provided by

    (A) ADP
    (B) ATP
    (C) FAD
    (D) NAD
    (E) vitamins

88. There is very little action during the latent period for which of the following reasons?

    (A) The stimulus is changing the permeability of the membrane.
    (B) ADP is being decomposed.
    (C) The resynthesis of glycogen is taking place.
    (D) The oxygen debt is being replaced.
    (E) Actin and myosin are being synthesized.

89. Rapid and repeated stimulation of the muscle results in a buildup of

    (A) alcohol
    (B) oxygen
    (C) glucose
    (D) lactic acid
    (E) malic acid

90. The conversion of ADP to ATP in the muscle takes place primarily during

    (A) the instant that contact is made with the stimulus
    (B) I and II
    (C) I and IV
    (D) II and III
    (E) III and IV

GO ON TO THE NEXT PAGE

Questions 91-92 refer to the diagram of the food web below.

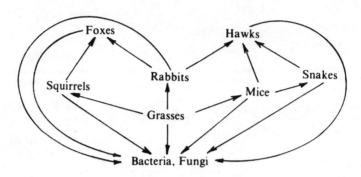

91. Which of the following organisms would probably be found in the fewest numbers?

    (A) Rabbits
    (B) Squirrels
    (C) Bacteria and fungi
    (D) Hawks
    (E) Snakes

92. One would expect to find a greater quantity, by weight, of

    (A) foxes than squirrels
    (B) rabbits than grasses
    (C) mice than snakes
    (D) hawks than foxes
    (E) hawks than mice

GO ON TO THE NEXT PAGE ➡

Questions 93-94

H.B. Kettlewell carried out careful experiments of industrial melanism as related to the moth *Biston betularia*. This moth has dark and light phenotypes that are genetically determined. In repeating one of these experiments, a student released 200 light-colored and 200 dark-colored moths in a forest adjacent to a coal-burning factory. The forest had birds that are predators of the moth. After several months, the student returned to the forest to collect data.

93. If the student could accurately sample this population, which of the following would be the most likely result?

   (A) The numbers of the surviving light-colored moths and the dark-colored moths would be approximately the same.
   (B) The number of the surviving dark-colored moths would be greater than that of the surviving light-colored moths.
   (C) The number of the surviving light-colored moths would be greater than that of the surviving dark-colored moths.
   (D) The ratio of the dark-colored moths to the light-colored moths that survived would be 3 to 1.
   (E) The ratio of the light-colored moths to the dark-colored moths that survived would be 3 to 1.

94. In the student's experiment, which of the following is the hypothesis being tested?

   (A) Natural selection favors organisms that are best adapted to their environment.
   (B) Predator-prey relationships fluctuate with the seasons.
   (C) Genetic dominance may be incomplete.
   (D) Industrial pollution kills plant and animal life.
   (E) Populations in equilibrium will remain unchanged.

Questions 95-96

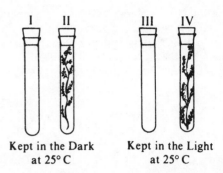

Kept in the Dark   Kept in the Light
    at 25° C   at 25° C

Four test tubes are set up as shown above. All of the tubes contain water to which a few drops of indicator have been added. The indicator used is yellow when the pH of the solution is less than 6.0, green when the solution pH is between 6.0 and 7.5, and blue when the solution pH is above 7.5. All tubes are greenish-blue at the beginning of the experiment. Tubes II and IV contain comparable sprigs of a green plant. Tubes I and II are kept in the dark; tubes III and IV are kept in the light. All are examined 24 hours later. At this time, the indicator in tube II is yellow; the indicator in tubes I, III, and IV is still greenish blue.

95. Which of the following statements about the experiment above is correct?

   (A) Tubes I and III represent experimental sets.
   (B) Tube II is the control for tube III.
   (C) Temperature is the independent variable.
   (D) Light is the independent variable.
   (E) pH is the independent variable.

96. After 24 hours, the indicator in tube II is yellow because the

   (A) plant photosynthesized and gave off O_2, which lowered the pH
   (B) plant respired and gave off CO_2, which formed carbonic acid and lowered the pH
   (C) plant could not photosynthesize and died, causing the H_2O to become alkaline
   (D) plant excreted nitrogenous wastes which caused the medium to become more alkaline
   (E) indicator decomposed in the dark causing the medium to become more acidic

GO ON TO THE NEXT PAGE

Questions 97-100

To test the effects of temperature on the metamorphosis and reproduction of a certain species of invertebrate, some investigators collected larvae from a creek and raised them to adulthood in the laboratory. They determined the average adult body weight, the average number of eggs laid by each female, and the time required for the adults to emerge from the larvae under five different growth temperatures. The average temperature of the creek was 18° C. The data are given in the table below.

Average Temperature	Average Body Weight (milligrams)	Average Number of Eggs	Days to Adult
18° C	0.66	248	11
16° C	1.28	350	16
14° C	1.46	380	40
13° C	0.91	289	56
11° C	0.48	212	82

97. Theoretically, the greatest number of generations of offspring per year could be produced at which temperature?

(A) 18° C
(B) 16° C
(C) 14° C
(D) 13° C
(E) 11° C

98. Theoretically, the greatest number of offspring in a single generation could be produced at which temperature?

(A) 18° C
(B) 16° C
(C) 14° C
(D) 13° C
(E) 11° C

GO ON TO THE NEXT PAGE

99. Which of the following graphs best represents the relationship between temperature and average adult body weight for the species studied in this experiment?

(A)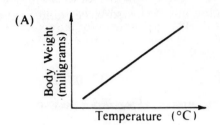

(B)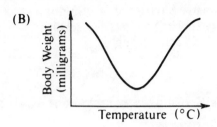

(C)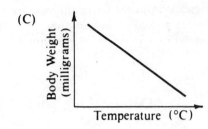

(D)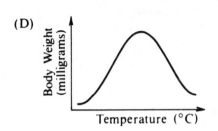

(E)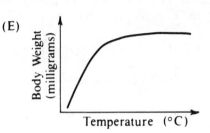

100. Suppose that some organisms of the same species had also been grown at 9° C. Which of the following would best describe the expected results?

(A) Low body weight, long developmental period

(B) Low body weight, short developmental period

(C) Low body weight, high egg production

(D) High egg production, long developmental period

(E) Low egg production, short developmental period

S T O P

**IF YOU FINISH BEFORE TIME IS CALLED, YOU MAY CHECK YOUR WORK ON THIS TEST ONLY.
DO NOT WORK ON ANY OTHER TEST IN THIS BOOK.**

How to Score the Biology Achievement Test

When you take the Biology Achievement Test, your answer sheet will be "read" by a scanning machine that will record your responses to each question. Then a computer will compare your answers with the correct answers and produce your raw score. You get one point for each correct answer. For each wrong answer, you lose one-fourth of a point. Questions you omit (and any for which you mark more than one answer) are not counted. This raw score is converted to a College Board scaled score that is reported to you and to the colleges you specify. After you have taken this test, you can get an idea of what your score might be by following the instructions in the next two sections.

Determining Your Raw Score

Step 1: Table A on the next page lists the correct answers for all the questions on the test.* Compare your answer with the correct answer and
  • Put a check in the column marked "Right" if your answer is correct.
  • Put a check in the column marked "Wrong" if your answer is incorrect.
  • Leave both columns blank if you omitted the question.

Step 2: Count the number of right answers and enter the number here . . . . _____

Step 3: Count the number of wrong answers and enter

the number here . . . . 4) ‾‾‾‾‾‾‾‾‾‾‾

Enter the result of dividing by 4 here . . . . _____

Step 4: Subtract the number you obtained in Step 3 from the number in Step 2; round the result to the nearest whole number (.5 is rounded up) and enter here . . _____

The number you obtained in Step 4 is your raw score. (The correction for guessing — subtraction of a quarter of a point for each incorrect answer — adjusts for the fact that random guessing on a large number of questions will result in some questions being answered correctly by chance.) Instructions for converting your raw score to a scaled score follow.

*The last column in Table A gives the percentage of students who took the test in November 1982 that answered the question correctly. (See page 319 for further explanation.)

TABLE A

Answers to Biology Achievement Test, Form 3EAC2, and Percentage of Students Answering Each Question Correctly

Question Number	Correct Answer	Right	Wrong	Percentage of Students Answering the Question Correctly	Question Number	Correct Answer	Right	Wrong	Percentage of Students Answering the Question Correctly
1	A			92%	51	B			34%
2	B			87	52	B			46
3	B			77	53	E			60
4	C			91	54	C			26
5	E			75	55	D			31
6	A			83	56	D			28
7	B			86	57	E			79
8	B			71	58	C			81
9	D			91	59	D			88
10	E			72	60	A			91
11	C			33	61	C			66
12	C			65	62	E			79
13	B			73	63	B			25
14	D			79	64	A			42
15	D			50	65	C			73
16	A			79	66	B			78
17	A			71	67	E			68
18	E			49	68	D			64
19	B			48	69	A			74
20	E			52	70	C			81
21	B			78	71	C			77
22	D			85	72	D			51
23	E			63	73	A			31
24	B			55	74	E			30
25	B			54	75	E			55
26	A			74	76	E			53
27	D			44	77	C			53
28	B			39	78	D			56
29	E			58	79	E			88
30	C			47	80	C			89
31	D			68	81	C			84
32	D			55	82	A			78
33	C			45	83	D			94
34	A			70	84	C			87
35	A			46	85	B			81
36	C			47	86	D			59
37	E			73	87	B			66
38	A			54	88	A			18
39	C			33	89	D			71
40	B			60	90	E			19
41	D			64	91	D			43
42	D			28	92	C			32
43	E			61	93	B			74
44	C			38	94	A			77
45	E			38	95	D			45
46	D			91	96	B			35
47	C			42	97	A			45
48	A			47	98	C			69
49	C			65	99	D			71
50	C			19	100	A			66

Note: The percentages are based on the analysis of the answer sheets for a random sample of students who took this test in November 1982 and whose mean score was 543.

Finding Your College Board Scaled Score ■

When you take Achievement Tests, the scores sent to the colleges you specify will be reported on the College Board scale, ranging from 200 to 800. The raw score that you obtained above (Step 4) can be converted to a scaled score by using Table B.

To find your scaled score on this test, locate your raw score in the left column of Table B; the corresponding score in the right column will be your College Board scaled score. For example, a raw score of 60 on this particular edition of the Biology Achievement Test corresponds to a College Board scaled score of 580. Raw scores are converted to scaled scores to ensure that a score earned on any one edition of the Biology Achievement Test is comparable to the same scaled score earned on any other edition of the test.

Because some editions of the Biology Achievement Test may be slightly easier or more difficult than others, statistical adjustments are made in the scores so that each College Board scaled score indicates the

TABLE B — SCORE CONVERSION TABLE					
Biology Achievement Test, Form 3EAC2					
Raw Score	College Board Scaled Score	Raw Score	College Board Scaled Score	Raw Score	College Board Scaled Score
100	800	60	580	20	360
99	790	59	570	19	360
98	790	58	570	18	350
97	780	57	560	17	350
96	780	56	560	16	340
95	770	55	550	15	330
94	760	54	550	14	330
93	760	53	540	13	320
92	750	52	540	12	320
91	750	51	530	11	310
90	740	50	530	10	310
89	740	49	520	9	300
88	730	48	510	8	300
87	730	47	510	7	290
86	720	46	500	6	290
85	720	45	500	5	280
84	710	44	490	4	270
83	700	43	490	3	270
82	700	42	480	2	260
81	690	41	480	1	260
80	690	40	470	0	250
79	680	39	470	−1	250
78	680	38	460	−2	240
77	670	37	450	−3	240
76	670	36	450	−4	230
75	660	35	440	−5	230
74	660	34	440	−6	220
73	650	33	430	−7	210
72	640	32	430	−8	210
71	640	31	420	−9 through −25	200
70	630	30	420		
69	630	29	410		
68	620	28	410		
67	620	27	400		
66	610	26	390		
65	610	25	390		
64	600	24	380		
63	600	23	380		
62	590	22	370		
61	590	21	370		

same level of performance, regardless of the edition of the test you take and the ability of the group you take it with. A given raw score will correspond to different College Board scores, depending on the edition of the test taken. A raw score of 40, for example, may convert to a College Board score of 470 on one edition of the test, but that raw score might convert to a College Board score of 490 on a slightly more difficult edition. When you take the Biology Achievement Test on the actual test day, your score is likely to differ somewhat from the score you obtained on this test. People perform at different levels at different times, for reasons unrelated to the test itself. The precision of any test is also limited because it represents only a sample of all the possible questions that could be asked. (See page 12, "How Precise Are Your Scores?" for further information.)

Reviewing Your Test Performance

After you have scored your test, you should take some time to consider the following points in relation to your performance on the test.

- *Did you run out of time before you reached the end of the test?*

   If you did, you may want to consider tactics that will help you pace yourself better. For example, you may have spent too much time working on one or two difficult questions. A better approach might have been to continue the test and return to those questions after you had attempted to answer the remaining questions on the test.

- *Did you take a long time reading the directions for the test?*

   The directions in this test are the same as those in the Biology Achievement Tests now being adminis-tered. You will save time when you read the directions on the test day if you become thoroughly familiar with them in advance.

- *How did you handle questions you were unsure of?*

   If you were able to eliminate one or more of the answer choices and you guessed from the remaining choices, then your approach probably worked to your advantage. On the other hand, omitting questions about which you have some knowledge or guessing answers haphazardly would probably be a mistake.

- *How difficult were the questions for you compared with other students who took the test?*

   By referring to Table A on page 317 you can find out how difficult each question was for the group of students who took the test in November 1982. The right-hand column in the table tells you what percentage of that group of students answered the question correctly. It is important to remember that these percentages are based on only one group of students; had this edition of the test been given to all students in the class of 1983 who took a Biology Achievement Test, the percentages would probably have been different. A question that was answered correctly by almost everyone in the group, obviously, is an easy question. Question 9, for example, was answered correctly by 91 percent of the students in the sample. On the other hand, question 50 was answered correctly by only 19 percent of the students. If you find that you missed several questions that would be considered easy, you may want to review those questions carefully. They may cover some aspect of the subject that you need to review. Perhaps you misunderstood the directions for one part of the test or you thought the questions were so easy that you did not spend as much time on them as you might have.

About the Chemistry Achievement Test

The Chemistry Achievement Test is a one-hour test that consists of 85 to 90 multiple-choice questions. The test assumes that you have had a one-year introductory course in chemistry and that the course content was at a level suitable for college preparation. The test covers the topics outlined in the description of test content given to the right. Different aspects of each topic are stressed from year to year. Because high school courses differ, both in the percentage of time devoted to each major topic and in the specific subtopics covered, you may encounter questions on topics with which you have little or no familiarity. However, in any typical high school chemistry course, more topics are usually covered — and in more detail — than there are questions in the Chemistry Achievement Test. So, even if high school chemistry curriculums weren't different, the questions in any particular test edition could be only a sample of all the questions that might be asked. The questions in all of the editions, however, test knowledge and abilities that might reasonably be expected of high school chemistry students intending to go to college.

Questions in the Chemistry Achievement Test have been tried out on entering college students who have had high school chemistry; the questions have also been approved by a committee of college and secondary school chemistry teachers appointed by the College Board. (See the section on "How the Tests are Developed" in the introduction of this book.)

No one instructional approach is better than another in helping you prepare for the test provided that you are able to recall and understand the major concepts of chemistry and to apply the chemical principles you have learned to solve specific scientific problems in chemistry. In addition, you should be able to organize and interpret results obtained by observation and experimentation and to draw conclusions or make inferences from experimental data. Laboratory experience is a significant factor in developing reasoning and problem-solving skills. Although laboratory skills can be tested only in a limited way in a standardized test, reasonable laboratory experience is an asset in helping you prepare for the Chemistry Achievement Test.

The Chemistry Achievement Test assumes that your preparation in mathematics enables you to handle simple algebraic relationships, to understand the concepts of ratio and proportions, and to apply these concepts to word problems.

You will *not* be allowed to use a periodic table during this test. The test is designed so that all necessary information regarding atomic numbers and atomic weights is given with the question concerned. Some editions of the test expect students to know the atomic weights and atomic numbers for hydrogen and oxygen. Also, you will *not* be allowed to use electronic calculators or slide rules during the chemistry test. Numerical calculations are limited to simple arithmetic. In this test, the metric system of units is used.

Content of the Test

Topics Covered	Approximate Percentage of Test
I. Atomic Theory and Structure, including periodic relationships	14
II. Chemical Bonding and Molecular Structure	10
III. States of Matter and Kinetic Molecular Theory	9
IV. Solutions, including concentration units, solubility, and colligative properties	6
V. Acids and Bases	9
VI. Oxidation-reduction and Electrochemistry	8
VII. Stoichiometry	10
VIII. Reaction Rates	2
IX. Equilibrium	5
X. Thermodynamics, including energy changes in chemical reactions, randomness, and criteria for spontaneity	4
XI. Descriptive Chemistry: physical and chemical properties of elements and their more familiar compounds, including simple examples from organic chemistry; periodic properties	16
XII. Laboratory: equipment, procedures, observations, safety, calculations, and interpretation of results	7

NOTE: Every edition contains approximately five questions on equation balancing and/or predicting products of chemical reactions. These are distributed among the various content categories.

Skills Specifications	Approximate Percentage of Test
Level I: Essentially Recall: remembering information and understanding facts	30
Level II: Essentially Application: applying knowledge to unfamiliar and/or practical situations; solving mathematical problems	55
Level III: Essentially Interpretation: inferring and deducing from available data and integrating information to form conclusions	15

Questions Used in the Test

Classification Questions

Each set of classification questions has, in the heading, five lettered choices that you will use to answer all of the questions in the set. The choices may be statements that refer to concepts, principles, substances, or observable phenomena; or they may be graphs, pictures, equations, numbers, or experimental settings or situations. The questions themselves may also conform to one of these formats or may be given in the question format directly. To answer each question you should select the choice in the heading that is most appropriate to it. You should consider all of the choices before answering a question. The directions for this type of question specifically state that you should not eliminate a choice simply because it is the correct answer to a previous question.

Because the same five choices are applicable to several questions, the classification questions usually require less reading than other types of multiple-choice questions. Therefore, this type of question is a quick means, in terms of testing time, of determining how well you have mastered the topics represented in the choices. The degree of mastery required to answer a question correctly depends on the sophistication of the set of questions. One set may test your ability to recall information; another set may ask you to apply information to a specific situation or to translate information from one form to another (descriptive,

graphical, mathematical). Thus, several types of abilities can be tested by a question of this type.

Following are the directions for and an example of a classification set.

Directions: Each set of lettered choices below refers to the numbered statements immediately following it. Select the one lettered choice that best fits each statement and then blacken the corresponding space on the answer sheet. A choice may be used once, more than once, or not at all in each set.

Questions 1-2 refer to the following aqueous solutions:

(A) 0.1 M HCl

(B) 0.1 M NaCl

(C) 0.1 M HC$_2$H$_3$O$_2$

(D) 0.1 M CH$_3$OH

(E) 0.1 M KOH

1. Is weakly acidic

2. Has the highest pH

These two questions belong to the topic category of acids and bases and require you to apply knowledge in this area to the particular solutions specified in the five choices.

To answer the first question, you must recognize which of the choices above are acid solutions. Only choices (A) and (C) satisfy this requirement. Choice (B) refers to a neutral salt solution, choice (D) is a solution of an alcohol, and choice (E) is a basic solution. Both choices (A) and (C) are acidic solutions, but (A) is a strong acid that is completely ionized in aqueous solution, while (C) is only partially ionized in aqueous solution. Since the concentrations of all the solutions are the same, you do not need to consider this factor. The hydrogen ion concentration of a 0.1-molar acetic acid solution is considerably smaller than 0.1-molar. The hydrogen ion concentration in (A) is equal to 0.1-molar. Thus (C) is a weakly acidic solution and is the correct answer to the question.

In order to answer the second question, you need to understand the pH scale, which is a measure of the hydrogen ion concentration in solution and is defined as pH = $-$ log [H$^+$]. The higher the pH, the lower the hydrogen ion concentration and the more basic the solution. Among the choices given above, choice (E) is the most basic solution and is the correct answer to this question.

Multiple-Completion Questions ▰▰▰▰

In the multiple-completion question, one or more of the three possible responses offered with the question may properly complete it. To answer this type of question correctly you must select the appropriate response or combination of responses. Thus, you can reach a correct answer only by deciding on the relevance or irrelevance of each one of the three possible choices. This selection process requires judgment in relating various considerations to the whole, and depends especially upon the completeness of your knowledge of any particular problem. Obviously, use of this question type normally is confined to situations in which several considerations of equal importance and plausibility can be suggested.

The multiple-completion type of question often is used when a problem involves any of the following: (1) a situation that may require you to consider several possible consequences; (2) a situation in which one or more conditions must be specified in order to define it adequately; (3) two situations that are alike (or unlike) with regard to one or more points of comparison; (4) a principle that may be applicable to one or more situations; or (5) several considerations that may bear upon a single result.

Directions: For each of the questions below, ONE or MORE of the responses given are correct. Decide which of the responses is (are) correct and on the answer sheet blacken space

(A) if 1, 2, and 3 are correct;

(B) if only 1 and 2 are correct;

(C) if only 2 and 3 are correct;

(D) if only 1 is correct;

(E) if only 3 is correct.

MARK ONE SPACE ONLY ON YOUR ANSWER SHEET FOR EACH QUESTION.

Directions Summarized				
(A)	(B)	(C)	(D)	(E)
1, 2, 3	1, 2 only	2, 3 only	1 only	3 only

3. In order to calculate the number of calories absorbed when 100 milliliters of a liquid is heated, one must know the

   (1) initial and final temperatures of the liquid

   (2) specific heat of the liquid

   (3) mass of the liquid

This is a question in which thermodynamic principles are applied to laboratory practices. When a substance absorbs energy (heat) without undergoing a change in state, there is a change in temperature. This change is directly proportional to the amount of energy added. Therefore both the initial and final temperatures are needed in order to calculate the number of calories a substance absorbs. Also the amount of energy absorbed is dependent on how much material is present, specifically what mass of the substance is present. Furthermore, the amount of energy absorbed depends on the chemical structure of the substance involved, a factor that determines the specific heat of the substance. Thus choices (1), (2), and (3) given with this question are all true. According to the directions given with this type of question, the correct answer is (A).

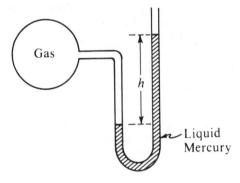

4. **The bulb of the open-end manometer shown above contains a gas. True statements about this system include which of the following?**

   (1) **Only atmospheric pressure is exerted on the exposed mercury surface in the right side of the tube.**

   (2) **The gas pressure is greater than atmospheric pressure.**

   (3) **The difference in the height, h, of mercury levels is equal to the pressure of the gas.**

This is a laboratory-oriented question pertaining to the measurement of gas pressures. It demands higher-level analytical skills that involve drawing conclusions from results obtained in an experiment. To answer this question correctly, you must first understand that, in an open type of manometer, the air exerts pressure on the column of liquid in the open side of the U-tube and the gas being studied exerts pressure on the other side of the U-tube. It is clear then that (1) is a true statement since the data given show that the manometer is open-ended and its right side is exposed to the atmosphere. Statement (2) is also a true statement because the level of liquid mercury is higher in the right side, which is exposed to the atmosphere, than in the left side, which is exposed to the gas. Thus the gas pressure is greater than atmospheric pressure. Statement (3) is not a correct statement because the pressure of the gas in the bulb, expressed in millimeters of mercury, is equal to the difference in height, h, of the two mercury levels, plus the atmospheric pressure. Thus only statements (1) and (2) are correct and the correct answer to the question is (B).

Relationship Analysis Questions

This type of question consists of a specific statement or assertion followed by an explanation of the assertion. The question is answered by determining if the assertion and the explanation are each true statements and if so, whether the explanation (or reason) provided does in fact properly explain the statement given in the assertion.

This type of question tests your ability to identify proper cause-and-effect relationships. It probes whether or not you can assess the correctness of the original assertion and then evaluate the truth of the "reason" proposed to justify it. The analysis required by this type of question provides you with an opportunity to demonstrate developed reasoning skills and the scope of your understanding of a particular topic.

Directions: Each question below consists of an assertion (statement) in the left-hand column and a reason in the right-hand column. On the appropriate line of the answer sheet blacken space

A if both assertion and reason are true statements and the reason is a correct explanation of the assertion;

B if both assertion and reason are true statements, but the reason is NOT a correct explanation of the assertion;

C if the assertion is true, but the reason is a false statement;

D if the assertion is false, but the reason is a true statement;

E if both assertion and reason are false statements.

Directions Summarized		
A-True	True	Reason is a correct explanation.
B-True	True	Reason is NOT a correct explanation.
C-True	False	
D-False	True	
E-False	False	

Assertion		Reason
5. The electrolysis of a concentrated solution of sodium chloride produces chlorine	BECAUSE	sodium chloride is a covalent compound.

The question above has several components. The first part of this question, the assertion, has to do

with an oxidation-reduction reaction, more specifically, an electrochemical reaction. This statement is true because the electrolysis of a concentrated sodium chloride solution yields chlorine gas at the anode (oxidation) and hydrogen gas at the cathode (reduction). The electrolytic solution gradually becomes alkaline with the accumulation of hydroxide ions (i.e., OH^- ions) as the reaction proceeds.

The second part of this question, the reason, is false because the type of chemical bonding in sodium chloride is ionic. According to the directions for the relationship-analysis questions, the correct answer to a question in which the assertion is true and the reason is a false statement is (C).

Assertion		Reason
6. Atoms of different elements can have the same mass number	BECAUSE	atoms of each element have a characteristic number of protons in the nucleus.

This is a question on atomic structure. The sum of the number of protons plus the number of neutrons contained in the nucleus of an atom is the mass number. However, atoms of the same element may have different numbers of neutrons in their nuclei and thus have different masses. Such atoms, which have the same number of protons but different numbers of neutrons, are called isotopes of an element ($^{12}_{6}C$ and $^{14}_{6}C$, for example). The existence of isotopes makes it possible for atoms of different elements, that is, with different numbers of protons, to have the same total mass or mass number ($^{14}_{6}C$ and $^{14}_{7}N$, for example). Thus the assertion in this question is true. The reason is also a true statement. The number of protons in the nucleus of an atom is a characteristic feature that identifies each element. But it is not the reason that explains the existence of isotopes and so does not properly explain the assertion. Thus, according to the directions for the relationship-analysis questions, the correct answer for this question is (B).

Assertion		Reason
7. When the system $CO(g) + Cl_2(g) = COCl_2(g)$ is at equilibrium and the pressure on the system is increased by decreasing the volume at constant temperature, more $COCl_2(g)$ will be produced	BECAUSE	an increase of pressure on a system will be relieved when the system shifts to a smaller total number of moles of gas.

The assertion is a true statement because whenever stress is applied to a system at equilibrium the system will tend to shift to relieve the stress (Le Chatelier's principle). In the system described, the stress is caused by an increase in pressure resulting from a decrease in the volume and will be relieved by the reaction of some CO and Cl_2 to form more $COCl_2$. The new equilibrium that will be established will contain a smaller total number of moles of gas, thereby reducing the pressure stress. This is the explanation given in the reason. The reason is not only a true statement but also correctly explains the phenomenon described in the assertion. Thus, according to the directions for this type of question, the correct answer is (A).

Five-choice Completion Questions

The five-choice completion question is widely used in objective tests and is probably the type of question with which you are most familiar. It is written either as an incomplete statement or as a question. In its simplest application, this type of question poses a problem that intrinsically has a unique solution. It is also appropriate when: (1) the problem presented is clearly delineated by the wording of the question so that you are asked to choose not a universal solution but the best of the solutions offered; (2) the problem is such that you are required to evaluate the relevance of five plausible, or even scientifically accurate, options and to select the one most pertinent; (3) the problem has several pertinent solutions and you are required to select the one inappropriate solution that is presented. In the latter case, the correct answer to the question is the choice that is *least* applicable to the situation described by the question. Such questions normally contain a word in capital letters such as NOT, LEAST, or EXCEPT.

The five-choice completion question also tests problem-solving skills. With this type of question, you are asked to convert the information given in a word problem into graphical forms or to select and apply the mathematical relationship necessary to solve the scientific problem. Alternatively, you may be asked to interpret experimental data, graphical stimulus, or mathematical expressions. Thus, the five-choice completion question can be adapted to test several kinds of abilities.

When the experimental data or other scientific problems to be analyzed are comparatively extensive, it is often convenient to organize several five-choice completion questions into sets, that is, direct each question in a set to the same material. This practice allows you to answer several questions based on the same material, compensating for the testing time required to read and interpret a large amount of scientific information. In no case, however, is the answer to one question necessary for answering a subsequent question correctly. Each question in a set is independent of the others and refers only to the material given for the entire set.

Directions: Each of the questions or incomplete statements below is followed by five suggested answers or completions. Select the one that is best in each case, and blacken the corresponding space on the answer sheet.

8. The hydrogen ion concentration of a solution prepared by diluting 50 milliliters of 0.100-molar HNO_3 with water to 500 milliliters of solution is

(A) 0.0010 $\underline{M}$

(B) 0.0050 $\underline{M}$

(C) 0.010 $\underline{M}$

(D) 0.050 $\underline{M}$

(E) 1.0 $\underline{M}$

This is a question that concerns solution concentrations. One way to solve the problem is through the use of ratios. In this question, a solution of nitric acid is diluted 10-fold; therefore, the concentration of the solution will decrease by a factor of 10, that is, from 0.100-molar to 0.010-molar. Alternatively, you could calculate the number of moles of H^+ ions present and divide this value by 0.50 liter: $(0.100 \times 0.050)/0.5 = \underline{M}$ of the diluted solution. In either case, the correct answer is (C).

9. A thermometer is placed in a test tube containing a melted pure substance. As slow cooling occurs, the thermometer is read at regular intervals until well after the sample has solidified. Which of the following types of graphs is obtained by plotting temperature <u>versus</u> time for this experiment?

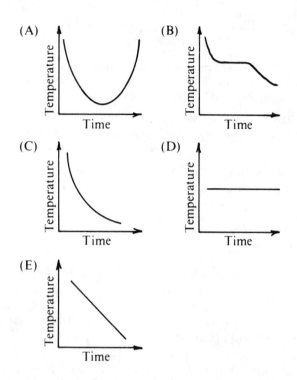

(A)

(B)

(C)

(D)

(E)

This is a question on states of matter. You must convert the description of the physical phenomenon given in the question to graphical form. When a liquid is cooled slowly, its temperature will decrease with time. Thus the first portion of a graph depicting this phenomenon must show a decrease when temperature is plotted against time. When a pure liquid substance reaches its fusion (melting) point, continued cooling will release heat with time as the substance solidifies. During this period there is no drop in temperature. After the substance has completely solidified, further cooling will cause an additional drop in temperature. The only graph above that accurately depicts the events described is (B), which is the correct answer.

10. From their electron configurations, one can predict that the geometric configuration for which of the following molecules is NOT correct?

(Atomic numbers: H = 1, C = 6, O = 8, F = 9, P = 15, Cl = 17)

(A) PF_3 trigonal planar

(B) CF_4 tetrahedral

(C) $CHCl_3$ irregular tetrahedron

(D) OF_2 bent (v-shaped)

(E) HF linear

This is a question on chemical bonding and requires you to apply the principles of molecular bonding. Each of the molecules given is correctly paired with the term describing its molecular geometry except (A). The geometry of PF_3 is not trigonal planar, but trigonal pyramidal, because this geometry corresponds to a maximum possible separation of the electron pairs around the central atom, phosphorus, and therefore yields the most stable configuration; the central atom of the molecule is surrounded by three single bonds and one unshared electron pair. Thus the correct answer is (A). Note that this is the type of question that asks you to identify the *one* solution to the problem that is *inappropriate*.

11. $\ldots SO_2 + \ldots O_2 \rightarrow \ldots$?

According to the reaction above, how many moles of SO_2, are required to react completely with 1 mole of O_2?

(A) 0.5 mole (B) 1 mole (C) 2 moles
(D) 3 moles (E) 4 moles

This is a question on descriptive chemistry that also tests your ability to balance chemical equations. The correct answer to this question depends first on your knowing that the combustion of sulfur dioxide, SO_2, produces sulfur trioxide, SO_3. The stoichiometry of the correctly balanced equation indicates that 2 moles of SO_2 are needed to react completely with 1 mole of O_2 to form 2 moles of SO_3. The correct answer is (C).

12. Analysis by weight of a certain compound shows that it contains 14.4 percent hydrogen and 85.6 percent carbon. Which of the following is the most informative statement that can properly be made about the compound on the basis of these data? (Atomic weights: H = 1.0; C = 12.0)

(A) It is a hydrocarbon.

(B) Its empirical formula is CH_2.

(C) Its molecular formula is C_2H_4.

(D) Its molecular weight is 28.

(E) It contains a triple bond.

This is a question on stoichiometry that tests the important skill of scientific reasoning based on experimental evidence. The question states that 100 percent of the composition of the compound analyzed can be accounted for with the elements hydrogen and carbon. Thus this compound is a hydrocarbon and (A) is a correct statement. It is not the correct answer to the question, however, because you can deduce more specific conclusions about this compound from the information given. The relative percentage composition provides evidence that the atomic ratio of carbon to hydrogen in the compound must be 85.6/ 12.0 : 14.4/1.0 or 1:2. Therefore, you can conclude that the empirical formula for the compound is CH_2, a hydrocarbon. Thus (B) is a better answer than (A). Since you do not know the total number of moles of the compound used for analysis, you cannot calculate the molecular weight or derive the molecular formula for this compound. Thus (C) and (D) cannot be determined from the information given and so they are not correct answers to the question. It is known, however, that a substance with an empirical formula of CH_2 cannot have a triple bond. Therefore, (E) is incorrect. The correct answer to the question is (B).

Chemistry Achievement Test

The test that follows is an edition of the Chemistry Achievement Test administered in December 1982. So that you will have an idea of what the actual test administration will be like, try to take this test under conditions as close as possible to those of the actual test. It will probably help if you

- Set aside an hour for the test when you will not be interrupted, so that you can complete all of it in one sitting.

- Sit at a desk with no other papers or books. You can't take a calculator, a dictionary, other books, or notes into the test room.

- Have a kitchen timer or clock in front of you for timing yourself.

- Tear out an answer sheet from the back of this book and fill it in just as you would on the day of the test. You can use one answer sheet for as many as three Achievement Tests.

- Read the instructions that precede the test. When you take the test, you will be asked to read them before you begin answering questions.

- After you finish the test, read the sections on "How to Score the Chemistry Achievement Test" and "Reviewing Your Test Performance," which follow the test.

CHEMISTRY TEST

The top portion of the section of the answer sheet which you will use in taking the Chemistry test must be filled in exactly as shown in the illustration below. Note carefully that you have to do all of the following on your answer sheet:

1. Print CHEMISTRY on the line to the right of the words "Achievement Test."
2. Blacken spaces 2 and 7 in the row of spaces immediately under the words "Test Code."
3. Blacken space 4 in the group of five spaces labeled X.
4. Blacken space 4 in the group of five spaces labeled Y.

You are to leave blank the nine spaces which are labeled Q.

When the supervisor gives the signal, turn the page and begin the Chemistry test. There are 100 numbered spaces on the answer sheet and 90 questions in the Chemistry test. Therefore, use only spaces 1 to 90 for recording your answers.

CHEMISTRY TEST

Part A

Directions: Each set of lettered choices below refers to the numbered questions, formulas, or statements immediately following it. Select the one lettered choice that best answers each question or best fits each formula or statement and then blacken the corresponding space on the answer sheet. A choice may be used once, more than once, or not at all in each set.

Questions 1-4

    (A) Thermometer
    (B) Separatory funnel
    (C) Flame spectrophotometer
    (D) Burette
    (E) Volumetric flask

1. Used to study the characteristic emission lines produced by excited atoms of elements

2. Used for the preparation of solutions of specific concentrations when a solid is used as the solute

3. Commonly used for removing the water layer from a system containing oil and water

4. Used for volume measurements during titration

Questions 5-9

    (A) Linear
    (B) Bent (V-shaped)
    (C) Trigonal, planar
    (D) Pyramidal
    (E) Regular tetrahedral

From the list above, select the shape that describes each of the following.

5. H_2O

6. BI_3

7. NH_3

8. Br_2

9. NH_4^+

Questions 10-12

    (A) $NaHCO_3$
    (B) H_2SO_4
    (C) CH_4
    (D) $Ca(OH)_2$
    (E) C_8H_{18}

10. A significant constituent of baking powders

11. A constituent of gasoline

12. A major constituent of natural gas

Questions 13-15

    (A) $3\ O_2(g) \rightleftarrows 2\ O_3(g)$
    (B) $OH^- + H_3O^+ \rightleftarrows 2\ H_2O$
    (C) $BaCl_2 \cdot 2\ H_2O(s) \overset{\triangle}{\rightarrow} BaCl_2(s) + 2\ H_2O(g)$
    (D) $Ca^{2+} + CO_3{}^{2-} \rightarrow CaCO_3(s)$
    (E) $Fe + Cu^{2+} \rightleftarrows Fe^{2+} + Cu$

13. Represents an oxidation-reduction reaction

14. Involves the formation of an ionic precipitate from a solution

15. Represents a Brönsted acid-base reaction

GO ON TO THE NEXT PAGE

Questions 16-19

    (A) 3*d* Transition metals
    (B) Alkali metals
    (C) Halogens
    (D) Noble gases
    (E) Actinides

16. Are the most readily oxidized elements within a given period

17. Have the highest first ionization energies (potentials) of the elements in their respective rows of the periodic table

18. Are all radioactive elements

19. Are the most electronegative of the elements above

Questions 20-22 refer to the following dilute solutions.

    (A) 0.010-molar HCl
    (B) 0.010-molar NaOH
    (C) 0.010-molar $Ba(OH)_2$
    (D) 0.010-molar H_2SO_4
    (E) 0.010-molar $C_{12}H_{22}O_{11}$ (cane sugar)

20. Which of the above has the lowest pH ?

21. Which of the above has the highest concentration of OH^- ions?

22. Which of the above has a freezing point closest to 0° C ?

Questions 23-25

(A)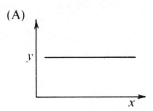

(B)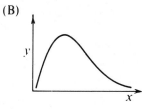

(C)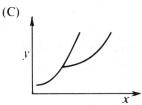

(D)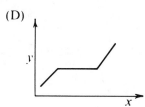

(E)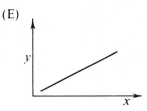

23. Shows how a plot of the pressure-volume product *y* varies with absolute temperature *x* for 1 mole of an ideal gas

24. Shows a plot of temperature *y* versus time *x* for the complete conversion, by uniform heating, of a pure liquid from below its boiling point to its vapor form above its boiling point

25. Shows a plot of the fraction of molecules in a gas sample *y* versus kinetic energy *x* at a given temperature

GO ON TO THE NEXT PAGE

CHEMISTRY TEST—*Continued*

Part B

<u>Directions:</u> For each of the questions below, ONE or MORE of the responses given are correct. Decide which of the responses is (are) correct and on the answer sheet blacken space

A if <u>1, 2, and 3</u> are correct;

B if only <u>1 and 2</u> are correct;

C if only <u>2 and 3</u> are correct;

D if only <u>1</u> is correct;

E if only <u>3</u> is correct.

MARK ONE SPACE ONLY ON YOUR ANSWER SHEET FOR EACH QUESTION

	Directions Summarized			
Ⓐ	Ⓑ	Ⓒ	Ⓓ	Ⓔ
1, 2, 3	1, 2 only	2, 3 only	1 only	3 only

26.
$$CaCO_3(s) \xrightarrow{\text{heat}}$$

Products resulting from the thermal decomposition of $CaCO_3$ indicated above include

(1) CaO
(2) CO_2
(3) C

27. A neutral atom, atomic number 33 and atomic mass 75, contains

(1) 75 neutrons
(2) 42 electrons
(3) 33 protons

28. When the temperature is increased, the speed of a chemical reaction usually increases because the

(1) pressure has decreased
(2) molecules collide less frequently
(3) fraction of the molecules possessing the activation energy for the reaction increases

29. When H_2S burns completely in oxygen, the products include

(1) S
(2) SO_2
(3) H_2O

30. A piece of zinc may be distinguished from a piece of magnesium by

(1) determining which conducts electricity
(2) determining which releases H_2 gas from a 1-molar hydrochloric acid solution
(3) measuring the density of each

31. Two 1-liter flasks contain hydrogen and oxygen, respectively, at the same temperature and pressure. It is true that the hydrogen and oxygen molecules have the same average

(1) kinetic energy
(2) mass
(3) speed

32. Molecules that involve both s and p orbital electrons in their bonding include which of the following? (Atomic numbers: H = 1, C = 6, N = 7, Cl = 17)

(1) NH_3
(2) CCl_4
(3) HCl

GO ON TO THE NEXT PAGE

DIRECTIONS SUMMARIZED ON THE OPPOSITE PAGE.

33. Species that, in water, can function as both a Brönsted acid and a Brönsted base include which of the following?

(1) $HClO_4$

(2) HCO_3^-

(3) HPO_4^{2-}

34. $$2 SO_2(g) + O_2(g) \rightleftarrows 2 SO_3(g) + heat$$

For the system above at equilibrium, increasing the temperature increases the number of moles of which of the following when equilibrium is reestablished?

(1) $SO_3(g)$
(2) $O_2(g)$
(3) $SO_2(g)$

35. $$\ldots CaO(s) + \ldots H_3O^+ + \ldots Cl^- \longrightarrow$$

Addition of solid calcium oxide to a solution of hydrochloric acid results in the formation of

(1) Ca^{2+}
(2) H_2O
(3) H_2

36. The $SiCl_4$ molecule is nonpolar and chlorine is more electronegative than silicon. From this information alone it can be deduced that the

(1) silicon-chlorine bond is nonpolar
(2) $SiCl_4$ molecule is planar
(3) $SiCl_4$ molecule is symmetrical

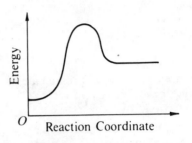

37. The diagram above shows how the potential energy changes as reactants are converted to products for a given reaction. From the diagram, it can be concluded that the

(1) overall reaction is endothermic
(2) activation energy of the forward reaction is greater than that for the reverse reaction
(3) forward reaction is a more rapid reaction than the reverse reaction

38. The number of moles of CO_2 that can be dissolved in a liter of water increases when the

(1) pressure of the CO_2 is increased
(2) temperature of the water is increased
(3) liquid is stirred

GO ON TO THE NEXT PAGE

CHEMISTRY TEST—*Continued*

Part C

<u>Directions:</u> Each question below consists of an <u>assertion</u> (statement) in the left-hand column and a <u>reason</u> in the right-hand column. On the appropriate line of the answer sheet blacken space

A   if both assertion and reason are true statements and the reason is a <u>correct explanation</u> of the assertion;

B   if both assertion and reason are true statements, but the reason is <u>NOT a correct explanation</u> of the assertion;

C   if the assertion is true, but the reason is a false statement;

D   if the assertion is false, but the reason is a true statement;

E   if both assertion and reason are false statements.

Directions Summarized		
A - True	True	Reason is a <u>correct explanation</u>
B - True	True	Reason is <u>NOT a correct explanation</u>
C - True	False	
D - False	True	
E - False	False	

Assertion		Reason
39. Element number 12 and element number 20 undergo similar chemical reactions	BECAUSE	element number 12 and element number 20 have similar valence electron configurations.
40. The element carbon forms the basic structural framework of more compounds than any other element	BECAUSE	the carbon-carbon bond is ionic.
41. The molecule CO_2 has a net dipole moment of zero	BECAUSE	the arrangement of atoms in the CO_2 molecule is linear and symmetrical, and the bond polarities within the molecule are canceled out.
42. A catalyst that increases the rate of a forward reaction also increases the rate of the reverse reaction	BECAUSE	the activation energy for a forward reaction is necessarily equal to that of the reverse reaction.
43. The boiling temperature of water is lower at high elevations than at sea level	BECAUSE	the atmospheric pressure is lower at high elevations than at sea level.
44. An element X with the electronic configuration $1s^2\,2s^2 2p^6\,3s^2 3p^4$ can be expected to form a compound of the type H_2X	BECAUSE	two additional electrons fill the valence shell of an element with outer electronic configuration $3s^2 3p^4$.
45. The heat of vaporization of water and the heat of fusion of water are numerically different	BECAUSE	when water freezes or vaporizes, its chemical composition remains unchanged.

GO ON TO THE NEXT PAGE

CHEMISTRY TEST—*Continued*

DIRECTIONS SUMMARIZED ON THE OPPOSITE PAGE.

46. When a piece of Zn is dropped into 1.0-molar $CuSO_4$ solution, metallic Cu appears BECAUSE Zn is more readily oxidized than Cu is.

47. HCO_3^- can act as a Brönsted acid or a Brönsted base BECAUSE HCO_3^- can donate a proton to form CO_3^{2-} or accept a proton to form H_2CO_3.

48. At 25° C and 1 atmosphere pressure, H_2O is a liquid but H_2S is a gas BECAUSE the molecular weight of H_2O is less than that of H_2S.

49. The equation
$$Fe^{2+} + NO_3^- + 4 H^+ \rightleftarrows Fe^{3+} + NO + 2 H_2O$$
is balanced BECAUSE all the atoms and charges in the equation shown for this reaction are conserved.

50. ^{50}Ti and ^{50}Cr are isotopes of each other BECAUSE atoms of ^{50}Ti and ^{50}Cr have the same mass number.

51. When the valve in the system shown above is opened and the system is allowed to reach equilibrium, most of the helium remains in the bulb on the left BECAUSE when two bulbs containing gases are connected, the randomness of the system decreases.

52. The first ionization energy of Li is less than that of Na BECAUSE Li is a smaller atom than Na.

GO ON TO THE NEXT PAGE

Part D

Directions: Each of the questions or incomplete statements below is followed by five suggested answers or completions. Select the one that is best in each case and then blacken the corresponding space on the answer sheet.

53. $\quad \ldots B_2O_3 + \ldots Mg \rightarrow \ldots MgO + \ldots B$

    According to the equation above, how many moles of magnesium would be required to react completely with 1 mole of B_2O_3? (Equation is not balanced.)

    (A) 0.2 mole
    (B) 0.3 mole
    (C) 1 mole
    (D) 2 moles
    (E) 3 moles

54. In the ionic solid NH_4NO_3, the ions present are

    (A) NH_4^+ and NO_3^-
    (B) N^{5+}, H^+, and O^{2-}
    (C) NH_4^+, N^{5+}, and O^{2-}
    (D) NH_3, H^+, and NO_3^-
    (E) N^{5+}, N^{3-}, H^+, and O^{2-}

55. All of the following are good laboratory practices EXCEPT:

    (A) Wait for a hot object to cool before weighing it.
    (B) Rinse a burette with the solution that will be used to fill the burette.
    (C) Wear goggles at all times.
    (D) Return unused chemicals to the reagent bottles.
    (E) To dilute H_2SO_4, pour it into water slowly.

56. Which of the following ions does NOT have a noble gas electron configuration? (Atomic numbers: $O = 8$, $Na = 11$, $Ca = 20$, $Mn = 25$, $I = 53$)

    (A) O^{2-}
    (B) Na^+
    (C) Ca^{2+}
    (D) Mn^{2+}
    (E) I^-

57. What volume of 0.20-molar HCl is required to exactly neutralize 40 milliliters of 0.10-molar NaOH?

    (A) 50 ml
    (B) 40 ml
    (C) 20 ml
    (D) 10 ml
    (E) 8 ml

58. All of the following are true of aluminum EXCEPT:

    (A) It is a good conductor of electricity.
    (B) It is a metal of high density.
    (C) It forms a protective coating in air that resists further corrosion.
    (D) It is an excellent reducing agent.
    (E) It forms a hydroxide that is soluble in both strong base and acid.

GO ON TO THE NEXT PAGE

59. $$^{212}_{84}Po \rightarrow \, ^4_2He + \, ?$$

The missing product in the equation above is

(A) $^{216}_{86}Pb$

(B) $^{212}_{86}Pb$

(C) $^{212}_{82}Pb$

(D) $^{208}_{84}Pb$

(E) $^{208}_{82}Pb$

60. $$9\,Fe_2O_3 + 2\,NH_3 \rightarrow 6\,Fe_3O_4 + N_2 + 3\,H_2O$$

According to the balanced equation above, when 1 mole of NH_3 reacts completely, which of the following is true?

(A) 1 mole of N_2 must be formed
(B) 1 mole of H_2O must be formed
(C) 3 moles of Fe_3O_4 must be formed
(D) 2 moles of Fe_2O_3 must react
(E) 4 moles of Fe_2O_3 must react

61. What is the percent composition of $CaBr_2$?
(Atomic weights: $Ca = 40$, $Br = 80$)

(A) 10% Ca and 90% Br
(B) 20% Ca and 80% Br
(C) 25% Ca and 75% Br
(D) 33% Ca and 67% Br
(E) 50% Ca and 50% Br

62. Two samples were weighed using different balances and the following data were obtained.

Sample #1 = 3.719 grams
Sample #2 = 0.42 gram

The total mass of the samples should be reported as

(A) 4 grams
(B) 4.1 grams
(C) 4.139 grams
(D) 4.14 grams
(E) 4.140 grams

63. A solution of a base that has a pH of 9.0 has a hydrogen ion concentration of

(A) $1 \times 10^{+9}$ molar
(B) $1 \times 10^{+5}$ molar
(C) 1×10^{-5} molar
(D) 1×10^{-7} molar
(E) 1×10^{-9} molar

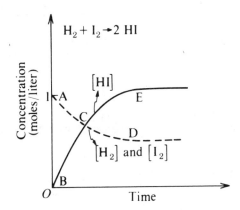

64. The graph above shows the variation in concentration of reactants and products as H_2 and I_2 react to form HI at a given temperature. Equilibrium is reached when the concentration of HI is

(A) A
(B) B
(C) C
(D) D
(E) E

65.

Element	Electronegativity
P	2.1
H	2.2
Br	2.8
O	3.5

On the basis of the electronegativity values given above, in which of the following are the bonds most polar?

(A) PH_3
(B) H_2O
(C) HBr
(D) P_4
(E) PBr_3

66. Potassium hydroxide is a good conductor of an electric current in the

(A) gaseous state only
(B) molten (fused) state only
(C) solid state only
(D) solid and molten (fused) states
(E) molten (fused) state and in aqueous solution

GO ON TO THE NEXT PAGE

67.

Liquid	Vapor Pressure (mm Hg), 25° C
A	20
B	35
C	56
D	112
E	224

In which of the liquids listed in the table above are the intermolecular forces of attraction the strongest?

(A) A
(B) B
(C) C
(D) D
(E) E

68. The range of oxidation states exhibited by most elements in group V of the periodic table (N, P, As, Sb, Bi) is

(A) −3 to +1
(B) −3 to +3
(C) −3 to +5
(D) −2 to +3
(E) +1 to +5

69.

Mass of Empty Flask	38.913 grams
Mass of Flask + KMnO₄	39.898 grams
Mass of Flask + Residue (after ignition)	39.773 grams

The data above were taken for the decomposition of $KMnO_4$ by ignition, which liberates oxygen and leaves a solid residue. The experimental mass ratio is

(A) $\frac{0.125}{0.985}$ gram residue/ gram $KMnO_4$

(B) $\frac{0.125}{0.860}$ gram residue/ gram $KMnO_4$

(C) $\frac{0.860}{0.985}$ gram residue/ gram $KMnO_4$

(D) $\frac{0.985}{0.860}$ grams residue/ gram $KMnO_4$

(E) $\frac{0.860}{0.125}$ grams residue/ gram $KMnO_4$

70. To find the concentration of a solution of a base by titration with a solution of an acid, which of the following represents the minimum data needed, assuming that the titration has been carried to the proper end point and that the equation for the reaction is known?

I. Volume of acid
II. Volume of base
III. Concentration of acid

(A) I only
(B) III only
(C) I and II only
(D) II and III only
(E) I, II, and III

71. $\ldots Cr(OH)_3\,(s) + \ldots OH^- \rightleftharpoons \ldots CrO_2^- + \ldots H_2O$

When the equation above is balanced, how many grams of water will be produced when 1.00 mole of CrO_2^- is formed?

(A) 9.0 grams
(B) 18.0 grams
(C) 27.0 grams
(D) 36.0 grams
(E) 45.0 grams

GO ON TO THE NEXT PAGE

72. Which of the following statements concerning fluorine and chlorine is FALSE?

    (A) Fluorine is more electronegative than chlorine.
    (B) The atomic radius of the fluorine atom is less than that of the chlorine atom.
    (C) Fluorine is a stronger oxidizing agent than chlorine.
    (D) Both fluorine and chlorine commonly exist in positive and negative oxidation states.
    (E) Both fluorine and chlorine are diatomic gases at room conditions.

73. How many moles of sodium oxalate, $Na_2C_2O_4$, are present in 6.7 grams of this compound? (Atomic weights: $C = 12$, $O = 16$, $Na = 23$)

    (A) 2.0 moles
    (B) 1.0 mole
    (C) 0.50 mole
    (D) 0.10 mole
    (E) 0.050 mole

74. A sample of 90.0 grams of glucose is dissolved in enough water to yield 200. milliliters of solution. What is the molar concentration of glucose (molecular weight 180.) ?

    (A) 0.500 M
    (B) 1.00 M
    (C) 2.00 M
    (D) 2.50 M
    (E) 10.0 M

75. $$CO_2(g) + C(s) \rightarrow 2\ CO(g)$$

    A sample of 100 liters of carbon dioxide at $25°$ C and 1 atmosphere pressure is reduced by being passed over hot coke according to the equation above. When measured at $25°$ C and 1 atmosphere pressure, the volume of carbon monoxide formed is

    (A) 22.4 liters
    (B) 44.8 liters
    (C) 50 liters
    (D) 100 liters
    (E) 200 liters

76. Which of the following acids, listed with their ionization constants at $25°$ C, is the strongest?

    (A) Nitrous acid (HNO_2) $K_i = 4.5 \times 10^{-4}$
    (B) Formic acid ($HCHO_2$) $K_i = 1.8 \times 10^{-4}$
    (C) Benzoic acid ($HC_7H_5O_2$) $K_i = 6.3 \times 10^{-5}$
    (D) Acetic acid ($HC_2H_3O_2$) $K_i = 1.8 \times 10^{-5}$
    (E) Hydrocyanic acid (HCN) $K_i = 4.0 \times 10^{-10}$

77. $$\ldots S_2O_8{}^{2-} + \ldots I^- \rightarrow \ldots SO_4{}^{2-} + \ldots I_2$$

    What is the maximum yield of iodine that can be obtained when 1 mole of $Na_2S_2O_8$ reacts completely with excess iodide ion according to the equation above? (Equation above is not balanced.)

    (A) 1 mole
    (B) 2 moles
    (C) 4 moles
    (D) 6 moles
    (E) 8 moles

78. The heat of formation for CO_2 is given as $\triangle H = -94.2$ kcal/mole. The negative value of $\triangle H$ indicates that

    (A) CO_2 is formed from its elements by an endothermic reaction
    (B) the reaction of carbon with oxygen occurs rapidly at $25°$ C
    (C) the enthalpy of the product CO_2 is less than that of the reactants, O_2 and C
    (D) no heat is liberated when carbon is oxidized
    (E) 94.2 kcal must be added to oxidize one mole of carbon

79. The oxidation number of the nitrogen atom in the ammonium ion is

    (A) +3
    (B) +2
    (C) +1
    (D) −2
    (E) −3

GO ON TO THE NEXT PAGE

80. Which of the following is a saturated hydro-carbon?

    (A) C_2H_2
    (B) C_2H_4
    (C) C_2H_6
    (D) C_6H_6
    (E) C_6H_{10}

81. The volume occupied by 0.50 mole of propane gas, C_3H_8, at a temperature of 27° C and a pressure of 2.0 atmospheres is best expressed by which of the following? ($R = 0.082$ liter-atm/mole° K)

    (A) $\dfrac{0.50 \times 0.082 \times 27}{2}$ liters

    (B) $\dfrac{0.50 \times 0.082 \times 300}{2}$ liters

    (C) $\dfrac{0.50 \times 0.082 \times 273}{300}$ liters

    (D) $\dfrac{0.50 \times 0.082 \times 300}{2 \times 760}$ liters

    (E) $\dfrac{0.50 \times 0.082 \times 27}{2 \times 760}$ liters

82. $$N_2(g) + 3 H_2(g) \rightleftarrows 2 NH_3(g)$$

    The correct equilibrium expression, K_c, for the formation of ammonia according to the equation above is

    (A) $K_c = \dfrac{[N_2][H_2]}{[NH_3]}$

    (B) $K_c = \dfrac{[NH_3]}{[N_2][H_2]}$

    (C) $K_c = \dfrac{[N]^2[H]^6}{[NH_3]^2}$

    (D) $K_c = \dfrac{[NH_3]^2}{[N_2][H_2]^3}$

    (E) $K_c = \dfrac{[N_2][H_2]^3}{[NH_3]^2}$

83. In qualitative analysis the separation of Ag^+ ions from Cu^{2+} ions by the addition of HCl depends on the fact that

    (A) Cu^{2+} forms an insoluble chloride and Ag^+ does not
    (B) Ag^+ forms an insoluble chloride and Cu^{2+} does not
    (C) Cu^{2+} forms a complex with HCl and Ag^+ does not
    (D) Cu reacts with HCl and Ag does not
    (E) Ag^+ is oxidized by HCl whereas Cu^{2+} is in its highest oxidation state

84. A battery jar contained a solution of copper sulfate. Two electrodes, one made of copper, the other a metal object to be copper plated, were placed in the jar and connected to a source of direct current. Which of the following statements concerning this system is correct?

    (A) The object to be plated is the anode.
    (B) Oxidation occurs at the anode.
    (C) The sulfate ions migrate toward the cathode.
    (D) The concentration of the copper sulfate solution increases as electrolysis proceeds.
    (E) The copper electrode increases in mass.

85. Which of the following contains the greatest total number of atoms?

    (A) One mole of CO_2 (molecular weight = 44)
    (B) One mole of H_2O_2 (molecular weight = 34)
    (C) One molecule of glucose, $C_6H_{12}O_6$ (molecular weight = 180)
    (D) One gram of helium (atomic weight = 4)
    (E) One gram of H_2O (molecular weight = 18)

GO ON TO THE NEXT PAGE

CHEMISTRY TEST—*Continued*

86.
$$\overset{\text{I}}{2s} \rightarrow \overset{\text{II}}{2p} \rightarrow \overset{\text{III}}{3d} \rightarrow \overset{\text{IV}}{3p} \rightarrow \overset{\text{V}}{4s} \rightarrow 2p$$

The electronic transitions shown above are observed when lithium atoms are sprayed into a hot flame. The various transitions are numbered for identification. Which of these transitions would result in emission of electromagnetic radiation (light)?

(A) I and II only
(B) I and III only
(C) I and V only
(D) III and IV only
(E) III and V only

87.

$P_4O_6 \xrightarrow{\text{I}} HPO_3$

$P_4O_6 \xrightarrow{\text{II}} PH_3$

$P_4O_6 \xrightarrow{\text{III}} H_3PO_3$

The compound P_4O_6 may be chemically converted into a variety of other species by processes I-III, indicated above. In which of the conversions above is phosphorus reduced?

(A) I only
(B) II only
(C) I and III only
(D) II and III only
(E) I, II, and III

88.
$$HS^- + OH^- \rightleftarrows S^{2-} + H_2O$$

In the system indicated by the equation above, which of the substances are Brönsted acids?

(A) HS^- and H_2O

(B) HS^- and S^{2-}

(C) HS^- and OH^-

(D) S^{2-} and H_2O

(E) OH^- and H_2O

89.
$$HCl(g) + NH_3(g) \rightarrow NH_4Cl(s)$$

If 3.0 moles of HCl gas and 5.0 moles of NH_3 gas, each measured at 20° C and 1.0 atmosphere pressure, are allowed to react completely according to the equation above, the final mixture will contain

(A) 3 moles of solid NH_4Cl only
(B) 5 moles of solid NH_4Cl only
(C) 3 moles of solid NH_4Cl + 2 moles of NH_3 gas
(D) 3 moles of solid NH_4Cl + 2 moles of HCl gas
(E) 2 moles of HCl gas, 4 moles of NH_3 gas, and 1 mole of solid NH_4Cl

90. In an electrolysis cell, the passage of 6.02×10^{23} electrons can produce

(A) 22.4 liters of H_2 gas (measured at standard conditions) from dilute H_2SO_4 solution
(B) 22.4 liters of O_2 gas (measured at standard conditions) from dilute H_2SO_4 solution
(C) 1 mole of Cl_2 gas from HCl solution
(D) 1 mole of metallic silver from $AgNO_3$ solution
(E) 1 mole of metallic copper from $CuSO_4$ solution

S T O P

IF YOU FINISH BEFORE TIME IS CALLED, YOU MAY CHECK YOUR WORK ON THIS TEST ONLY. DO NOT WORK ON ANY OTHER TEST IN THIS BOOK.

How to Score the Chemistry Achievement Test

When you take the Chemistry Achievement Test, your answer sheet will be "read" by a scanning machine that will record your responses to each question. Then a computer will compare your answers with the correct answers and produce your raw score. You get one point for each correct answer. For each wrong answer, you lose one-fourth of a point. Questions you omit (and any for which you mark more than one answer) are not counted. This raw score is converted to a College Board scaled score that is reported to you and to the colleges you specify. After you have taken this test, you can get an idea of what your score might be by following the instructions in the next two sections.

Determining Your Raw Score

Step 1: Table A on the next page lists the correct answers for all the questions on the test.* Compare your answer with the correct answer and
- Put a check in the column marked "Right" if your answer is correct.
- Put a check in the column marked "Wrong" if your answer is incorrect.
- Leave both columns blank if you omitted the question.

Step 2: Count the number of right answers and enter the number here . . . . _____

Step 3: Count the number of wrong answers and enter

the number here . . . . 4) ‾‾‾‾‾‾‾‾

Enter the result of dividing by 4 here . . . . _____

Step 4: Subtract the number you obtained in Step 3 from the number in Step 2; round the result to the nearest whole number (.5 is rounded up) and enter here. . _____

The number you obtained in Step 4 is your raw score. (The correction for guessing — subtraction of a quarter of a point for each incorrect answer — adjusts for the fact that random guessing on a large number of questions will result in some questions being answered correctly by chance.) Instructions for converting your raw score to a scaled score follow.

*The last column in Table A gives the percentage of students who took the test in December 1982 that answered the question correctly. (See page 347 for further explanation.)

Answers to Chemistry Achievement Test, Form 3EAC, and Percentage of Students Answering Each Question Correctly

Question Number	Correct Answer	Right	Wrong	Percentage of Students Answering the Question Correctly	Question Number	Correct Answer	Right	Wrong	Percentage of Students Answering the Question Correctly
1	C			87%	46	A			38%
2	E			57	47	A			57
3	B			87	48	B			41
4	D			59	49	E			42
5	B			80	50	D			32
6	C			49	51	E			41
7	D			46	52	D			24
8	A			83	53	E			83
9	E			69	54	A			79
10	A			62	55	D			60
11	E			60	56	D			46
12	C			64	57	C			71
13	E			51	58	B			57
14	D			38	59	E			73
15	B			72	60	C			78
16	B			50	61	B			63
17	D			40	62	D			56
18	E			61	63	E			55
19	C			46	64	E			37
20	D			24	65	B			47
21	C			65	66	E			48
22	E			27	67	A			47
23	E			55	68	C			32
24	D			79	69	C			48
25	B			30	70	E			48
26	B			85	71	D			46
27	E			76	72	D			43
28	E			85	73	E			51
29	C			67	74	D			37
30	E			30	75	E			29
31	D			61	76	A			35
32	A			36	77	A			42
33	C			31	78	C			26
34	C			45	79	E			34
35	B			41	80	C			37
36	E			34	81	B			29
37	B			47	82	D			39
38	D			20	83	B			19
39	A			62	84	B			19
40	C			62	85	B			22
41	A			41	86	E			15
42	C			23	87	B			14
43	A			65	88	A			20
44	A			57	89	C			31
45	B			49	90	D			11

Note: The percentages are based on the analysis of the answer sheets for a random sample of students who took this test in December 1982 and whose mean score was 550.

Finding Your College Board Scaled Score ■

When you take Achievement Tests, the scores sent to the colleges you specify will be reported on the College Board scale, ranging from 200 to 800. The raw score that you obtained above (Step 4) can be converted to a scaled score by using Table B.

To find your scaled score on this test, locate your raw score in the left column of Table B; the corresponding score in the right column will be your College Board scaled score. For example, a raw score of 41 on this particular edition of the Chemistry Achievement Test corresponds to a College Board scaled score of 580. Raw scores are converted to scaled scores to ensure that a score earned on any one edition of the Chemistry Achievement Test is comparable to the same scaled score earned on any other edition of the test.

Because some editions of the Chemistry Achievement Test may be slightly easier or more difficult than others, statistical adjustments are made in the scores so that each College Board scaled score indicates the same level of performance, regardless of the edition of the test you take and the ability of the group you take it with. A given raw score will correspond to

TABLE B — SCORE CONVERSION TABLE					
Chemistry Achievement Test, Form 3EAC					
Raw Score	College Board Scaled Score	Raw Score	College Board Scaled Score	Raw Score	College Board Scaled Score
90	800	50	640	10	390
89	800	49	630	9	380
88	800	48	620	8	370
87	800	47	620	7	370
86	800	46	610	6	360
85	800	45	610	5	360
84	800	44	600	4	350
83	800	43	590	3	340
82	800	42	590	2	340
81	800	41	580	1	330
80	800	40	570	0	320
79	800	39	570	−1	320
78	800	38	560	−2	310
77	800	37	560	−3	310
76	800	36	550	−4	300
75	790	35	540	−5	290
74	790	34	540	−6	290
73	780	33	530	−7	280
72	770	32	520	−8	270
71	770	31	520	−9	270
70	760	30	510	−10	260
69	750	29	510	−11	260
68	750	28	500	−12	250
67	740	27	490	−13	240
66	740	26	490	−14	240
65	730	25	480	−15	230
64	720	24	470	−16	230
63	720	23	470	−17	220
62	710	22	460	−18	210
61	700	21	460	−19	210
60	700	20	450	−20 through −22	200
59	690	19	440		
58	690	18	440		
57	680	17	430		
56	670	16	420		
55	670	15	420		
54	660	14	410		
53	660	13	410		
52	650	12	400		
51	640	11	390		

different College Board scores, depending on the edition of the test taken. A raw score of 40, for example, may convert to a College Board score of 570 on one edition of the test, but that raw score might convert to a College Board score of 590 on a slightly more difficult edition. When you take the Chemistry Achievement Test on the actual test day, your score is likely to differ somewhat from the score you obtained on this test. People perform at different levels at different times, for reasons unrelated to the test itself. The precision of any test is also limited because it represents only a sample of all the possible questions that could be asked. (See page 12, "How Precise Are Your Scores?" for further information.)

Reviewing Your Test Performance

After you have scored your test, you should take some time to consider the following points in relation to your performance on the test.

- *Did you run out of time before you reached the end of the test?*

  If you did, you may want to consider tactics that will help you pace yourself better. For example, you may have spent too much time working on one or two difficult questions. A better approach might have been to continue the test and return to those questions after you had attempted to answer the remaining questions on the test.

- *Did you take a long time reading the directions for the test?*

  The directions in this test are the same as those in the Chemistry Achievement Tests now being administered. You will save time when you read the directions on the test day if you become thoroughly familiar with them in advance.

- *How did you handle questions you were unsure of?*

  If you were able to eliminate one or more of the answer choices and you guessed from the remaining choices, then your approach probably worked to your advantage. On the other hand, omitting questions about which you have some knowledge or guessing answers haphazardly would probably be a mistake.

- *How difficult were the questions for you compared with other students who took the test?*

  By referring to Table A on page 345 you can find out how difficult each question was for a selected sample of the students who took the test in December 1982. The right-hand column in the table tells you what percentage of that group of students answered the question correctly. It is important to remember that these percentages are based on only one group of students; had this edition of the test been given to all students in the class of 1983 who took a Chemistry Achievement Test, the percentages would probably have been different. A question that was answered correctly by almost everyone in the group, obviously, is an easy question. Question 26, for example, was answered correctly by 85 percent of the students in the sample. On the other hand, question 86 was answered correctly by only 15 percent of the students. If you find that you missed several questions that would be considered easy, you may want to review those questions carefully. They may cover some aspect of the subject that you need to review. Perhaps you misunderstood the directions for one part of the test or you thought the questions were so easy that you didn't spend as much time on them as you might have.

About the Physics Achievement Test

The Physics Achievement Test is a one-hour test consisting of 75 multiple-choice questions. The test assumes that you have had a one-year introductory course in physics and that the course content was at a level suitable for college preparation. Questions appearing in the test have been tried out on students just entering college who have had high school physics; the questions have also been approved by a committee of high school and college physics teachers appointed by the College Board (see the section "How the Test Is Developed" in the introduction to this book).

The approximate percentages of the questions on each major topic in the Physics Achievement Test are listed in the description of test content given to the right. The test emphasizes the topics that are covered in most high school courses. However, because high school courses differ, both in the percentage of time devoted to each major topic and in the specific subtopics covered, you may encounter questions on topics with which you are not familiar.

In any high school physics course, more material is usually covered and in more detail than can be covered in any single Physics Achievement Test. So, even if high school physics curriculums weren't different, the questions in any particular test edition could be only a sample of all the questions that might be asked. The questions in every edition of the test, however, test knowledge and abilities that might reasonably be expected of high school physics students intending to go to college.

The test is not based on any one textbook or instructional approach, but concentrates on the common core of material found in most texts. You should be able to recall and understand the major concepts of physics and to apply physical principles to solve specific problems. You also should be able to organize and interpret results obtained by observation and experimentation and to draw conclusions or make inferences from experimental data. Laboratory experience is a significant factor in developing reasoning and problem-solving skills. Although laboratory skills can be tested only in a limited way in a standardized test, there are occasional questions that ask you to interpret laboratory data. Reasonable laboratory experience is an asset in helping you prepare for the Physics Achievement Test.

The Physics Achievement Test assumes that you understand simple algebraic, trigonometric, and graphical relationships and the concepts of ratio and proportion, and that you can apply these concepts to word problems.

You will *not* be allowed to use an electronic calculator or a slide rule during the test. Numerical calculations are not emphasized and are limited to simple arithmetic. In this test, metric units are used predominantly.

Content of the Test

Topic	Approximate Percentage of Test
I. Mechanics	40
A. Kinematics (such as velocity, acceleration, motion in one dimension, motion of projectiles, and circular motion)	
B. Dynamics (such as Newton's laws, centripetal force, and statics)	
C. Energy and Momentum (such as work, power, impulse, and conservation laws)	
D. Other (such as gravity and orbits of planets and satellites, vibrations, and simple harmonic motion)	
II. Electricity and Magnetism	20
A. Electrostatics (such as Coulomb's law, electric field and potential, and capacitance)	
B. Circuits (such as Ohm's law, Joule's law, and direct-current circuits with resistors and capacitors)	
C. Electromagnetism (such as production and effects of magnetic fields, and electromagnetic induction)	
III. Optics and Waves	20
A. Waves (such as general wave properties and sound)	
B. Physical Optics (such as interference, diffraction, and properties of light)	

C. Geometrical Optics (such as reflection, refraction, mirrors, and lenses)

IV. Heat, Kinetic Theory, and Thermodynamics   10
   A. Thermal Properties (such as mechanical equivalent of heat, temperature, and specific and latent heats)
   B. Kinetic Theory and Ideal Gas Law
   C. Laws of Thermodynamics (first and second laws)

V. Modern Physics   10
   A. Atomic (such as the Rutherford and Bohr models, energy levels, and atomic spectra)
   B. Nuclear (such as radioactivity and nuclear reactions)
   C. Other (such as photons, photoelectric effect, and relativity)

Some questions are of a general nature and overlap several topics, illustrating the unified structure of physics.

Abilities	Approximate Percentage of Test
1. Recall (generally involves only remembering the desired information)	20-33
2. Single-concept problem (generally involves recall and use of a single physical relationship)	40-53
3. Multiple-concept problem (generally involves recall and use of two or more physical relationships that must be combined)	20-33

Questions Used in the Test

Classification Questions ▬▬▬

Each set of classification questions begins with five lettered choices that you will use to answer all of the numbered questions in the set (see sample questions 1-4). In addition, there may be descriptive material that is relevant in answering the questions in the set. The choices may be words, phrases, sentences, graphs, pictures, equations, or data. The numbered questions themselves may also be any of these, or they may be given in the question format directly. To answer each numbered question you should select the lettered choice that is most appropriate to it. You should consider all of the lettered choices before answering a question. The directions for this type of question state specifically that a choice cannot be eliminated just because it is the correct answer to a previous question.

Because the same five choices are applicable to several questions, the classification questions usually require less reading than other types of multiple-choice questions. Therefore, classification questions provide a quick means, in terms of testing time, of determining how well you have mastered the topics represented. The set of questions may ask you simply to recall appropriate information, or the set may ask you to apply information to a specific situation or to translate information between different forms (descriptive, graphical, mathematical). Thus different types of abilities can be tested by this type of question.

Directions: Each set of lettered choices below refers to the numbered questions or statements immediately following it. Select the one lettered choice that best answers each question or best fits each statement and then blacken the corresponding space on the answer sheet. A choice may be used once, more than once, or not at all in each set.

Questions 1-2

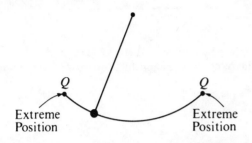

Extreme
Position

Extreme
Position

A small sphere attached to the end of a string swings as a simple pendulum. The sphere moves along the arc shown above. Consider the following properties of the sphere.

(A) Acceleration

(B) Kinetic energy

(C) Mass

(D) Potential energy

(E) Velocity

1. Which property remains constant throughout the motion of the sphere?

2. Which property goes to zero and changes direction at each extreme position Q?

To answer question 1, you may know that in classical mechanics mass is a fundamental property of an object that does not depend on the position or velocity of the object. Thus the best answer is (C). Alternately, you may realize that, since a pendulum during its motion repeatedly speeds up, slows down, and changes direction, the sphere's velocity, kinetic energy, and acceleration must also change. Also since the height of the sphere varies, so must its potential energy. Thus you can also obtain the best answer by process of elimination.

To answer question 2, you must know some specific details about the motion of the pendulum. At each extreme position Q, the velocity and the kinetic energy (which is proportional to the square of the velocity) are both zero, but kinetic energy has magnitude only and thus no direction to change. Velocity does have direction, and in this case the velocity of the sphere is directed away from the center, or equilibrium position, just before the sphere reaches Q, but directed toward the center just after passing

through Q. The velocity changes direction at each point Q, so the best answer is (E). The only other choice that has direction is acceleration, but acceleration is at its maximum at each point Q and is directed toward the center, both shortly before and shortly after the sphere is at Q.

Questions 3-4 relate to the following characteristics of images formed by mirrors or lenses.

(A) Erect and larger than the object

(B) Erect and smaller than the object

(C) Erect and the same size as the object

(D) Inverted and larger than the object

(E) Inverted and smaller than the object

Select from the list above the characteristics of the image formed in each of the cases described below.

3. The image of a bulletin board on the wall of a room is formed by a plane mirror on the opposite wall.

4. The image of print in a book is formed by a converging lens (focal length = 15 centimeters) placed 10 centimeters from the book.

This set of questions tests your knowledge of the formation of images by different types of lenses and mirrors. To answer question 3, you should recall that images formed by plane mirrors are erect (not inverted) and are the same size as the object, so the correct answer is (C).

Question 4 is more difficult. It requires recognizing that the object distance of 10 centimeters is less than the focal length of the lens. You may recall that under this condition, similar to that of a magnifying glass used for reading, the image formed will be erect and magnified and so the correct answer is (A). If you do not recall this fact, you can sketch a ray diagram to locate the image, or you can use the lens equation to compute the image distance and then find the magnification by comparing image and object distances.

Five-Choice Completion Questions ▬▬

The five-choice completion question is the most widely used in objective tests. This type of question is written either as an incomplete statement or as a question. In its simplest application, it poses a problem that intrinsically has a unique solution. It is also appropriate when: (1) the problem presented is clearly delineated by the wording of the question so that you choose not a universal solution but the best of the five offered solutions; (2) the problem is such that you are required to evaluate the relevance of five plausible, or scientifically accurate, choices and to select the one most pertinent; or (3) the problem has several pertinent solutions and you are required to select the one that is *inappropriate* or *not* correct from among the five choices presented. Questions of this latter type (see sample question 6) will normally contain a word in capital letters such as NOT, EXCEPT, or LEAST.

A special type of five-choice completion question is used in some tests to allow for the possibility of more than one correct answer. Unlike many quantitative problems that must by their nature have one unique solution, situations do arise in which there may be more than one correct response. In such situations, you should evaluate each response independently of the others in order to select the most appropriate combination. (See sample question 7.) In questions of this type several (usually three) statements labeled by Roman numerals are given with the question. One or more of these statements may correctly answer the question. The statements are followed by five lettered choices, with each choice consisting of some combination of the Roman numerals that label the statements. You must select from among the five lettered choices the one that gives the combination of statements that best answers the question. In the test, questions of this type are intermixed among the more standard five-choice completion questions.

The five-choice completion question also tests problem-solving skills. With this type of question, you may be asked to convert the information given in a word problem into graphical forms or to select and apply the mathematical relationship necessary to solve the scientific problem. Alternatively, you may be asked to interpret experimental data, graphs, or mathematical expressions. Thus, the five-choice completion question can be adapted to test several kinds of abilities.

When the experimental data or other scientific problems to be analyzed are comparatively long it is often convenient to organize several five-choice completion questions into sets, with each question in the set relating to the same common material that precedes the set (see sample questions 8-9). This practice allows you to respond to several questions based on information that may otherwise take considerable testing time to read and comprehend. Such sets also test how thorough your understanding is of a particular situation. Although the questions in a set may be related, you do not have to know the answer to one question in a set to answer a subsequent question correctly. Each question in a set can be answered directly from the common material given for the entire set.

Directions: Each of the questions or incomplete statements below is followed by five suggested answers or completions. Select the one that is best in each case and then blacken the corresponding space on the answer sheet.

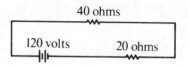

5. If the internal resistance of the 120-volt battery in the circuit shown above is negligible, the current in the wire is

(A) 0 A

(B) 2 A

(C) 3 A

(D) 6 A

(E) 9 A

In question 5, you must apply two concepts to solve the problem. First, you must recognize that the two resistors are connected in series, and thus are equivalent to a single resistor whose resistance is 60 ohms, the sum of the two component resistances. Next, applying Ohm's law, you will find that current is given by the potential difference divided by this equivalent resistance. Thus the answer is $\frac{120 \text{ volts}}{60 \text{ ohms}}$, which equals 2 amperes. Therefore, (B) is the best answer.

6. All of the following are vector quantities EXCEPT

(A) force

(B) velocity

(C) acceleration

(D) power

(E) momentum

Question 6 is a straightforward question that tests your knowledge of vector and scalar quantities. A vector quantity is one that has both magnitude and direction. All five quantities have a magnitude associated with them but only quantities (A), (B), (C), and (E) also have a direction. Power, a rate of change of energy, is not a vector quantity, so the best answer is (D).

7. A sample containing radioactive material emits alpha particles. Quantities that decrease with time include which of the following?

 I. The half-life of the radioactive nuclei that remain in the sample

 II. The average number of nuclei that decay per unit time

 III. The average electric charge of all nuclei, decayed and undecayed, that remain in the sample

(A) I only

(B) III only

(C) I and II only

(D) II and III only

(E) I, II, and III

In question 7, several of the statements represented by the Roman numerals may be correct. You must evaluate each in turn. The half-life of a radioactive sample, the time required for half the nuclei to decay, is a fundamental property of any particular radioactive isotope and does not change with time. Thus statement I is not correct. However, the rate of decay of radioactive nuclei is proportional to the number of undecayed nuclei in the sample. As nuclei decay, this number will decrease and so will the rate of decay (the average number of nuclei decaying per unit time). Thus statement II is correct. Each alpha particle contains two protons and two neutrons, so it is positively charged. As the alpha particles are emitted, conservation of charge requires that after decay each nucleus will have two fewer protons, hence less charge, than before decay. As nuclei continue to decay, the average charge of all the nuclei in the sample, both decayed and undecayed, will decrease. Thus statement III is also correct. Since statements II and III are both correct, but I is not, the best response to the question is (D).

Questions 8-9

In the following graph, the speed of a small object as it moves along a horizontal straight line is plotted against time.

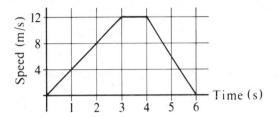

8. The magnitude of the acceleration of the object during the first 3 seconds is

(A) 3 m/s²

(B) 4 m/s²

(C) 6 m/s²

(D) 12 m/s²

(E) 36 m/s²

9. The average speed of the object during the first 4 seconds is

(A) 1.9 m/s

(B) 3.0 m/s

(C) 4.0 m/s

(D) 6.0 m/s

(E) 7.5 m/s

Questions 8 and 9 are a set of questions, both based on the graph provided. To answer question 8, you need to know that the magnitude of the acceleration is equal to the magnitude of the slope of a graph of speed *versus* time. In this situation, from time = 0 to time = 3 seconds, the graph has constant slope of $\frac{12 \text{ m/s}}{3 \text{ s}}$ = 4 m/s², which is the magnitude of the acceleration. So the best answer is (B).

The average speed of an object during a certain time is equal to the total distance traveled by the object during that time divided by the time. In question 9, the total distance traveled by the object during the first 4 seconds is equal to the area under the graph from time = 0 to time = 4 seconds. This area is $\frac{1}{2}(3 \text{ s})(12 \text{ m/s}) + (1 \text{ s})(12 \text{ m/s}) = 18 \text{ m} + 12 \text{ m} = 30 \text{ m}$. The average speed is therefore $\frac{30 \text{m}}{4 \text{s}}$ = 7.5m/s, which is answer choice (E).

Physics Achievement Test

The test that follows is the edition of the Physics Achievement Test administered in May 1983. So that you will have an idea of what the actual test administration will be like, try to take this test under conditions as close as possible to those of the actual test. It will probably help if you

- Set aside an hour for the test when you will not be interrupted, so that you can complete all of it in one sitting.

- Sit at a desk with no other papers or books. You can't take a calculator, a dictionary, other books, or notes into the test room.

- Have a kitchen timer or clock in front of you for timing yourself.

- Tear out an answer sheet from the back of this book and fill it in just as you would on the day of the test. You can use one answer sheet for as many as three Achievement Tests.

- Read the instructions that precede the test. When you take the test, you will be asked to read them before you begin answering questions.

- After you finish the test, read the sections on "How to Score the Physics Achievement Test" and "Reviewing Your Test Performance," which follow the test.

PHYSICS TEST

The top portion of the section of the answer sheet which you will use in taking the Physics test must be filled in exactly as shown in the illustration below. Note carefully that you have to do all of the following on your answer sheet:

    1. Print PHYSICS on the line to the right of the words "Achievement Test."

    2. Blacken spaces 2 and 8 in the row of spaces immediately under the words "Test Code."

    3. Blacken space 3 in the group of five spaces labeled X.

    4. Blacken space 3 in the group of five spaces labeled Y.

To provide information on your training in physics, please answer the question below. Indicate your answer by blackening one of the first four spaces labeled Q on your answer sheet. Your response will not influence your test score.

How many semesters of instruction have you had in a high school physics course or courses? (There are two semesters in a school year. If you are taking physics in the current semester and the semester is more than half over, count this current semester as a full semester.)

Space 1: One semester

Space 2: Two semesters

Space 3: Three semesters

Space 4: Four semesters

Spaces 5 to 9: (Leave blank)

When the supervisor gives the signal, turn the page and begin the Physics test. There are 100 numbered spaces on the answer sheet and 75 questions in the Physics test. Therefore, use only spaces 1 to 75 for recording your answers.

PHYSICS TEST

Part A

Directions: Each set of lettered choices below refers to the numbered questions immediately following it. Select the one lettered choice that best answers each question and then blacken the corresponding space on the answer sheet. A choice may be used once, more than once, or not at all in each set.

Questions 1-3 refer to two marbles that are released next to each other at the same time from the same height above level ground. One marble is shot horizontally from a spring gun; the other is dropped from rest. Air resistance and the curvature of the Earth are negligible and g, the acceleration due to gravity, is constant for both balls and directed perpendicular to the ground.

    (A) The marble that is shot
    (B) The marble that is dropped
    (C) It is a tie.
    (D) It cannot be determined without knowing the height.
    (E) It cannot be determined without knowing the value of g.

1. If the marbles are identical, which one hits the ground first?

2. If the marbles are identical, which one hits the ground with the greater speed?

3. If the dropped marble has twice the mass of the shot marble, which marble hits the ground first?

Questions 4-7 relate to the following properties of waves.

    (A) Frequency
    (B) Wavelength
    (C) Speed
    (D) Intensity
    (E) Direction of propagation

4. Which property is inversely proportional to the square of the distance from a point source of a wave?

5. Which property is equal to $\frac{1}{T}$, where T is the period of the wave?

6. Which property is equal to the product of two of the others for a traveling wave?

7. Which property is a minimum along a nodal line created by waves from two point sources?

Questions 8-9 relate to the lettered components in the following circuit diagram.

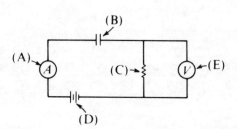

8. Which component is a capacitor?

9. Which component measures electric potential difference?

Questions 10-11 relate to a flat object lying on a frictionless table. Two forces, 1 and 2, are separately applied to the object as shown below. The line of action of each force is shown by a dashed line.

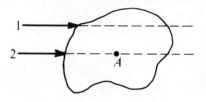

Top View

    (A) 1 only
    (B) 2 only
    (C) Neither
    (D) Both, but 1 will be greater than 2
    (E) Both, but 2 will be greater than 1

10. If the object is free to rotate about a fixed axis through point A, which force will produce a rotation?

11. If the object is not fixed and point A is the object's center of mass, which force will produce purely translational motion?

GO ON TO THE NEXT PAGE

Questions 12-13 refer to the following three diagrams each showing a light ray from an object at *O* that passes through a lens having focal points *F*. Assume that the thin lens approximation is used in drawing the diagrams.

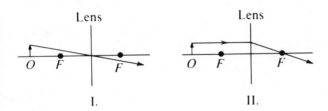

I.   II.

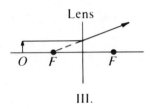

III.

(A) I only
(B) III only
(C) I and II only
(D) I and III only
(E) II and III only

12. Which of the diagrams above can be correct for a converging lens?

13. Which of the diagrams above can be correct for a diverging lens?

Questions 14-15 relate to five objects that are moving in parallel straight-line paths. The objects all cross a starting line at the instant a clock is started. The distances from the starting line in meters after 1, 2, 3, 4, and 5 seconds are as follows:

| | Time (seconds) | | | | |
Object	1	2	3	4	5
(A)	1 m	1 m	2 m	2 m	3 m
(B)	1 m	2 m	3 m	4 m	5 m
(C)	1 m	4 m	9 m	16 m	25 m
(D)	4 m	10 m	18 m	28 m	40 m
(E)	6 m	11 m	15 m	18 m	20 m

14. Which object is moving with zero acceleration?

15. Which object has constant nonzero acceleration and appears to have started from rest?

GO ON TO THE NEXT PAGE

Part B

Directions: Each of the questions or incomplete statements below is followed by five suggested answers or completions. Select the one that is best in each case and then blacken the corresponding space on the answer sheet.

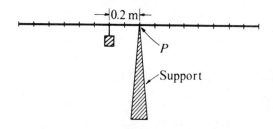

16. A massless rod is supported at point P as shown above. A block weighing 40 newtons is attached to the rod 0.2 meter from P. How far from P must a block weighing 80 newtons be attached in order to balance the rod?

    (A) 0.1 m
    (B) 0.2 m
    (C) 0.4 m
    (D) 0.5 m
    (E) 0.8 m

Questions 17-18

A rock weighing 10 newtons is lifted a distance d from the ground. The work done by the force that lifts the rock is 10 joules. The rock is then dropped on a wooden stake, thus driving the stake into the ground.

17. The distance d is most nearly

    (A)   0.01 m
    (B)   0.1 m
    (C)   1 m
    (D)   10 m
    (E)   100 m

18. The work done by the rock in driving the stake into the ground is most nearly

    (A)   0.01 J
    (B)   0.1 J
    (C)   1 J
    (D)   10 J
    (E)   100 J

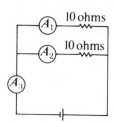

19. A_1, A_2, and A_3 are the readings on the three ammeters in the circuit shown above. What is the correct relationship among A_1, A_2, and A_3?

    (A) $\dfrac{A_1}{A_2} = A_3$

    (B) $\dfrac{A_2}{A_1} = A_3$

    (C) $A_2 - A_1 = A_3$

    (D) $A_1 - A_2 = A_3$

    (E) $A_1 + A_2 = A_3$

20. Which of the following statements is (are) true in the region of a positive point charge?

    I.   The electric field is directed toward the point charge.
    II. A negatively charged body experiences a force directed toward the point charge.
    III. The force on a second point charge is inversely proportional to the square of its distance from the first point charge.

    (A) I only
    (B) III only
    (C) I and II only
    (D) II and III only
    (E) I, II, and III

GO ON TO THE NEXT PAGE

21. Two metal spheres of equal radius are each
charged and mounted on insulated stands.
Sphere 1 has a charge of +20 coulombs; sphere
2 has a charge of −4 coulombs. The two spheres
are touched together and then separated. The
charge on sphere 2 will now be

   (A)   0
   (B)   +4 C
   (C)   +8 C
   (D) +16 C
   (E) +20 C

22. All of the following are forms of electromagnetic radiation EXCEPT

   (A) microwaves
   (B) infrared
   (C) ultraviolet
   (D) x-rays
   (E) sound

23. The half-life of one isotope of radium is about
1,600 years. In a given sample of this isotope,
15/16 of the radium atoms will decay in a time
most nearly equal to

   (A) 1,000 years
   (B) 1,500 years
   (C) 1,600 years
   (D) 3,200 years
   (E) 6,400 years

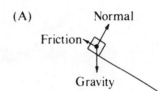

24. A block of mass *M* slides down a plane
inclined at an angle of 30° to the horizontal as
shown above. Which of the following diagrams
shows the sources and directions of the three
forces acting on the block in any real situation?

(A)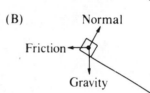

(B)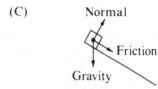

(C)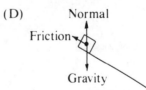

(D)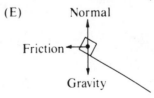

(E)

GO ON TO THE NEXT PAGE

25. An object of mass 5 kilograms has a momentum of 20 kilogram·meters per second. Its speed is most nearly

    (A)   0.25 m/s
    (B)   0.4 m/s
    (C)   4 m/s
    (D)   10 m/s
    (E)   100 m/s

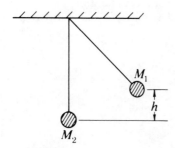

26. Two small objects of masses M_1 and M_2 are suspended from massless, unstretchable strings of equal length. The object with mass M_1 is raised through a height h as shown above and released. If the objects stick together after colliding, they will swing on the other side to a height that is

    (A) greater than h
    (B) equal to h
    (C) less than h
    (D) greater than, equal to, or less than h depending on the value of h
    (E) greater than, equal to, or less than h depending on the ratio M_2/M_1

27. The following graphs show displacement as a function of distance for pairs of traveling waves. Which pair of waves would result in total destructive interference when superimposed?

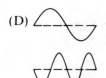

28. Lenses form images because they

    (A)   absorb light
    (B)   diffract light
    (C)   emit light
    (D)   refract light
    (E)   reflect light

GO ON TO THE NEXT PAGE

29. Atoms are said to be ionized when which of the following occurs?

   (A) Electrons are added to or removed from the atoms.
   (B) Protons are added to or removed from the atoms.
   (C) The atoms are accelerated to a very high velocity.
   (D) The atoms are projected into a cloud chamber.
   (E) One or more electrons in the atoms are raised to higher orbits.

30. Which of the following particles travels at the speed of light?

   (A) Alpha particle
   (B) Electron
   (C) Neutron
   (D) Proton
   (E) Photon

31. The photoelectric effect can be described by which of the following?

   (A) Electrons striking the surface of a metal and atoms of the metal being emitted
   (B) Neutrons striking the surface of a metal and other neutrons being emitted
   (C) Photons striking the surface of a metal and electrons being emitted
   (D) Positive ions striking the surface of a metal and negative ions being emitted
   (E) Protons striking the surface of a metal and alpha particles being emitted

32. As a child wearing wool pants slides down a plastic slide, gravitational potential energy may be converted to which of the following?

   I.   Thermal energy
   II. Kinetic energy
   III. Electrostatic potential energy

   (A) I only
   (B) II only
   (C) I and III only
   (D) II and III only
   (E) I, II, and III

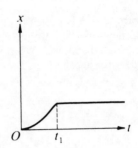

33. The graph above shows position x as a function of time t for a particle moving along the x-axis. Which of the following graphs of velocity v as a function of time t describes the motion of this particle?

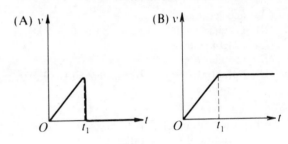

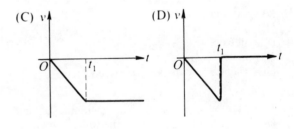

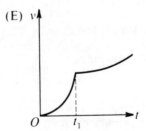

GO ON TO THE NEXT PAGE

34. A 15-kilogram wagon is pulled to the right with a force of 45 newtons. The wagon accelerates at 2 meters per second squared. What is the net (unbalanced) force accelerating the wagon?

    (A) 3 N
    (B) 15 N
    (C) $22\frac{1}{2}$ N
    (D) 30 N
    (E) 45 N

35. A 75-kilogram astronaut sits in a 1,000-kilogram satellite as it orbits the Earth. In an inertial frame of reference, the astronaut and the satellite have the same

    (A) acceleration
    (B) gravitational force exerted on them
    (C) kinetic energy
    (D) momentum
    (E) potential energy (assume zero at the Earth's surface)

36. When the volume of a given mass of gas is decreased at constant temperature, the molecules of the gas undergo a decrease in

    (A) volume
    (B) mass
    (C) density
    (D) average speed
    (E) the average distance between them

37. If the temperature of an ideal gas increases, one can be certain that which of the following also increases?

    (A) The average kinetic energy of the gas molecules
    (B) The rest mass of each gas molecule
    (C) The volume occupied by the gas
    (D) The pressure exerted by the gas
    (E) The number of moles of the gas

38. A person normally weighing 500 newtons steps on a bathroom scale in an elevator. If later, the scale reads 450 newtons, this indicates that the elevator is

    (A) moving downward with a constant velocity
    (B) accelerating downward
    (C) moving upward with a constant velocity
    (D) accelerating upward
    (E) at rest

39. A satellite moving in a circular orbit with respect to the Earth's center experiences a gravitational force. If the radius of the orbit is decreased, how will the gravitational force and the speed of the satellite change, if at all?

	Gravitational Force	Speed
(A)	Decrease	Decrease
(B)	Decrease	Increase
(C)	Remain the same	Remain the same
(D)	Increase	Decrease
(E)	Increase	Increase

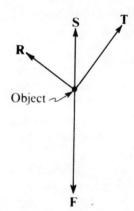

40. Forces **R**, **S**, **T**, and **F** are all in the plane of the paper. The forces act on an object, as shown above, and have magnitudes proportional to the lengths of the vectors. Which combination of forces would yield a zero net force on the object?

    (A) **S** and **F** only
    (B) **R**, **S**, and **F** only
    (C) **S**, **T**, and **F** only
    (D) **R**, **T**, and **F** only
    (E) **R**, **S**, **T**, and **F**

GO ON TO THE NEXT PAGE

Questions 41-42

Q_1 Q_2
$\bullet$ $\bullet$
M_1 M_2

Two isolated point particles of masses M_1 and M_2 have charges of magnitude Q_1 and Q_2, respectively. The gravitational force between the particles is balanced by the electrostatic force between them.

41. Which of the following is true about the signs of the charges?

    (A) Q_1 must be positive and Q_2 must be negative.
    (B) Q_1 must be negative and Q_2 must be positive.
    (C) Both Q_1 and Q_2 must be positive.
    (D) Both Q_1 and Q_2 must be negative.
    (E) Q_1 and Q_2 must have the same sign but it does not matter whether they are both positive or both negative.

42. If G is the universal gravitational constant and k is the Coulomb's law constant, which of the following must be true about the magnitudes of the charges?

    (A) $Q_1 = Q_2$

    (B) $\dfrac{Q_1}{Q_2} = \dfrac{M_1}{M_2}$

    (C) $\dfrac{Q_1}{Q_2} = \dfrac{M_2}{M_1}$

    (D) $Q_1 Q_2 = \dfrac{G}{k} M_1 M_2$

    (E) $Q_1 Q_2 = \dfrac{k}{G} M_1 M_2$

---

43. A volt is defined as one joule per coulomb and an ampere as one coulomb per second. A volt times an ampere is a unit of

    (A) energy
    (B) force
    (C) heat
    (D) power
    (E) work

44. The magnitude of the current produced by a generator depends on all of the following EXCEPT the

    (A) direction in which the coil is turned
    (B) rate at which the coil is turned
    (C) number of loops in the coil
    (D) length of the wire in the coil
    (E) diameter of the wire in the coil

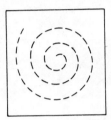

45. The illustration above represents a photograph of the spiral path of an electron in a bubble chamber. Which of the following is a possible direction of the magnetic field?

    (A) Counterclockwise in the plane of the paper
    (B) Clockwise in the plane of the paper
    (C) From left to right in the plane of the paper
    (D) From right to left in the plane of the paper
    (E) Perpendicular to the plane of the paper

46. A beam of light in air is incident onto a glass plate. Which of the following diagrams best indicates the behavior of the beam?

(A)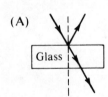
(B)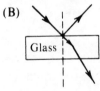

(C)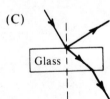
(D)

(E)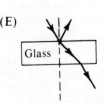

GO ON TO THE NEXT PAGE

Questions 47-48 relate to the figure below that represents a photograph of a wave propagating along a string.

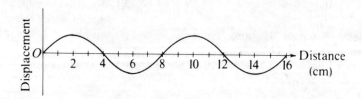

47. This wave is an example of a

   (A) torsional wave
   (B) transverse wave
   (C) diffracted wave
   (D) longitudinal wave
   (E) refracted wave

48. If the frequency of the wave is 80 hertz, the speed of the wave is

   (A) 640 cm/s
   (B) 320 cm/s
   (C) 20 cm/s
   (D) 10 cm/s
   (E)   0.1 cm/s

GO ON TO THE NEXT PAGE

Questions 49-50

An object with mass m and speed v_0 directed to the right strikes a wall and rebounds with speed v_0 directed to the left.

49. The change in the object's kinetic energy is

(A) $-mv_0^2$

(B) $-\frac{1}{2}mv_0^2$

(C) zero

(D) $\frac{1}{2}mv_0^2$

(E) mv_0^2

50. The change in the object's momentum is

(A) $2mv_0$ directed to the left

(B) mv_0 directed to the left

(C) zero

(D) mv_0 directed to the right

(E) $2mv_0$ directed to the right

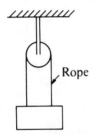

51. A block weighing 200 newtons is suspended from both ends of a massless rope that goes over a pulley, as shown above. What is the tension in the rope?

(A) 50 N

(B) 100 N

(C) 150 N

(D) 200 N

(E) 400 N

52. Two positive charges of magnitudes q and Q ($Q > q$) are located as shown above. If a negative charge is to experience no electrical force, at which point is it most likely to be located?

(A) a

(B) b

(C) c

(D) d

(E) e

53. The voltage across a 20-ohm resistor carrying 2 amperes of current is

(A) 0.1 V

(B) 5 V

(C) 10 V

(D) 40 V

(E) 80 V

54. A bar magnet is placed near a coil of wire. A current will be generated in the coil in which of the following cases?

   I. The magnet and coil move relative to each other.
   II. The coil has a constant charge and the magnet and coil are stationary.
   III. The magnet has a constant charge and the magnet and coil are stationary.

(A) I only

(B) II only

(C) III only

(D) II and III only

(E) I and III only

55. Some metal rods are to be used to transfer heat from a furnace to a container of water. To increase the rate of transfer of heat, quantities that could be increased include which of the following?

   I. Temperature of the furnace
   II. Cross-sectional area of each rod
   III. Number of rods

(A) I only

(B) III only

(C) I and II only

(D) II and III only

(E) I, II, and III

GO ON TO THE NEXT PAGE

56. If 200 grams of water at 48° C is mixed with 100 grams of water at 30° C, the resulting temperature of the water is

    (A) 18° C
    (B) 36° C
    (C) 39° C
    (D) 42° C
    (E) 78° C

57. Oxygen molecules are enclosed in a container. Which of the following is primarily responsible for the pressure on the walls of the container?

    (A) Collisions between the molecules
    (B) Collisions of the molecules with the walls of the container
    (C) The force of attraction between the molecules
    (D) The force of repulsion between the molecules
    (E) The force of attraction between the molecules and the walls

58. When 1 kilogram of water initially at 20° C has 42,000 joules of work done on it by stirring the water, its temperature rises 10° C. If that same water initially at 20° C has 21,000 joules of heat flow into it and also 21,000 joules of work done on it by stirring, what will be its final temperature if the pressure is the same in both cases?

    (A) 20° C
    (B) 25° C
    (C) 30° C
    (D) 40° C
    (E) It is impossible to calculate from the data given.

59. You are inside a windowless, vibration-free van. You release a steel ball and observe that it strikes the floor directly beneath the point of release. Which of the following could be the van's condition at this time?

    I.   The van is at rest.
    II. The van is moving with constant velocity.
    III. The van is accelerating uniformly on a horizontal plane.

    (A) I only
    (B) III only
    (C) I or II but not III
    (D) I or III but not II
    (E) II or III but not I

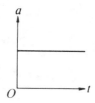

60. The graph above shows acceleration a as a function of time t for a particle moving in a straight line. Graphs of speed v *versus* time t that are consistent with the a *versus* t graph above include which of the following?

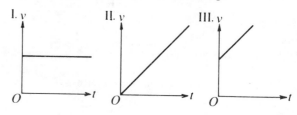

    (A) I only
    (B) III only
    (C) I and II only
    (D) II and III only
    (E) I, II, and III

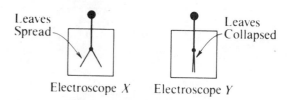

Electroscope X Electroscope Y

61. Electroscopes X and Y are shown above. Electroscope X is charged and electroscope Y is uncharged. Of the following three procedures, which would be necessary to determine the sign of the charge on electroscope X?

    I.   Touching electroscope Y to electroscope X and observing what happens to the leaves of electroscope Y
    II. Bringing a positively charged rod near electroscope X and observing what happens to its leaves
    III. Grounding electroscope X and observing what happens to its leaves

    (A) I only
    (B) II only
    (C) I and II only
    (D) I and III only
    (E) II and III only

GO ON TO THE NEXT PAGE

62. Total internal reflection will occur when the angle of incidence is

   (A) equal to zero
   (B) equal to the angle of polarization
   (C) equal to the angle of refraction
   (D) greater than the angle of refraction
   (E) greater than the critical angle

63. The electric force of repulsion between the protons of a nucleus does not cause the nucleus to break up because

   (A) the electric force disappears inside the nucleus
   (B) the short-range nuclear force of attraction is stronger than the electric force
   (C) the gravitational force between the protons overcomes the electric force
   (D) some of the protons turn into neutrons and electrons thus canceling the electric force
   (E) the protons are moving rapidly inside the nucleus and thus produce a magnetic field which holds the nucleus together

n	Energy Above Ground State
3	———— 7 eV
2	———— 3 eV
1	———— 0 eV

64. The three lowest energy levels of an atom are shown above. An atom in the $n = 3$ state can, in a single transition, spontaneously emit a photon having an energy of

   (A) 3 eV only
   (B) 4 eV only
   (C) 7 eV only
   (D) 4 eV or 7 eV only
   (E) 3 eV or 4 eV only

65. A camera has a mass of 40 kilograms on the Moon. The acceleration due to gravity on the Moon is approximately one-sixth that on Earth. The weight of the camera on Earth is most nearly

   (A)   7 N
   (B)   40 N
   (C)   65 N
   (D) 240 N
   (E) 400 N

66. A curved wave front could result from all of the following EXCEPT

   (A) a disturbance emanating from a point source
   (B) the passage of a plane wave through a very small opening
   (C) the reflection of a plane wave from a concave surface
   (D) the reflection of a plane wave from a convex surface
   (E) the reflection from a parabolic surface of a circular wave originating at the focus of the parabola

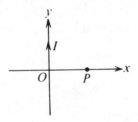

67. A wire on the y axis of a coordinate system has a current I in the $+y$ direction as shown above. What is the direction of the magnetic field resulting from this current at point P?

   (A) →
   (B) ↑
   (C) ←
   (D) ↓
   (E) Perpendicular to the xy-plane

GO ON TO THE NEXT PAGE

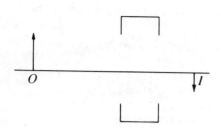

68. A box with holes in opposite sides contains an optical element. A real inverted image is formed at I of an object placed at O as shown above. The optical element contained in the box is a

    (A) diverging lens
    (B) converging lens
    (C) diverging (convex) mirror
    (D) converging (concave) mirror
    (E) prism

69. A source emits sound of frequency f_0 in air. A person moving toward this source at a uniform speed would measure a frequency that is

    (A) constant and lower than f_0
    (B) constant and the same as f_0
    (C) constant and higher than f_0
    (D) continually decreasing
    (E) continually increasing

70. A hollow metal sphere that has a diameter of 50 centimeters has a positive charge of 8×10^{-5} coulomb. The electric field at the center of the sphere has magnitude

    (A) 0 N/C
    (B) 3.2×10^{-4} N/C
    (C) 6.4×10^{-4} N/C
    (D) 3.2×10^{6} N/C
    (E) 6.4×10^{6} N/C

Questions 71-73

An aluminum block with a mass of 1 kilogram moves to the left with a constant velocity of 8 meters per second, as shown in the diagram above. After striking the spring, the block is brought to rest in 0.005 second as the spring is compressed.

71. The magnitude of the momentum change of the block in coming to rest is

    (A) 2 kg·m/s
    (B) 4 kg·m/s
    (C) 8 kg·m/s
    (D) 16 kg·m/s
    (E) 32 kg·m/s

72. The average force exerted on the spring by the block as the block is brought to rest is

    (A) 200 N
    (B) 400 N
    (C) 800 N
    (D) 1,600 N
    (E) 3,200 N

73. The energy of the spring at its maximum compression is most nearly

    (A) 2 J
    (B) 4 J
    (C) 8 J
    (D) 16 J
    (E) 32 J

GO ON TO THE NEXT PAGE

74. The colors seen in a soap bubble are primarily due to

    (A) polarization
    (B) interference
    (C) absorption
    (D) fluorescence
    (E) phosphorescence

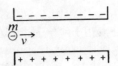

75. A negatively charged particle of mass m and speed v is projected into an electric field between the plates of a charged capacitor as shown above. Which of the following vectors best represents the direction of the acceleration of the charged particle?

    (A) ↑
    (B) →
    (C) ↘
    (D) ↓
    (E) ←

S T O P

IF YOU FINISH BEFORE TIME IS CALLED, YOU MAY CHECK YOUR WORK ON THIS TEST ONLY.
DO NOT WORK ON ANY OTHER TEST IN THIS BOOK.

How to Score the Physics Achievement Test

When you take an actual Physics Achievement Test, your answer sheet will be "read" by a scanning machine that will record your responses to each question. Then a computer will compare your answers with the correct answers and produce your raw score. You get one point for each correct answer. For each wrong answer, you lose one-fourth of a point. Questions you omit (and any for which you mark more than one answer) are not counted. This raw score is converted to a College Board scaled score that is reported to you and to the colleges you specify. After you have taken this test, you can get an idea of what your score might be by following the instructions in the next two sections.

Determining Your Raw Score

Step 1: Table A on the next page lists the correct answers for all the questions on the test.* Compare your answer with the correct answer and
- Put a check in the column marked "Right" if your answer is correct.
- Put a check in the column marked "Wrong" if your answer is incorrect.
- Leave both columns blank if you omitted the question.

Step 2: Count the number of right answers and enter the number here . . . . _____

Step 3: Count the number of wrong answers and enter

the number here . . . . 4)‾‾‾‾‾‾‾‾

Enter the result of dividing by 4 here . . . . _____

Step 4: Subtract the number you obtained in Step 3 from the number in Step 2; round the result to the nearest whole number (.5 is rounded up) and enter here . . _____

The number you obtained in Step 4 is your raw score. (The correction for guessing — subtraction of a quarter of a point for each incorrect answer — adjusts for the fact that random guessing on a large number of questions will result in some questions being answered correctly by chance.) Instructions for converting your raw score to a scaled score follow.

*The last column in Table A gives the percentage of students who took the test in May 1983 that answered the question correctly. (See page 375 for further explanation.)

TABLE A

Answers to Physics Achievement Test, Form 3FAC, and Percentage of Students Answering Each Question Correctly

Question Number	Correct Answer	Right	Wrong	Percentage of Students Answering the Question Correctly	Question Number	Correct Answer	Right	Wrong	Percentage of Students Answering the Question Correctly
1	C			82%	41	E			79%
2	A			51	42	D			47
3	C			65	43	D			64
4	D			54	44	A			66
5	A			77	45	E			39
6	C			59	46	D			65
7	D			40	47	B			55
8	B			69	48	A			50
9	E			72	49	C			57
10	A			82	50	A			26
11	B			62	51	B			56
12	C			67	52	B			50
13	D			24	53	D			69
14	B			82	54	A			50
15	C			48	55	E			57
16	A			82	56	D			70
17	C			85	57	B			71
18	D			83	58	C			45
19	E			80	59	C			76
20	D			42	60	D			57
21	C			62	61	B			55
22	E			91	62	E			55
23	E			53	63	B			39
24	A			69	64	D			32
25	C			86	65	E			26
26	C			69	66	E			40
27	A			83	67	E			31
28	D			72	68	B			47
29	A			78	69	C			34
30	E			69	70	A			37
31	C			62	71	C			58
32	E			70	72	D			28
33	A			52	73	E			20
34	D			43	74	B			31
35	A			49	75	D			20
36	E			65					
37	A			51					
38	B			63					
39	E			66					
40	D			47					

Note: The percentages are based on the analysis of the answer sheets for a random sample of students who took this test in May 1983 and whose mean score was 596. The analysis sample was selected to represent the students for whom the test is intended. Only those students who had at least two semesters of physics were included.

Finding Your College Board Scaled Score ▰

When you take Achievement Tests, the scores sent to the colleges you specify will be reported on the College Board scale, ranging from 200 to 800. The raw score that you obtained above (Step 4) can be converted to a scaled score by using Table B.

To find your scaled score on this test, locate your raw score in the left column of Table B; the corresponding score in the right column will be your College Board scaled score. For example, a raw score of 33 on this particular edition of the Physics Achievement Test corresponds to a College Board scaled score of 570. Raw scores are converted to scaled scores to ensure that a score earned on any one edition of the Physics Achievement Test is comparable to the same scaled score earned on any other edition of the test.

Because some editions of the Physics Achievement Test may be slightly easier or more difficult than others, statistical adjustments are made in the scores so that each College Board scaled score indicates the same level of performance, regardless of the edition of the test you take and the ability of the group you take it with. A given raw score will correspond to different College Board scores, depending on the edition of the test taken. A raw score of 40, for example, may convert to a College Board score of 610 on one edition of the test, but that raw score might convert to a College Board score of 630 on a slightly more difficult edition. When you take the Physics Achievement Test on the actual test day, your score is likely to differ somewhat from the score you obtained on this test. People perform at different levels at different

TABLE B — SCORE CONVERSION TABLE					
Physics Achievement Test, Form 3FAC					
Raw Score	College Board Scaled Score	Raw Score	College Board Scaled Score	Raw Score	College Board Scaled Score
75	800	40	610	5	400
74	800	39	610	4	400
73	800	38	600	3	390
72	800	37	590	2	380
71	800	36	590	1	380
70	790	35	580	0	370
69	780	34	580	−1	370
68	780	33	570	−2	360
67	770	32	560	−3	350
66	770	31	560	−4	350
65	760	30	550	−5	340
64	760	29	550	−6	340
63	750	28	540	−7	330
62	740	27	530	−8	320
61	740	26	530	−9	320
60	730	25	520	−10	310
59	730	24	520	−11	310
58	720	23	510	−12	300
57	710	22	500	−13	290
56	710	21	500	−14	290
55	700	20	490	−15	280
54	700	19	490	−16	280
53	690	18	480	−17	270
52	680	17	470	−18	260
51	680	16	470	−19	260
50	670	15	460		
49	670	14	460		
48	660	13	450		
47	650	12	440		
46	650	11	440		
45	640	10	430		
44	640	9	430		
43	630	8	420		
42	620	7	410		
41	620	6	410		

times, for reasons unrelated to the test itself. The precision of any test is also limited because it represents only a sample of all the possible questions that could be asked. (See page 12, "How Precise Are Your Scores?" for further information.)

Reviewing Your Test Performance

After you have scored your test, you should take some time to consider the following points in relation to your performance on the test.

- *Did you run out of time before you reached the end of the test?*

  If you did, you may want to consider tactics that will help you pace yourself better. For example, you may have spent too much time working on one or two difficult questions. A better approach might have been to continue the test and return to those questions after you had attempted to answer the remaining questions on the test.

- *Did you take a long time reading the directions for the test?*

  The directions in this test are the same as those in the Physics Achievement Tests now being administered. You will save time when you read the directions on the test day if you become thoroughly familiar with them in advance.

- *How did you handle questions you were unsure of?*

  If you were able to eliminate one or more of the answer choices and you guessed from the remaining choices, then your approach probably worked to your advantage. On the other hand, omitting questions about which you have some knowledge or guessing answers haphazardly would probably be a mistake.

- *How difficult were the questions for you compared with other students who took the test?*

  By referring to Table A on page 373 you can find out how difficult each question was for the group of students who took the test in May 1983. The right-hand column in the table tells you what percentage of that group of students answered the question correctly. It is important to remember that these percentages are based on only one group of students; had this edition of the test been given to all students in the class of 1983 who took a Physics Achievement Test, the percentages would probably have been different. A question that was answered correctly by almost everyone in the group, obviously, is an easy question. Question 22, for example, was answered correctly by 91 percent of the students in the sample. On the other hand, question 50 was answered correctly by only 26 percent of the students. If you find that you missed several questions that would be considered easy, you may want to review those questions carefully. They may cover some aspect of the subject that you need to review. Perhaps you misunderstood the directions for one part of the test or you thought the questions were so easy that you did not spend as much time on them as you might have.

COLLEGE BOARD — ACHIEVEMENT TESTS
Side 1

Use a No. 2 pencil only for completing this answer sheet. Be sure each mark is dark and completely fills the intended space. Completely erase any errors or stray marks.

1.
YOUR NAME: _____
(Print) Last   First   M.I.

SIGNATURE: _____ DATE: __/__/__

HOME ADDRESS: _____
(Print) Number and Street

_____
City   State   Zip Code

CENTER: _____
(Print) City   State   Center Number

IMPORTANT: Please fill in these boxes exactly as shown on the back cover of your test book.

FOR ETS USE ONLY

5. YOUR NAME

First 4 letters of last name | First Init. | Mid. Init.

(Columns of bubbles A through Z)

2. TEST FORM

3. FORM CODE

4. REGISTRATION NUMBER
(Copy from your Admission Ticket.)

6. DATE OF BIRTH

Month	Day	Year
Jan.		
Feb.		
Mar.		
Apr.		
May		
June		
July		
Aug.		
Sept.		
Oct.		
Nov.		
Dec.		

7. SEX
- Male
- Female

8. TEST BOOK SERIAL NUMBER

BE SURE EACH MARK IS DARK AND COMPLETELY FILLS THE INTENDED OVAL. IF YOU ERASE, DO SO COMPLETELY. YOU MAY FIND MORE ANSWER SPACES THAN YOU NEED. IF SO, PLEASE LEAVE THEM BLANK.

TEST CODE

X (1)(2)(3)(4)(5) Y (1)(2)(3)(4)(5)

Q (1)(2)(3)(4)(5)(6)(7)(8)(9)

FOR ETS USE ONLY | R | W | FS | CS

ACHIEVEMENT TEST: _____
(Print)

(Answer grid, questions 1–100, each with options A B C D E)

1–20, 21–40, 41–60, 61–80, 81–100

Q1206   Copyright © 1983 by Educational Testing Service. All rights reserved. Princeton, N.J. 08541   I.N. 574002 — 110VV33P388

COLLEGE BOARD — ACHIEVEMENT TESTS Side 2

Use a No. 2 pencil only for completing this answer sheet. Be sure each mark is dark and completely fills the intended space. Completely erase any errors or stray marks.

You may find more answer spaces than you need. If so, please leave them blank.

TEST CODE

FOR ETS USE ONLY | R | W | FS | CS

ACHIEVEMENT TEST:

(Print)

9. SIGNATURE:

COLLEGE BOARD — ACHIEVEMENT TESTS
Side 1

Use a No. 2 pencil only for completing this answer sheet. Be sure each mark is dark and completely fills the intended space. Completely erase any errors or stray marks.

1.
YOUR NAME: (Print) Last First M.I.

SIGNATURE: _____ DATE: ___/___/___

HOME ADDRESS: (Print) Number and Street

City State Zip Code

CENTER: (Print) City State Center Number

IMPORTANT: Please fill in these boxes exactly as shown on the back cover of your test book.

FOR ETS USE ONLY

5. YOUR NAME
First 4 letters of last name | First Init. | Mid. Init.

2. TEST FORM

3. FORM CODE

4. REGISTRATION NUMBER
(Copy from your Admission Ticket.)

6. DATE OF BIRTH

Month	Day	Year
Jan.		
Feb.		
Mar.		
Apr.		
May		
June		
July		
Aug.		
Sept.		
Oct.		
Nov.		
Dec.		

7. SEX
Male
Female

8. TEST BOOK SERIAL NUMBER

BE SURE EACH MARK IS DARK AND COMPLETELY FILLS THE INTENDED OVAL. IF YOU ERASE, DO SO COMPLETELY.
YOU MAY FIND MORE ANSWER SPACES THAN YOU NEED. IF SO, PLEASE LEAVE THEM BLANK.

TEST CODE

FOR ETS USE ONLY | R | W | FS | CS

ACHIEVEMENT TEST: _____ (Print)

Copyright © 1983 by Educational Testing Service. All rights reserved. Princeton, N.J. 08541

Q1206

I.N. 574002 — 110VV33P388

COLLEGE BOARD — ACHIEVEMENT TESTS   Side 2

Use a No. 2 pencil only for completing this answer sheet. Be sure each mark is dark and completely fills the intended space. Completely erase any errors or stray marks.

You may find more answer spaces than you need. If so, please leave them blank.

TEST CODE

① ② ③ ④ ⑤   ⑥ ⑦ ⑧ ⑨ ⓪
X ① ② ③ ④ ⑤   Y ① ② ③ ④ ⑤
Q ① ② ③ ④ ⑤ ⑥ ⑦ ⑧ ⑨

FOR ETS USE ONLY   R   W   FS   CS

ACHIEVEMENT TEST:

(Print)

1 Ⓐ Ⓑ Ⓒ Ⓓ Ⓔ	21 Ⓐ Ⓑ Ⓒ Ⓓ Ⓔ	41 Ⓐ Ⓑ Ⓒ Ⓓ Ⓔ	61 Ⓐ Ⓑ Ⓒ Ⓓ Ⓔ	81 Ⓐ Ⓑ Ⓒ Ⓓ Ⓔ
2 Ⓐ Ⓑ Ⓒ Ⓓ Ⓔ	22 Ⓐ Ⓑ Ⓒ Ⓓ Ⓔ	42 Ⓐ Ⓑ Ⓒ Ⓓ Ⓔ	62 Ⓐ Ⓑ Ⓒ Ⓓ Ⓔ	82 Ⓐ Ⓑ Ⓒ Ⓓ Ⓔ
3 Ⓐ Ⓑ Ⓒ Ⓓ Ⓔ	23 Ⓐ Ⓑ Ⓒ Ⓓ Ⓔ	43 Ⓐ Ⓑ Ⓒ Ⓓ Ⓔ	63 Ⓐ Ⓑ Ⓒ Ⓓ Ⓔ	83 Ⓐ Ⓑ Ⓒ Ⓓ Ⓔ
4 Ⓐ Ⓑ Ⓒ Ⓓ Ⓔ	24 Ⓐ Ⓑ Ⓒ Ⓓ Ⓔ	44 Ⓐ Ⓑ Ⓒ Ⓓ Ⓔ	64 Ⓐ Ⓑ Ⓒ Ⓓ Ⓔ	84 Ⓐ Ⓑ Ⓒ Ⓓ Ⓔ
5 Ⓐ Ⓑ Ⓒ Ⓓ Ⓔ	25 Ⓐ Ⓑ Ⓒ Ⓓ Ⓔ	45 Ⓐ Ⓑ Ⓒ Ⓓ Ⓔ	65 Ⓐ Ⓑ Ⓒ Ⓓ Ⓔ	85 Ⓐ Ⓑ Ⓒ Ⓓ Ⓔ
6 Ⓐ Ⓑ Ⓒ Ⓓ Ⓔ	26 Ⓐ Ⓑ Ⓒ Ⓓ Ⓔ	46 Ⓐ Ⓑ Ⓒ Ⓓ Ⓔ	66 Ⓐ Ⓑ Ⓒ Ⓓ Ⓔ	86 Ⓐ Ⓑ Ⓒ Ⓓ Ⓔ
7 Ⓐ Ⓑ Ⓒ Ⓓ Ⓔ	27 Ⓐ Ⓑ Ⓒ Ⓓ Ⓔ	47 Ⓐ Ⓑ Ⓒ Ⓓ Ⓔ	67 Ⓐ Ⓑ Ⓒ Ⓓ Ⓔ	87 Ⓐ Ⓑ Ⓒ Ⓓ Ⓔ
8 Ⓐ Ⓑ Ⓒ Ⓓ Ⓔ	28 Ⓐ Ⓑ Ⓒ Ⓓ Ⓔ	48 Ⓐ Ⓑ Ⓒ Ⓓ Ⓔ	68 Ⓐ Ⓑ Ⓒ Ⓓ Ⓔ	88 Ⓐ Ⓑ Ⓒ Ⓓ Ⓔ
9 Ⓐ Ⓑ Ⓒ Ⓓ Ⓔ	29 Ⓐ Ⓑ Ⓒ Ⓓ Ⓔ	49 Ⓐ Ⓑ Ⓒ Ⓓ Ⓔ	69 Ⓐ Ⓑ Ⓒ Ⓓ Ⓔ	89 Ⓐ Ⓑ Ⓒ Ⓓ Ⓔ
10 Ⓐ Ⓑ Ⓒ Ⓓ Ⓔ	30 Ⓐ Ⓑ Ⓒ Ⓓ Ⓔ	50 Ⓐ Ⓑ Ⓒ Ⓓ Ⓔ	70 Ⓐ Ⓑ Ⓒ Ⓓ Ⓔ	90 Ⓐ Ⓑ Ⓒ Ⓓ Ⓔ
11 Ⓐ Ⓑ Ⓒ Ⓓ Ⓔ	31 Ⓐ Ⓑ Ⓒ Ⓓ Ⓔ	51 Ⓐ Ⓑ Ⓒ Ⓓ Ⓔ	71 Ⓐ Ⓑ Ⓒ Ⓓ Ⓔ	91 Ⓐ Ⓑ Ⓒ Ⓓ Ⓔ
12 Ⓐ Ⓑ Ⓒ Ⓓ Ⓔ	32 Ⓐ Ⓑ Ⓒ Ⓓ Ⓔ	52 Ⓐ Ⓑ Ⓒ Ⓓ Ⓔ	72 Ⓐ Ⓑ Ⓒ Ⓓ Ⓔ	92 Ⓐ Ⓑ Ⓒ Ⓓ Ⓔ
13 Ⓐ Ⓑ Ⓒ Ⓓ Ⓔ	33 Ⓐ Ⓑ Ⓒ Ⓓ Ⓔ	53 Ⓐ Ⓑ Ⓒ Ⓓ Ⓔ	73 Ⓐ Ⓑ Ⓒ Ⓓ Ⓔ	93 Ⓐ Ⓑ Ⓒ Ⓓ Ⓔ
14 Ⓐ Ⓑ Ⓒ Ⓓ Ⓔ	34 Ⓐ Ⓑ Ⓒ Ⓓ Ⓔ	54 Ⓐ Ⓑ Ⓒ Ⓓ Ⓔ	74 Ⓐ Ⓑ Ⓒ Ⓓ Ⓔ	94 Ⓐ Ⓑ Ⓒ Ⓓ Ⓔ
15 Ⓐ Ⓑ Ⓒ Ⓓ Ⓔ	35 Ⓐ Ⓑ Ⓒ Ⓓ Ⓔ	55 Ⓐ Ⓑ Ⓒ Ⓓ Ⓔ	75 Ⓐ Ⓑ Ⓒ Ⓓ Ⓔ	95 Ⓐ Ⓑ Ⓒ Ⓓ Ⓔ
16 Ⓐ Ⓑ Ⓒ Ⓓ Ⓔ	36 Ⓐ Ⓑ Ⓒ Ⓓ Ⓔ	56 Ⓐ Ⓑ Ⓒ Ⓓ Ⓔ	76 Ⓐ Ⓑ Ⓒ Ⓓ Ⓔ	96 Ⓐ Ⓑ Ⓒ Ⓓ Ⓔ
17 Ⓐ Ⓑ Ⓒ Ⓓ Ⓔ	37 Ⓐ Ⓑ Ⓒ Ⓓ Ⓔ	57 Ⓐ Ⓑ Ⓒ Ⓓ Ⓔ	77 Ⓐ Ⓑ Ⓒ Ⓓ Ⓔ	97 Ⓐ Ⓑ Ⓒ Ⓓ Ⓔ
18 Ⓐ Ⓑ Ⓒ Ⓓ Ⓔ	38 Ⓐ Ⓑ Ⓒ Ⓓ Ⓔ	58 Ⓐ Ⓑ Ⓒ Ⓓ Ⓔ	78 Ⓐ Ⓑ Ⓒ Ⓓ Ⓔ	98 Ⓐ Ⓑ Ⓒ Ⓓ Ⓔ
19 Ⓐ Ⓑ Ⓒ Ⓓ Ⓔ	39 Ⓐ Ⓑ Ⓒ Ⓓ Ⓔ	59 Ⓐ Ⓑ Ⓒ Ⓓ Ⓔ	79 Ⓐ Ⓑ Ⓒ Ⓓ Ⓔ	99 Ⓐ Ⓑ Ⓒ Ⓓ Ⓔ
20 Ⓐ Ⓑ Ⓒ Ⓓ Ⓔ	40 Ⓐ Ⓑ Ⓒ Ⓓ Ⓔ	60 Ⓐ Ⓑ Ⓒ Ⓓ Ⓔ	80 Ⓐ Ⓑ Ⓒ Ⓓ Ⓔ	100 Ⓐ Ⓑ Ⓒ Ⓓ Ⓔ

You may find more answer spaces than you need. If so, please leave them blank.

TEST CODE

① ② ③ ④ ⑤   ⑥ ⑦ ⑧ ⑨ ⓪
X ① ② ③ ④ ⑤   Y ① ② ③ ④ ⑤
Q ① ② ③ ④ ⑤ ⑥ ⑦ ⑧ ⑨

FOR ETS USE ONLY   R   W   FS   CS

ACHIEVEMENT TEST:

(Print)

1 Ⓐ Ⓑ Ⓒ Ⓓ Ⓔ	21 Ⓐ Ⓑ Ⓒ Ⓓ Ⓔ	41 Ⓐ Ⓑ Ⓒ Ⓓ Ⓔ	61 Ⓐ Ⓑ Ⓒ Ⓓ Ⓔ	81 Ⓐ Ⓑ Ⓒ Ⓓ Ⓔ
2 Ⓐ Ⓑ Ⓒ Ⓓ Ⓔ	22 Ⓐ Ⓑ Ⓒ Ⓓ Ⓔ	42 Ⓐ Ⓑ Ⓒ Ⓓ Ⓔ	62 Ⓐ Ⓑ Ⓒ Ⓓ Ⓔ	82 Ⓐ Ⓑ Ⓒ Ⓓ Ⓔ
3 Ⓐ Ⓑ Ⓒ Ⓓ Ⓔ	23 Ⓐ Ⓑ Ⓒ Ⓓ Ⓔ	43 Ⓐ Ⓑ Ⓒ Ⓓ Ⓔ	63 Ⓐ Ⓑ Ⓒ Ⓓ Ⓔ	83 Ⓐ Ⓑ Ⓒ Ⓓ Ⓔ
4 Ⓐ Ⓑ Ⓒ Ⓓ Ⓔ	24 Ⓐ Ⓑ Ⓒ Ⓓ Ⓔ	44 Ⓐ Ⓑ Ⓒ Ⓓ Ⓔ	64 Ⓐ Ⓑ Ⓒ Ⓓ Ⓔ	84 Ⓐ Ⓑ Ⓒ Ⓓ Ⓔ
5 Ⓐ Ⓑ Ⓒ Ⓓ Ⓔ	25 Ⓐ Ⓑ Ⓒ Ⓓ Ⓔ	45 Ⓐ Ⓑ Ⓒ Ⓓ Ⓔ	65 Ⓐ Ⓑ Ⓒ Ⓓ Ⓔ	85 Ⓐ Ⓑ Ⓒ Ⓓ Ⓔ
6 Ⓐ Ⓑ Ⓒ Ⓓ Ⓔ	26 Ⓐ Ⓑ Ⓒ Ⓓ Ⓔ	46 Ⓐ Ⓑ Ⓒ Ⓓ Ⓔ	66 Ⓐ Ⓑ Ⓒ Ⓓ Ⓔ	86 Ⓐ Ⓑ Ⓒ Ⓓ Ⓔ
7 Ⓐ Ⓑ Ⓒ Ⓓ Ⓔ	27 Ⓐ Ⓑ Ⓒ Ⓓ Ⓔ	47 Ⓐ Ⓑ Ⓒ Ⓓ Ⓔ	67 Ⓐ Ⓑ Ⓒ Ⓓ Ⓔ	87 Ⓐ Ⓑ Ⓒ Ⓓ Ⓔ
8 Ⓐ Ⓑ Ⓒ Ⓓ Ⓔ	28 Ⓐ Ⓑ Ⓒ Ⓓ Ⓔ	48 Ⓐ Ⓑ Ⓒ Ⓓ Ⓔ	68 Ⓐ Ⓑ Ⓒ Ⓓ Ⓔ	88 Ⓐ Ⓑ Ⓒ Ⓓ Ⓔ
9 Ⓐ Ⓑ Ⓒ Ⓓ Ⓔ	29 Ⓐ Ⓑ Ⓒ Ⓓ Ⓔ	49 Ⓐ Ⓑ Ⓒ Ⓓ Ⓔ	69 Ⓐ Ⓑ Ⓒ Ⓓ Ⓔ	89 Ⓐ Ⓑ Ⓒ Ⓓ Ⓔ
10 Ⓐ Ⓑ Ⓒ Ⓓ Ⓔ	30 Ⓐ Ⓑ Ⓒ Ⓓ Ⓔ	50 Ⓐ Ⓑ Ⓒ Ⓓ Ⓔ	70 Ⓐ Ⓑ Ⓒ Ⓓ Ⓔ	90 Ⓐ Ⓑ Ⓒ Ⓓ Ⓔ
11 Ⓐ Ⓑ Ⓒ Ⓓ Ⓔ	31 Ⓐ Ⓑ Ⓒ Ⓓ Ⓔ	51 Ⓐ Ⓑ Ⓒ Ⓓ Ⓔ	71 Ⓐ Ⓑ Ⓒ Ⓓ Ⓔ	91 Ⓐ Ⓑ Ⓒ Ⓓ Ⓔ
12 Ⓐ Ⓑ Ⓒ Ⓓ Ⓔ	32 Ⓐ Ⓑ Ⓒ Ⓓ Ⓔ	52 Ⓐ Ⓑ Ⓒ Ⓓ Ⓔ	72 Ⓐ Ⓑ Ⓒ Ⓓ Ⓔ	92 Ⓐ Ⓑ Ⓒ Ⓓ Ⓔ
13 Ⓐ Ⓑ Ⓒ Ⓓ Ⓔ	33 Ⓐ Ⓑ Ⓒ Ⓓ Ⓔ	53 Ⓐ Ⓑ Ⓒ Ⓓ Ⓔ	73 Ⓐ Ⓑ Ⓒ Ⓓ Ⓔ	93 Ⓐ Ⓑ Ⓒ Ⓓ Ⓔ
14 Ⓐ Ⓑ Ⓒ Ⓓ Ⓔ	34 Ⓐ Ⓑ Ⓒ Ⓓ Ⓔ	54 Ⓐ Ⓑ Ⓒ Ⓓ Ⓔ	74 Ⓐ Ⓑ Ⓒ Ⓓ Ⓔ	94 Ⓐ Ⓑ Ⓒ Ⓓ Ⓔ
15 Ⓐ Ⓑ Ⓒ Ⓓ Ⓔ	35 Ⓐ Ⓑ Ⓒ Ⓓ Ⓔ	55 Ⓐ Ⓑ Ⓒ Ⓓ Ⓔ	75 Ⓐ Ⓑ Ⓒ Ⓓ Ⓔ	95 Ⓐ Ⓑ Ⓒ Ⓓ Ⓔ
16 Ⓐ Ⓑ Ⓒ Ⓓ Ⓔ	36 Ⓐ Ⓑ Ⓒ Ⓓ Ⓔ	56 Ⓐ Ⓑ Ⓒ Ⓓ Ⓔ	76 Ⓐ Ⓑ Ⓒ Ⓓ Ⓔ	96 Ⓐ Ⓑ Ⓒ Ⓓ Ⓔ
17 Ⓐ Ⓑ Ⓒ Ⓓ Ⓔ	37 Ⓐ Ⓑ Ⓒ Ⓓ Ⓔ	57 Ⓐ Ⓑ Ⓒ Ⓓ Ⓔ	77 Ⓐ Ⓑ Ⓒ Ⓓ Ⓔ	97 Ⓐ Ⓑ Ⓒ Ⓓ Ⓔ
18 Ⓐ Ⓑ Ⓒ Ⓓ Ⓔ	38 Ⓐ Ⓑ Ⓒ Ⓓ Ⓔ	58 Ⓐ Ⓑ Ⓒ Ⓓ Ⓔ	78 Ⓐ Ⓑ Ⓒ Ⓓ Ⓔ	98 Ⓐ Ⓑ Ⓒ Ⓓ Ⓔ
19 Ⓐ Ⓑ Ⓒ Ⓓ Ⓔ	39 Ⓐ Ⓑ Ⓒ Ⓓ Ⓔ	59 Ⓐ Ⓑ Ⓒ Ⓓ Ⓔ	79 Ⓐ Ⓑ Ⓒ Ⓓ Ⓔ	99 Ⓐ Ⓑ Ⓒ Ⓓ Ⓔ
20 Ⓐ Ⓑ Ⓒ Ⓓ Ⓔ	40 Ⓐ Ⓑ Ⓒ Ⓓ Ⓔ	60 Ⓐ Ⓑ Ⓒ Ⓓ Ⓔ	80 Ⓐ Ⓑ Ⓒ Ⓓ Ⓔ	100 Ⓐ Ⓑ Ⓒ Ⓓ Ⓔ

9. SIGNATURE: